The Aesthetics of Culture
in *Buffy the Vampire Slayer*

The Aesthetics of Culture in *Buffy the Vampire Slayer*

by MATTHEW PATEMAN

McFarland & Company, Inc., Publishers
Jefferson, North Carolina, and London

LIBRARY OF CONGRESS CATALOGUING-IN-PUBLICATION DATA

Pateman, Matthew.
    The aesthetics of culture in Buffy, the vampire slayer / by Matthew
Pateman.
        p.   cm.
    Includes bibliographical references and index.

    ISBN 0-7864-2249-1 (softcover : 50# alkaline paper) ∞

    1. Buffy, the vampire slayer (Television program).   I. Title.
PN1992.77.B84P38   2006
791.45'72 — dc22   2005024678

British Library cataloguing data are available

Cover photograph: ©2006 Ingram Publishing

Manufactured in the United States of America

*McFarland & Company, Inc., Publishers
  Box 611, Jefferson, North Carolina 28640
  www.mcfarlandpub.com*

To Kelly,
the one girl in all the world

Acknowledgments

First and foremost, thank you to Joss Whedon and the whole *Buffy* team, for giving us seven wonderful seasons about which to ponder and write. Once *Buffy* became established as the phenomenon it is, scholars such as David Lavery, Rhonda Wilcox, Roz Kaveney, and Sue Turnbull provided an academic environment in which studies could flourish, so thanks are due to them and to the many others who have written or spoken so compellingly on the show over the last few years.

The writing of the current book took place in Scarborough, United Kingdom, and Cleveland, Ohio. For making my stay at John Carroll University in Cleveland so enjoyable, and productive, thanks are due to the students who were such a joy and to members of the English Department, especially Chris Roarke, Amy Roarke, Anna Hocevar, Tom Pace, Peter Kvidera, Francis Ryan, Phil Metres and Steven Heyward. For *Buffy* nights and great conversations, thank you to Melissa Milavec, Courtney Tunmore and Sharon Kaye. Special thanks to George Bilgere and Jody Rufus.

Closer to home, thank you to Charles Mundye and Anna Fitzer, for coping with my distractions over the last months, and to Martin Arnold and Maria Arnold for consistent splendor. Everybody needs a gang, so to the Scarborough Scoobies who fueled enthusiasm and sparked debate — Pete Massey, Rach Massey, Lee Taylor, and Kate Marriott — thank you. And for nights hunched over the computer screen with red wine and friendship, my thanks to Kerry Ward and Claire Matson.

Untold gratitude to my parents and to all of my family for their continued support and love. And, for the house that appeared around me, the as-if-by-magic food, the love and, above all, the patience, while I was busy doing this, thank you, Kelly, my very own Power That Be.

Contents

Acknowledgments　　　　　　　　　　　　　　　　　　　vii

A Note on the Text　　　　　　　　　　　　　　　　　　xi

Introduction: "What kind of name is Buffy?"　　　　　　　1

**Part I: Aesthetics and Cultures
in *Buffy the Vampire Slayer***

1. Aesthetics, Culture and Knowledge: "Everyone forgets,
　Willow, that knowledge is the ultimate weapon"　　　　15

2. Aesthetics, Culture and Ethnicity: "Silly, silly British Man"　　38

3. Aesthetics, Culture and History: "She lives very much in
　the 'now'"　　　　　　　　　　　　　　　　　　　62

4. Aesthetics, Culture and Ethics: "You can tell it's not gonna
　have a happy ending when the main guy's all bumpy"　　85

**Part II: Restless Traditions: The Aesthetics
of Involution in *Buffy the Vampire Slayer***

5. The Aesthetics of Involution: "I've got a theory"　　　　109

6. Willow's Dream: "It's exactly like a Greek tragedy"　　　126

7. Xander's Dream: "It's all about the journey, isn't it?"　　146

8. Giles's Dream: "There's a great deal going on. And all at once"   164

9. Buffy's Dream: "You think you know what you are?"   183

Conclusion: "I'd call that a radical interpretation of the text"   208

Appendix: Episode Listing   213
Notes   221
Bibliography   247
Index   263

A Note on the Text

Buffy the Vampire Slayer as a title is usually shortened to *Buffy*, except where a particular point about the title is being made, or confusion with the character, Buffy, may occur.

Episode titles are given in full, followed by their season and episode number, unless an episode is being referenced many times on a single page, in which case the season and episode numbers only will be given. For example, "'Welcome to the Hellmouth' (1.1)" would be referenced simply as "(1.1)" if mentioned again very soon after the initial reference.

Episodes from *Angel* will also be given full titles with season and episode numbers prefixed by *AtS* to signify their provenance. For example, "Spin the Bottle" (*AtS* 4.6).

Slayage: The Online International Journal of Buffy Studies is referred to as *Slayage* throughout.

Introduction

"What kind of name is Buffy?"

Rarely has a television series had such a seemingly silly-sounding name as *Buffy the Vampire Slayer*. Whether taken individually or in juxtaposition, the two main phrases that make up the name invite, it would appear, derision. "Buffy" conjures images of the inconsequential, blonde, fluffy, intellectually insipid, mall-worshiping fashion junky who is the quintessential postmodern American middle-class teen. "Vampire slayer" is little better. Locating itself in a historical halfway house between modernity's revisiting of the early modern in tales of the vampire, and a premodern pseudo-mythic world of dragons and knights with the notion of the slayer, the phrase sounds like cultural eclecticism run mad. Placed next to the name Buffy, this hybrid title, with all its apparent disregard for history, offers a cartoon aesthetic and is just another example of disposable pop: a vacuous product for a diminished culture.[1]

By the time the high school girl with the even more preposterous name — Aphrodisia — asks her friend, "What kind of name is Buffy?" in the first episode of the first season, "Welcome to the Hellmouth" (1.1), any notion of the vacuous has been dispelled. As we will have seen in the opening few minutes of this episode, and as the remaining 143 will go on to enforce, *Buffy* is one of the most important contributions to the presentation and analysis of contemporary American culture,[2] and it undertakes this with a televisual aesthetic virtuosity that is unrivaled. So why the silly name?

In part, the answer to that question is simple. It offers itself up as part of the very critique of culture that the show is undertaking; it revels in its

1

own ostensible shallowness in order to demonstrate that popular culture, however frivolous it may seem, is worthy of more serious attention, but that only those who are willing to forego deeply embedded hierarchies of taste will be welcome on the ride. In what amounts to an inversion of Umberto Eco's famous rebuke to those who found the opening to his fabulous novel *The Name of the Rose* too difficult, and to whom he replied that only those willing to endure the initial difficulty were welcome as fellow travelers on Adso's and William's journey,[3] *Buffy* shows its barefaced embrace of the popular and demands that this be accepted before the viewer come aboard.[4]

However, this itself would be little more than a pleasing but slight game if that is all there was to it. The title of the show is more than simply a celebration of popular culture: it is a precise and extraordinarily careful introduction to the show's aims both in terms of its aesthetic practice and its cultural claims. The eclecticism mentioned above, that appears to be an effacement of history and a recapitulation of the postmodern delight in depthlessness, is very far from this. It is, of course, possible to argue, as Jean-François Lyotard does, that:

> Eclecticism is the degree zero of contemporary general culture: one listens to reggae, watches a western, eats McDonald's food for lunch and local cuisine for dinner, wears Paris perfume in Tokyo and "retro" clothes in Hong Kong; knowledge is a matter for TV games. It is easy to find a public for eclectic works.[5]

However, eclecticism need not be so disturbing. The great champion of the avant-garde, Lyotard, at this moment, mistook the dangers of a "general cultural" phenomenon as translatable to particular manifestations. When general culture is also dominated by niche markets that require clearly defined objects of consumption that conform to preestablished modes of expression (another aspect of contemporary culture that, rightly, irked Lyotard), then the eclectic-minded (or genre-busting) product is a welcome and necessary antidote.[6] *Buffy the Vampire Slayer* as title and, therefore, probably the first introduction to the show's aesthetic, exerts this refusal of generic singularity from the outset. Simply repudiating genre is not the point, though. Rather, it is using a variety of genres to create something that is creatively thrilling, that avoids blunt formalism while celebrating formal innovation, and that invigorates two genres (high school drama and gothic horror[7]) by producing something new that pays homage to both. This is what *Buffy* does, and what its title, teasingly, proposes. But even this, exciting and desired though it may be, is not enough.

A generic amalgam that still flattened out history, as the title may be thought to do, would be aesthetically pleasing but culturally only a symptom of a more pervasive dehistoricization.[8] *Buffy*'s title, though, is, yet again, surprisingly, exact in what it signifies. A postmodern girl (Buffy) will engage with the legacy of modernity and its immediate antecedents (the demonic possibilities of the early modern)[9] and will, in so doing, invoke and interrogate more archaic forms of cultural understanding (the Slayer). The title does not flatten out history as much as it compresses the show's various relationships with differing approaches to historicity.[10] The generic fusion of high school drama and gothic horror (to mention only the two most prominent of the staggering number of genres present in the show) supplies the aesthetic corollary of this cultural undertaking.

Before examining how the aesthetics of culture will be addressed in this book, it is important not to forget other ways in which the title *Buffy the Vampire Slayer* works. While the advertisement of the television show that ran from 1997 to 2003 for 144 episodes (or over 100 hours of quality television) is the primary understanding of it, the name moves in excess of this. There is also the 1992 film. Widely regarded as unsuccessful, both in terms of box office numbers and quality, there is little that unites the film and the television show. The film's only mode is parody, and, once the comedy of the vapid girl being a reluctant Slayer is established, it is not even a very funny parody. By losing any sense of the horror that Joss Whedon's script had included, the film can only aspire to a knowing debunking of the teen and horror movies it was trading on. The subtlety, genuine scariness, and potential for horror that the television show provides are absent, and, therefore, almost all of the latent power is missing. Primarily this is due to the preponderance of the parodic. Joss Whedon explained it most pithily when he said, "When you wink at the audience and say nothing matters, then you can't have peril."[11]

It was not only peril that was missing but also the sense of strength and capability with which Buffy was supposed to be endowed. By parodying films in which the blonde girl always dies at the hand of the villain, the filmic *Buffy* may have laid bare some of the aesthetic clichés, but it did nothing to try to provide a new aesthetic. The drift toward a more empowered notion of the female protagonist needed another film that, in some senses, allowed the television *Buffy* to come into being:

> The first step towards the modern reclaiming of horror as a genre in the name of Girl Power occurred in 1996's *Scream* [which] existed as a milestone in Girl Power, the first real mass media document to champion it. *Scream* set off the cinematic arm of the media wave that Girl Power rode and, like the teen media wave before it, this one would soon come to be dominated by romantic comedies and gore-filled horror outings.[12]

While film would return to rom-com and gore, television was about to have its first Girl Power teen horror show. But this had required an evolution too. While Whedon's original template for what *Buffy* could be remains massively important to its eventual appearance as a television show, the immediate history of television in terms of high quality, intelligent teen drama and high-quality, intelligent sci-fi was needed to convince networks of the viability of such a show. For *Buffy*, the antecedents were *My So-Called Life* and *The X-Files*: "creator Joss Whedon himself has referred to it [*Buffy*] as a cross between *My So-Called Life* and *The X-Files* (Tracy 22)—*Buffy* debuted in the midst of Girl Power cinematic prime but was the first television show of the late nineties teen media wave."[13]

So the title includes not just the television show and the film but also the development from one to the other, and this has to be figured as part of broader cinematic and television trends, themselves the product of (and contributors to) shifting cultural assumptions about the representation of young women. The aesthetic choices made are not solely the consequence of the media used (indeed, the television show is far more interesting in terms of its production values and willingness to experiment than the film was) but also are the direct result of a desire to engage with particular facets of contemporary American culture, with this engagement requiring specific aesthetic choices, not the least of which was to minimize parody.

If the film version and the television show are the most obvious ways in which the title operates, they are not the only ones. *Buffy the Vampire Slayer* is now a brand name as much as the title of a series. And this brand name covers an enormous range of products: VHS and DVD sets of the seasons; VHS and DVD sets of episodes themed by character; individual episodes on VHS and DVD (at this time, only the musical episode "Once More with Feeling" [6.7]) has been released in this way); CDs of music from the show; script books; official guides; card games; board games; posters; novels; the official website; comics; video games; conventions. Unofficial merchandising includes books, t-shirts, posters and, most contentious, fan websites. All of these products operate under the name of *Buffy the Vampire Slayer*.[14]

And then there is the name of our heroine herself. The astonishing array of products all derive from the show, and the show takes its name from its main character, Buffy Summers, Vampire Slayer. As with the show's title, its main character is an expression of the tensions inherent in the juxtaposition of the terms "Buffy," "vampire" and "Slayer." While the generic and general cultural concerns of the title exist in all aspects of each episode, they find special depth and resonance through their articulation via Buffy. The problems of being a teenager in late 1990s America, being the only child of a broken home, starting a new school, making friends, developing one's sexuality, finding a sense of coherence and meaning, moving to university, making new friends, developing one's sexuality further, discovering you have a sister, experiencing the death of your mother, losing loves, seeing other friends depart and die, watching addiction take hold of your closest confidante, losing your surrogate father: these are the life experiences that Buffy, the teenager and young adult, confronts. Fighting the forces of evil, and defending friends and family and the broader community from monsters, vampires, rampaging gods, malevolent witches, zombies and others: these are the perils for the Slayer. But for Buffy, these two disparate worlds are united, not only because she lives both of them but also because the monster may turn out to be her boyfriend, her best friend might try to destroy the world, she herself might die and return as something different, or nihilism might overtake her. And, further, the decision to kill or not to kill a vampire might not be simply a matter of stopping the bad guy but will entail a recognition of moral values and ethical choices derived from these values that are in conflict with other moral systems and the ethical choices that derive from those systems. A vampire might be an old school friend, or a monster could in fact be a kind-hearted uncle-figure. Archaic, mythical values that determine the Slayer's role are often in conflict with contemporary questions regarding ethnicity; Enlightenment thought can be incredibly obtuse when confronted by premodern forms of understanding; scientific rationalism cannot account for mystical phenomena; and Buffy and her friends constantly have to negotiate the emotional implications of their actions on each other and their families as well as the antagonistic ethical, epistemological, ontological, and historical consequences and predicates of their decisions. In other words, they are individuals who are in constant struggle with all aspects of their culture and who relentlessly battle to understand it and to save it. While they achieve the second aim with fraught regularity, the former aspect is much more difficult.

As Raymond Williams observed, culture "is one of the two or three most complicated words in the English language."[15] Partly due to its intricate history and development through a number of European languages, the word's main difficulty lies in the fact of its use in different, and often contradictory, disciplines and systems of thought. It can be used to mean the artistic productions, and appreciation of them, that determine good taste; it can offer ethnographic differentiation between groups of people; it can mean the processes of understanding and communication within a group; it can mean an ethos within an organization; it can refer to particular examples of mass-produced entertainment; it can be a whole field of inquiry into "the popular"; it can also describe the changing relations of a group of people to itself over time. And it can mean an uneasy admixture of all of the above.

To talk of "culture" in relation to *Buffy*, then, is to invite in a decidedly un–Arnoldian anarchy. Yet a tentative containment of these heterogeneous meanings is possible, because *Buffy* itself is so determined to encounter each of them and to provide stories in which each of them comes into contact with the other so that a culture of *Buffy* develops out of this commingling.

Perhaps the most straightforward sense of culture that we find in *Buffy* is the ethnographic one. Buffy and her friends combat demons. There is a sense, very general for the moment, in which the demons represent a different, and threatening, culture and Buffy's job is to protect her known culture. This conceptually easy division of the world into two cultures (human and demon) is the starting point for much of the subtle analysis of culture in this sense with which the show deals. Not only is it the case that the recognition of significant variegation within the two assumed total cultures is required, it is also apparent that the philosophical underpinnings that provide the justification for the initial division have to be interrogated too. The construction of the categories of human and demon and the consequent construction of ethnic differentiation within those categories becomes a dominant aspect of the series and will be discussed in greater detail in chapter 2.

The ethnographic sense of culture has, in part, relied on the philosophical traditions of Enlightenment and post–Enlightenment Europe, which contributed to the idea of a European culture. This culture, mired in the history that produced it, itself created "that ahistorical nineteenth-century polarity of the Orient and the Occident which, in the name of progress, unleashed the exclusionary imperialist ideologies of self and other."[16] These exclusionary categories, which *Buffy* seeks to interrogate in some respects, nevertheless provide one of the other ways in which a notion of culture influences the program. This is the very general notion of a contemporary, postmodern American culture, which is set against an assumed culture of an older Europe. The different relationships to history that these two cultures are perceived to have form part of the argument for chapter 3, especially insofar as one can be seen to represent a notion of modernity and the other a notion of postmodernity, though these terms are contested and also appear in other chapters too.

Questions pertaining to modernity and postmodernity and the different ways in which these terms imply an understanding, or knowledge, of the relations of culture in all that term's polysemic variation will be addressed in chapter 1. Here also the ways in which a self-defined culture chooses to disseminate its knowledge about itself to itself through a variety of institutional forms will be discussed. The extent to which an institution, or a less clearly demarcated group, determines an ethos that will support its well-being and operations, and the ways in which this functions as another version of culture, will constitute part of this chapter, as well as others.

One of the ways in which a group understands itself as a homogeneous entity, as a culture, is through its adherence to a moral system and the ethical choices that the individual members of that group make as a response to that moral system. Different moral systems and, therefore, different ethical choices, mark out clear distinctions that operate as cultural boundaries. *Buffy*'s concentration on the centrality of ethical choices and their consequences, and the different ways in which groups choose to undertake these choices, will form a major part of chapter 4.

The chapters in part I, then, are all organized around a prominent aspect of *Buffy*'s confrontation with culture: the claims made for knowledge and its dissemination to (or withholding from) others in chapter 1; ethnographic distinctions and the articulation of identities in chapter 2; the changing relationship of a people with itself, and the competing claims made between and about people over time, in chapter 3; and the decisions made with regard to ethics in chapter 4. Each chapter will address other points, and there will be some crossover between chapters, especially in relation to the uses made by the show of other forms of cultural references in the sense of high art and popular production. These chapters will be concerned with the generality of *Buffy*, ranging across characters, episodes and seasons. Part II is located more at the level of character. These character studies are still concerned to situate both the individual and the show in the broad realm of cultural analysis, and to develop the notion of "the aesthetics of involution," which I see as such a dominant part of the show's production value, as well as being the method of criticism used to discuss it. Each chapter, then, presents a discussion of *Buffy* in the light of a facet of the aesthetics of culture. Broad categories of cultural thought make up the first four, and a specific aesthetic determination on behalf of the show (involution) is the main focus of the last five where the relationship between aesthetics and character is a prominent feature. Each of the last five chapters begins from, and returns at various points to, the episode "Restless" (4.22) for reasons that are explained in chapter 5. Part I tends to focus on culture (in all the complex ways that *Buffy* treats that term) and analyzes how aesthetics contribute to an understanding and articulation of these various ideas. Part II tends to be more explicitly focused on notions of the aesthetic and is interested to show how different cultural and character concerns are derived from this.

"Aesthetics," like culture, is a complex term with a set of disputed meanings. For Terry Eagleton, in his desire to insist on the material conditions of the emergence of the term in the first place and, thus, to refuse the bourgeois ideality of an autonomous realm of culture that is seemingly self-contained and free of any material influence whatsoever, the aesthetic is "the very secret prototype of human subjectivity in early capitalist society, and a vision of human energies as radical ends in themselves which is the implacable enemy of all dominative or instrumentalist thought."[17] A less vibrant definition comes from Hegel who is less than sanguine in the introduction to his thesis on aesthetics about being able to provide a definition of his subject: "We shall, therefore, permit the name Aesthetic to stand, because it is nothing but a name, and so is indifferent to us, and, moreover, has up to a certain point passed into common language."[18]

If one yokes the freedom of usage allowed by Hegel to the insistence on a material culture that determines an understanding of the aesthetic in Eagleton, then the aesthetics of culture in *Buffy* can be explained as follows. In the first instance, the aspects of culture with which this book is operating all carry their own aesthetic component. Assuming that Eagleton's rather narrower conception of culture (art) is no less able to claim autonomy and the autotelic self-referential illusion than other parts of culture, then these other parts of culture will, too, have a materially present aesthetic that will also carry its own ideological weight. For the moment I am less concerned with the ideological implication than with the materially present fact of the aesthetic.

With regard to knowledge as an aspect of culture, its aesthetic operates in a variety of ways, not the least of which is the formal restraint placed on the transmission of knowledge by virtue of the media used. I shall return to this point in the discussion of aesthetics and television a little later in this introduction. Additionally, however, is the rather more banal point that knowledge as a concept is intimately bound up with ideas of narrative through its etymology. That knowledge should be so deeply implicated in a device that is itself central to artistic creation (and, therefore, any understanding of aesthetics that includes narrative art) means that one does not have to talk of an aesthetics of knowledge so much as recognize that knowledge is already an aesthetic category. Chapter 1 works to show how knowledge distribution and maintenance operate though a narrative strategy in *Buffy* such that the two become integral parts of each other in the show.

Ethnicity might appear to be less immediately susceptible to the aesthetic, but in some ways it is brutally aesthetic from the outset with the ideological ramifications equally as blatant. Among the markers of ethnic difference, the most prominent and immediate tend to be physical: skin color; hair color, texture and style; eye color and so on. An aesthetics of color allied to a symbology of good and evil and an ideology of European progress provides ample grounds for ethnic discrimination. While this forms part of the discussion of chapter 2, the major focus is on the way in which the show proposes a conception of ethnicity (and a broader understanding of identity) as performative. To this extent, ethnicity is a process and a construct that insists on the aesthetic as a material aspect of becoming, not simply an abstract constituent of criticism.

History, like knowledge, is a predominantly narrative undertaking, and the ways in which narratives of progress are developed and imposed exerts a huge influence on the ways in which, for example, ethnicity, knowledge and ethical choices are formed. Chapter 3 examines *Buffy*'s uses of history as narrative and shows how the program once again draws culture and aesthetics together in its treatment of these histories, refusing to sequester the aesthetic into an ahistorical, dematerialized abstraction.

The chapter on ethics, chapter 4, draws on *Buffy*'s alertness to the cultural processes that have developed an ethical register of aesthetic attributes, most notably color but other visual and discursive regimes as well. In the show, these registers are played with, inverted, destabilized and otherwise recognized as historically situated products of cultural processes whose aesthetic-ethical dimension is open to scrutiny and reassignment, even though the show does not always do this.

Chapter 5 will expand on the ways in which aesthetics and culture combine at the level of character, and through the technique of involution, to provide arresting and important contributions to any analysis of contemporary American culture.

The notion of the aesthetic is not being used only as an aspect of a cultural feature as described above. It is important to insist on a specifically televisual aesthetic, one whose modes of production and eventual product are the result of television itself. This returns us to Eagleton. If, as Eagleton asserts, there has been a consolidated effort to obscure the material effects of culture (especially with regard to the structures of economic dependence and patronage) in order to elevate a supposed pure and uncontaminated aesthetic that stands apart from the grubbiness of such mean affairs as money, then television is its own anti-aesthetic. Primarily an object that acts as the medium through which aesthetic forms can be displayed (rarely thought of as an object of beauty in its own right), the medium itself determinedly foregrounds the material culture that allows the aesthetic to be. Whether it be through a mixture of state-owned licensing and independently financed private companies, or whether wholly through one or the other, everybody is all the time made aware of the financial aspect of television. It can never rise above, or pretend to rise above, the economic. Additionally, the necessarily collective nature of television production denies the possibility of the individual genius: clearly, television can be an expression of neither abstract, dematerialized, "pure" aesthetics nor the unadulterated communion with a rarefied artistic spirit. It can never be art because its aesthetic is always *of* culture (materially conceived in economic terms) and not *for* culture (abstractly revered in terms of high artistic achievement).

Only a perverse refusal to recognize the primacy of the economic concerns of art allows this ill-informed denial of television anything like a true appreciation in terms of its aesthetic qualities; but this refusal is not only perverse, it is pervasive. Among those who seek to challenge its curious power is Sue Turnbull. At the *Slayage* conference held in Tennessee in 2004, she presented a clarion call for a serious analysis of television in aesthetic terms. Published as "Not Just Another *Buffy* Paper: Towards an Aesthetics of Television,"[19] Turnbull's paper outlines a typology of television criticism, specifically related to *Buffy* but potentially open to a general method, that not only recognizes but celebrates its materially cultural production of an aesthetic (or range of aesthetics). A brief summary of the areas such a criticism would involve is, according to Turnbull, as follows:

1. Industry and production context — being alert to network constraints, advertisers' concerns and contributions, contractual issues and so on. For *Buffy* this would include such questions as the move from the WB to UPN; the advertiser-driven concerns over the representation of fast-food outlets in "Doublemeat Palace" (6.12); and the location, for example, of Amber Benson's name in the opening credits.

2. Auteurism — not the celebration of an individual genius, but a knowledge of the roles and histories of those people who have contributed to the creation of a show including producers, directors, writers and so on. This would refer to Joss Whedon, evidently, but also to David Fury, Marti Noxon, David Greenwalt, Jane Espenson and all of the writers, directors, producers and so on who have contributed to the show.

3. Genre and narratology — an understanding of the different forms that television can take and an appreciation of what a genre is able to achieve, as well as its limitations, allied to a strong awareness of certain

techniques relating to, for example, editing. Much of the discussion of the present book is concerned with these areas but a good example in relation to *Buffy* would be the episode "Pangs" (4.8) in which the "soap opera" row between Giles, Willow and the rest is placed in front of Buffy who seems to be from a sitcom as she stirs the mixture in the cooking bowl in a frantic denial of what is taking place.

4. Postmodern cultural turn — an awareness of and openness to the allusive and referential quality of television productions that accommodates both the popular cultural and the classical, the high-, middle- and low-brow. This is ever present in *Buffy*, and much of part II is given over to its analysis.

5. Televisual aesthetic — a recognition of the specific styles used by a program and these styles' indebtedness to previous television. In *Buffy*, as Turnbull points out, the shift between the *Buffy* aesthetic standard (or its realist techniques) and the stylistic choices relating to horror, sitcom, soap opera, silent movie, musical and so on is part of this process.

6. The aesthesis of performance — the interaction of the viewer with the show that pays heed not only to intellectual analysis but also to emotional response or, as Turnbull says following Eagleton's return to the Greek root, "the whole region of human perception and sensation."

These areas of critical inquiry combine the immediate material conditions of networks, advertisers and the industry requirement of making money with the histories of television production and the developing and changing technological and artistic possibilities (often with the one — artistic expression — being dependent on the other — technological advance), emotive and intellectual responses, the creative process and the people involved in that process as well as the interrelationship between television and other areas of cultural production.

The current book was begun well before I heard Turnbull's lecture, but the general remit is broadly similar. I try, at least, to recognize and incorporate the material aspects of the production of *Buffy* and, to insist on and delight in the show's most obvious aspect, which is that it is television. It has obligations to its network and its advertisers but is also prepared to recognize and play with the inevitable limitations that this imposes; it has as its creator a man who had little practical knowledge of making a television show [20] but who, with a marvelous production team and writing staff, transformed the potential of genre television through its quick-fire genre-shifting and staggering storylines that trade on, mock, celebrate and invigorate television history and the aesthetics that have developed it. By refusing to limit its scope to either high or pop cultural references, *Buffy* demonstrates the broadly democratizing possibility of mass-mediated information without treating democratizing as a synonym for "banalizing"; it constantly encourages its viewers to interrogate their beliefs and systems of thought while terrifying them, delighting them or breaking their hearts.

Buffy the Vampire Slayer engages with American culture at the end of the twentieth and beginning of the twenty-first centuries. Alert to the multiple meanings of culture, and even more alert to the plethora of possibilities within each of these meanings, *Buffy* is culturally polyglot. It recognizes and utilizes the aesthetic categories inherent in the different modalities of culture and delights in asserting the materially cultural influences on the creation of its own aesthetic. *Buffy* is television as art, not because it tries to hide its materiality or to ape the supposed purer realms of literature or even film but because it lays its aesthetic bare, declares its indebtedness to culture in both its material and abstract forms and refuses to be cowed by either. *Buffy* has propelled the possibilities of televisual aesthetics and has done so by embracing and critiquing the cultures that inform, sustain and sometimes threaten it.[21] The aesthetics of culture have never looked so good.

◆ PART I ◆

Aesthetics and Cultures
in *Buffy the Vampire Slayer*

Aesthetics, Culture and Knowledge

*"Everyone forgets, Willow,
that knowledge is the ultimate weapon"*

Xander's comment to Willow in "Never Kill a Boy on the First Date" (1.5), the subtitle of this chapter, is somewhat undermined as an assertion by the fact that he is actively trying to avoid researching (gaining knowledge) with Giles. He wants to follow Buffy and her new paramour and pretends that the knowledge he will discover by doing this is in someway generally useful, rather than simply personally desired. His use of the axiom-turned-cliché is his rather desperate argumentative ploy. Knowledge is a weapon, of course, but not always (actual weapons are often much more useful in this regard), but the problem lies not so much with when knowledge may or may not be the group's major strength in battle, but with what knowledge actually is. *Buffy* continually poses this question, always resisting any claims that it and its characters know knowledge.

Recent theorists have been keen to assert that knowledge is intimately related to notions of power. The veracity of this is debatable, but it is essential that knowledge require narrative as the vehicle through which it is expressed. In *The Postmodern Condition: A Report on Knowledge*, Lyotard is emphatic about the relationship of knowledge and narrative, claiming narrative as the pre-eminent "form in the formulation of traditional knowledge."[1] This is not to claim that Lyotard and other theorists are in any way discovering something new about the relationship between the two, simply that they are developing a sophisticated theory from an established etymology: "**narrate** (næ'reɪt), *v.* [f. L. *narrāt-*, ppl. stem of *narrāre* to relate, recount, supposed to be for **gnārāre*, related to *gnārus* knowing, skilled, and thus ultimately allied to KNOW *v.*]."[2]

This etymological link provides a clear and unambiguous sense of the interconnectedness of knowledge and narrative; in other words, knowledge has, at least in part, an aspect that is aesthetic.[3] Indeed in *Buffy*, much of the development of plotlines (of episodes' and seasons' narrative trajectories) is predicated on the different ways in which knowledge is distributed and disseminated. The earlier part of this chapter will look at a number of examples where knowledge of this sort is used in the show. In addition to this, though, there are other concerns that are less specific. Among these are the ways in which knowledge as a facet of social organization functions, especially as it is tied in with institutional centers of authority, be they educational (school, university), political (local government), or military (the army). Beyond these questions, however, there are also issues of knowledge that operate in a fashion that is not only internal to the show (even if that internality has external, real-world homologues) but also external in the sense of requiring viewer knowledge of a range of cultural processes and practices to be brought to bear on a reading.

To begin with, though, I would like to present a number of examples of the way in which the having or not-having of knowledge, and the desire to keep secret or discover that knowledge, is used as a principle of narrative organization in *Buffy*. And most pertinent to that has to be the role and nature of Buffy herself.[4] The opening episode is largely, though far from exclusively, organized around Buffy's desire to maintain the secret of her identity. Believing herself to be the only person who knows what she is, her initial meeting with Giles, who knows she is the Slayer (1.1), is a great shock and forces her to run away. The discovery of a dead boy in the locker room encourages her reluctant return to Giles, and brings forth the first explicit mention of her identity to the audience and also, as it transpires, to Xander who, inexplicably (given his lackluster engagement with school) is in the library and overhears what has been said. The audience now has knowledge that neither Xander nor Buffy does (we know for a fact Buffy is the Slayer, unlike Xander who is skeptical; and we know of Xander's knowledge of the conversation, unlike Buffy); the importance of this audience knowledge for an aesthetics of knowledge in the show will be addressed later.

Xander's skepticism is enforced when he picks up one of Buffy's stakes after having bumped into her. After Willow's abduction by a vampire from the Bronze, Buffy begins to search for her and she asks for Xander's help. Xander's response that he hopes the guy is not a vampire as then Buffy would have to slay him prompts her exasperated question as to whether or not there is anyone who does not know she is the Slayer. He replies that he knows she "thinks" she is (1.1). There are two aspects worth noting here. First is the wonderful humor derived from the failure of Buffy to keep her knowledge secret (first Giles, then Angel, then Xander know). To this extent, the "retention-of-the-secret-identity" trope (a staple of narrative from Odysseus's return to Ithaca up to *Alias* and beyond) is delightfully parodied and the show's agenda of warping genre for comedic effect is highlighted from the first.[5] The second aspect, which I shall return to, is the extent to which Xander initially acts as a conduit for a common-sense, rationalist response to being presented with such seemingly improbable claims. The competing claim for rational knowledge against those of seemingly irrational ones is addressed again and again in the show,[6] and finds its representational apotheosis in season 6's "Normal Again" (6.17), one of the best episodes ever and one that I shall discuss later in that chapter.

Willow's extremely traumatic discovery that vampires exist, that Buffy slays them and that Giles is Buffy's Watcher almost completes the group. Now the secret knowledge is shared by four people.[7] The group soon increases to five with the inclusion of Cordelia. Now the entire group has knowledge that it is imperative they keep secret — this knowledge is a whole realm of existence utterly outside the lived experience of everyone else in Sunnydale and, by extension, the world. The extent to which this is itself complicated as the Buffyverse expands will be another area addressed later in this chapter.

Having set up the initial group of those who know Buffy's secret, episodes are able to present stories that have a twin narrative structure. On the one hand, the group is responsible for discovering the causes of violence, death or other forms of disruption in a manner that is a mixture of the whodunit and the thriller,[8] and on the other they have to maintain the knowledge of their secret. This means that the group always has to work outside of officially sanctioned law enforcement and, occasionally, outside of the law itself. The former of these two requirements is stated bluntly in response to Willow's question:

> WILLOW: Uh, this may be the dumb question, but shouldn't we call the police?
> GILES: And they'd believe us, of course.
> WILLOW: Well, we don't have to say vampires. We, we could just say that there's a, a bad man.

BUFFY: They couldn't handle it even if they did show up. They'd only come with guns [1.2].

The police would be incredulous and also a volatile addition to the situation. Having dismissed the idea of police involvement the group is soon happy to dismiss certain sorts of legal restrictions on their access to information. They need access to plans of the city and Willow "accidentally decrypted the city council's security system" (1.2). The sort of knowledge they have makes official law enforcement useless, and the sort of knowledge they need makes the law itself malleable. This has led some commentators to assert that *Buffy* is essentially anarchist in outlook, refusing the sanctions of state law. However, as Bradney points out,

> because they are aware of its [the law's] limitations, [this does not mean] they have no regard for it at all. The acknowledgement that "the human world has its own rules" is real and not merely rhetorical. It leads Buffy to be willing to turn herself into the police when she thinks she has killed Katrina in "Dead Things" [6.13] and it means that her initial reaction to Warren's murder of Tara is to let human law take its course ("Villains" [6.20]). Nonetheless, at the same time, state law is regularly broken by Buffy and the Scooby Gang; their relationship with state law is thus a complex one.[9]

And this complexity is largely due to the different categories of knowledge with which the Scoobies work. Their knowledge of the world of demons and their requirement to protect people from apocalypse and strife mean that they are under an obligation to a greater moral law: one that supervenes state law and allows the breaking of state law. Here knowledge is the predicate of a morality, and the morality is the driving force of the show insofar as it can be reduced to two words: "slay vampires." The morality itself, however, which has been institutionalized by the Watchers' Council into a law of its own, becomes prey to ambivalence and relative application as Buffy especially, but others, too, gain more knowledge of a variety of demons.

This happens in the first instance with Angel. He, like Buffy, has his secret identity. The mysterious noir hero of the first episodes is able to maintain his secret much more effectively than Buffy, both from her and the audience. When she and we discover his vampiric side in "Angel" (1.7) it is a truly shocking moment.[10] We have already seen Jesse killed off in the second episode and Principal Flutie killed in "The Pack" (1.6) so we have a knowledge of the show's capacity to upset our expectations of character development and we, no less than Buffy, remain unsure about Angel's intentions until the end of the episode. Like Buffy, the audience is forced to realize that the seeming moral simplicity of her title and function is significantly more complicated than might have appeared to be the case: Angel is a vampire, but he is also an ally, if not a friend.

Knowledge serves to make the world more complex. Not only are categories such as law and morality placed under severe scrutiny, but this scrutiny has its own power to complicate the emotional level. Xander's infatuation with Buffy means that he is predisposed to dislike Angel because he is already a rival for Buffy's affections. The discovery that he is a vampire allows Xander to use the supposed supremacy of the moral law (slay vampires, protect humans) as a means by which he can eradicate that rival. Buffy's refusal to allow that law its position as supreme, based on her experiential knowledge, offers an opportunity for questions of knowledge and morality and questions of friendship and characterization to be played out in impressively sophisticated and symbiotic fashion. The show's constant commitment to narrative complexity as an adjunct to aesthetic sophistication is here manifest and marvelous. Xander's continued resentment toward Angel is increased when Angel becomes Angelus in season 2. In the final episode of that season, Willow attempts a spell to return Angel's soul and thus prevent Angelus from awakening Acathla and ushering in eschatology's achievement. Xander has been sent to tell Buffy to stall killing Angelus in order that Angel might be restored before Acathla is awakened. Xander, instead, simply says that Willow's message is "kick his ass" (2.22). This lie, this withholding of information, means that Buffy eventually has to kill Angel who is re-ensouled too late to stop Angelus carrying out his plan. The extreme pathos and beauty of this scene, the bewildered Angel facing the sword-wielding Buffy, who, in tears, tells him to close his eyes as she kills him, is wonderful. It is made all the more poignant by virtue of the fact that the audience knows it was avoidable.

Knowledge, and its withholding, continues at the intersections of morality, loyalty, friendship and narrative and is also now an extreme emotional intensifier. Our sadness about Angel's death and about Buffy's grief and despair (she has also been expelled from school and forced out of her home) is massively augmented by our disbelief at Xander's selfishness. This lie is reprised five seasons later in "Selfless" (7.5). Anya has returned to her demon ways and has killed some frat boys. The increasingly isolated Buffy decides that the only possible option is to kill her. The debate about the rights and wrongs of this has Xander and Buffy occupying completely opposite positions from those they held in "Angel" (1.7). Where Xander used the supremacy of moral law as a weapon with which to try and dispatch Angel, Buffy used her knowledge of him to save him. Here,

Buffy addresses her need to kill Anya to a supreme law that Xander argues against. The main difference here is that Buffy has learned to recognize the futility of moral absolutes, has become so embroiled in the difficulty of moral relativity that she has foregone its subtleties and nuances and, in its place, installed herself as the final arbiter of moral choices. When Faith had claimed in "Consequences" (3.15) that "we are the law," Buffy's response was emphatic and simple: "No." Having fallen into an emotional and spiritual abyss through season 6, and encountered her own form of nihilism, she now occupies a space not dissimilar to that of Faith, and like Faith, her isolation from friends forces her more and more onto her own capacities.[11] Xander recognizes the pattern, and the conclusion he draws is that Buffy has stepped away from everything human and is acting "like [she's] the law" (7.5). Buffy reminds him and Willow that she killed Angel despite loving him, and that the pair of them were cheering her on, repeating Xander's message from Willow. Willow begins to dispute that she ever said that, but the argument continues.

Knowledge of the show at this point brings the two episodes and the arguments about Buffy's responsibility as a Slayer and her responsibilities as a friend into focus. We remember Xander's betrayal of her (and Willow, too, as a result of his misrepresentation of her) and remember, too, Buffy's selflessness, a memory that chimes with this episode's title. By having Buffy, seconds after the above exchange, assert without reserve or remorse "I am the law," we are also encouraged to locate Buffy alongside Faith. The selfless and the selfish Slayer are here united in one multilayered moment of analeptic congruence. The arguments about the right thing to do exist not simply as an aspect of an episode but as part of a dialogue that has been in process since, at least, the fifth episode of the first season. This dialogue is explicitly located as an aesthetic unraveling, through story arcs and characterization, of a moral dilemma that has knowledge as its predicate.

This notion of knowledge, however, is a comparatively limited one that relates specifically to an awareness of the variegated nature of demons and the consequent recognition of the need to continually redefine the moral standards that had seemed to be absolute. The question of knowledge in *Buffy* operates in a number of other spheres.

One of the spheres has already been intimated, and that is the role of the viewer in reading the text of *Buffy* from a position of knowledge. The second part of this book, with its notion of involution, which relies heavily on questions of intertexts and allusions, evidently assumes a considerable level of viewer knowledge in a number of areas. However, the question of the viewers' knowledge is apparent in other ways too. One of these is comparatively straightforward and is put to good use by the writers of the show. Throughout the seasons, there are occasions where the viewer has possession of knowledge that one or more members of the cast do not. Xander's mendacity is an early example of this, and it is one whose function is to raise the emotional force of the season's conclusion. Similarly, in a scene from the same season, the appalling sense of impending tragedy is produced by the audience knowing what Giles does not ("Passion" [2.17]). He is returning home, having finally reconciled his and Jenny Calendar's split, which was provoked by her having kept knowledge secret. She had known of Angel's curse (because she was a member of the Gypsy clan that had instituted it). Her failure to make this common knowledge contributed to Angel's becoming Angelus and, thence, Buffy's and Giles's anger at her.

Giles comes home, expecting Jenny to be there and is welcomed by his home having been dressed in the signs of luxuriant, overwhelming sensuality: a bottle of champagne cooling, red rose petals strewn, an invitation to go upstairs and *La Bohème* being played on the stereo (complementing the already operatic atmosphere of high-blown passion). The intra-diegetic music provides the devastatingly intense soundtrack to both Giles's ascent to what he believes will be love, and the audience's simultaneous descent into what it knows will be tragedy. Jenny has been killed by Angelus earlier in the episode, her neck broken in a beautiful and macabre shot framed by the huge windows, which are dark with the night. We know she is dead, but Giles believes she is waiting for him. The music, which he believes has been put on by Jenny, provides a torturous counterpoint for anyone who knows the opera (Angelus's torture of Giles being preceded by the show's own torture of the audience so that we not only know the facts that will become clear to Giles but also the emotions that he will be facing, a fully realized aesthesis). The part playing as he goes up the stairs is the end of act 1 with Rodolfo and Mimi declaring their love:

O soave fanciulla, o dolce viso	Oh! Lovely girl! Oh, sweet face
Di mite circonfuso alba lunar	bathed in the soft moonlight
In te ravviso il sogno	I see you in the dream
Ch'io vorrei sempre sognar	I'd dream forever

As Giles arrives at the moment of his devastation, he drops the bottle and Mimi sings "Ah love, you rule alone" while Rodolpho responds, "Already I taste in spirit, the height of tenderness." The layers of dramatic irony produced by the general audience's knowledge of Jenny's death, a less general recognition of the sumptuous operatic scene dressing and the more specific recognition of the opera and its words provoke a level of emotional distress rarely matched again on the show.

Possibly more interesting than those areas of the program where the audience is invited to know something that the characters do not is when the program leaves the audience without knowledge that the characters may or may not also know. Often this has the effect of opening up the possible world of the Buffyverse in ways hitherto unexplored, additionally reasserting the show's manipulation of the aesthetics of representational realism.

Realism as a mode of artistic representation has been much challenged in the twentieth century by artists and theorists alike. From Joyce's narrative complications in *Ulysses* and wholesale linguistic jamboree in *Finnigan's Wake*, to Picasso's fragmentation of space, to Rothko's huge blocks of color, to Jarman's entirely blue screen, to a plethora of others, realism across the arts has been undermined. From the point of view of postmodern theory, realism is regarded skeptically because of assumed political and philosophical claims inherent in its very being. In the place of realism, many critics prefer an aesthetic that draws attention to its own methods of construction, thereby effacing any sense of a supposed transparent window onto the world. In fiction this process of self-conscious recognition of the process of fictionalizing within the fictional work itself is termed metafiction.

Drawing on the theories of Linda Hutcheon, the theorist Alison Lee claims for metafictional texts a cultural or ethical engagement because they subvert realist codes and conventions. For Lee, as for Hutcheon, these codes and conventions have broader ideological implications. There is a sense in which realism is seen as upholding, or at least enforcing, a set of claims about the nature of the world and humanity's relationship with it. Lee discusses some of the "untenable assumptions"[12] that she sees as implicit in realist writing. Included among these are the ideas that "'empirical reality' is objectively observable through pure perception" and that "there can exist a direct transcription from 'reality' to novel." Underpinning both of these is the belief that there "is a common, shared sense of both 'reality' and 'truth.'"[13] Beyond the confines of the novel, this assumed sharing of a worldview is the point at which realism's assumed conservatism is demonstrated.

A shared sense of the real and the true would seem to suggest a common set of moral and ethical principles. The realist writer, therefore, is not simply describing the world, he is judging it. In turn the world will judge his art not, according to Lee, in terms of its aesthetic achievements or processes, but in terms of its morality. "The essential equation is that 'good' men will produce 'good' art."[14] Lee quotes a dictum of Ruskin's and then criticizes it:

In "The Queen of the Air," he is insistent that "Great art is the expression of the mind of a great man, and mean art, that of the want of mind of a weak man" (1903–12b:19: 389).

It is easy to see how this kind of criticism loses sight of the processes and structures of art except in so far as the art is the reflection of a good man whose example will offer appropriate moral instruction to the reader. Art develops, then, the status of religion, and the artist becomes a moral guide. This is certainly one of the aspects of Realism which has intruded into the twentieth century.[15]

It is this intrusion that Lee would appear to see as having its corrective in metafiction. By challenging the realist codes of objectivity, transparent language, pure perceptions and moral instruction, the metafictionalist is also challenging the worldviews that support, and are in turn supported by, them. This challenge is termed by Linda Hutcheon as "de-naturalizing critique,"[16] which is expanded to mean that "postmodernism works to 'de-doxify' our cultural representations and their undeniable political import."[17] This is to say that by rejecting a literary expression that was predicated on a conception of language and representation that was both philosophically flawed and ethically dubious (in that it reflected the views of the dominant culture and pretended this was nature), the metafictionalist is inevitably making a (radical) political gesture.

When Xander expresses disbelief that the room the Scoobies spend all their time planning and researching in is actually the school library ("Passion" [2.17]), he is the mouthpiece for the writer's response to fan criticism regarding the lack of students in the library. When an amnesiac Buffy scoffs at the idea of a vampire with a soul falling in love with a Slayer ("Tabula Rasa" [6.8]) it is difficult to imagine a more self-referential, metafictional moment of comedic-ironic self-deprecation. Andrew's moment as the would-be documentary maker of "Buffy: Slayer of the Vampyres" ("Storyteller" [7.16]), and the psychiatrist's reflections on Buffy's mental illness in "Normal Again" (6.17) all proffer grand examples of the metafictional nature of the show.[18] Yet its realism remains vital.

Realism is, of course, no more than a technique. It is a technique that may well have political and philosophical implications, but it is a technique first and foremost. As a technique it aims to represent its object in a fashion that means that a viewer or reader will be as little distracted as possible by the act of representation so that the world offered will be as unmediated and, therefore, as real-seeming as possible. Realism is not a representation of the real but a technique for the greatest possible level of real-seeming-ness.

In a show like *Buffy* the real-seeming-ness of the world presented as normal is vital if its susceptibility to supernatural threat is to work. Sunnydale has to be believable (real-seeming) in order that we have some level of connection through recognition of our real world. The costumes, sets, lighting, and language all have to work as unobtrusively as possible so that the representation works,[19] analogously to realist fiction, such that the camera lens really is just a window onto a world and we do not see the lens "working" (through, for example, effects such as slow motion, foreshortening, dramatic lighting effects such as noir shadows, overexposure and so on). The production techniques need to be as little visible as possible so that the buildings, streets, exteriors and so on (which all carry the recognizable reality of Southern California[20]) are as unexceptional as possible. This is, itself, an exceptional feat.

With the establishment of a "real" Sunnydale, produced via representationally realist techniques (which is to say techniques that become the habituated norm or what Sue Turnbull refers to as the *Buffy* "standard"[21]), the unreal world of monsters and demons can be allowed into it with the expectation of a firmer sense of the grounding of the show such that these elements are both more plausible and more frightening than if Sunnydale itself were also unreal. A Sunnydale introduced in swirling fog, empty houses with clattering shutters, or howling wolves on the periphery would immediately have marked it as a horror town in a horror show; our Sunnydale places it in the remit of other realist genres such as the cop show (*Law and Order*) or the thriller (*The Lyon's Den*). The generic disturbances that arrive as a result of a shift in production techniques do move us away from the realism of the show. This is in part because realism does not work as a composite: either a show *is* realist in which case the production techniques it sets up at the beginning remain in place throughout, or the techniques shift and vary in which case it is a composite and realism is simply one set of techniques among many. The interlacing of techniques with regard to production (different uses of sound effects, of lighting, of camera angles, of acting styles) all make *Buffy* a generically mongrel show, impure in terms of technique yet based absolutely on an initial technical realism, that allows the marvelous uses of filmic pastiche and parody to be exploited to the full. Indeed, McNeilly et al. aver that "what remains real about the show is its insistence on acknowledging its own formal limits as television: its reality effect inheres in its parodic style."[22] Without that foundation, all the other games played would fail.

The complete importance of the initial proposition of representational realism is that it allows an enormous presumption of knowledge. By recognizing the world presented the viewer is also assumed to know about it. He or she will know what that world is supposed to be like and will, therefore, recognize those elements that are alien or intrusive. The aesthetic effect of the realist production technique is to offer a secure, known, recognizable world whose safety we care about. When there are aspects, then, about which we are ignorant, that are offered without explanation or comment, the simple fact of their unknownness is liable to provide cause for concern. Insofar as the demons are concerned, their connection to the world of *Buffy* of which we are now insiders (having been given the knowledge of the Slayer's heritage) means that they are not unknown as such. Or even when they are, we can expect the group to find out about them and through knowledge of them, learn how to defeat them. Much more unsettling are the extensions to the world of *Buffy* itself that undermine our sense of what it is or is meant to be.

The first example of this occurs in the penultimate episode of season 1, "Out of Mind, Out of Sight" (1.11). The season typically offered us a set of episodes in which the monsters and demons act as metaphors and allegories for growing up in an American high school.[23] The traumas of dating loom large, as do parental pressure, peer pressure, gangs, physical abuse, intractable authority and so on. The metaphors are recognized as such by the audience by the wonderful imposition of the supernatural onto the real world of Sunnydale such that the representational conflict between realism and horror is resolved at the point of allegorical recognition. The world, then, remains understood and knowable; the demons are a threat to that world, are defeated, and the emotional metaphor is registered. Largely, this is because, Sunnydale is "real"— the techniques of its representation allow us to understand it as an American town where we could also live. However, in (1.11) this cozy representation is massively subverted, and it is a subversion that marks the beginning of the audience's awareness that the realism that underpins the show and provides us with a real Sunnydale is truly only a technique and belies the fact that Sunnydale is in fact not what we thought we knew at all.

When Marcie Ross is so ignored by students and teachers at Sunnydale High that she becomes invisible, the metaphor is clear. Buffy and friends chase down the mystery, uncover the cause and try to right the wrongs. As Scott Westerfeld has discussed in "A Slayer Comes to Town," the resolution of this sort of story, a "trespass story" as he calls it, tends toward a restitution of the normal, the explanation of the event and the covering up of the awkward supernatural elements. Most pertinently for *Buffy*, the gang of the original *Scooby Doo*, from whom our Scoobies take their name, were always able to demonstrate that the supernatural was, in fact, simply a ruse created by a criminal.[24]

Buffy has had its cover-up stories, the implication of which (like the necessary secret of Buffy's role and the Scoobies' knowledge) is that the residents of Sunnydale and of the wider world are unaware of, and need to remain unaware of, the existence of the supernatural. The earliest of these is Cordelia's explanation for the events in "The Harvest" (1.2), which she reasons away:

> Well, I heard it was rival gangs. You know, fighting for turf? But all I can tell you is they were an ugly way of looking. And Buffy, like, knew them! Which is just too weird. I mean, I don't even remember that much, but I'm telling you, it was a freak show! [1.2].

Giles's response to the incredulous Scoobies is simply, "People have a tendency to rationalize what they can and forget what they can't" (1.2). So, the show is playing with the notion of a normal town besieged by monsters that no one except our heroes and the audience know about.

The case of Marcie Ross is different, however. Having figured out the cause of the attacks and discovered Marcie's condition, we have a subversion of narrative expectation insofar as the discovery (knowledge) does not bring success (restitution) because Marcie cannot be saved by Buffy. Among other plausible reasons for this is Buffy's own assertion that Marcie is a "thundering loon" (1.11). This pleasingly amusing undermining of expectations is then drastically amplified when we see Marice being led into a classroom (or we see a seemingly empty classroom with books rustling, desks opening and chairs moving and infer from that that Marcie is there with other people) and discover that this is a spy training class for the FBI and today's lesson is "assassination and infiltrations" to which invisible Marcie's response is "cool" (1.11). Suddenly the premise of the show, its expression of a sophisticated trespass story is shifted. Trespass stories work by virtue of the secret, which is absolute. Yet here, the world in which Sunnydale is situated is now not one where only we and the Scoobies know of the town's supernatural, potentially demonic, aspect, but the FBI does too. Apart from being a nod to *The X-Files*, this causes the audience to shift its response to the world of the show. It is no less realistic in terms of its techniques of representing Sunnydale, but the reality that is being presented is a lot less stable, and much more open to change than had appeared to be the case until now.

The audience is never given an explanation for the fate of Marcie. We are simply presented with a fact and left to infer our own response. We are left in a state of unknowing. This is a ploy that the show uses on a number of occasions and it is one of the reasons for the sustaining interest in it. Unlike the simple restoration of order at the end of a trespass tale where the real is unproblematically maintained in a mythical state of sameness, the Buffyverse is malleable, changeable and unknowable in an absolute sense; it is conceptually monstrous such that the world itself is a constituent part of the potential for surprise and shock.

The way in which the world presented to us in *Buffy* shifts and alters is very well discussed in Westerfeld's essay mentioned above as well as Margaret L. Carter's "A World Without Shrimp."[25] I want to focus, rather than on the construction of alternative realties, on the extent to which the audience's knowledge and the program's manipulation of it upset our reading of the Buffyverse.

If the FBI can know about Marcie, then the secret is evidently less well kept than previously assumed. This can be accommodated in our experience of Sunnydale (and maybe even, as Giles suggests, forgotten about) only at the expense of foregoing the belief in the reality of Sunnydale as somehow equivalent to a world that we could plausibly inhabit. The fictionality of the world has been explicitly reinforced through the expansion of the knowledge of the supernatural beyond Sunnydale but, importantly, beyond our ken too. So, at the same time that the show's fictional element has been reasserted, it *feels* truer than ever because, like our own world, it refuses to explain aspects of itself. It is both familiar and strange, known and inscrutable. Using this as an aesthetic premise, our hero's *unheimlich* homestead is able to surprise and disorient us more and more, and to do so with increasingly sophisticated representational tools.[26]

Buffy is not just the five acts that offer us that episode's story. It is comprised of a "previously on" segment (from about one-third of the way through season 2 this becomes an almost ever-present feature), a teaser and the credits.[27] This is as much a part of the experience of a *Buffy* episode on television as the story itself, and it is as much a part of its world too, in the sense of providing the aesthetic "edges" of the text that separate it from what has been on the television before and what will come after. We are welcomed into the world through the familiar door of its opening form, especially the opening credit sequence.

Season 4's "Superstar" (4.17) uses the audience's familiarity with the show's structure to present one of the most aesthetically radical subversions of a television world that has ever occurred. There is a short "previously on" that seems to return us to "Earshot" (3.18), in which the previously minor character Jonathan is central to part of the story, with little that would be troubling or unusual. We then are launched into the teaser, which has Buffy and friends trying to fight a nest of vampires and deciding they need help. The unusual need for assistance is itself quite strange but their arrival at Jonathan's mansion (when did he get a mansion, how did he get so rich, why would they go to *him*?) is just incomprehensible. This enormously defamiliarized set-up is as nothing to what comes next, however.[28] The opening credits to each season alter and show a montage of elements from the season to come and some snippets from seasons past. They focus primarily on Buffy herself with the other Scoobies having a reasonably large segment too, under which their names are credited. "Superstar" (4.17) has as its opening credits ten shots of the character Jonathan, played by Danny Strong, in postures of heroic or starlike quality. Not only, then, has the world within the show been altered, but the world that would usually be regarded as at the edges of the show, its paratexts, has been altered too. The wholesale magical shift of reality that, we discover, has occurred in Sunnydale and moreover around the world (Jonathan has invented the Internet and starred in *The Matrix*, for example) is true not just for the fictional reality of Sunnydale but for *our* reality too. Another way of reading it is that what appears to be extraneous to the representation of the *world* of *Buffy* but necessary to its *branding* (in other words, emphatically located in our world of merchandising) is dragged into the fictional world. This profoundly unsettles our relationship with the program by defamiliarizing one of the seemingly least important parts of the show's apparatus.

Our knowledge of the show and our knowledge of what we understand the opening credits to be there for are both confounded. In so doing, the relationship between aesthetics and knowledge becomes involved in questions not just internal to the episode's story (with all the attendant metaphorical relationships with the real world), but extends beyond that to questions of branding, merchandise, contracts and the rest.[29]

The coincidence of "our" world and the increasingly different and differentiated world of *Buffy* is forced into the foreground again in season six's excellent "Normal Again" (6.17). In this episode Buffy has been seemingly drugged by a demon summoned by Andrew, Warren and Jonathan (who constitute the season's pretend Big Bad — Willow, of course, assuming that role with vehemence as it unfolds) and is suffering from hallucinations in which she is an inmate in a mental institution suffering from schizophrenia. The representational economy with which the show has worked in presenting Sunnydale to us retains all the techniques of realism such that we still believe in its integrity and truth. The very same techniques, though located entirely in the interior of the institution, are used for the "insane Buffy" sections. Neither is afforded any greater sense of aesthetic verisimilitude than the other and, as such, the viewer is given no aesthetic grounds (tenebrous lighting, overextended shadows for a gothic[30] insane asylum, for example) from which to choose which of the realties is truer. We, having invested so much time and emotion in the Sunnydale Buffy, almost certainly wish that to be the real world that she should live in, but we are given no representational clues that will allow us to *know*.

The situation becomes more complicated when her psychiatrist, in explaining Buffy's state and likelihood of recovery to her parents (in the Sunnydale world, of course, one of them — her mother — is dead and the other — Buffy's father — is absent) tells them, and us, the following:

> The Slayer, right, but that's only one level. She's also created an intricate latticework to support her primary delusion. In her mind, she's the central figure in a fantastic world beyond imagination. She's surrounded herself with friends, most with their own superpowers ... who are as real to her as you or me. More so, unfortunately. Together they face ... grand overblown conflicts against an assortment of monsters both imaginary and rooted in actual myth. Every time we think we're getting through to her, more fanciful enemies magically appear [6.17].

The doctor, then, provides the audience with the absolute expression of the skepticism that must be kept in abeyance when entering into the fantastical world of *Buffy* and which each viewer does try to keep hidden. By this point in season 6, some viewers were becoming increasingly restless about the absence of a true Big Bad and, in its stead, the geeks, Jonathan, Andrew and Warren. The doctor's comments resound as both wonderful metafictional commentary and as an assertion of "our" world, a world in which Buffy is not a superhero (how could she be, there are no such things, let alone monsters and demons) but a mentally ill young girl: "Buffy, you used to create these grand villains to battle against, and now what is it? Just ordinary students you went to high school with. No gods or monsters ... just three pathetic little men ... who like playing with toys."

Additionally, Dawn's role in the show, her abrupt and extraordinary appearance that necessitated the audience's revision of the last four seasons, and the characters to have the intellectual understanding of her mystical nature while retaining the memories of her whole life, is critiqued by the doctor:[31]

> A magical key. Buffy inserted Dawn into her delusion, actually rewriting the entire history of it to accommodate a need for a familial bond. Buffy, but that created inconsistencies, didn't it? Your sister, your friends, all of those people you created in Sunnydale, they aren't as comforting as they once were. Are they? They're coming apart [6.17].

At this point, the doctor's comments are so much a part of our world (in the general sense of the world we inhabit but in a more precise sense, too, of the collection of *Buffy* fans watching the show) that to see Buffy in it, fragile, frightened, insane is to recognize the plausibility of the proposition that the entire world of *Buffy* is the hallucination of Buffy. Indeed, the writer and the director of the episode, on the DVD commentary, both indicate that they would have been pleased for this to be the final episode of the season, thereby leaving the audience in an ontological limbo, especially as the very last shot is of the insane, real Buffy, blank-eyed and unresponsive to care.

The location of the insane asylum presents a different way that the show engages with questions of knowledge, and this is to do with the institutions that are supposed to have it: notably schools, universities, hospitals, and various arms of government. The insane asylum represents a version of knowledge closely related to ideals of scientific rationalism. These ideals are, for Michel Foucault in his famous *Madness and Civilization*, the result of an event occurring between the Renaissance and the Classical Age (or the post–Descartes world) in which madness is silenced as a legitimate form of expression. Madness becomes medicalized and, through psychiatry, a discourse *about* madness occurs, which excludes madness itself any point of entry into the discussion. Foucault writes of the silencing of madness, "[T]he language of psychiatry, which is a monologue of reason about madness, has been established only on the basis of such a silence."[32] Buffy, in "Normal Again" (6.17) is silenced throughout the asylum scenes, only being able to assent to recommendations given to her by the extremely kind doctor.

The fact that the proposition that Buffy is mad and that her role as Slayer is the product of mental illness is so plausible is largely due to the production values of the show but is equally due to the show's expression of a cultural practice that has been established as cultural fact: irrational-seeming behavior can and, indeed, must always be explicable through rational means. *Buffy* exists as an expression of the irrational-seeming and any episode that is able to challenge that premise through recourse to a rational discourse (even at the expense of the show's entire history) is likely to be able to achieve its goal. The fact that this episode decides to employ not only knowledge of the real world but, moreover, to assert the primacy of the *mode* of knowledge most prevalent in the real world (scientific rationalism) is an index of just how secure the show's belief in its own fictional world is.

What is interesting is just how sympathetic the doctor is. The episode refuses the easy gothic horror of the mad scientist and also eschews the equally easy contemporary example of the blinkered scientist who fails to engage with humanity or see potential ethical complexity. Here, the scientific rationalism with which we are presented is part of a genuine desire to cure Buffy of her illness and this, from the evidence of the show, is a medical-pharmaceutical endeavor and not Freudian-oriented talk therapy. Knowledge is put to the aide of humanity via scientific research into neuroscience in order that a young girl with delusions can be made better. It is intriguing, of course, that (if we are to assume that the continuation of the series in Sunnydale rather than the institution implies that the asylum was imaginary) the scientific rational explanation is part of a mystically induced hallucination in the Sunnydale world. Rationalism has never fared very well in the Buffyverse.

The dissemination of knowledge to as many people as possible through a system of institutions designed for the sole purpose of that very dissemination is one of the most notable achievements of contemporary social practice. Increasingly democratized throughout most countries that have it in the twentieth century, education systems tend to offer education of at least a minimal level to people from the age of three or so upwards. In order to achieve this, the full weight of social systems, infrastructures, taxation and so on has to come into effect. Mass education not only expresses the ideals of versions of post–Enlightenment liberalism but it also requires those very ideals in order to come into being. The American high school, whatever else it may be, however socially or financially troubled, represents one of the great achievements of rationalism. To place one of these monuments above a Hellmouth is immediately to imply a critique.

The Hellmouth, the portal to chaos and the irrational, is kept in check, at least symbolically, by the school. The school imparts knowledge to the students who, at first at least, along with the citizens of Sunnydale, are oblivious to the dangers beneath them. Chaos is reigned in by rationalism. The experience is different, of course. The Hellmouth's power seems to have the capacity to literalize metaphor and make manifest that which had existed only as language: chaos bleeds into the rational.

The school itself, as far as the audience is concerned, is very little engaged in education. There is a very good pragmatic reason for this: television drama is unlikely to remain very exciting if it simply stays in the classroom. The few visits we do have to a classroom are usually brief and never to learn what the students are learning in terms of institutional knowledge. The school is the location for the drama, and the drama is located, primarily, in the free time of the students; Xander's crush on a teacher requires a certain time in class, but the real story is during the breaks and after school ("Teacher's Pet" [1.4]), for example. The trouble that Buffy finds herself in at home is because of the limitations that school places on her ability to function as the Slayer by not letting her leave school grounds during specified times. The conflict between the school as expression of rational ideals and its location above the Hellmouth, in addition to Buffy's need to have access to other forms of knowledge, provides one of the great tensions in the show.

It is not just the school in general but the library in particular that sits atop the Hellmouth for the first three seasons. A school library is intended as a shared resource where the safekeeping and dissemination of knowledge can occur. That Sunnydale High's is so frequently empty is comment enough, but that it is the locus for the research undergone by the Scoobies allows for a number of interesting questions about knowledge to be articulated.

The library at Sunnydale is, as part of sanctioned institutional authority,[33] there to provide the texts necessary for a student to complete his or her studies. The books and other items, then, are part of orthodox knowledge and Giles's job is to enable access to them for the students and, presumably, faculty. He is the custodian of an "open" knowledge environment. However, the library, as part of an unofficial but equally institutional authority in relation to the Watchers' Council, is determinedly "closed."[34] The knowledge there is heterodox (both from secular education and theological inquiry) and deemed to be dangerous by the Council and its Watcher. It is deemed equally dangerous by the authorities when, under the auspices of Mothers Opposed to the Occult in "Gingerbread" (3.11), the stocks of the "secret" library are cleared and burned. Giles, then, operates under curiously similar, if ostensibly opposed, edicts: hide the heterodox knowledge from the world in order to protect them from the truth of what lies beneath; but also protect that orthodox knowledge from those from the Hellmouth who would seek to destroy it.

The knowledge may be heterodox by virtue of its being concerned with the irrational world of demons, alternative dimensions, and magic but it is susceptible to all the rigors of modern interrogation and research. Indeed, it is as scholars or detectives that the Scoobies function in the library. They seek out clues, sketch hypotheses, and arrive at conclusions that are counterfactually verifiable. The first season, especially, with its generic affinity to the thriller or whodunit, has the gang engaged in discussions that are formally congruent with anything that may be seen on *Law and Order* or read in Sherlock Holmes stories or Wilkie Collins's *The Moonstone*.[35] This is true even if the content is significantly different. Taking this initial notion of the rational and the irrational confronting each other at the intersection of the school library and the Hellmouth, McNeilly et al. offer a further assessment that includes the very fact of television, and its organization of channels, in its argument:

> The Hellmouth-library subtends to a necessary contradiction; to stop an unruly disclosure of demonic power and an over-writing of self by forces beyond its grasp, a counterflow of information, of kissing, of narrative works to be let loose. Knowledge, and sometimes blood, wants to be streamed through proper channels. And these channels—circulatory systems, discursive constructs—both shape and are shaped by the channel structure of television.[36]

Television as both the medium through which ideas about knowledge in the show are being transmitted and as an integral part of contemporary dissemination of information is looked on as an object of disdain at times on *Buffy*. Xander's jubilation at finding a television in Giles's house and Giles's tremulous look as Xander gleefully pronounces, "Look, he's shallow. Like us" ("The Harsh Light of Day" [4.3]) indicates this, and even Oz admits to being a little "disappointed" in Giles whose only defense is that he watches "public television." By contrast, books are assumed to have, in addition to their pragmatic function, a sense of high cultural capital.[37] The repositories of the knowledge, the books themselves, are also interesting insofar as they are nearly all heavy, leather-bound, hand-printed, hand-sketched old books. Their authority resides partly in their age (and almost unfailing accuracy) but also in their aesthetics. They are objects of beauty and delight in themselves (even if the engravings and description produce a welter of "ews" from the gang). This is juxtaposed by Giles to modern systems of information retrieval and dissemination, not only the television but also the computer which has, crucially, no smell. It is, for Giles, at least as important that knowledge have a sensory aspect (be subject to aesthetics) as an epistemological one; knowledge affects the body as well as the mind:

> I know! Smell is the most powerful trigger to the memory there is. A certain flower or a, a whiff of smoke can bring up experiences ... long forgotten. Books smell. Musty and, and, and, and rich. The knowledge gained from a computer, is, uh, it ... it has no, no texture, no, no context. It's, it's there and then it's gone. If it's to last, then, then the getting of knowledge should be, uh, tangible, it should be, um ... smelly ["I Robot, You Jane" (1.8)].

The person to whom he makes this remark is the "techno-pagan," Jenny Calandar, played by Robia La Morte. As a member of the gypsy clan who cursed Angel, she is evidently, in terms of the show's representational economy, part of a long tradition of mysticism and magic. She is also, however, very much a part of the technological age and is, in addition, beautiful. Michelle Callander uses this to provide a sexualized reading of the mysticism versus modernity debate that pervades *Buffy* and finds one of its most trenchant presentations here. She says, drawing on Robia La Morte's physicality as well as the simple fact of newness, "Whedon wants his audience to find technology more attractive because more modern."[38]

Giles's knowledge is, then, heterodox, aesthetically rich, irrational in content but open to rational inquiry and central to the saving of humanity. Buffy is aided in her fights by this knowledge, all of which is, for the first three seasons, housed in the center of what should be the bastion of official, orthodox, rational knowledge. The two realms come into conflict, especially through the figure of Principal Snyder. The fact that he is working for the mayor, who is himself embroiled in the mystical, means that Snyder cannot be read simply as an expression of repressed rationality trying to subdue unruly irrationality, though the extent to which Snyder knows of the mayor's secret means that it is not possible to say that one cannot at least imagine this as a reading too. The conflict between the two versions of knowledge is, however, largely played out as a function of other conflicts, rather than being the battle in itself.

This changes in season four, where the Initiative are emphatically marked as an example of scientific rationalism who are opposed, explicitly, to the occult, irrational world of knowledge used by Buffy. The Initiative is a secret government-military group whose aim is to hunt down and capture for research, or kill, "hostile subterrestrials." One of the many differences in approach is outlined by Maggie Walsh, Buffy's psychology lecturer, the Initiative's head scientist and, it would appear, commander. When Buffy chooses to work with them, Maggie says, "We use the latest in scientific technology and state-of-the-art weaponry and you, if I understand correctly, poke them with a sharp stick" ("A New Man" [4.12]). The purposeful belittling of Buffy's methods when set against all that technology can buy and provide sets up one of the ongoing battles of the season: whose methods are better? The fact that both have remained unaware of each other's presence for so long suggests a certain myopia on both sides. Buffy is astonished to discover Riley Finn (her psychology TA, Maggie Walsh's graduate student, member of the Initiative, and soon-to-be Buffy's boyfriend) has never heard of her, especially given all the resources they must have:

> I thought a professional demon chaser like yourself would have figured it out by now. I'm the Slayer. Slay-er? Chosen One. She who hangs out a lot in cemeteries? You're kidding. Ask around. Look it up: Slayer comma the ["Doomed" (4.11)].

The wonderful demand that he use the dictionary (the great monument to rational and taxonomic thought) to find out about her is a glorious moment. More important, though, is the clear sense of hostility felt between the two methods. Buffy's relationship with Riley means that first she joins forces with the Initiative and then he chooses to join the Scoobies.

The Initiative's methods are seen to be wrongly focused on two grounds. The first is because of a structural feature of the organization. Maggie Walsh appears to be in charge of the operation on the ground, though she is clearly answerable to people higher up the chain of command as seen in "Primeval" (4.21). She is represented as part of a tradition of scientists made popular by such texts as *Frankenstein* and *Dr. Jekyll and Mr. Hyde.* The scientist's belief in their work's worth blinds them to any and all other considerations. For Maggie, the Initiative is really just a front for creating her part-human, part-cyborg super soldier Adam. Her delusions and self-importance lead her to try and kill Buffy, which in turn means that her favorite, Riley, rejects her. The second problem, it is strongly implied, would lead to the failure of the project even were it run by someone less dangerous. This problem is neatly presented by Toby Daspit in "Buffy Goes to College, Adam Murders to Dissect: Education and Knowledge in Postmodernity." In this essay, Daspit writes, "In knowing the 'true' nature of demons, the Initiative's goal appears to be to 'solve' the demon problem, echoing modernism's faith in the ability of science and reason to remedy all ills."[39] Modernity's claim to mastery seen in many of its epistemological models[40] is seen as potentially problematic in and of itself. The resolute belief in material explanations and remedies to problems via mastery of knowledge produces Adam and, importantly, produces his own belief in the same structures of thought. His mutilation of the little boy (as I have said before, *Buffy* is never afraid to wear its references on its sleeve) is explained by Adam as a desire for knowledge ("Goodbye Iowa" [4.14]). Adam becomes the manifest danger of a modernist epistemology that finds its apotheosis in scientific rationalism.[41]

Against this is Giles's occult knowledge. As mentioned, this is open to the very same modernist methods of scrutiny. This implies that the show is not necessarily opposed to contemporary modes of knowledge (Willow is, after all, a computer geek before she is a Wiccan and remains one after her magic has turned bad, and Jenny Calander is a techno-pagan) but that it resists the institutionalizing aspect of that knowledge in systems that appear to promote certain sorts of standardized behaviors (school, the army, for example). Even the apparently more liberal and open environment of the university has Maggie Walsh as one of its professors, and within this environment Buffy is humiliated by a popular culture lecturer.

Occult knowledge is no less prone to forms of absolutism and coercion, however. While Maggie Walsh may desire to have mastery over knowledge in order to create Adam, there are versions of mastery from the supernatural world that Buffy and her friends must constantly combat. The most obvious of these are prophecies that, by their very nature, assume foreknowledge that is unquestionable. *Angel* is much more dedicated to playing with the idea of prophecies, especially to the extent that they are seen to be malleable or inscrutable,[42] but *Buffy* does too. When Buffy dies at the end of season one, the prophecy foretelling her death has come true: a supervening power that exceeds all human intervention or knowing has proved its dominion on earth.

Buffy is revived, however, by Xander, of all people. At the very least, the status of the prophecy is questioned with regard to its completeness (did someone lose the second half that read "and then she will be revived"?). Alternatively the supposed immutability of certain prophecies (this is from the Codex, and therefore unimpeachable) is open to other more local and controllable forces. The prophecy is, after all, fulfilled: Buffy does die.

The completion of the prophecy's descriptive utterance (something like "It is fore-told that the Slayer will die") implies a prescriptive that is carried within it. To use a descriptive as a prescriptive is a part of strategy of totalitarian politics and linguistic domination that has been analyzed by, among others, Lyotard following Austin. *Buffy* does not fundamentally dislocate the descriptive from the prescriptive, but it does render a possible supplement, whereby an additional level of description in excess of the seemingly hermeneutically closed utterance is possible. By so doing, the implied total knowledge of the prophecy is undermined and made open to reinterpretation and revision.[43]

Neither Maggie Walsh's drive for total knowledge through scientific rationalism nor age-old prophecies with their claims to omniscience are seen as viable models for knowledge, at least not insofar as any threat to the continuation of the Slayer is concerned. Ancient or modern, knowledge is dangerous when its claims are totalizing.

Buffy engages with these different ideas of knowledge and always comes down against totalizing forms of knowledge. If Buffy claims for herself the position of lawgiver, thereby concentrating knowledge and power in herself alone, she is expelled by the rest of the group ("Empty Places" [7.19]); if Maggie Walsh seeks to create Adam as the culmination of her methods, she is killed; when the show presents a world as true and known (if growing) it upsets our reading by offering a plausible alternative; if we think we recognize its genre, an episode shifts somewhere else; and, as I discuss in part II, if we think we, unlike Anya, are able to get all the references and know the show entirely, we are very much mistaken.

Buffy delights in making things complex, refusing simplification. Knowledge that seeks total answers tends also toward a simplified universe. The Buffyverse does not allow this to happen. This places strain on narrative and credulity at times (Dawn's introduction), and it can frustrate us when the show becomes something other than what we thought we knew (the Slayers in Training in season 7), but this is a small price to pay for a show that insists upon the openness and expansiveness of knowledge and represents this in an aesthetic that provides formal expression of one of the central concerns of any notion of culture.

♦ CHAPTER 2 ♦

Aesthetics, Culture
and Ethnicity

"Silly, silly British man"

When Andrew calls Giles a "silly, silly British man," mocking his capacity to play Dungeons and Dragons in "Chosen" (7.22), we are reminded, in the finale to the whole show, of *Buffy*'s fascination with Englishness in particular and Britishness in general. From Giles to Wesley to Gwendolyn Post to Spike to The Watchers' Council and a host of others, the representation of Britishness is a continual and significant thread in the program's engagement with the presentation of culture. While Englishness might be the most prominent ethnicity in terms of the show's particular fascination with it as an object of curiosity, it is far from being alone. More prominent even than Englishness, but not recognized as an object of curiosity in quite the same way by the show's producers or its U.S. audience, is Americanness. The aesthetics of representation with respect to Americanness has led Charlaine Harris to lament *Buffy*'s deeply homogenized view of Americanness as white and middle class[1] and this shall be addressed later in the chapter. In addition to Americanness and Englishness, there are representations of other ethnicities in the Buffyverse, including Irishness through the character of Angel,[2] Jewishness (itself a problematic term in relation to ethnicity) via Willow, seemingly nonspecific Afro-Caribbeanness through Kendra and, from a different perspective, vampireness as a category of ethnic exclusion.[3] This chapter will attempt to trace some of the reflections on ethnicity that the show engages in, and to see how, despite many obvious and problematic lapses in its representations of ethnic difference, the manner of these representations provides a subtle and arresting view of ethnic construction.

To view ethnicity as a construction is to see it, and its contribution to a more comprehensive notion of identity, in broadly performative terms, which is to say aestheticized. Julie Rivkin and Michael Ryan provide a discussion of ethnicity as performance (or, as a de-ontologized approach to ethnicity that sees it as a cultural production rather than a physical attribute). They say,

> ethnicity would seem to be culturally rehearsed and performed into an imaginary ontological status; indeed, as the contrived (through constant and repeated endogamous marriage) repetition of traits such as facial characteristics that are merely external, representational graphics without meaning or signifiers that signify nothing more than themselves, ethnic identity consists of the performance into imaginary being of something which has no existence outside of the repetition of traits.[4]

The extent to which external characteristics are as "mere" as suggested here or that they have no meaning in themselves are points of evident dispute (the discussion of ethics in chapter 4 engages with this question to some extent). However, the performative aspect of ethnicity is one that, through its de-ontologized aspect disavows, for example, the blatant racism of the Watchers' Council with respect to demons, as well as tempering many of the claims made on behalf of abstract universal humanity by concentrating on cultural practices as definitional of, rather than ancillary to, ethnic identity. This chapter is going to argue that *Buffy* is largely concerned with offering a performative understanding of ethnicity (and identity more broadly conceived). It will begin, though, with one of the most surprising comments ever made on the show in relation to this concept. It comes as part of Giles's effort to reassure Willow, as she is due to head back to Sunnydale after recuperating in England. This recuperation follows her murder of Warren and her attempt to destroy the world toward the end of season 6. Giles says, "In the end, we all are who we are, no matter how much we may appear to have changed" (7.1). In a series that has seen Willow, for example, transform from a geek in season 1 to a goddess in season 7; that has witnessed Anya's strenuous efforts to overcome having been a demon, in order to construct an amalgamated postmodern American identity that can also accommodate her Dark Age Scandinavian incarnation; that has seen Faith reconstituted as a penitent, responsible person after her homicidal havoc; and that has allowed Dawn to be invented out of nothing in order to live the life of Buffy's sister, it is odd, to say the least, to have an assertion of such steadfast ontological security. While the series' increasing reliance on the concept of the soul as a guarantor of humanity may well explain a certain insistence on a core identity, the metaphysical awkwardness of the soul itself should give us pause for thought before it can be seen as an instrument of ontological grounding.[5] And if there is no ontological grounding, or if the fashion of its being is such an insubstantial thing, then Giles's comment seems remarkably out of place in the Buffyverse.

The importance of Giles's comment in relation to *Buffy* and its representation of ethnicity is that it proffers a worldview of the indelibly and absolutely human, which, in its turn, leads into an attitude toward ethnicity that the show does not seem to allow. Which is not to say that the world of the show is in any sense a multiethnic one, but it is to say that, even in its restricted representation of ethnicities, the method of representation is one that disavows an ontologically secure foundation for identification.

My own terminology already indicates one of the difficulties concerning questions of ethnicity, and that is what, exactly, ethnicity is. To talk of Englishness is to imply a state or condition that makes a person English. And any attempt to define that state or condition soon falls prey to exceptions, complications, contradictions and failure. In the 1860s the problem seemed less pronounced as Victorian writers defending colonial practice such as Luke Owen Pike could claim that

> there are probably few educated Englishmen living who have not in their infancy been taught that the English nation is a nation of almost pure Teutonic blood, that its political constitution, its social custom, its internal prosperity, the success of its arms, and the number of its colonies have followed necessarily upon the arrival, in three vessels, of certain German warriors under the command of Hengist and Horsa.[6]

The utterly spurious nature of this claim (hinted at by the adverbial hesitancy of "almost pure") and its espousing of a foundation myth of Teutonic origins with all the implied racial purity that lends to the success of England are, of course, demented. It is not least a lie because it utterly fails to look inward to the plight of many of the English in the emergent cities and depleted villages. More important for my argument, is that Pike[7] locates ethnicity through blood, or heredity, which is then allied with a history. An ontological security (blood determines ethnicity) is derived from, and simultaneously contributes to, the history that tells the story of how that blood came to be English in the first place. This self-fulfilling circularity occludes the aporetic structure so that ontologically grounded ethnicity is guaranteed by history and vice versa. It is not a particularly big step to yoke this myth of ethnic purity with prevailing ideas concerning European modernity in order to translate the myth of an originary moment of ethnic foundations into the discourse of progress and the narratives of Enlightenment. This translation then places Englishness as a representative of European humanism, which, supported by philosophy and science, asserts Man as an evolving creature whose aim is perfectibility and whose European expression is its current apotheosis. Even commentators who were appalled by the events of colonization were, nevertheless, assured of its inevitability. A decade and a half before the previous quotation was written, Robert Knox wrote *The Races of Men* in 1850. Incidentally, apart from being published exactly in the mid-century this was also the moment when Romanticism had its last major flowering at precisely the point when a new Victorian vision of the modern came into play with posthumous publication of Wordsworth's *The Prelude* and the publication of Alfred Lord Tennyson's *In Memoriam*. It is throughout the latter part of the nineteenth century, and mainly in Europe, that Angelus, Spike, Drusilla and Darla are most active in terms of what we see on *Buffy*. This massively important era, from industrialization to colonialism, is the formative time for our family of anti-heroes: they are, in effect, the living residue of European modernity's claims for power and superiority, at the same time as being part of the premodern, irrational world of demons and vampires. Knox, while berating the capture and colonization of parts of North Africa and New Zealand also maintained that the peoples of these countries were physically and mentally inferior and would die while "feebly contending against the stronger races for a corner of [the] earth."[8]

The secure ontological foundation of ethnicity provides a justification, even an imperative, for the colonial project, which is to civilize and humanize. Half a century later Joseph Conrad published his extraordinary tale of Marlowe's journey into the heart of darkness to find the elusive Kurtz. This story provides a neat insight into a critical reflection on modernity that in turn leads us back to the question of ethnicity. *Heart of Darkness* will feature in my discussion of Xander's dream in chapter 7, and it is a curiously prevalent intertext throughout much of *Buffy* and also *Angel*. For the moment, though, I would like to concentrate on general questions regarding modernity as discussed by Jean-François Lyotard. These will seek to locate some current speculations with regard to ethnicity (speculations that are central to this discussion of *Buffy*) in the context of modernity and its subsequent supposed mutation into the postmodern. While focusing on modernity generally, it is, I hope, clear that questions pertaining to notions of the truly human (the Ur-category of any ethnic conceptualization) are as centrally and life-threateningly important in *Buffy*, especially when considering the Chumash tribe,[9] the vampires, Willow's Jewishness, Kendra, and, finally, Giles's ontologically secure identity.

For the great French thinker Jean-François Lyotard, a defining characteristic of modernity is its use of what he has famously called "grand narratives."[10] These narratives, so Lyotard argues in various ways, operate in such a way that they orient the individual within a society toward a future point, a goal. This future point or *telos* will be the culminating point of human history, its final achievement, a space and time where all the wrongs that are thought to be current will have been eradicated. Importantly for Lyotard, and this is a point that can be overlooked too easily by some commentators, this "grand narrative" aspect of modernity has its roots in Christian thought: "The traits of modernity can be seen to appear in the work done by Paul of Tarsis (the apostle), then by Augustine to make an accommodation between the pagan classical tradition and Christian eschatology."[11] The importance of eschatology is that it marks not only a *telos* but also promises that a "lack" felt by the individual will be fulfilled, will finish at the end of time through the remission of evil and the forgiveness of the Father.[12] While later versions of this narrative may not include the Father as such (Marxism, for example), the promise-prophecy of this fulfillment and remission still exists as a principle. The Father, in Lyotard's notion, is "full signifier."[13] This means, roughly, that where an individual had experienced lack or partial knowledge, the Father promises fullness and total knowledge. While it would be tempting to try and read Giles as font of knowledge and Willow's desire to reconcile with him after the events of season 6 in eschatological terms, this would miss the importance of eschatology as an aspect of metanarrative, and to reduce this to a rather banal synecdoche. In other words, narratives in the West since the inception of Christianity have promised a future point that will fulfill history: this is the *historicity* inherent to modernity.

In the same essay from which the above quotation was taken, Lyotard makes the relationship between eschatological thought in Christianity and the historicity of modernity plain:

> [L]ay modernity maintains this temporal device, that of a "great narrative," as one says, which promises at the end to reconcile the subject with itself and the overcoming of its separation. Although secularised, the Enlightenment narrative, Romanticist or speculative dialectics, and the Marxist narrative deploy the same historicity as Christianity, because they conserve the eschatological principle. The completion of history, be it always pushed back, will re-establish a full and whole relation with the law of the Other (capital O) as this relation was in the beginning: the law

of God in the Christian paradise, the law of Nature in the natural right fantasized by Rousseau, the classless society, before family, property, and state imagined by Engles. An immemorial past is always what turns out to be promised by way of an ultimate end.[14]

The claim here is that modernity draws on the idea of eschatology in Christian thought, which posits an initial separation and promises a future reconciliation back into wholeness. European modernity *looks forward* (importantly, then, further occluding the myth of ethnic purity — a backward-looking, mythic attitude — presented by Pike). Not only that, but modernity strives to achieve this hoped-for land of the full and presents to itself a number of possible routes there. This is where we begin to see modernity proper. Modernity is almost inevitably secular. On the one hand it designates a relation to temporality (the eschatological structure); on the other, it is an attempt to find a narrative capable of delivering the promise of that structure. There have been a number of these narratives, which, in combination, could be thought to define modernity.

> The "metanarratives" I was concerned with in *The Postmodern Condition* are those which have marked modernity: the progressive emancipation of reason and freedom, the progressive or catastrophic emancipation of labour (source of alienated value in capitalism), the enrichment of all humanity through the progress of capitalist technoscience, and even — if we include Christianity itself in modernity (as opposed to the classicism of antiquity) — the salvation of creatures through the conversion of souls to the Christian narrative of martyred love. Hegel's philosophy totalises all of these narratives and, in this sense, is itself a distillation of speculative modernity.[15]

What each of these narratives does, in different ways and for particular reasons (all bound up in the eschatological principle), is provide a goal, or in Lyotard's terms an Idea. This Idea (the enrichment of all humanity, for example) is to be achieved through the use of the narrative (capitalist technoscience in this case) and the Idea legitimizes the narrative and any action carried out in its name. An example that Lyotard returns to on a number of occasions to demonstrate this is the Terror after the French Revolution. The Terror was what the leaders of the new French Republic conducted against those it considered enemies of the new republic and its most clear manifestation in popular consciousness is the guillotine. The sheer scale and seeming arbitrariness of the actions would appear on any usual grounds to be a sign of barbarity, wickedness, cruelty and perversion, quite contrary to a supposed "wholeness" or "fullness" for all people. Yet an important aspect of the Idea, for Lyotard, is that there is no object that one can attach to it: it exists as a future hope, a promise and so all that one can say in relation to it is by way of analogue, hypothesis, metaphor. This being so, the Idea can only exist as a part of a culture, as the unifying sign that all language and thought aspires toward: the Idea is a product of cultivation. In some respects, the ultimate expression of an aesthetics of culture is the Idea that provides that culture's eschatological principle. This cultivation, of necessity, believes that the culture it represents is improving, moving toward its *telos*. The French Revolution claimed to be a movement for freedom, the freedom of all people from the yoke of monarchic tyranny. Freedom here is the Idea that legitimizes the narrative and the actions of the Terror. It cannot be seen to "exist," there is no object that can be held up as "freedom": it is a future goal, an eschatological point of hope. The enthusiasm with which the Revolution and the Terror were received (at least at first) can be seen then to be a consequence of a belief in this Idea of freedom. Lyotard discusses Kant's *Conflict of the Faculties* to show how the Terror was justified or explained, and, paraphrasing the Kant book, he says that it was explained that "although the reality of the Terror (its empirical factuality) cannot of course be recognised as legitimate on an ethical or even political level, at least in its effect it is a sign of humanity's progress towards the better."[16]

The French Revolution is not, of course, the same thing as Europe's colonialist enterprise with which *Heart of Darkness* deals nor the same as the constant supernatural threat that threatens civil society in *Buffy*. Different sorts of motivations, different strategies, different ideas and Ideas urged these things. However, the analogy with the Terror is instructive as it indicates the ways in which acts that might be considered from a number of perspectives to be abhorrent can be reconciled with and legitimated through the narratives of modernity and the Ideas that sustain them.

Buffy's rather complex relationship with modernity and postmodernity is significant to much of the argument of this book, and the concept of the Idea is one such complex point. The Idea in *Buffy* is always the saving of the world, and actions that promote this can be defended, even if they are in opposition to human (by which is inevitably meant U.S.) laws and social organizations. The awkwardness of eschatology in *Buffy* is a subject for chapter 3, but for the time being one needs only to think of Giles's murder of Ben at the end of season 5 ("The Gift" [5.22]), or Buffy's terrorizing of Andrew in season 7 ("Storyteller" [7.16]), or, more problematically, the decision of Angel to work for Wolfram and Heart in the final season of *Angel* to see how the Idea supervenes in questions of moral legitimacy.

The Idea in *Buffy*— to save the world from demons who want to destroy humanity — is the ordering principle that informs and demands the actions undertaken in its name. Any action that is undertaken in its name is justified by virtue of that fact. There is a moral absolute good (saving humanity) and any person, thing or action that attempts to countermand that good is, therefore, evil. The ethical implications of this will be discussed in chapters 3 and 4, but the implications for ethnicity are of more immediate concern here; not the least of which is how *Buffy* figures humanity and the human in the first place. To have the saving of humanity as the Idea that predicates the action of the show is to presuppose the notion of what humanity is. In *Buffy*, this is presented as a quality, even the essence, of what it means to be human. Giles tells the Scoobies in "Surprise" (2.3) that the monster called The Judge literally burns the humanity out of people and that while a creature who is truly evil will survive the process, "no human ever has." Humanity, then, defines the human and, irrespective of race, sex or any other marker of cultural difference, anyone with humanity is human. This rather amorphous, even circular, proposition becomes increasingly complicated as the seasons progress, but it provides a partial explanation, defense even, of the overwhelmingly Caucasian grouping in the show. The philosophical question concerning the nature of the human is also caught up in a set of questions regarding aesthetics, especially aesthetic questions pertaining to the presentation of a cultural and social realism.

By choosing to locate Buffy in Sunnydale, the show immediately presents itself with one of two general choices. Either it can forego a certain notion of realism in order to present an ethnically diverse cast who would be unlikely to live in such an affluent Southern Californian town, or it can risk accusations of exclusion in favor of the demands for its realism.[17] The realism is, ultimately, essential. In order for the demons and vampires to appear credible as a threat they have to exist in an environment that has been established as real, as believable, indeed almost "known" to the viewer. Given the power and world reach of U.S. television, and its tendency to present either New York or Los Angeles/Southern California (or SoCal) as the locales for its shows, setting *Buffy* in Sunnydale is an obvious and proper choice.

The shooting script for episode one indicates that, although the students going to school "could be from anywhere in America" they are still demonstrably "SoCal."[18] The "anywhere in America" aspect has been well documented by David Lavery[19] and the specifically SoCal nature of the show has been analyzed by Boyd Tonkin in "Entropy as Demon: Buffy in Southern California."[20] These two essays provide a geographical, topographical, cultural and geological analysis of *Buffy* that is essential to anyone wanting to understand the concept of a global product set in the SoCal region.

The main American characters in the show are white and, with the exception of Willow, are simply American. The commonplace hyphenated American is absent, with no self-defined Irish-Americans, Italian-Americans, Polish-Americans and very few African-Americans.[21] This denial of hyphenated ethnicity is recognized in a fashion that is both playful and knowing as well as potentially offensive (especially in the light of Ono's commentary of the racialized aspect of vampires— see note 3 of this chapter) in "When She Was Bad" (2.1). Utilizing her enormous power of the quip as she is about to stake a vampire Buffy says, "You're a vampire. Oh, I'm sorry, was that an offensive term? Should I say 'undead–American'" (2.1). The episode's title perhaps invites us to critique Buffy's choice of terms here, but the clear use of its intentions as a joke that we should share indicates otherwise. The family names of Buffy's group indicate a lack of ethnic diversity (Summers, Harris, Chase) that is confirmed on the bodies of the actors. The ethnic makeup of the group is, then, hardly representative of "anywhere in America" and yet it is supposed to stand in as precisely that and, by virtue of that fact to extend to include all of humanity. The main difficulty with this arrives at the articulation of the "we." Buffy's job is to save "us," which is to say humanity, but the objective case "us" is clearly of a very different order from the subjective case "we" as expressed by the group. Either the "we" presents an oddly homogenous version of the human — white, middle-class American — or it extends well beyond the human such that the "we" includes a greater section of humanity (though still restricted: English, Jewish) but also demons and vampires such as Angel, Spike, Clem, Oz and Anya.[22] The second version of the "we" appears to be a much more inclusive and expansive one, and indeed it is, and this is because of the way in which ethnicity, identity and moral worth are figured here. To berate the show for failing to present a multiethnic spectrum of characters is understandable from the point of view of a sociology of representation. However, a cultural aesthetic that sees a plurality of ethnicities included in any representation as a positive expression of racial inclusivity misses the point. The assumption behind this is that representational heterogeneity at the level of ethnicity is equivalent to an expression of liberal inclusivity. While this may be true, it fails itself to recognize the aporia that is at the core of this liberal inclusivity. Giles's comment to Willow at the opening of this chapter is part of an agenda of ontological fixity, which is part of liberal inclusivity. The problem with this, though, is that the very nature of this claim to inclusion is predicated on a stable category of the human, which is part of what Lyotard calls the "republican we." This will be discussed in greater detail in chapter 7 but a quotation from Bill Readings provides one point of conclusion that might mitigate against a too-quick celebration of liberal inclusion and the aesthetics of representational heterogeneity that support it: "acts of great terror have been committed not simply in the name of but *as a result of* a common, abstract, universal humanity."[23]

If *Buffy* presents a homogeneous ethnicity at the level of those represented (white American), it is much more interesting at the construction of identities whose inclusion into the "we" is allowed. The role of the demons as part of the Scooby Gang is most important here. While there is a clear expression of Buffy's role as protector of humanity (a humanity figured very much in a liberal tradition of equal moral worth for each person, which poses the problems raised before), it is equally as clear that her job is also to kill demons. This is due to her position in relation to the Watchers' Council, which acts as the supreme authority and lawgiver. As Anthony Bradney states in his "I Made a Promise to a Lady: Law and Love in *BtVS*," "Central to the law of the Council is the proposition 'kill vampires and demons.' Buffy finds herself unable wholly to obey this rule from very early on when she realizes that Angel, even though he is a vampire, will never hurt her" ("Angel," 1007).[24]

This law assumes, in fact insists upon, an absolute ontological identity that is not susceptible to any form of alteration or change. A demon is not bad by degree or action, a demon simply *is* and by virtue of that fact needs to be killed. The state of being is itself a moral category, one that is unambiguous, total and given. Buffy's love for Angel, and her realization that he poses no threat, is a minimal but fundamental refusal to accept the Council's law and, therefore, its philosophical predicate. Once this shift in the legal status of demons has been accepted (the exception made for Angel implies the general possibility of exceptions[25]) then, even if there were no more, that shift undoes the assumptions relating to identity that allowed the law in the first place. If the absolute division between human and demon, which is expressed as an absolute function of ontology, is false, then we can infer that the claims for the ontological fixity of both demon and human are also false.

While the demons themselves come in a range of guises that can easily be seen as different ethnicities,[26] the category of "demon" has lost for Buffy and her friends its simplifying focus as "enemy." Clearly many demons and types of demons do remain enemies, but that is as a consequence of their actions, and not by virtue of their being. The reduction of an individual (demon or otherwise) to the position of representative of a group, which is to say that the group is assumed in totality in the body of an individual, and the individual is never more than a local expression of that grouping, is a clear example of racism.[27] Denying ontologically fixed definitions of a group is one step to refusing this simplification-cum-discrimination. To then address the individual as a performative being and to recognize the same in oneself is to disallow the reduction of a being simply on the grounds of difference. As Rob Breton and Lindsey McMaster assert, the Scooby Gang's "deeply personal relationship with the supernatural, wherein discrimination against werewolves can be a form of bigotry, and elevation of the human a form of Nazism" means that it is the individual's performative expressions rather than his or her supposed nature that grounds Buffy and her friends' ethical choices.[28] Set against this, the Initiative of season 4 uses technological advancement allied with a ferocious ontological separation between humans and demons such that its "activities bear a striking resemblance to the Nazi research agenda in World War II."[29] Locating identity, then, as much in action (performance) as in being, the show presents a version of ethnicity that, at least in part, disallows an ontological fixity and opens up a much more flexible possibility.

While the claims for a performative ethnicity, especially in relation to the demons, may be compelling this does not entirely obviate some of the concerns regarding ethnicity in the Buffyverse. One of these has been made most tellingly by Naomi Alderman and Annette Seidel-Arpaci. Describing the Jewishness of Willow, the writers comment on the extent to which Jewishness is represented as the negative of other aspects of U.S. culture:

> Willow has, in fact, become a reverse–Marrano: she appears to be Jewish, but has taken on Christian practices, hiding her paraphernalia. After a fashion, as we have seen, *Buffy the Vampire Slayer* and *Angel* have similar traits: they appear to be "multicultural" programmes, with characters of various backgrounds, but the Buffyverse is, in many ways, a distinctly Christian, "white" place.[30]

I am not sure that *Buffy* can have many pretensions to multiculturalism for the reason of its refusal to accede to an aesthetic of representational heterogeneity. The demands on its realistic portrayal of Sunnydale deny its multicultural possibilities but instigate very interesting debates regarding a more subtle (and, therefore, more contentious) notion of ethnicity. Willow's Jewishness is one example of this, at least so far as it is contentious.

Beyond the negative representation of her Jewishness, it is the relative infrequence with which it is mentioned at all on the show that concerns

Alderman and Seidel-Arpaci. As I shall move on to shortly, Giles is quintessentially English and retains his ethnic identity even after bouts of amnesia, and his sense of cultural belonging is ever-present, even when he is mocked. Willow has no such sense of her ethnicity as a positive expression of identity. Indeed, as the above-quoted essay goes on to say, despite the performative aspect of ethnicity I applauded earlier, it is noticeable that the performance is itself rather limited. While demons may not be categorically evil, the de-ontologized performance of ethnicity is not necessarily any less restrictive for that:

> We hear of "breeds" and "half-breeds." Literal "non-humans" come from "other dimensions," or from South America, "ancient Egypt," from Pakistan, the Middle East and so on: in other words, "from outside." And vampires do regularly come from England or Ireland, hence "from within." Various "tribes" of demons and monsters have "ancient" and weird cultural practices. "Doing good," for ex-demons, such as Angel, Anya and, latterly, Spike, is inextricably linked to becoming part of a new, acceptable group, and giving up old associations. The weird "tribes" and individuals in *Buffy* and *Angel* have to either drop their cultural habits and history to be assimilated, or remain "other" and face the ultimate sanction of the stake.[31]

And the assimilation is into a Christian worldview, dominated by WASP sensibilities and cultural expectations, even as the show seems to try so hard to undermine many of these stereotypes and constructions:

> This leaves the non–WASP characters in *Angel* and *Buffy*, standing on ever-eroding ground, unable to access parts of their own cultural background for fear of being dubbed "evil," but unable fully to assimilate into the homogeneous, white Christian world represented by *Buffy*. It seems that even shows that are produced with an ambition to deconstruct racialized "identities," may still reproduce them, unable to escape the internalized forces of the dominant culture.[32]

Willow's Jewishness, such as it is, has evidently been eroded to the point where it is not assimilated so much as eradicated.[33] In each case, there is a worry that, despite itself, the show is rehearsing and perpetuating cultural practices that lead to the exclusion or assimilation of groups outside of the norm. For Lyotard, writing in "Heidegger and 'the jews'" the fact of cultural exclusion is part of a process of forgetting at the core of Western thought. The term "jews" is used by Lyotard in a nonethnically specific fashion (the quotation marks and lack of a capital letter make this clear) but as a term which nevertheless signifies under the inevitable specificity of Jewish history. It refers to all those who, wherever they are, seek to remember and to bear witness to something that is constitutively forgotten, not only in each individual mind, but in the very thought of the West. And it refers to all those who assume this anamnesis and this witnessing as an obligation, or a debt, not only toward thought, but toward justice.[34]

Following Freud, Lyotard calls this forgotten thing the "unconscious affect." As long as the unconscious affect remains forgotten, remains undiscovered, "it will give rise to inexplicable formulations (expressions, symptoms) [...] Its 'expressions' form a tissue of 'screen memories' that block the anamnesis."[35] The affect of this memory has played itself out in expulsions, assimilations and, of course, in the Final Solution where even the "assimilated Jew was forced to remember that he stood as a witness, however involuntarily, for something about himself which Europe did not want to remember":

> Through mass extermination, Nazi Germany attempted to eliminate without trace or memory the physical presence of all Jews in Europe; and [...] by doing so it also sought to eliminate from within Western thought (and therefore within the thought and political project of Nazism itself) the unrepresentable itself "represented" by "the jews," namely, what Lyotard argues is a relation to what is always already forgotten in all thought, writing, literature, and art, to a "Forgotten" that was never part of any memory as such and which memory, as memory, forgets in turn by representing (that is, by giving form to it or producing an image for it).[36]

Willow's Jewishness, by its almost complete disappearance, offers a sense of this forgetting that is rather more literal than that outlined by Lyotard but which, nevertheless, is part of a representational economy that occludes certain ethnicities at the moment of seemingly engaging with them. The concern of Alderman and Seidel-Arpaci that *Buffy* is "unable to escape the internalized forces of the dominant culture" would appear to have a significant level of validity when that dominant culture is not simply the U.S. majority culture but something as vast and historically embedded as Western thought.

Willow is the most conspicuous Other in the show's main body of human characters, but there are others. Jenny Calendar and the members of her family that we see are gypsies and offer a curiously hybridized admixture of the exotic and alien with normative Americanness. Ms. Calendar is a schoolteacher, part of the Internet generation; she is deeply, therefore, embedded in the modern (social organization put to the use of the dissemination of rational knowledge), the postmodern (knowledge distribution as a concomitant of technology through both official and unsanctioned means), and the pre-modern (she is a pagan and part of a generations-long tradition of gypsy culture). And she dies. Mr. Trick is a vampire but an African-undead–American. His (and obviously the writers') pointed observation concerning the "Caucasian persuasion" of Sunnydale when he arrives in "Faith, Hope and Trick" (3.3) underscores his verbally sharp, witty, thoroughly modern attitude. He is a businessman vampire, street-smart and hip. His position as a semi-major Big Bad makes his death inevitable, and he dies. Slayers have to die, it is part of their role, but, as Lynne Edwards mildly puts it, "[E]qually suggestive is the fact that only two slayers known to be killed by a vampire (Spike) are both women of color, one black and the other Chinese" ("Fool for Love").[37] The other black Slayer that we know to have been killed by a vampire is Kendra, who was killed by Drusilla.

If the notion of performativity in relation to ethnicity is supposed to be a safeguard against ontologically determined modes of discrimination, it cannot avoid its own modes of equally pervasive models of exclusion. Performativity as a function of identity presumes there to be social categories into which a subject can place him- or herself. These subject positions, many and various and including such aspects as gender, ethnicity, class, age, occupation, relationship position and so on, are themselves then subject to their articulation through cultural practices. These cultural practices (primarily aesthetic in nature) can range from fairy tales, to folk stories, to epic poems, to small-scale local anecdotes, to legends and so on. Novels, movies, and television shows are all part of this acculturation process, being both informed by them and perpetuating them. For Edwards, Kendra's character is performed into a set of subject positions (black, female Slayer) that are partly informed by *Buffy*'s own sets of stories—by the Slayer myth; by general U.S. versions of youth and gender; and also by a specific cultural process of identity construction that is the "tragic mulatta myth." For Edwards, Kendra's position within this myth (the circumscription of her gendered and ethnic performance of identity, or her very real subjection to the aesthetics of culture) means that her death is inevitable. However, her death has to come after an eventual inclusion into the group, which finally results in her assimilation. Only once the threat of the sexualized, exotic Other has been achieved can her danger be finally eradicated: "Symbolically, this suggests that assimilation equals deaths for blacks. As in the tales of tragic mulattas everywhere, by attempting to be something she is not, Kendra suffers the ultimate punishment."[38] The performative is no more a guarantor of inclusivity than ontology, although the recognition of the performative aspect of ethnic construction allows for the potential for change. Edwards's essay ends with an assertion of this, though expressed in different terms:

However, it would be a mistake to dismiss these representations as per-petuating cultural stereotypes of people of color. Since blacks have histor-ically been and continue to be marginalized in society, their depiction as such in Whedon's mythic world may serve, as Joseph Campbell suggests, to illustrate and to illuminate historical "truths" from which black and white viewers can learn how to transcend their ordinary existence.[39]

The extent to which Edwards assumes society to be American indicates a certain seduction by modernity that is almost impossible to escape, and it is at least possible that the rehearsing of such myths as the tragic mulatta simply affirms their power rather than acting as a subtle pedagogic tool. However, Edwards' essay is a shrewd and important engagement with ques-tions of ethnicity in *Buffy*, and the extent to which it attempts to negoti-ate the boundary between the ontologically given and the performatively produced is welcome.

As mentioned above, one of the ways in which the occlusion of Wil-low's Jewishness is brought into stark relief is through the very concen-trated notion of Giles's Englishness. It is not simply that other cultures are all ignored in favor of a dominant version of the United States, but rather that majority cultures and their ethnic representatives are given space to be expressed. It is also true that Englishness, as portrayed through Giles and also through Wesley and Spike, is often the brunt of an affectionate mockery.

It is through the mocking of Englishness that a large part of the show's humor is derived. The humor of *Buffy* is one of its greatest features and the range of different sorts of comedy is highly impressive,[40] but its capac-ity to trade on stereotyped Englishness without any sense of hostility or judgment (a pastiching rather than a parodying) is especially good. In addi-tion to very witty dialogue (which I shall discuss) and other forms of phys-ical comedy, much of the show's comedic value derives precisely from the situations in which the characters find themselves. It is not then, simply, that the situation allows the characters to perform funny acts or say amus-ing things, but more interestingly, that the situation is often in a position of generic tension with what is happening. By placing two sets of generic codes side by side, or by juxtaposing one set of generic expectations in one scene with a different set in the next scene, much of the humor is predi-cated on structural incongruity as much as it is on character interaction or dialogue. The hybrid nature of the show's aesthetic (its performative disruption of genre in order to create a shifting, pluralized version of itself) acts (at least analogously) as a celebration of the performative nature of ethnicity and identity more generally. A brief and early example of this occurs in "Welcome to the Hellmouth" (1.1). Buffy has spotted a vampire who is looking to attack Willow. She is looking for the vampire in a dark and eerie nightclub. The camera tracks her in a close shot; shadows are cast long from the lighting. Buffy opens a door, there is nothing there, the music builds, she passes us, close to the camera, we track the back of her head and see the shadow of a person or thing, Buffy turns and grabs the monster. It is Cordelia Chase, just another girl at the school whose first response is "Geez, what *is* your childhood trauma" and follows this up with a remark to her three friends, "I have to call everyone I have ever met, right now" (1.1). The comedy here derives from the rapid shift from a scene from a horror movie (replete with all the usual production requirements—lighting, music, camera angles and so forth, as well as the situation that has been set up) to a scene from a farce where the mistaken identity motif is augmented by the callous and witty one-liners from Cordelia (who is now framed in a portrait shot with more light and different music).

This juxtaposing of different genres as a mechanism of comedic possibility (among other things) is mirrored in the program's characters and story by a number of other juxtapositions that enable not only the comedy but also the action, the suspense and the drama both in terms of plot development and character interaction. The dominant juxtaposition is probably that between human and nonhuman, natural and supernatural. Also there are the juxtapositions and collisions between male and female questions of youth and age, responsibility and rights, right and wrong and, most prescient in the current context, American and British ethnicities.[41]

Buffy, as the vampire Slayer, has a Watcher who guides, trains and looks after her. Her Watcher, Rupert Giles, is also the librarian at Sunnydale High. He is in his forties and British. Our first introduction to him is in the library with Buffy coming in to find some books. She is oblivious to the fact that he is the Watcher. Interestingly, she is coming from a lesson that had been on the Black Death. While the first season revolves around the resurrection of the Master and his desire to wipe humanity off the face of the earth, the reference to the Black Death immediately raises a European dimension to the program and a depth of history that is essential insofar as the vampire myth is a predominantly European one.[42] Buffy sees the librarian in his tweed jacket, his glasses and his slightly gauche poise and he surprises her, and us, by knowing who she is: "Miss Summers?" (1.1). The accent is clearly English, quite upper-class, and the formal exchange identifies him as a quintessential Englishman in terms of discursive expectations derived from other horror shows and cinematic representations. However, he is also a handsome man and one, about whom we quickly discover, there is significantly more than parody and exposition.

Not only is he English, though; he is also old enough to be Buffy's father. To this extent, the program at least allows, if it doesn't actively encourage, a reading of the relationship between Buffy and Giles (as we come to know him) as one between Watcher and Slayer, one between teacher and student, one between father and daughter, and one between Old England and the New World in a fashion not dissimilar to that seen by some critics of *Lolita*.[43] The father-daughter relationship is quickly posited when Buffy rejects her position as Slayer and Giles reprimands her with the very fatherly fashion by exclaiming, "I really don't understand this attitude" (1.1). Later, in the nightclub where he has gone searching for her, just before the incident with Cordelia Chase, Giles's Britishness and age are highlighted. Amid a discussion about vampires, Giles laments the noise of the club and asserts that he would "much rather be at home with a cup of Bovril and a good book" (1.1).[44] The culture-specific reference to Bovril and the desire for quiet serve to reinforce his position as older and English. Buffy's response a little later that he is like a "textbook with arms" heightens his position as authority and teacher while simultaneously undermining him. Giles himself is painfully aware of these attributes. As the series progresses, his relationship with Buffy becomes very close and fatherly, and she responds in kind. He also is seen to be a much richer and more rounded character than we may at first imagine. He has been, in his younger days, involved in the death of friend, has been in bands, has his own love life and so on.[45] Initially, however, he and we are forced to recognize that his injunction to Willow to "wrest some information from that dread machine ... was a bit, er, British, wasn't it?" (1.2).

Giles's Britishness (which is, of course, Englishness, itself perhaps a conflation that marks a certain attitude to and distance from Britain on behalf of the makers or viewers of the show in the United States) is provided with interesting tonal comparisons from other English characters on the show. One of these is another Watcher, Wesley Wyndham Price, who arrives in the third season after Giles has been relieved of duty by the Watchers' Council. The other is Spike. Wesley provides a comparison in kind. He too is a Watcher; he too is upper-class and smartly dressed, often in tweeds, but he is a much more effete version of the type. If Giles might be thought in some ways to reflect and trade on a sort of self-controlled, stiff-upper-lip spirit of an Empire avuncular Victorian version of Englishness, then Wesley is much more closely allied to a bumbling, cowardly, effeminate *Brideshead Revisited* Edwardian sort of character. The interaction between the two provides a great source of humor for the program and also presents a surprisingly variegated version of Englishness, a variegation, as we have seen, sadly lacking in relation to Willow's Jewishness.

The entry of Wesley opens up its own comedic possibilities. The Watcher-Slayer, father-daughter partnership has been forcibly split by an external and distanced institution whose representative is bound to be resented. The bonds between Buffy and Giles are stronger than the impositions from the Council and into this mixture one must also add the anomalous new Slayer, Faith, who was called after the brief death of Buffy (the strains on credulity that the storylines throw up are often a starting point for the writers in their own self-referential jibes). Wesley is first seen wearing tweed, a tie and glasses much like Giles at Giles's entrance. At one point, after a small row, both Giles and Wesley, unseen by the other, simultaneously take off their glasses, wipe them with a handkerchief taken from a top pocket, and replace the glasses in identical fashion (3.14). These two, then, share a scene that mocks and draws parallels but that has been at pains to highlight differences, not least among which is the fact that Wesley is about ten years younger.

Wesley is, initially, patronizing, over-bearing, rule-bound and very proper. He laments the emotional attachments between Giles and Buffy and criticizes Giles's methods. The avuncular Giles comes up against the repressed head boy, a self-definition given much later in *Angel* in an episode of almost pure comedy called "Spin the Bottle" (*AtS* 4.6). Inevitably, Wesley is going to have to face his failings and later in the episode he and Giles are captured by the henchmen of the demon Balthazar. Like Giles who, we discover, has been less than enamored of Buffy's use of language ("Her abuse of the English language is such that I understand only every other word in a sentence" [3.14]), Wesley deploys a range of very English phrases and constructions. This typically English response to American English is compounded by his use of a very quaint British English expression, "Don't fret" (3.14). After their capture by the henchmen, Wesley's language remains very British and his cowardly attempt to strike a deal with Balthazar expresses another aspect of a perception of Englishness that Wesley has already demonstrated: his effeminacy. The alignment of Englishness with effeminacy is moderated in "Checkpoint" (5.12). The Watchers' Council is coming to Sunnydale in order to give Buffy information regarding Glory, the Big Bad of season 5. Buffy's clear discomfort at the thought of their arrival prompts Tara to wonder whether they can be English at all as she believes English people to be "gentler" than "normal, er [people]" (5.12). Wesley, however, is effeminate.[46] He semi-moans "Oh God, oh God, oh God, stay calm, Mr. Giles" (3.14), thereby being both afraid and proper at the same time. Giles maintains the calm poise of the gentleman as well as his verbal sharpness and ironic capacity: "Thank God you're here, I was planning to panic" (3.14). Wesley's spectacularly underscored "No need to get snippy" presents him as thoroughly English but also immature and boylike while Giles's "Be quiet you twerp" (3.14) insists on his own superiority in both moral charge and age by reducing Wesley to the position of child — "twerp" being a phrase of the mildest sort of chastisement; its use here is clearly an emphatic belittling of Wesley.

The entire situation is a comic restatement of the Western or mafia movie[47] where the good guys are captured by the forces of evil. The pairing of a coward and the hero is evidently a stock scenario and is deployed by scriptwriters for all that it is worth. What is interesting here is that the opportunity has been taken to play off two similar versions of Englishness in a context that allows an expression of conviviality and contempt: the English are both stalwart and cowardly, elegant and gauche, powerful and weak, admirable and contemptible. In addition, the generic situation requires that they should try and escape whereas each, in different ways, is too concerned with asserting his Englishness as "real" or most worthy.

Giles in the "dread machine" episode mentioned earlier has self-consciously realized his position as alien, a recognition that has prompted the affectionate response, "Welcome to the New World" (1.2). Wesley, just arrived from Britain, holds the notion of the New World as something that America still is. He describes Balthazar as being "brought ... to the New World" (3.14). He appears to be unable to distance himself from a notion of England as superior to the United States. Giles, for all his Old World ways and reluctance to use computers and so on, is much more modern than Wesley, though his lexical choices demonstrate his undeniable refusal to pander to political correctness.[48] To this extent there is a version of Englishness in terms of attitude that is being commended in the program and one that is clearly being mocked. Both, however, belong to a rather idealized notion of the English gentleman-scholar in a style not very far removed from, for example, Captain Jean-Luc Picard in the series *Star Trek: The Next Generation*, who, despite his ancestry possibly being French, is still the Victorian English gentleman.

The other main Englishman in Buffy's view is Spike. He is introduced in season 2 as the main source of evil with his English, mad, vampire girlfriend Drusilla. Absent from season 3, with one guest appearance, he is a regular through the last four seasons. In these last seasons he is reduced as a threat via a number of plot mechanisms, but his potency as a character remains. This is partially due to the particular sort of Englishness he portrays. With Drusilla, his entrance is reminiscent of Sid Vicious, the musician with the '70s punk band the Sex Pistols and Sid's girlfriend, Nancy Spungen, who scandalized the British media with their antisocial behavior, drug taking, violence and eventual deaths.[49]

Spike, then, offers a version of reasonably recent Englishness as exemplified through youth culture. This finds its expression in subcultural musical forms (mods and rockers, glam, punk, new wave, indie and dance in a rough timeline from the '60s to the present), as well as in the related fashions, or antifashions, and of course in forms of violence, most usually associated with football. This last point is reinforced in one of the episodes where Xander, on returning to the scene of a demonic attack, wryly asks, "Who sponsored careers day, the British Soccer Fan Association?" (2.10).

There is, between Spike and Giles, a cultural and historical gap. Giles is an image of Englishness that owes its status to cultural representations from, and of, the Victorian period through to films of the second World War and up to icons such as James Bond. He is intelligent, well mannered, courageous but not unduly violent, thoughtful and witty. Spike owes his Englishness to violent counterculture, to antiheroes, antiestablishment values and a certain brutality. Curiously, Spike begins life as a late nineteenth-century member of precisely the class from which Giles seems to draw some of his representational power. Spike, then called William, is a softly spoken, rather effete poet. His poetry is so bad he is dubbed William the Bloody Awful. After he becomes a vampire, he is William the Bloody as a consequence of the appalling violence and tortures he instills. The similarity of nicknames neatly conjoins these two seemingly opposed representations of Englishness in the one epithet, which is a tiny but excellent example of the care and subtlety of the aesthetics of culture in *Buffy*.

As with the resemblance between Giles and Wesley, the program insists on representational similarities between Spike and Giles. The most noticeable of these occurs in the final episode of season 4, "Restless" (4.22). Having vanquished the evil, Buffy and her friends are relaxing and watching videos. They all fall asleep and dream a variety of surreal events that seem to have physically damaging properties. Xander's dream includes a sequence where Spike and Giles are both dressed in tweed — Spike with a particularly fetching deer-stalker hat — and they are sitting side by side on a set of swings. They look very similar, engage in the same activity of childhood innocence and Giles asserts Spike as his son and potentially a watcher of sorts.[50]

This small episode is reprised two seasons later in "Tabula Rasa" (6.8). A small amount of scene setting will be necessary in order to demonstrate the ways in which the episode works with tonal and generic juxtaposition in order for the full humor and pathos to be evident, especially in its portrayal of Englishness. Willow and her girlfriend Tara have fallen out because of the amount of magic that Willow has been using. This draws on the love story, teen romance and fantasy genres. Giles has told Buffy that he must leave Sunnydale and return to England. This is after Buffy has had the trauma of being killed, sent to heaven and then ripped out of heaven by Willow and Xander, who mistakenly believe she is in Hell. Buffy feels lost and, now, betrayed by Giles. This draws on fantasy and family drama. Both of these issues, and the ways they are played, lead to genuine emotional turmoil and an engagement with the viewer at this level. Spike and Buffy have been drawn into a physical relationship that has confused Buffy (he is a vampire, after all) and at the beginning of the episode Spike's negative characteristics are humorously compounded by the fact that he owes a kittens to a demon because of a betting debt. Seeking refuge from the demon's men, Spike runs to The Magic Box where all have gathered for Giles to tell them of his decision to return to England. To avoid being burned by the sun, Spike has borrowed a tweed suit and deer-stalker hat just like that from Buffy's dream in "Restless" (4.22). This is clearly blackly funny in the context of a potentially damaging relationship for an already damaged Buffy. Willow wants to make everyone forget their bad experiences and so casts a spell, which comes into operation at the precise point that Buffy is making a speech of farewell and pain.

Up to this point, the episode has been a relationship-led story that has been, at best, downbeat and that tends toward the tragic. The spell makes everyone pass out and when they wake the spell has proven too powerful and they have all lost their memories entirely. We have seen small moments of Giles's Englishness (repeating Buffy's angry injunction to "cut to the chase" with a sense of sadness and disdain), and Spike has twice used the word "bloke" in reference to the demon (unless otherwise stated, all subsequent quotations are from [6.8]). Once they wake from the spell, the camera shows Giles lying slumped against Anya (who is engaged to Xander) and Giles rearranges his glasses and wipes some drool from Anya's back. The motifs of his Englishness and age are here already being deployed as comic tools. Spike, who was sitting on the cash counter, wakes and falls off with a high-pitched squeak. His violent, punk Englishness is mocked both through his ridiculous costume and his frightened yelp; in fact he is much more like William the Bloody Awful poet at this moment.

Giles's role as guide is briefly asserted when he tries to comfort Xander, who is very scared, and to explain the situation, which, he reasons, is probably the result of having got "terribly drunk": the old-fashioned adverb indicating once more his distance both in terms of cultural expectation and age. Anya mentions a pop-culture American star, which simply baffles Giles. Having ascertained that they are in a magic shop, Giles, the grand exponent of magics and the one-time member of the Watchers'

Council, declares that magic is all "balderdash and chicanery." Again, his Englishness is manifest through his lexical choice and this is presented as skeptical, patronizing and aloof.[51] In other words, he represents late nineteenth-century Enlightened modernity. The aloofness is also expressed through understated self-irony when he states, "We don't know a bloody thing except I seem to be British, don't I? With glasses. Well, that narrows it down significantly." The great expositor and source of knowledge becomes little more than a teller of the obvious and unwitting expression of his own stereotype. Yet, *contra* Willow, it is his ethnicity that defines him. Willow at no point remarks on her being Jewish; the episode is much more concerned to locate her identity through her sexuality.[52] Giles's Englishness remains intact; indeed his comment to Willow mentioned earlier here seems to be true for him: he has remained the same, at least in terms of ethnic identification.

Spike, having recovered something of his punk identity, attempts to mock Giles through recourse to a further stereotyped vision of Englishness. He says, "Oh, listen to Mary Poppins." Apart from the clear cultural reference to Englishness and an implied feminization, this is also amusing for long-time *Buffy* fans to the extent that many people have criticized the actor who plays Spike, James Marsters, for his accent sounding a little too much like Dick van Dyke from the film *Mary Poppins.*[53] The show manages to present and subvert stereotypes of Englishness by drawing attention to its own implicit collusion with some of them. Spike continues (all the while in his tweeds and deer-stalker hat and English accent), "He's got his crust all stiffened up with that nancy boy accent," once again asserting a sense of English masculinity as effete ("nancy boy" being a term used to imply effeminacy in British English and an assertion made against him in his William days). Carrying on, he says, "You Englishmen are always so...," which is intended to be the precursor to a racial slur but which is abruptly halted as he realizes his own voice: "Bloody hell: sodding, blimey, shagging, knickers, bollocks. Oh God. I'm English." The short list of English swear words, with varying degrees of offense, is the ideal lexical marker not just for Spike's being English but also for his diminished punk credentials. Verbal offense has always been a marker of punk. Famously, the Sex Pistols said "fuck" on a British television show, which led to the presenter being sacked and the tabloids fulminating against the state of the nation's youth. Spike's choice of words are, for the most part, primary school insults with little shock value, except, perhaps, "bollocks." Interestingly, when the show was aired by the BBC in its prime-time slot, this scene was cut.[54] Apparently Spike is more punk than we might have believed. Giles, demonstrating dignity through irony, simply retorts, "Welcome to the nancy tribe."

This exchange has allowed for a presentation of the clichés that Giles and Spike represent. Clearly, the viewers are aware of their prehistories but the characters are allowed to act simply as ciphers for their competing claims to Englishness. One of the elements that separates these two versions of being English is age. Giles is both an older man and, therefore, in terms of the representational economy being used, more likely to subscribe to the values that are seen as quintessentially English. Spike, who is younger (he has lived a lot longer, of course, but is permanently the same age as he was when turned into a vampire), is able to represent the claims of youth and rebellion and the subversion of these. Not only that, the two characters are synecdochic of broader cultural and historical versions of Englishness, or, more particularly, English masculinity.

These ideas are brought together in the conceit that they inadvertently assume each other to be a relative: son and father. Spike, misreading the positions in which Giles and Anya awoke calls her a "trollop" and Giles, irked at being called "old," says, "You're not too old to put across my knee, you know, sonny," thereby fulfilling the role of a stern father and teacher.

Not knowing his name, Spike looks in his clothes in a fashion not dissimilar to a child at school who has a name tag written inside. What he sees is the label "Randy." Simultaneously both English and an aggrieved son, Spike laments, "Randy Giles? Why not just call me Horny Giles or desperate for a shag Giles," once again drawing attention to lexical difference between British and American English ("randy" being a term to mark sexual desire and "shag" being a slang term for sexual intercourse) but also emphasizing an assumed preoccupation with sex as well as an emasculating dread.

The episode resolves itself into a searingly painful denouement with Giles leaving, Tara and Willow breaking up and Spike and Buffy being entangled and confused. A "situation comedy" has occurred amid one of the darker storylines of *Buffy* and has served again to demonstrate the genre-busting wishes of Joss Whedon. In doing this, the comedy has also enabled a self-conscious examination of the sorts of representations of English masculinity that the program has been undertaking. These aspects of the show rarely fall prey to moralizing or to promoting one sort of discursive framework as being better than another. In many ways, the juxtapositions of Englishness operate in the same way as the generic or thematic collisions insofar as they expand the possibilities of the show. Giles, Wesley and Spike are all simply characters, of course, but in their interactions with each other and the other characters, *Buffy* offers up a range of notions of English masculinity that trade upon but also contribute to the store of clichés, stereotypes and models that allow for a discursive notion of the concept in the first place.

Buffy's engagement with ethnicity, then, is fraught. In its representation of a performative notion of ethnic identity that seeks to de-ontologize the category, thereby also providing an oblique critique of an aspect of modernity, the show is subtle, careful and seemingly progressive. The fact that the ethnicities performed tend to marginalize non-majority ones (be they Jewish, African or other) means that the series is also rehearsing the very categories of exclusion that it seeks to confront elsewhere. Its use of ethnic identity to provide an interrogative humor that both compounds and challenges stereotypes is very skillful (and very funny) but its assertion via Giles of the reimposition of fixed identities that would have to include ethnicity cannot help but leave one feeling that Andrew's assessment is right and that, on this issue at least, Giles is a silly, silly British man.

♦ Chapter 3 ♦

Aesthetics, Culture and History

"She lives very much in the 'now'"

The uses of history in *Buffy* are, as one would expect, various and multi-faceted. Staying mainly in a representation of contemporary America, of "now," the show nevertheless also presents us with histories that either explicitly or implicitly take us to classical Greece, Dark Age Europe, medieval Europe, nineteenth-century Europe, early twentieth-century America, turn-of-the-century China, an alternative present-day America, eighteenth- and nineteenth-century America and others. Often, these historical (and geographical) shifts provide us with the backstory of a character, most notably of Spike and Angel, though also of Anya. This element is clearly very important and I shall comment on it later, as I shall also comment on some of the ways in which the series engages with past U.S. cultural and political history (something that happens curiously rarely). For the moment, however, I want to concentrate on the ways that the representation of these different historical moments provides for a set of some-times related, often conflictual, *attitudes* to history. Most especially, I want to assess the show's overt games with eschatology and the ways in which the different histories contribute to this.

Death, judgment, heaven and hell — the science of these is eschatol-ogy — have figured as part of many religions, but in the Western world they are most commonly associated with Christian ideas. *Buffy* is not a reli-gious show per se[1] and so the use of the term "eschatology" may appear somewhat arbitrary. The point, however, is not that the term is religious and that *Buffy* is not; rather, it is the power that the concept of eschatology has had on Western thought, through its specifically Christian usages over the last two thousand years and especially on its relationship with an idea of history as a narrative leading to a specified and determinable end point. Related to, though in important ways different from, the notion of apocalypse, whose meaning of revelation has been so closely identified with John's gospel that it tends to be used as an expression of violent endings, eschatology provides the sense of an ending: absolute and pure.

Buffy, as David Lavery has pointed out, uses the word "apocalypse" or versions thereof in no fewer than 26 episodes.[2] This is a show predicated on eschatological concerns and apocalyptic devices. Each of the seasons sees Buffy fighting an evil whose main goal is the eradication of humanity and Buffy's job in each season is to avert the apocalypse, to postpone the eschatological.[3]

This postponing serves an obvious need in *Buffy*, which is the continuation of the show and the narratives and histories internal to it. If the apocalypse were to succeed, if historical finality were achieved, then *Buffy* would end or, as in the case of the final season, the ending of the series *Buffy* would necessitate the ending of the character — which eschatological completion would have done, but in a less pleasing way for the viewer. However, it is not this which is of most concern to me here, though I will return to it later. What I am eager to do for the time being is explain how different historical representations exist in relation to each other, and how these representations carry with them certain *attitudes* to narrative, teleology and eschatology.

The world of *Buffy* exists in a representational framework that is primarily a recognizable Southern Californian town with recognizable American people. This is the primary historical site represented in the show. It is represented to us in such a normal fashion that for the most part we do not even recognize the signs as signs, as representation or aesthetics. David Lavery, however, has enumerated in quite some detail the aesthetics of this historical representation in his conference paper "Fatal Environment: *Buffy the Vampire Slayer* and American Culture."[4] While mainly concerned to demonstrate a certain insularity to the Buffyverse that sees the outside or extraneous as threatening, it does this by brilliantly showing the aesthetics of representing the cultural and social history of contemporary America. From the mall, to Thanksgiving, to cartoons, to Twinkie bars, to television, to Hollywood, to musicals, to language, to "to do" lists, to miniature golf, to RVs, to (homicidal) preachers, to baseball, this is contemporary America. In addition to this, as Roz Kaveney states, the show "takes place in something like real time ... closely tied to the rhythms of the American High School Year."[5] Moreover, it is a contemporary America that exists in a continual state of the present; de-historicized, skimming the past with no real attachment to it except through allusion and nostalgia.

The extent to which the Buffyverse acts as an uncomplicated presentation of America itself (representation and represented little more than one and the same thing — the ultimate realism) is addressed at various times throughout the book and is a moot point, yet it is essential at the aesthetic level so that the other orders of history can be recognized as such.[6] In a different way from that explained in Lavery's analysis, but equally as forcefully, not only extraneous people and things but also extraneous times are seen as potentially fatal in the Buffyverse.

The most demanding historical intrusion into Buffy's world is that which provides her title of Vampire Slayer. Even with the appearance of the first Slayer in season 4, it is never quite clear when the Slayer came into existence. The Shadowmen of "Get It Done" (7.15) seem to have made the first Slayer by placing a demon's heart in a woman, the power of which has persisted through the generations. They also say that they were there at the beginning and now it is nearly the end (7.15). In other words, Buffy, as Slayer, exists in a history that is almost antipathetical to the contemporary, de-historicized present: she is part of a mythical history that goes back into prehistory but has a definite, if unknowable, beginning and has a certain, if unknowable, end. This is not a history of progress, however. The end and the beginning are effectively instances of the same — the Slayer; and all intervening instances have not *progressed* the history, simply maintained it. This is mythical history where all sorts of magic and impossibilities can occur (not the least of which is the Shadowmen's continued existence).

Between the postmodern, depthless history of contemporary America and the mythical history of the Slayer, other histories come into play. Before briefly looking at those, it may be useful to make an observation about Buffy at this point. As a young American (already identified by David Bowie in his 1975 song "Young Americans" as a category of person whose amnesiac relation with history was worrying), Buffy exhibits a typical reluctance to engage with history.[7] Giles's comment to her mother, which opens this chapter, is one of many testaments to that. However, as the Slayer, her relationship with history is no more informed. Her job, mythically ordained and existing in mythical time, is strictly speaking ahistorical: all Slayers do the same job to the same ends irrespective of cultural context or historical period. Buffy's particular anxiety stems from trying to keep her job secret in a de-mythologized age and to that extent conflicting historical perspectives create significant tension. An awareness, then (a deeply felt, painfully present awareness) to antagonistic attitudes to historical organization influences the character and the show enormously; the specific facts and narratives of those histories are, for the most part, unimportant. I shall examine one very clear exception to this assertion in the episode "Pangs" (4.8) later in the chapter.

If contemporary America is de-historicized (either unconcerned with history or believing itself to be history's culminating point, its apogee[8]) and the Slayer's history is really ahistorical, there are other histories and attitudes to history that make this already quite awkward and refreshingly subtle relationship that the program has with history very complex. Among these are medieval European history, which is quietly but importantly present from the very first episode of the first season where the students are given a history lesson on the Black Death. From the outset, then, the medieval period in *Buffy* is marked as potentially threatening and its presence in the series typically endorses this. The medieval menace can be seen in a version of overarching Catholic hegemony (the Watchers' Council's relation to Buffy), the Crusades against Islam (season 5's Knights of Byzantium), and, for that matter, vampires and monsters. The vampire can be traced back to 1047 through the Russian word "upir" and then through the twelfth century with Walter Map's 1190 "De Nagis Curialium," which includes accounts of vampirelike beings in England, and on to William of Newburgh's 1196 "Chronicles," which record several stories of vampire-like revenants in England. It is, of course, not until the later Middle Ages that the vampire myth becomes most prevalent and the most famous vampire of them all enters folklore. The history of Vlad Dracul, which laid the foundation of much of what we understand the vampire to be today, has additional interest simply because of the broader context of later medieval eastern European history and its relationship with western European medieval history and its continuing fascination. A brief chronology of it is as follows.

In 1428–29 Vlad Tepes, the son of Vlad Dracul, is born. Vlad Tepes becomes prince of Wallachia in 1463 and moves to Tirgoviste. In 1442 Vlad Tepes is imprisoned with his father by the Turks. Vlad Tepes becomes a hostage by the Turks in 1443. Vlad Dracul is beheaded in 1447. Vlad Tepes briefly attains the Wallachian throne the following year. After he is dethroned, he goes to Moldavia and befriends Prince Stefan. In 1451 Vlad and Stephan flee to Transylvania. Constantinople falls four years later. In 1456 John Hunyadi assists Vlad Tepes to attain the Wallachian throne. Vladislav Dan is executed. In 1458 Matthias Corvinu succeeds John Hunyadi as king of

Hungary. In 1459 there is an Easter massacre of boyers and rebuilding of Dracula's castle. Bucharest is established as the second governmental center. There is a 1460 attack on Brasov, Romania. In 1461 a successful campaign is waged against Turkish settlements along the Danube, then there is a summer retreat to Tirgoviste. In 1462, following the battle at Dracula's castle, Vlad flees to Transylvania. Vlad begins 13 years of imprisonment. In 1475 summer wars in Serbia against Turks take place. Vlad resumes the throne of Wallachia that November. Vlad is assassinated in 1476–77.[9]

This offers a glimpse of the character that will be written about by Bram Stoker in 1897, but Vlad's involvement in the period of the fall of Constantinople and the fights against the Turks make Stoker's version of the historical figure curiously (if not explicitly) part of the fight for souls raging between Islam and Christianity during the period.[10]

The important thing for *Buffy* is not just that there are historical connections that (intentionally or not) have interesting parallels with current U.S. political and cultural concerns, most notably the emergence of radical Islam as the new "force for evil" after the demise of the Communist bloc in the twentieth century, but also there are the ways in which medieval relations with history operate. To talk this loosely about medieval history will doubtless displease many scholars who will be quick to alert us to the fact that a period that covers a thousand years is only reducible to such generalizations through an act of outrageous philistinism. However, the medieval history most pertinent for *Buffy* is, in some senses, precisely this attenuated, even denuded, vision of the Middle Ages that is transmitted primarily through literary and visual reformations drawn from the nineteenth century onwards. *Buffy*'s medieval history in its content largely draws on the "familiar concepts of barbarism and superstition"[11] common to many popular cultural engagements with the period, which, in their turn draw less on the history qua history and more on other popular cultural representations echoing the "postmodern call to revisit the past with a mixture of nostalgia and irony [...] by deploying the 'prior textualization' of the cinematic history of the 'Middle Ages' as pastiche."[12]

Whether Catholic hegemony and papal authority or, later, reformed Protestantism with individual salvation is at its root (in *Buffy*, The Watchers' Council or Caleb), medieval and renaissance history tended toward an inevitably eschatological viewpoint. And this eschatological model is also very much part of *Buffy*'s world. Even when the historical allusion, reference or plotline moves forward to the later Enlightenment and industrialized Europe (especially Britain and Ireland) of the nineteenth century with Spike and Angel, the historical attitude being traded on is still eschatological. Spike, as William, the late nineteenth-century gentleman and would-be poet, is clearly marked as a member of the class that benefited enormously from British colonial expansion. Whether he is actively a part of the process (and we never find out), he represents a part of British history that was predicated on Enlightenment values of spreading civilization and prosperity under a *pax Britannica*.[13] An aspect of this part of European history (the colonial project as envisioned by Joseph Conrad) is discussed in relation to Xander's dream in chapter 6, but the eschatological element in *Buffy* is central.

To get to the heart of this matter I want to look at a notion of eschatological historical thought and then return, via other forms of contemporary cultural production, to *Buffy* in order to see the way the program's conflicting historical attitudes nevertheless resolve into a version of the eschatological that is an important aspect of its cultural significance.

I shall begin a very long way away from *Buffy* indeed with the third-century theologian Tertullian and fifth-century St. Cyril, and their discussions of catechumens. Tertullian describes these would-be initiates into the early Catholic Church in *De praescriptione haereticorum*:

> Among them it is doubtful who is a catechumen and who a believer; all can come in alike; they hear side by side and pray together; even heathens, if any chance to come in. That which is holy they cast to the dogs, and their pearls, although they are not real ones, they fling to the swine.[14]

Two centuries later, St. Cyril continues:

> Should a catechumen ask what the teachers have said, tell nothing to a stranger; for we deliver to thee a mystery ... see thou let out nothing, not that what is said is not worth telling, but because the ear that hears does not deserve to receive it. Thou thyself wast once a catechumen, and then I told thee not what was coming. When thou hast come to experience the height of what is taught thee, thou wilt know that the catechumens are not worthy to hear them.[15]

At the beginnings of the Catholic Church, the mystery of Christ's second coming and the redemption of humanity at the end of historical time was a guarded secret. Though there is a clearly different content and context, Buffy has her own catechumen whose involvement with her operates in an analogous set of structures of secrecy and exclusion. Heathens and even would-be initiates were excluded from the heart of the Catholic mystery. Before the conversion of Rome to Christianity, when persecution was rife, and then even after, when Christianity was the state religion and sought as a matter of principle to exclude pagan worship,[16] Christian doctrine, especially its specifically eschatological element, was hidden. Two of the most closely kept secrets were the Lord's prayer and the creed. Catechumens would be told the one eight days before baptism and would learn the other on the day of baptism. While both the Lord's prayer and the creed offer different points of contact to the faith, they clearly share a delineated worldview and expression of belief in that worldview. Whether it was the apostolic creed of the very early Church or the Nicene creed of slightly later (itself a response to the Arian heresy), the eschatological principle is absolute: "He will come again in glory to judge the living and the dead."

This aspect of Christian theology derives from a number of biblical sources. Most vividly, of course, in Revelation, but it is also a central part of the gospels, particularly of Paul's letters. In his first letter to the Thessalonians, he writes:

> because at the word of command, at the sound of the archangel's voice and God's trumpet-call, the Lord himself will descend from heaven; first the Christian dead will rise, then we who are left alive shall join them, caught up in clouds to meet the Lord in the air. Thus we shall always be with the Lord.[17]

Matthew had explained what this moment would be like with the righteous being welcomed into the kingdom of heaven while those who did not offer help or support to those in need would go to "the eternal fire that is ready for the devil and his angels."[18] Similar accounts are also given in Mark and Luke, all of which proclaim the risen Lord, the judgment and the fact that by believing in Christ and by living a life worthy of that belief "you will win true life for yourselves."[19] In other words, the life currently being lived is but a prelude to that which awaits at the end of history with the second coming of Christ and the judgment and reconciliation of the righteous. Buffy's continual thwarting of the end of days (even if it is to stave off the demon invasion) is in stark contradistinction to the pivotal aim of Christian eschatological thought.

Evidently, neither Paul nor Revelation nor Christianity invents eschatology. Concerns about life after death, judgment, the relationship of this existence to any possible later one had been prevalent in many previous religions, not least Judaism. But Christian doctrine exerted an extraordinary force on the notion that moves it so far in excess of any of the earlier manifestations as to make it almost new. Paul establishes a belief in the material resurrection of the body, which will find bliss in its reunification with God and all other worthy people. There will be a restitution of the many to the One, of the individual to the Cosmos. Paul's eschatology is both individual and cosmic, predicated on the soul's worth but manifested in the materiality of the body. Judgment is total and unflinching; reward, eternal and unchanging; punishment, absolute. When writing to the Romans he explicitly invokes a cosmic rebirth and a bodily rebirth in the spirit of God:

> For the created universe waits with eager expectation for God's sons to be revealed [...] because the universe itself is to be freed from the shackles of mortality and enter upon the liberty and splendor of the children of God.[...] Not only so, but even we, to whom the Spirit is given as first-fruits of the harvest to come, are groaning inwardly while we wait for God to make us his sons and set our whole body free.[20]

And this newness of the future is what is maintained as a secret by the early Fathers of the Church under the discipline of the secret.

The Christian secret, which is nothing other than the mystery of the God incarnated in the resurrected Christ and the promise of salvation at His return and judgment of us, is kept from but yet open to all people. It is, in essence, an inclusive doctrine. Buffy's by contrast is utterly (if ineptly) exclusive. But this inclusivity is restricted to those who are initiated into its secrets. John writes in his first letter, "You, no less then they, are among the initiated; this is the gift of the Holy One, and by it you all have knowledge."[21] Knowledge is reserved for an elect, an elect who, unlike the makers of the first covenant, can expect redemption and forgiveness at the fulfillment of the Word. From the vantage point of those who have this belief the others are, to quote Peter, "ignorant and unstable."[22] Those who choose to ignore the secret to salvation demonstrate also their status as nonpersons: "Above all he will punish those who follow their abominable lusts.[...] These men are like brute beasts, born in the course of nature to be caught and killed."[23] Once the mystery is accepted and the secret has been revealed, however, those members of the Christian faith, which is to say, humans, are to be regarded as the same under God. Paul offers a great paean to the homogeneity of people under God in his letter to the Collossians: "There is no question here of Greek and Jew, circumcised and uncircumcised, barbarian, Scythian, slave and freeman; but Christ is all, and is in all."[24] Once the secret has been uncovered, each person is the same.

The point of this, however, is not a theological investigation of these ideas. Rather, I would like to look at their historiological ramifications and how these are mirrored in *Buffy*. If one accepts that post-conversion Rome solidified and entrenched Christianity at the heart of a political and military power in Western Europe and, further, one allows for a Christianization that continued in excess of the collapse of the Roman Empire such that Christianity provides the primary conceptual apparatus from the Mediterranean to northern Europe, then it can be argued that the eschatological principle as envisioned by Paul becomes the dominant mode of relating to historical time throughout the continent.

It can be seen that even cultures that may have been thought to be peripheral to both the Roman Empire and, later, Christianization, have both a knowledge of and, it would appear, a relation to history that is emphatically eschatological in the Christian sense.[25] What this indicates is that from about the fourth century onward Europe has not only been Christian in the sense of having that as its primary faith but also that this faith fundamentally presents a notion of historical time that is finite; that history, for Europe, has always been awaiting its conclusion and, with it, our reconciliation.

Many people have noted the structural similarities between historico-political thought such as Marxism, and Christian thought, and, less homologous, between Christian eschatological principles and the ideas of a Hegel or a Rousseau. Indeed, for the Jean-François Lyotard of *The Postmodern Condition*, all of these species of thought (Christian, Marxist, Hegelian, liberal, etc.) fall under the general rubric of "grand narratives." Later Lyotard, however, modified this thinking. In "A Postmodern Fable," he no longer sees Christianity as a subspecies of a grand narrative, but rather sees eschatology itself as the predicative requirement of grand narratives:

> But eschatology, properly called, which governs the modern imaginary of historicity, is what the Christianity rethought by Paul and Augustine introduced into the core of Western thought.[...] Although secularised, the Enlightenment narrative, Romanticist or speculative dialectics, and the Marxist narrative deploy the same historicity as Christianity, because they conserve the eschatological principle. The completion of history, be it always pushed back, will re-establish a full and whole relation with the law of the Other (capital O) as the relation was in the beginning: the law of God in the Christian paradise, the law of Nature in the natural right fantasized by Rousseau, the classless society, before family, and state, imagined by Engels.[26]

If this is so, then the mystery of parousia, initially kept secret to thwart heathens and heretics, becomes the secret of history. It is the orienting principle of the notion of historical progress and human fulfillment. Further than this, Christian eschatology becomes the base of modernity's historicity. Modernity is not then an epoch or a period that can be demarcated as coinciding with the Enlightenment or colonialism or the Industrial Revolution. Rather modernity is an *attitude* to historical time that has coexisted with Catholic hegemony, with the Reformation, with the Enlightenment and so on. Modernity — which orients historical time to a future point of reconciliation, indivisibility, full signification — is what provides the other models of historical and political organization with their power. Whatever the contingent, material, economic and political differences that separate these models, they all share the requirement of the fulfillment of the project, whatever that project might be. With the project's fulfillment, historical time ceases because history is precisely that time during which the project exists. At its completion, the project is no more: history is fulfilled because reconciliation has occurred. As I shall mention later, in the Buffy-verse it is the demons who most eagerly work toward this reconciliation.

The reconciliation, as with Christianity, is of all of humanity, either with God or with itself. The universal or cosmic aspect of eschatology qua modernity requires, then, the reconciliation of humanity. However, humanity is, as was demonstrated earlier, a self-fulfilling category: those who are reconciled are human, those who are not are not. The projects of modernity are universal in scope, but universality is contextual in definition. Indeed, humanity is that which can be defined as having been initiated into the secret. While *Buffy*'s conceptualization of the human appears to be a liberally all-inclusive one that causes its own problems (see chapter 2), Christianity's specifically contextualized human is equally as awkward. Another way of phrasing this would be to say that modernity assumes an initial alienation and the true human is he or she who has overcome this in order to fully be himself or herself by reviving the initial state in a later manifestation: whether the formal expression of this be through prayer or the shedding of ideology is immaterial to the structure of modernity.

Modernity, as an attitude toward historical time, provides the futurity necessary for social and political models of organization to be developed that are eschatological in essence and as such are universal in scope. *Buffy*, for all its worldwide appeal, is a show whose world is highly parochial. She may be fighting, in absolute terms, to save the world, but this is nearly always represented as, initially, a fight to save her friends and Sunnydale. Any universal application of her victory is a happy offshoot. Neither Buffy the American teenager nor the Slayer has the historical imagination or desire to see her fight in eschatological terms. Indeed, as noted, her job is to avert any event that might bring about an ending of any sort.

Despite this requirement, Buffy's attitude to impending catastrophe is often one of complacent irony, best exemplified by her comment to Giles in "Never Kill a Boy on the First Date" (1.5): "If the apocalypse comes, beep me." This casual disinterest can be seen as part of what Mark Dery calls the "*Scream* meme," which, he claims, suggests "that we're so ironic that we can't even take our own apocalypse — our lurking sense, on the eve of the future, of social disintegration and simmering discontent — seriously."[27] Dery locates a *fin de siècle* (even *fin de millennium*) social malaise as the productive component of cultural forms of the malaise's recapitulation. In relation to *Buffy* it is clearly the case that the show is a late-century phenomenon and that the general concerns regarding what this means will have had some influence on the writers' expressions of apocalyptic and eschatological concerns. As Catherine Siemann notes, it is almost impossible to ignore the "something symbolic about a century's closing decade that suggests a winding down, even an apocalypse"[28] and, in an essay that offers a truly thoughtful comparison of *Buffy* with other end-of-the-century texts as well as the mid-century U.S. comedy *Gidget*, she continues, "[A]pocalyptic notions abound: the end of society, the end of culture, the end of morality and the family, then end, in fact, of the world as we know it."[29] Buffy's desire to thwart the apocalypse and to stem the eschatological tide could then be seen as a simple antidote to millennial fears — the world as we know it (or at least she knows it) will continue. Or her refusal to take seriously the real possibility of an apocalypse could be an index of her postmodern positioning: ironic to dangerous degrees, part of a culture (and existing as a person) so alienated from itself (and herself) that droll denial is all that can be hoped for. However, Buffy's placement in the postmodern is only part of her being; she is also a part of a premodern and early-modern tradition, while the constant emergence of modernity itself means that her negotiations of these historicities cannot be read solely as reflective of her contemporary characterization (though this is obviously important).

It is the maintenance of the present, not any sustaining concern with the future, that is her remit. Buffy has disavowed the eschatological and with it *Buffy* maintains a tense relationship with modernity — a relationship that can be glossed as a version of postmodernity. While postmodernity has been described in many, many ways, one of the factors that seems to be consistent is the sociological shift toward the individual and away from the collective or the community. *Buffy*'s fraught presentation of the conflict between individual and collective responsibility is one of the ways it engages with postmodernity. Generally suspicious of large, officially sanctioned organizations, *Buffy*, nevertheless, is not a simple celebration of the individual.

Liberalism, in its many guises, assumes the centrality of the individual and, whether this is represented by psychology or consumerism, individual fulfillment is an ordinary aspect of contemporary Western life. Indeed, it is the emphasis on the category of the individual that in many ways is the dominating notion of the postmodern in its sociological sense, and which provides much of the dramatic impulse for *Buffy* at the level of interpersonal relationships and character development (as opposed to the drama derived from demon fighting). Away from the Buffyverse, political or social movements that have attempted to maintain a collective vision of the future are seen as increasingly redundant, be they communist, socialist or even imperialist. The eschatological underpinnings of such movements are, likewise, less and less prevalent as markers of historical, political or social ideas.

Modernity, evidently, still exists to the extent that there are still people who have a historical consciousness that is predicated on eschatological models, but the important point is that it is now in the minority. The attitude, for that is all modernity is, persists but is outweighed by stronger currents of localized, foreshortened models of political, historical and social action. Or this, at least, appears to be the accepted description of events. Self-fulfillment of the crassest kind has replaced any longer-term notion of salvation, return to paradise or judgment (Xander's TV and food obsessions spring immediately to mind); salvation is a trip to the analyst (heroically, mostly avoided by the writers of *Buffy* until Buffy herself becomes a school counselor in season 7); paradise is induced by narcotics or alcohol (the U.S. government's paranoid fear of which is wonderfully parodied in a much berated episode "Beer Bad" [4.5][30]); and judgment is a purely local event of legalism. In addition, the future is regarded as the life span of the individual (and maybe his or her family) and the far-off event of reconciliation is a defunct vestigial nostalgia.

However, the consumer-oriented individual, vibrant in the new skin of the singular present, having sloughed off the mottled carapace of the collective future, is not necessarily anything more than a historical quirk. Assuming that arguments that posit techno-science and late capitalism as the motors of individualism (and, therefore, as the eventual cause of eschatology's decline) are correct, they are also the motors of emergent forms of thought that could just as easily prompt the eventual coalescing of collectivity. The beautiful joining together of Buffy, Willow, Xander and Giles to defeat Adam in "Primeval" (4.21) offers a small, but potent, example of *Buffy*'s oscillating undecidedness between the individualistic hero and the collective group working together for good. The emergence of the new Slayers at the ultimate end of the show is a further version of this unresolved tension. The tension between individualism and some larger category of social cohesion is addressed by a number of writers in relation to *Buffy*, and a particularly insightful comment is made by Tanya Krzywinska. Identifying one of the many tensions in the show, Krzywinska indicates how a metaphysical concept such as fate (Buffy being "chosen" without any opportunity to resist her role as Slayer; the presence of the "powers that be") is sustained and in turn rejuvenates moral categories such as good and evil in the guise of Manicheanism. The problem of fate is that it so overwhelms individual choice or action that the notion of individualism becomes defunct. To avert this, many cultural products rely on a hero figure whose individual refusal to be a part of such a spectacular denial of self locates him or her (usually) as a champion of "aggressive individualism present in many Hollywood films where heroic protagonists often transcend the limitations of determination (social, psychological or otherwise) and are liable to control life rather than life controlling them."[31] *Buffy*'s insistence on some level of fate (though one that is not absolute[32]) denies its protagonists, and especially its hero, the postmodern peak of individualistic idol.[33] The postmodern teenager may aspire to atomized individualism but the premodern Slayer and her modernity-bound Watcher cannot allow this. Competing claims for historical supremacy are fought out in the body of Buffy and are most often manifested in her (and the show's) intricate dealings with the eschatological.

In relation to eschatology, *Buffy* is perhaps the most interesting of many recent engagements from popular culture with the subject. These range from *X-Men* to *The Matrix* but none is so deeply involved or deeply ambivalent as *Buffy* (in part, of course, because of the sheer scale of the *Buffy* enterprise). *Buffy*'s main characters occupy a realm that in some senses is akin to the environments in which eschatology in its Christian form secured its centrality in Europe. While the Catholic Church attempted to wrest power away from local lords and even kings in the eleventh to fifteenth centuries, and codified doctrine and teaching, the mass of the populace practiced Christianity against the backdrop of witches and demons, spirits and all manner of the devil's armies. (It would, of course, be prudent to point out that vampires as we have come to understand them were not yet as prominent in the general consciousness.) In other words, history was an all-encompassing battle for Christ that would one day find resolution in His return. The popular enthusiasm for the harsh and brutal world of the Crusades can partly be explained by the realization that the Crusades were explicitly linked to a greater chance for redemption. *Buffy*, as mentioned, is not a Christian program (indeed, its vilification by many in the Christian right in America seems to imply quite the contrary) but its framework implies this sort of a world. There is the Watchers' Council, a remote authority that codifies doctrine and attempts to control practice. Buffy and her friends live in a realm of witches, demons, vampires and the general massed armies of hell. Buffy does not necessarily seek redemption, but she is on a sort of crusade, and apocalypse is a constant threat (although the promise of reconciliation with the Other is not always promised).

While the aspects of eschatology described above may be said to exist in *Buffy* as some type of deep cultural memory, their presence can be determined by a much more overt expression that is as structuring principle. Each season, as mentioned, operates as a movement toward Buffy's confrontation with the monster or evil whose goal is to bring about the end of days. The narrative logic of each season, then, has a strict teleological aspect that Lavery calls narrative eschatology.

At a structural level, a Slayer who is ahistorical and existing in mythical time attempts to avert the destruction of the world of Buffy and her friends, which is dehistoricized or postmodern, by destroying the evil whose goal is apocalyptic. This is represented in a narrative whose teleological momentum is eschatological, or an expression of modernity. The demons' desires are, properly speaking, eschatological, even though they seek a restitution of mythical time. They are aware of their past and use the present to plan a future, and this is seemingly the epitome of rationalist post–Enlightenment historiography but is, however, importantly different. There is no real teleological agenda beyond killing humans and returning to the previous state: in other words, a desire to delete history and return to a myth of beginnings. They regard human history as an obstacle to be overcome in order to allow mythic time to resume. This is most explicitly stated by Luke, the Master's henchman, in "The Harvest" (1.2) where he joyfully asserts, "Today will be history at its end" thereby seeking to bring about human apocalypse, but this is to restore an ancient mythical time of demons and so is, in fact, backward looking (or, seemingly anti-eschatological, which always looks forward). However, if eschatology is that which "will re-establish a full and whole relation with the law of the Other (capital O) as the relation was in the beginning: the law of God in the Christian paradise, the law of Nature in the natural right fantasized by Rousseau, the classless society, before family, and state, imagined by Engels,"[34] then the demons are working with a perverse, monstrous eschatology.

If the explicit narrative structure is eschatological and, therefore, exhibits an attitude that is characterized as part of modernity, but if the eschatological activity of the story is always thwarted in the show (if the demons seem to desire it and Buffy seeks to delay it), then the show's own relation to modernity is itself evidently fraught. Indeed, even the seeming structural dominance of the eschatological is, inevitably, played with by the show calling its penultimate episode "End of Days" (7.21), which undermines the apocalyptic intent of the title by having it precede any possibility of the series' narrative eschatological conclusion. More explicit difficulties with modernity can be seen in two very different episodes that have very different relations to history and push the characters' stories in different directions. One is "The Wish" (3.9) and the other is "Pangs" (4.8).

"The Wish" (3.9) sees a still-smarting Cordelia blame Buffy for her sudden fall from social grace, which was precipitated by Cordelia going out with Xander. Unwittingly, she makes a wish to Anyanka, a vengeance demon, that Buffy had never come to Sunnydale. Anyanka grants the wish and we are in one of science fiction's staple worlds: the alternative reality.[35] It is still historically the same time and geographically the same place but things are, inevitably, different. The major difference from which all others occur is the absence of Buffy. Due to her never having come to the town, the Master, whom she defeated at the end of season 1, has risen and unleashed his reign of terror. Giles fights with those who are able, though no one knows he is a Watcher; Xander and Willow have become vampires and enjoy a relationship of sadomasochistic orientation that echoes Spike and Drusilla, foreshadows Spike and Buffy and is a prelude to Bad Willow of season 6.

The joy of the episode is largely derived from seeing the familiar crew being unfamiliar and thereby testing their acting skills, the writer's capacity to retain certain character traits while perverting them enough for this episode, and the director's vision with regard to lighting and costume, which will be discussed in relation to ethical concerns in chapter 4. There is also the interest in seeing a character who had seemingly disappeared come back to life, especially one so excellently played by Mark Metcalf. There is, too, the intertextual pleasure of keeping *It's a Wonderful Life* in view. While all of these aspects of the episode are interesting in terms of narrative play and the idea of involution that will be explored in part II, they do not have a huge impact on the general notion of history or the specific concerns of eschatology and modernity that I look at here.

Where concerns regarding modernity come into their own is with the Master's plan. Mention has been made periodically to a plant opening, most memorably by Vamp Willow as she is torturing Angel (or "the puppy" as he is called in this episode just in case the S&M overtones were not already strongly present). The plant, then, is marked within a context of evil and pain and is looked forward to by the demons and torturers. It is not explained by any of them, except that it is set to mark the new era of something. Finally, we see what they have been heralding, and the Master makes the inaugural speech:

Vampires, come! Behold the technical wonder, which is about to alter the very fabric of our society. Some have argued that such an advancement goes against our nature. They claim that death is our art. I say to them ... well, I don't say anything to them because I kill them. Undeniably we are the world's superior race. Yet we have always been too parochial, too bound by the mindless routine of the predator. Hunt and kill, hunt and kill. Titillating? Yes. Practical? Hardly. Meanwhile, the humans, with their plebeian minds, have brought us a truly demonic concept: mass production! [3.9].

The Master's new plan to mechanize and automate the bleeding of victims is both very funny in an otherwise quite bleak episode but also an unambiguous attack on one of the mainstays of twentieth-century techno-scientific and manufacturing progress. Indeed, its very notion as progress makes it one of the defining characteristics of modernity, especially in its twentieth-century guise of techno-scientific advancement.[36]

The twin concerns of automated technology and planned societies that is evident in much of early twentieth-century literature are most frighteningly expressed, perhaps, by Aldous Huxley's *Brave New World*, a text explicitly mentioned by Anyanka ("I had no idea her wish would be so exciting: Brave New World" [3.9]) and which locates the Master's plan in a general critique of the elision of progress and technology allied with a concern over what it means to be human (Huxley's novel entering that especially provocative area with stunning insight). The Master forestalls any debate about how technology and progress ("advancement") might alter the fabric of vampire society, or even the very nature of vampires themselves, by killing the dissenters (eschatology is open to all but only if the individual accepts the definition of what it means to be part of "the all" in the first place).

The satire here is not especially subtle, but its point is clear — mass production is a dehumanizing concept (the literalization of this metaphor by Marti Noxon is one of the many delightful moments of the episode). The historical concern is that twentieth-century mass production has been hurtful. While there may be much to agree with here, the show cannot so easily chastise an innovation (an American innovation, at that) that has produced the very culture and society that it is Buffy's duty and responsibility to protect each week. Once again the program provides a wonderful aporia: the world that created Sunnydale is in many ways bad but the world created needs to be saved. The obvious response to this is historical forgetfulness: regret the demonic activity but ignore its relation to anything present. If progress and technology become the bywords for twentieth-century modernity, then leave that behind and enter the postmodern. For Lyotard this is what has happened anyway. The alliance of science, social planning and a version of rationality came together in a horrifying admixture under the Nazis and led directly to the Holocaust, an event (or set of events) that in its terror and abjection — an abjection made more so by virtue of being predicated on the rational and progressive — liquidated modernity. This is far from a generally accepted thesis and many argue that modernity continues apace and the Nazis, rather than being a horrific inevitability of modernity, were a disgraceful anomaly.[37]

It may seem that the move from the Master's mass production to the Holocaust is, at least out of proportion and at worst offensive. However, *Buffy* makes a similar step itself and engages with another one of the horrors on modernity's name and one that has a specifically American complexion. "Pangs" (4.8) confronts the genocide of the indigenous peoples. In itself this makes the episode unusual in the *Buffy* corpus. There are episodes that offer an oblique confrontation with U.S. history but none that is as direct as "Pangs" (4.8). "Gingerbread" (3.11), through the auspices of Joyce's concerned-parent group Mothers Opposed to the Occult, or MOO, parodies such recent groups as the Parents Music Resource Center, which was Tipper Gore's attempt to limit the sales of what she considered to be obscene records. More tellingly, the near-burning at the stake of Buffy, Willow and Amy alludes to Arthur Miller's *The Crucible* and thence to the McCarthy witch hunts of the late 1940s onwards. The burning of the books in this episode also forces a relation between McCarthyism and Nazism. Many other episodes offer metaphorical versions of contemporary social concerns that might face an American teenager or young adult (indeed much of the first season can be seen as doing precisely this), but these are not engagements with particular historical events so much as general social concerns.

"Pangs" (4.8) is different. After the accidental discovery of an old mission on the site which is to house a new cultural center, Hus, the spirit of the Chumash tribe of Native Americans, is released and proceeds to seek vengeance for the wrongs done to his people. Among those targeted is Xander, as it was he who initially digs through the ground and falls into the mission. He is infected with a range of diseases that had afflicted the Chumash after exposure to Europeans. The problem for the Scoobies is threefold: first, Buffy is desperate to have a nice Thanksgiving dinner (her previous few Thanksgivings having all been rather violent or grim affairs) and she does not want anything (Hus or otherwise) to spoil it; second, Hus's vengeance clearly needs to be halted, not least because of Xander's near-fatal accumulation of illnesses; third, Willow's sense of historical guilt that she feels (and believes the others should also feel) means that she refuses to aid the group in killing Hus. Alongside this triangular tribulation, other factors are noteworthy: the episode is the first half of the newly possible *Buffy–Angel* crossover; the newly neutered Spike seeks sanctuary at Giles's house where the Thanksgiving dinner is to take place; and Giles himself is trying to adjust to his seeming lack of purpose now that he is no longer either Watcher or librarian.

Buffy's position as typical teen, the would-be fun-loving American girl whose knowledge of history and awareness of its continuing presence is somewhat lacking, is made clear in the first scene. Here, she, Anya and Willow are awaiting the ceremonial first dig of the new site, and Xander is part of the construction team (which allows Anya's sexually charged personality some marvelous moments of expression). Buffy's simple pleasure in the cultural center's seeming liberal agenda and in the fact of its being Thanksgiving and therefore a time for friendship and fun is quickly undercut by Willow's passionate diatribe concerning the plight of the Indians. Buffy's response, which is to assert that Willow is acting as her mother's mouthpiece, and Willow's concession that this might be partly true, immediately presents some difficulties. Buffy's reluctance to accept Willow's version is not necessarily surprising; the show's subtle endorsement of that reluctance persists throughout, despite some excellent writing by Jane Espenson whose capacity for dialogue-as-debate is very impressive.

Anya provides a surprisingly insightful anthropological slant on Thanksgiving (which avoids the question of the role of the Indians altogether), which, again, Buffy is unwilling to accept:

> ANYA: I love a ritual sacrifice.
> BUFFY: Not really one of those.
> ANYA: To commemorate a past event you kill and eat an animal. A ritual sacrifice ... with pie [4.8].

The real debate begins once it is clear that Hus is a Chumash vengeance demon and Xander's life is in peril. Each of the main actors in the debate (Buffy, Willow, Giles and Spike) offers arguments that are as much reflections of their relationships with history as they are aspects of personality, though the one may be reasonably inferred from the other.

Buffy, as has been said, is the least involved in history of any of the characters, except perhaps Xander. As Buffy, she exists in a permanent historical present where the immediate concern of love, family and friends, and the simple facts of high school or university occupy most of her time. As the Slayer her duty is to protect the world from demons and not to be especially concerned about the historical circumstances of their being. She is also a decent person and Willow's friend and is, therefore, eager to try and fulfill her Slayer's duty while celebrating the day and keeping Willow happy. Her pragmatic and unconcerned response to the situation is very funnily presented and is an excellent portrayal of general social values and concerns through a specific character. Trying to assure Willow of the deep emotional sympathy she feels for the plight, Buffy simply cuts away, tells Anya how much brandy is needed for a recipe and then continues without missing a beat: the rhetoric of historical concern is wonderfully juxtaposed with the reality of immediate need.

Questions of rhetoric as an aspect of political responses to historical dilemmas is nicely funneled through Giles. Trying to make Buffy ignore the preparation of the meal in favor of considering what to do about Hus, Giles calls him an Indian.[38] Amid her search for a kitchen appliance[39] Buffy reprimands Giles's use of language. Giles shall come unstuck again when he meets Maggie Walsh four episodes later and calls Buffy a "girl" rather than a "young woman," prompting him to exclaim, "Woman, of course. How wrong of me to choose my own words" (4.12). Here, his linguistic lapse leads to his caustic aside, "Yes, always behind on the terms. Still trying not to refer to you lot as 'bloody colonials'" (4.8). And immediately we have a different relationship with history. Giles is explicitly English (as discussed in chapter 2) and this allows the program makers and especially the writers to trade on that fact. There is a presumption, it seems, that by virtue of being English, Giles is inevitably closer to an idea of the historical, both in the sense of living in a country that has centuries of history itself but also in the sense that this offers a continuing idea of the presence of the past. This general notion is augmented by the fact that Giles not only has a national association with a long heritage but his position as a Watcher also locates him in a specific context that is bound to an ages-old history, albeit a hidden and secret history. He reads about history, exists in history, and is part of an organization that is saturated by history. Despite this, he, more than Buffy, is deeply pragmatic about Hus. While recognizing the depredations suffered by the Chumash, he is unwilling to allow that fact to deflect Buffy from her Slayer's duty. He is unusually blithe when arguing the case with Willow. She has come stacked with books that tell of the atrocities and that have stoked her indignation and historical sympathy. A little later she demands that the atrocities be brought to light. Giles retorts that if the books are full of them then they have been brought to light and that would seem to be that.

Giles, then, is seen to have a historical consciousness by virtue of national allegiance, and this provides him with the recognition of the wrongs done. This however, is simply one aspect of his being and other allegiances (to the Slayer, most especially) allow him to make a reasoned choice that asserts the primacy of the immediate danger over the legacy of the Chumash history. Buffy's ironic claim that he is the patriarch and needs to understand her country's customs with regard to Thanksgiving dinner is felt forcefully by Willow when the older man with rationality seemingly on his side implies strongly that her response is irrational and emotional. Willow rejects this.

Willow's own response to the historical dilemma is perhaps the most interesting. Despite the curious way in which her initial concerns about the genocide are dissipated by Buffy's comment about her mother, this does at least provide Willow's position with some, however attenuated, historical depth of its own. Willow's character has been marked as an outsider from the start. Each of the characters is, to some degree, alone and alienated, but Willow is especially so. Her very first appearance in the dowdiest of school clothes in "Welcome to the Hellmouth" (1.1) and her love of learning and computer skills place her firmly in the nerd camp. More than this, though, her own occult interests and her family's cultural heritage place her in a marginal position. The fact of her Jewishness is rarely drawn out in the seasons,[40] yet it cannot be ignored here. While there is no point at which the fate of the Indians is equated with that of the Jews in Europe during World War II, it is impossible for a viewer not to make that connection. Willow's absolute conviction that some sort of restitution of the wrongs is necessary and her single-minded commitment to trying to find one present us with a historical doubling that is at times very moving. In addition to her Jewishness is the fact of her being a witch. Once again, she is a member of a group that faced persecution, ostracism, torture and death, and her recognition of social injustice is not merely an emotional and flimsy whim but an aspect of her deep association with groups whose own histories stand in cruel alignment with that of the Chumash.

It is disconcerting, then, that the episode does not maintain Willow's historical integrity. While a resolution to the show in which the demon was talked out of his mission by promises of land renewal or formal apologies would have been frankly silly, and given the necessity of narrative completion—for many reasons but most pressingly the fact that Buffy had to appear on *Angel* immediately after the commercials—it is understandable if regrettable that the demon is killed. What is less understandable is Willow's turnaround. She fights the demons and attempts harm to them with almost no sign of the guilt she had shown earlier. Some sort of principled conscientious objection would have been plausible, even as the fight raged, but she simply joins in. Her own worry about this later is far too easily explained away by Giles at the dinner table who states that "that's what violence does" (4.8).

Violence is, of course, what Spike is good at, or at least has been good at. His inclusion in the debate is due to his need for shelter after his escape from the Initiative. He is incapable of harming humans and poses no physical threat. His relationship with history is unusual. On the one hand his existence as a vampire indicates a lack of historical consciousness insofar as the purpose of vampires and other demons, as has been seen, is the bringing about of the end of human time. Spike's position as a particular vampire, rather than simply an example of the genus, is rather different. In the final episode of season 2, "Becoming II" (2.22), Spike proposes an alliance with Buffy to stop Angel. Refusing the tough guy talk of vamps who claim to want to "destroy the world" he instead presents a version of the world that he wants to save, which includes the fact that there are billions of people walking around like Happy Meals on legs. Additionally, though, are specific cultural (especially English) aspects that he likes for their own sakes. Unconvincingly from this London-based would-be punk vampire he presents Manchester United as one reason; more interestingly, dog racing as another. Either way, Spike is unusual as a vampire for actually wanting the maintenance of the very thing he is supposed to try to destroy. He would not phrase it like this, but he wants to continue history; his reasons are self-interested and deeply pragmatic, but they are real.

His pragmatism can be seen in "Pangs" (4.8). Unlike any of the other characters, he is unwilling, initially, to engage in the "namby-pamby boo-hooing about the bloody Indians." Locating the U.S. westward expansion and conflict with the indigenous peoples in the context on imperial expansion he simply states the historical fact of what has happened and the pointlessness of regretting it: "You had better weapons, and you massacred them. End of story" (4.8). More than this, however, is the sense in which apology is not only futile but itself offensive. "You exterminated his race. What could you possibly say that would make him feel any better?" (4.8).

While Spike's pragmatism is partly due to his vampirism, and to the particular brand of masculinity that he trades off via his self-appointed bad-boy punk image, there is another relationship to history he has that has an influence on his response to colonial expansion. This is his position, before being turned into a vampire, of being an English gentleman in 1880s London. While we do not get the full story of this until season 5, most fully in "Fool for Love" (5.7), its contribution to Spike's persona seems strong. He keeps the nickname he had at that period ("William the Bloody") but re-casts its initial designation (bloody awful poet) into his new incarnation where it is his bloody use of railway spikes that becomes dominant.

The pampered English mummy's-boy, would-be paramour and ineffectual fop of the English aristocratic classes shows no sign of engagement with worldly affairs, preferring to leave any unpleasantness to the police (5.7). It is interesting to note that the shift to Yorkshire, in the north of England has him repudiate the "frilly cuffs-and-collars" crowd in favor of fighting and violence; this is a wonderfully curtailed representational critique of the north-south split in English culture and the attendant masculinities that are thought to go along with that. However, his simple belonging to that class at that time implies a strong historical connection, at least at the level of benefit, to the British Empire's expansion. I discuss this further in the chapter on ethnicities, but Spike's pragmatic rejection of guilt in favor of historical necessity is deeply implicated in his imperial background. While Giles appears every inch the English gent, Spike was one and both seem to proffer pragmatism as a substitute for restitution.

Spike ultimately wails out an apology as the arrows start to fly but Angel's secret presence ensures that the spirit is killed and Thanksgiving can continue as Buffy desired: peripherally aware of the plight of the Indians but much more concerned with the immediacy of the domestic.

It is true that the show offers a range of debating points that at least provide a position from which one of the great historical silences of U.S. history can be addressed. However, while the sympathies of the show are almost certainly with President Ulysses S. Grant, who stated in 1869 that "the history of the Government connections with the Indians is a shameful record of broken treaties and unfulfilled promises ... murder, outrage, robbery, and wrongs,"[41] the resolution of the episode and, therefore, its unambiguous aesthetic conclusion with regard to the history, is much closer to Philip Sheridan, the infamous nineteenth-century army general, whose comment that the "only good Indian is a dead Indian" is disturbingly mirrored in "Pangs" (4.8) even if his less well known, and equally as important caveat is also present: "we took away their country and their means of support.... Could anyone expect less?"[42]

Buffy clearly has a generally liberal agenda and seeks to engage with a number of different contemporary aspects of social and cultural concern. Its relationship with history and the representation of history serves to complicate this agenda. Whether an individual episode fails to provide an aesthetic resolution to a question that moves beyond one of the most ignominious expressions in U.S. history, or whether it provides a witty and disturbing attack on curtailments of civil liberties and free expression from 50 years ago, the demands of the story will always outweigh the overarching historical sensibility. Lavery's term, narrative eschatology, requires (even though he might not agree with this point) the supercession of the story over other factors. Self-contained storylines within an episode that has backward- and forward-looking narrative trajectories in a teleologically oriented seasonal structure have to be closed off.[43] They may provide hints for future developments or reflect back on previous actions, but they need resolution within the episode. This simple structural requirement disallows genuine and sustained treatment of specific historical subjects. While this presents certain problems (of which "Pangs" is the most extreme example), it also provides a much more prolonged, subtle and complex involvement with ideas *about* history and our participation with and in it.

Buffy continues to thwart the apocalypse and maintain the "now." Her mythical past and postmodern present have an equally spectral involvement with history. Yet the eschatological modernity implicit in the show's structure, as well as through other characters (especially Giles and Spike), allied with other relationships to history expressed by, for example, Willow's Jewishness and her being a witch, gives *Buffy* a breadth and depth of historical concern and representation that makes it one of the most challenging and intelligent shows on television.

♦ CHAPTER 4 ♦

Aesthetics, Culture and Ethics

"You can tell it's not gonna have a happy ending when the main guy's all bumpy"

Tara's comments to Willow in "Crush" (5.14) about the inevitable demise of Quasimodo due to his physiognomy alerts us to one of *Buffy*'s great strengths: it is never afraid to point out its own indebtedness to, and reliance on, earlier moments of horror. In this instance, it is horror's usual reliance on external physical attributes as signs of moral degeneracy that is being asserted. Tara's analysis of the character, however, seems to imply that the moral choices made by Quasimodo (his "actions were selfishly motivated. He had no moral compass, no understanding of right" [5.14]) are separate to his physicality; the physical characteristics are further visual signs for the reader.

Visual signs are vital for any television show. The extent to which we are able to read a scene or a character and understand a set of actions is always going to be circumscribed by the visual (as well as music and other sound effects). *Buffy* is no different, except that in this show there is a huge effort made to move beyond the medium's usual rather black-and-white use of such signs. The closed economy of signs that would typically assert black as evil and white as good is opposed to an open economy of signs by Frances Early, drawing on the work of Sharron MacDonald. Early writes:

> Open images, in contrast, "are to be interpreted, read and to an extent repopulated [and] the form of condensation that they employ [is] not meant to reflect or define the social life itself" (21–23). In other words,

open images are inherently unsettling to the ways things are. Significantly, MacDonald argues, utilization of open images permits their creators to focus on human agency and the potential for social change.[1]

While it is largely true that, even in *Buffy*, the bumpy guys are likely to end up in a bad place, the economy of representation that is utilized to produce Sunnydale and its various inhabitants moves us far beyond the codifications for good and evil found in similar, though deeply different, shows, such as *Charmed*, *Xena* and even *The X-Files*.

Two interesting essays that look at questions of the visuality of evil and the aesthetics of ethics are Camille Bacon-Smith's "The Color of the Dark"[2] and "A Reflection on Ugliness" by Charlaine Harris.[3] What both of these writers engage in, in very different ways both thematically and methodologically, is an attempt to read *Buffy*'s ethical positions through its aesthetic constructs. In large part, this chapter will attempt a similar reading, paying attention not so much to broader questions of ethical decision making (though some analysis of that is present) but rather focusing on the ways in which representational strategies present their own ethical vision. To that extent, the ethical is not seen in *Buffy* as a result only of character action but is recognized as intrinsic to the aesthetic choices made by the production teams: the aesthetic is already ethical, it already asserts a relationship to culture in terms of the encoding (and revisions of the encoding) of good and bad, right and wrong.

While the aesthetic may have an irreducible relationship to the ethical, it is still important to realize that ethical choices are made by characters, and so some understanding of what these choices are, and how they are chosen, will be useful. The general ethical dimensions that I am most interested in for the purposes of this chapter are the choices made at the moral intersections of the grand categories of good and evil with which the show works. These categories remain the locus for much of the decision making for Buffy and her friends, and it is always the overarching impulse toward the good that acts as the primary impulse. However, while the categories remain in place as both structural narrative necessity and metaphysically abstracted constant, their presentations allow for a complex and fraught set of negotiations such that their appearance is often confused, both for the characters and for the viewers. Discussing a specifically Kantian reading of the show, Scott R. Stroud places these individual dilemmas within the context of a complete moral universe and asserts:

> The ideal version of this plan also involves individual agents continuously struggling to order their lives and their actions through maxims based not in inclination, but instead in the moral law.[4]

Refusing such a clear realm of moral law, at least one located in metaphysical structures, Greg Foster prefers the Platonic conception of eudaemonism or the assertion that, based on the premise that people will always do that which they believe will make them happy, it is the job of moral philosophy to show that the morally good life is also the happiest life. For Foster the benefit of this is that this morality is rooted in "real experience" and has as "little dependence as possible on abstraction and metaphysics."[5] While the show's presentation of the metaphysical realm of good and evil is certainly inconsistent (and even more so when one introduces *Angel*'s own particular versions), the realm is not nonexistent. Eudaemonism is certainly part of the moral structure, but, for *Buffy*, it is not as divorced from the metaphysical as Foster asserts.

The fact that these two writers can see such divergent positions in relation to moral law and the ethical decisions that are derived from these in *Buffy* demonstrates both the complexity and, to a certain extent, inconsistency of morality in the show.[6] Whether it is a conscious choice on behalf of the program makers, or whether it is the result of a number of different writers with differing moral perspectives of their own trying to invent a moral order in the series, this inconsistent moral universe is one of the show's great strengths. As mentioned in chapter 1, *Buffy* tends to deny totalizing systems of thought, and this is as true of its relationship with morality as it is of its relationship with other forms of knowledge. The viewer is never in any doubt about the strenuous efforts of the characters to discern the right course of action and the extreme difficulty that this poses. Devoid of any overarching religious principle, bereft of a secure metaphysical grounding yet still subject to metaphysically oriented structures, the characters' choices are always made on a case-by-case basis. Sometimes the choices are deemed wrong by other characters (Buffy's decision to kill Anya [7.5]), sometimes by the audience (Xander's lie to Buffy [2.22]) but we, as much as they, are forced to consider the positions from which we are reaching our own judgments. By denying the viewer the consolation of comfortable and known moral structures, the show insists on the experience of ethical doubt and care. Brian Wall and Michael Zryd place the moral ambivalence of *Buffy* in the context of a modernity that itself is deeply skeptical about the possibility of totalizing moral principles. They claim that *Buffy* "does not, in its narrative universe, presume to imagine a moral utopia [...] a failure which notably mimics modernity itself."[7] Modernity's deeply conflicting claims to moral authority, discussed in various ways in the preceding three chapters, have given rise to a supposed postmodern moral free-for-all. While *Buffy*'s undoubted moral eclecticism might be thought to be a part of this, it is, in fact, much more closely allied with a postmodern strain of deeply committed philosophical and moral thought. Jean-François Lyotard sought a moral position in a metaphysical desert and consistently refused the presumed solace of the preexisting. In both aesthetic and ethical considerations, his work is a testament to the power of laborious thought and the importance of rejecting the relief of the ready-made. In a quotation that refers primarily to art, but which has a definite validity for Lyotard's notions of ethical judgments too, he states, "The artist and writer therefore work without rules, and in order to establish the rules for what *will have been made*."[8] *Buffy*'s struggle with ethical decisions is due to the realization that it is often only retrospectively that the moral rules governing the ethical choice can be discerned, and then only murkily. Yet despite this, choices have to be made, and it is to the show's credit that it rarely opts for the easy option.

However, it is not only through the characters' choices and decisions that the show presents a reflection on ethical possibility. Its own aesthetic is steeped in ethical assumptions drawn from the representational traditions of cinema, television and literature. These, through their iconographic immediacy, seem initially to be comparatively straightforward: dark and night equates with danger and, subsequently, evil; light and sunshine equate with day and, subsequently, good, to take a rather simplistic starting point. One of the ways that *Buffy* moves beyond its position as simply a horror-genre show is its willingness to play with these categories, sometimes letting the expected ethical outcome from a particular aesthetic moment run its course, other times subverting it, other times still offering both aesthetic and ethical obscurity. As this chapter shall argue, the ethical complexity of the show that is derived from the aesthetic games makes a simple reading of *Buffy* very awkward, especially at the political level. And this is to its credit.

This discussion of the specifically aesthetic aspect of ethics will begin by looking at the uses of light and dark as ethical markers, then at color coding (especially in terms of hair and clothes). A brief discussion of discourses of masculinity as signs of evil, or, at least, as signs of a failure to achieve normativity, will then be undertaken. I shall end with an account of monsters and vampires and try to extend the discussion of ethics and aesthetics to incorporate a notion of contemporary cultural practices and processes as developed through the representation of these creatures.

The opening scene of "Welcome to the Hellmouth" (1.1) encapsulates the myriad ways that *Buffy* deploys aesthetics. The involutional aspects, that shall be discussed in part II, accrue around the shot of the high school. While it may not be apparent to all, and it is certainly not marked out as such by the scene, the school is the same as that used in *Beverly Hills 90210*.[9]

Perhaps insignificant in itself, the fact that the *Buffy* school is shown at night means that it has a relation to *90210* that is inverted and semi-parodic. The highlife glamour, troubled-teen trauma that was endemic to that show is here obscured by the night — that show's template of blue skies and bitches (which, indeed, constitutes a part of *Buffy*) is only half the story: a darker, violent, unknown and unknowable quality also resides in the seemingly straightforward world of high school drama. The intertextual marker (importantly, and irreducibly, visual — itself a central aspect of the aesthetics of *Buffy*) extends the program beyond itself to another program. The involutional strain that is such a dominant feature of *Buffy*'s remarkable aesthetic enterprise is apparent in its very first shot.

In addition to the aesthetics of involution that are introduced, we are also offered the show's engagement with the aesthetics of culture. Much of this has been discussed in previous chapters, especially the American, and more particularly Southern Californian geographical and cultural markers. The two people to whom we are introduced are unmistakable American high school kids — the clothes, the speech patterns, and the setting itself all immediately propel us into high school. While the aesthetics of culture are often much more interesting than this, their inclusion as an aspect of the requirement of the show to deploy the strategies of televisual realism even as it yanks us out of our reality to the realm of monsters and fiends is essential to its economy of representation.

For the purposes of the current chapter, it is the relationship of the scene to the aesthetics of ethics that is most important. Given the show's title and an expectation on behalf of the program makers that there will be, at least, a minimal awareness of the sort of program that includes "vampire Slayer" in its title, the opening scene presents a copybook exercise in setting the stage for a vampire. The time is night, darkness pervades, the school is empty, the girl is blonde and seemingly hesitant ("Are you sure this is a good idea?") (1.1) and the boy is bad. Vampire legends, books and movies, for all the clear differentiation between them, require these staples before the lonely girl in the secluded castle, house or, here, school, is bitten by the vampire. The blondeness of the girl here marks her as an all–American sweetheart and maintains the inevitable rainbow of goodness: the nearer to white, the better; the boy, who is bad, we are led to believe, has dark hair and a dark leather jacket. This neat and utterly expected opening soon presents its own inversion, as the simple presentation of the high school has already done: the sweet, blonde victim turns out to be the vampire and it is she who sinks her fangs into the boy. Apart from debunking the generic expectation of the girl as victim (and generic variability will be discussed below), this opening also asserts the ways in which the less obviously generic aspects of the show will also be either (perhaps too easily) inverted or (much more interestingly) confused, intermingled and made complex, or monstrous.

In this instance, it is not just a structural feature of the horror genre that is inverted (male victim slain by female monster), but an aesthetic that, while seeming to be simply an ancillary attribute of that structure, is itself constitutive of the horror genre and *Buffy*'s extraordinary revisions of it. One of the obvious signs of evil is darkness. This has been true of many genres, not only horror, and can be seen in both the natural and cultural aspects of the term. Natural darkness would include nighttime, unlit interiors, shaded exteriors such as forests; cultural darkness would include the color of clothes, of hair and the range of acculturated inferences drawn from the natural in terms of descriptors of people: "he's a dark one," "his heart's as black as night" and so on.

In the opening scene, we have the natural dark of night — the time of demons and ghosts, murderers, rapists and all sorts of terror — as well as the seeming color scheme of victim and killer. Except, of course, the scheme is inverted: the blonde girl in light clothes is in fact the one with no soul and a hunger for blood. It is plausible that many people watching the show for the first time may have believed that there would be an inversion of the expected simply by virtue of the girl being the fabled Buffy; that the bad vamp would find his comeuppance at the hands of a sprightly and strong Slayer. And it is one of the strengths of the show that, right at its opening, we are teased with expectation being met (the dark night) and then being inverted (the blonde girl as killer) but also, then, muddled. For our heroine, we know little other than that she has had bad dreams,[10] has just moved to Sunnydale with her mother and is also a blonde girl. While it is doubtful that the mixing of the aesthetic palette will lead many people to assume that Buffy herself is anything other than the sweet all–American girl she appears to be, we have been given cause to be a little less easily seduced by the seeming signs of innocence and evil.

So the opening few minutes of the show have posited one of its aesthetic attributes, which is that expected signifying practices will not be adhered to. This is not simply a case of inverting them, however, as that would itself become just another predictable premise. Also, the inversion of a system of only two terms does little more than maintain that system and, additionally, serve to reinforce through repetition the initial structure's dominance. Rather, what *Buffy* does is to invert and then invert again, to muddle the expectations such that one can never discount the possibility that dark will equate with evil and light with good, but equally one can never trust that this will be the case. By doing so, the initial two-term system becomes multiplied beyond itself and in so doing this broadens the palette of possible colors for good and evil.

The garb and coloring of characters will be addressed again shortly, but it is not the only spectrum that operates at the level of an ethical sign system in film and television: there is also lighting. The darkness of the school at nighttime is very quickly juxtaposed with the amazing sunshine of the school by day. Once again, this leads us into the realism of the show; its location in a Southern Californian town whose inhabitants can expect sunshine and warmth all year round. However, this is not just any SoCal town, this is Sunnydale. Its very name insists upon its relationship with a benevolent nature that spreads warmth and light over the open river valley. Less bizarre than "Buffy," the town's name is itself a sign that connotes the sort of world that bespeaks peace, prosperity and sunny days. And during the day this certainly seems to be true: the colors are bright, the clothes are lightweight and appealing, the skins are tanned and the teeth are white. It is obvious that juxtaposing this against the terrors of the dark provides a clear contrast, a dividing line between the world of demons that, we assume, Buffy will have to slay, and the world of school and normalcy, which, we assume, will be the usual sort of strain or joy as it is for most young people. And it is true that, for the most part, the monsters that Buffy slays are creatures of the night and the darkness but the world of day and light is far from free from the infestations of the shadows: the panning shot from the Master's lair beneath the school (right in the famed Sunnydale Hellmouth) upwards toward light, day and the normal world beautifully makes this seamless intermeshing of the two worlds (as opposed to their utter differentiation) visually apparent, with all the attendant prelude to horror that this will unleash (1.1).

In the light of day, during this episode, the remaining main characters who will inhabit the world of the show are introduced. Xander and Willow, the two ever-present members of the Scooby Gang are far from fashionable: in Willow's case the plaid dress is a terrifying indictment of what parents can do. However, they are shot in bright sunshine outside. Xander's shirt, though less than cool, is colorful and bright and the two friends, both outsiders, are attractive in nonstereotypical ways. Cordelia, the enemy-turned-helper-turned-friend, is dressed in a fashionable and chic dress and is much more obviously good looking and aware of that fact. High school fashion being what it is, Cordelia mocks Willow's clothes and seems much more drawn to new-girl Buffy whose trendy yet unassuming (if very short) attire marks her out as cool and worthy of attention. Giles, the school librarian and Buffy's Watcher, sports a tweed jacket and shirt and tie and looks and acts every inch the stuffy early-middle-aged Englishman.

The point for the time being is that they are normal; indeed, visually they are barely distinguishable from characters who may have been in *90210* or *Dawson's Creek*, or, more pertinently, the young characters from Wes Craven's horror parody *Scream*. The costume designer for *Scream* was Cynthia Bergstrom who went on to become the costume designer for *Buffy* because "as I recall, Joss really liked the way the kids looked because they were so believable; they were so real."[11] Sarah Michelle Geller's appearance in the sequel *Scream 2* is another example of the involution that shall be discussed in part II.

In the world of the seemingly normal is, of course, Buffy: cute, pretty and blonde.[12] She exudes the wholesomeness of a thousand American teen girls. Despite her seeming representational indebtedness to a mawkish media, fetishistically recalling a 1950s America wonderfully and tenderly critiqued in *Pleasantville,* directed by Gary Ross (a film that included other members of the *Buffy* cast, another involutional link), Buffy is very much of the 1990s. Her parents are divorced, she is an only child, she has been kicked out of her previous high school and she is troubled. She is also able to engage in social semiotics, a capacity that becomes invaluable later when she is able to distinguish a vampire by the fact that his clothes are unfashionable (1.1). Our first encounter with this is when she is choosing clothes in which to go to the Bronze, the local nightclub. Here, the representational history of teenage girls is marvelously reduced to two choices of dress, one of which prompts Buffy to assert that she looks like a seller of *The Watchtower*, the other of which makes her look like a "slut." Virgin or whore, '50s teen-dream or '90s teenage tramp: the program not only disallows Buffy to be cast into one light or the other but it is also able to reflect on the aesthetic practices and televisual and cinematic traditions that have upheld the culturally dominant categories of youthful femininity for so long. In addition, this also alerts the viewer to what we have already seen: the categories of signification are powerful but subvertable. And Buffy, herself, operates as an aesthetic sign throughout the seasons, especially in her relationships with other characters.

That the girl in the opening scene, who we come to know as the vampire Darla (sire of Angelus), had to be blonde is known from Joss Whedon's comments that he wanted to begin the show by genre busting.[13] It is less clear that Buffy had to be blonde, though continuing the motif of turning the defenseless blonde teenager into a fighting force for good makes this likely. Our two initial encounters with blonde girls, then, both serve to undermine a staple aesthetic of the genre. Additionally, Darla's Catholic schoolgirl outfit offers a sexualized, fetishized counterpoint to Willow's dowdy outfit. *Buffy*, then subverts one notion (the defenseless, and often dumb in the sense of voiceless, blonde) but upholds another (that light is good).

When we encounter the shadowy figure that is following Buffy, there is a sense in which we know, given her aptitude for fighting that we have already seen, that this will probably be another bad guy, a vampire: he is stealthy, unseen and it is dark. Indeed, when they finally confront one another it is obvious that he also has dark hair and is wearing black. All of the necessary conditions for badness are there and yet, it appears, he is good, if somewhat gnomically so. The culturally allowable tall, dark and handsome man here meshes with the shadowy and furtive as well as the mad, bad and dangerous to know. Angel occupies an area that is traditionally complex though aesthetically resolved on the side of good[14] (male sexuality and desirability) and makes it even more complex as the seasons develop.

Angel's first appearance is aesthetically what he is as a character: confused, contradictory and unexpected. As Buffy moves through the seasons and develops a range of emotional and ethical complexity, a number of things about her change — clothes style, body shape, hair style but never her hair color (at least it never shifts entirely out of the blonde range). However dark she becomes, she never loses the capacity for knowing right from wrong and as such always remains good (some of the philosophical aspects of the show will be discussed later). Accordingly, and in keeping with the aesthetic tradition, her hair stays light. Angel, by contrast, keeps his dark hair. In the reduced world of most televisual iconography this would not be surprising for an evil character, but Angel is not evil.

Angel was once simply a louche and rather disinterested young man in Ireland whose predilection for drink and women possibly indicated a lack of socialization in a deeply Catholic country but this did not make him evil. He only became evil, Angelus, when his desire for women led him to be willingly seduced by the blonde, beautiful white-wearing Darla (2.21). Innocent if foolhardy, black is corrupted by the pure evil hiding in the virginal garb of the vampire; the prowling man in his territory of darkness is killed (and made immortal) by the girl in the light's glow. The archetypes are once more maintained and once more made complex. Once he is Angelus, however, the black hair, dark eyes, black coats and cloaks confer the costume of the corrupter most impressively.

After re-ensoulment, Angel (the name, of course, demands to be read warily: is he the innocent enclosed by the monster's wrap, or the custodian of the monster within?) strives for atonement. His sole purpose is to try and repay for all the appalling havoc he discharged whilst a vampire (though he is still a vampire). Unlike the other vampires in the show, with a few notable exceptions, especially Spike, Angel is normally seen in his human form which is, as is well known, very appealing. The shift from sexy Angel to evil Angelus is indicated by a physiognomic change: his forehead becomes bumpy, his eyes change color and his teeth grow into fangs. This metamorphosis is true of all the vampires and is an obvious visual indicator of their evilness. This indicator itself, however, is problematic as Charlaine Harris has pointed out. In her article Harris discusses the fact that evilness on Buffy is nearly always physically ugly. There is a direct correspondence between an ethical position and an aesthetic appearance. The Scooby Gang is good, even when the Scoobies are riven with doubt, hate, jealousy and so on. As a consequence, they are all good looking. The supposedly geeky Xander is a very handsome man and nerdy Willow is, nevertheless, very cute. Giles has a chiseled attractiveness; Buffy is blonde and sweet; Dawn is a pretty, young girl; Joyce, a good-looking woman; Wesley, despite his early buffoonery, is also striking; even Faith, the Slayer-gone-wrong, is very sexy. It may be that many of the assumptions regarding horror are overturned in this show, but in the area of the aesthetics of good (at the most obvious and superficial level) beauty wins.

Against these models of salvation are ranged the evildoers, the monsters and the villains. The vampires and other monsters are all, with important exceptions, ugly. From the vampire faces of even the most beautiful women (Darla, for example) to the fish monsters,[15] the troll Olaf,[16] the praying mantis woman[17] and so on, monsters are ugly. This in itself is understandable: one of the characteristic traits of a monster is that it is monstrous looking and one of the most monsterly of all monsters (the Frankenstein monsteresque Adam) fits the bill perfectly. When we see him devoid of his hewn-together body (4.22), he is another good-looking man, but as the monster he becomes he has to be ugly. I will discuss the monsters more below. What is less obvious is why the other evil characters have to be so too. The dinner lady who is trying to poison the students in "Earshot" (3.18)[18]; Principal Snyder with his ratlike demeanor; Mayor Wilkins whose avuncular bearing is counterpoised by his becoming a huge snake; even the Willow of season 6 is all veins and grimness. It appears as though, amid the generally sophisticated and subtle work being done elsewhere, the production team has decided that one of the most common areas of the genre will not be tampered with. This is a shame, as it perpetuates one of the stock conceits of the genre but also inculcates, along with the advertisers who finance the show, a belief in a clear aestheticization of morality at the level of human appearance. For a show that excels at allowing the terror of everyday existence to be as important as the possibility of Hellmouth invasion this propensity for the pretty is a little disappointing.

There are exceptions, however, in the later seasons. Glory, the rampagingly malevolent god of season 5 is attractive, though this is modulated, rather, by the look of insanity that she carries around with her and the signs of physical degeneration that precede her need to suck the brains out of her victims. In this instance, once again (which serves to illustrate the point that a more complex representation is nearly always going to provide a greater sense of depth and resonance), her similarity to Buffy makes for some interesting drifts. The blonde-haired, beautiful, extremely powerful Buffy who fights for good is pitched against a blonde-haired, very beautiful, extremely powerful god who fights for evil. The signifiers of goodness and badness are here enmeshed in a visual cross-fertilization that allows certain aspects of Buffy's character to be rendered more intriguing simply by virtue of its congruence with Glory.[19] The fact that Glory's minions are extremely ugly little creatures, all warty and long-nosed, however, proves her demarcation within the evil group as the two blonde leaders exist in worlds of friends or minions whose ethical position is stamped unambiguously on their bodies.

More ambiguous still in terms of an aesthetic expression of ethical position is the pseudo–Big Bad of season 6. The trio of Warren, Jonathan and Andrew do not, generally, carry the stigma of ugly with them. Jonathan is, it is true, a very short man, but his face is pleasant and Andrew and Warren are also, if not extremely good looking, at least not ugly. Despite their not wearing the typical visual signs of evil, they have been written into a discursive space that has its own ethical overtones. We first meet Warren as a sad and pitiable figure who has created a robotic girlfriend because he is unable to find a real one himself, although later in the episode it appears he has ("I Was Made to Love You" [5.15]). Jonathan is always put upon, feeling himself to be outside and unlovable. This comes to a point of crisis in "Earshot" (3.18) when he attempts to commit suicide and again in "Superstar" (4.17) when he casts a spell to make everyone believe that he is powerful and talented. Andrew is a new addition — he is the brother of a student who tried to release hellhounds at the prom — and it is clear that he is effeminate and probably in love with Warren. Each of the three, then, is an example of a failure to achieve a notion of normative masculinity and, as in many aesthetic forays into this area in a variety of genres, this is going to prompt them to evil. One need only think of the, perhaps, rather more extreme examples of Buffalo Bill in *The Silence of the Lambs* (Jonathan Demme, 1991) or John Doe in *Seven* (David Fincher, 1995) to see where failed normative masculinity ends up in much cultural production. It is perhaps not a surprise that the most heinous crimes committed by members of the trio are the murder of Warren's girlfriend ("Dead Things"

[6.13]) and the killing of Tara ("Seeing Red" [6.19]). Both of these are really Warren's crimes (and he appears to be the most sexually disturbed), but the other two are also culpable. While the visual representation might not be quite as easily locatable as evil, the aesthetic choices regarding the discourses of masculinity that the characters inhabit present an equally predictable, and in some senses, disappointing decision regarding the representational strategies of evil. The show's deployment of the aesthetics of culture is here at its most conservative with both the aesthetic strategies and the cultural categories reinforced.[20]

If the troika are the pseudo–Big Bad of season 6, then Willow is the real deal. Her growing addiction to magic, the break-up with Tara and the eventual killing of Tara by Warren all lead Willow to a space of destruction. James B. South argues convincingly that there are no obvious or discernible reasons that would explain Willow's desire to destroy the world (her anger and so on, yes, but the absolute destruction, no). While this may be true, the program makes sure that we are under no illusion as to the potential evil of Willow, even if it is not rationally explicable.[21]

When Willow holds the dead Tara in her arms, with blood-soaked clothes and the sun pouring into the room we have a quintessentially dramatic moment ("Seeing Red" [6.19]). Outside, Buffy lays wounded and Xander is oblivious to the events that are unfolding. We, the audience, see through the window in Willow's room the brightness, almost too bright; the vivid bloodstain; we feel, too, the shock of the unexpected (a shock that is disabling and mortifying — Tara is dead, Willow is in agony — but also thrilling and delightful, the frisson of a drama blowing us and Tara away); and then we see Willow turn. Before our eyes, her eyes become deep, liquid and jet-black; her hair becomes raven-colored; her face ruptures with protruding veins. There is no doubting the way in which the aesthetic is leading us. It is clearly the case that Willow's transformation into an irrational, world-destroying uber-witch is mirrored by her physicality.

Within the economy of representation that the program has been working with, this is an inevitable and necessary step. Her potential for misuse of magic and, therefore, her scary behavior has been demonstrated by her warning to Giles not to mess with her earlier in the season (6.3)[22] and, unlike the more straightforward examples of ugly equals bad, Willow offers a chance of a much more playful and involuted strategy. Willow has already, if only obliquely, been shaded evil by Darla's and her clothes in the very first episode (1.1). Teasingly, the possibility of Willow losing herself if she allows herself to become unrestrained has been hinted at in "Halloween" (2.6) when, at Buffy's insistence, Willow dresses up in semi-goth clothes only to hide under a sheet and pretend to be a ghost. When a spell turns everyone into what they are wearing she becomes a ghost, incorporeal, and walks through walls in her skimpy outfit. The outfit and the ontological dislocation are then reprised in substantially modified form in season 3's "The Wish" (3.9) and "Doppelgangland" (3.16). In these episodes, Willow, from an alternate reality in which Buffy never arrived in Sunnydale, is turned into a vampire. With yellow eyes, bumpy face and shocking red hair as well as a black leather bustier, vamp Willow is a goth-girl dream. Her attitude is one of laconic boredom, a sinuous devil with sex on her mind. The sex, though, is "kinda gay" according to "our" Willow — still resplendent in fluffy pink pullovers and dimmer henna hair. Willow, of course, is gay as the seasons unfold, which presents, at least, a sense of the possible interrelationship of the two Willows; of normal Willow's potential for evil. This is not due to her lesbianism, of course (though some on the Christian right may disagree), rather it is a function of the drawing together of the two characters in terms of dialogue, clothes and scenography such that their aesthetic coincidence implies an ethical corollary.

This is exacerbated by the episode "Tabula Rasa" (6.8) in which Willow, addicted to magic, casts a spell to make Tara and Buffy forget how miserable they are. The spell does not succeed as planned and all the characters lose their memory. Once again, an ontologically disturbed Willow shares something with vamp Willow; this time it is her own sense that she is "kinda gay." The relationship between the two is made explicit when season 6's grieving and evil Willow captures Warren and tortures him. After a long and agonizing session, evil Willow directly quotes vamp Willow by intoning "bored now" (6.20), one of vamp Willow's expressions. Evil Willow's return to normalcy is shown to us through her morphing back into henna-haired, sweet-eyed, smooth-faced Willow; the black jacket and trousers are now little more than part of a young woman's wardrobe.

Willow's journey is not over, however. In season 7, despite her reluctance, she is cajoled into performing a major feat of magic. The spell this time does go according to plan (and thereby brings about the demise of the First Evil, the destruction of Sunnydale and Spike's ascendance to absolute hero) and, during it, Kennedy, her new lover, is present. At the height of the spell, at the height of her powers which are being used for absolute good, Willow transforms again. This time, she turns an almost translucent, bright white from head to toe. Kennedy calls her "my goddess" (7.22) and the good triumphs. The apotheosis of good in the aesthetics of the Buffyverse is light and white and Willow's shining performance presents us with the climax of moral and ethical excellence.

If Willow achieves a moment (the moment?) of moral excellence as represented in aesthetic terms, then Spike gets the same treatment in terms of sacrifice. Having been central to the plans of the First Evil, and then of Buffy to defeat the First Evil, it is perhaps fitting that he should be the conduit through which the First Evil is defeated. The shot of Spike's final sacrifice (until he reappears in *Angel* in the next season) is a beautiful moment. Buffy expresses her love for him, which Spike is both delighted at but skeptical of. Buffy rushes up the collapsing tunnel as the forces of the First Evil attempt to continue their fight. A sudden rod of light passes through Spike's body and we see his flesh begin to fall off, the vampire flesh that has terrorized, attacked, loved, hated, raped and benighted the Scooby Gang for five seasons. But inside we see the light, the violently bright white light at the center of Spike's being, which is, of course, his soul. Like Willow, Spike's action is presented as ultimately good through the extravagant excess of luminescence. As his body is stripped away, his hard-won, newly earned soul shines wildly: after all, he is a good man.

He has not always been, though. Spike's journey from season 2's resident evil to season 7's majestic savior can be traced, like Willow's, through his presentation, or his aesthetic. Most noticeable, from the outset, was his dress and hairstyle, which remained largely unchanged. The long leather black coat and the peroxided hair immediately call to mind the 1980s punk rocker Billy Idol, though the sneering violence and casual cruelty of Spike seems more indebted to a harder-edged punk aesthetic from the U.K. of the 1970s rather than the glam-camp version that Idol expresses. In addition to the antisocial bad boy image that his garb provides, the ethical implications are complex and often wanly amusing. In season 2, this is most noticeable in his relation with Drusilla, his vampire girlfriend. Drusilla has long, dark hair and often wears ethereal white flowing dresses (though occasionally she is darker and more gothic than pre–Raphaelite).[23] Their relationship provides an obvious counterpoint to Buffy's and Angel's but so does their fashion. Spike and Dru invert the hair coloring of Buffy and Angel, while maintaining a certain coded dress symbolism. Angel wears black leather as does Spike (both have been and are still capable of being evil) but Spike gets the blonde hair. It, though, is peroxided, false, a simulacrum of the supposed goodness that the color carries with it.[24] Angel maintains an honest darkness, refusing to adopt symbology as an antidote to salvation. Dru's winsome madness belies the hyperfeminine aspect of her clothes; her lunatic ramblings that have the edge of innocence betray her viciousness. Spike and Dru are not simple inversions of Buffy and Angel, but they are modulations, complex tonal and thematic variations that, while unambiguously evil in action, are multivalent creatures in aesthetic. Indeed, even their actions are less clearly evil than might at first appear, simply due to the capacity for love that the pair share, a capacity that has its own perverse violent and murderous obverse, which tends, rather, to complicate love as a category than to simplify Spike and Dru.

Spike's movement from enemy to hero is caused initially by the chip planted in his brain by the secret government agency The Initiative, and then by his own efforts to restore his soul. While he has the chip he has to live in Xander's basement for a while, and the extent of his captivity, his neutered potential and puppyfication can be seen in the episode where he ends up wearing Xander's clothes ("Doomed" [4.11]). The punk sociopath is now a parody of hopeless white trash: what on Xander was endearingly goofy is for Spike a humiliation. Season 5's Spike, through his love for Buffy, becomes noble and self-sacrificing, enduring torture for Dawn's sake.[25] While still predominantly in black, and still wearing the long leather coat that we discover later he stole as a trophy from a Slayer he killed in New York in 1977, he is also now more likely to wear simple black sweaters and jeans; the growing chic of his wardrobe acting as a somber reflection of his growing stature ethically. The torn and broken man who sobs uncontrollably at Buffy's death at the season finale (5.22) not only acts good, he looks good: a sure sign of his rise.

While the aesthetic relation between Spike and Buffy prompts each to be read in the other's reflection, it is the specific quality of being a Slayer that is the most apparent way that Buffy and the replacement Slayer Faith are placed in juxtaposition.[26] Within this, however, the aesthetic is also crucial. Faith, like Buffy, is beautiful, but where Buffy frets with awkward reconciliation of living as Buffy and being the Slayer, Faith relishes the latter. Buffy aims to uphold a greater conception of good through her slaying while also living a general life that would be considered ethically balanced. For all her stylishness and beauty, her clothes are, for the most part, quite moderate as exemplified by the comment mentioned earlier about her clothes seeming to be Jehovah's Witness–like or slutty. Faith's fashion, like almost all her visual signs, is different from Buffy's. She enjoys sexually alluring clothes, and she has long, dark hair and dark eyes. While Andrew in "Dirty Girls" (7.18) uses color coding metaphorically, his description of her ethical position operates just as well (in fact, literally, better) for her appearance: "But like so many tragic heroes, Faith was seduced by the lure of the dark side" (7.18). Her openness, sexual excitement, sense of adventure and fun in killing all mark her out as being Buffy's opposite. Not as explicit as Willow's vampiric other half, Faith acts in a similar fashion for Buffy and her look is one of the major indicators of this. After coming out of her coma and finding out that the mayor has died, the high school has been blown up, Angel has left town and Buffy is going out with Riley, Faith's capacity for giving pain seems unabated ("This Year's Girl" [4.15]). When a posthumous present from the mayor allows her to switch bodies with Buffy it is *as* Buffy that we watch Faith. This provides for some especially fine acting from both actresses, who are able to adopt the mannerisms, speech patterns and body postures of each other's roles perfectly, never more so than when Faith-in-Buffy stands before the mirror and comically chastises herself (though seeing Buffy, of course) for being naughty and wrong ("Who Are You?" [4.16]).[27] This wonderful moment of comedy has its ethical-aesthetic aspect, however. Faith is seeing good Buffy (blonde hair and all) tell her (bad Faith) how naughty she is. It takes a while, but living the life, receiving the friendship, enjoying the love and being contextually constrained to acts of goodness, dark-souled and dark-haired Faith in the body of good-souled and blonde-haired Buffy discovers that she is unhappy being bad. Evidently, many factors of characterization enable this moral makeover but the fact that she is inhabiting the body of virtue in a specifically visual sense means that her continuing recovery, when back in her own body, is inevitable.

Faith's time in Buffy's body allows her to experience and witness ethical consideration that she has not felt before, and this moves her toward the possibility of goodness that we then witness in the final season where her rehabilitation continues. Again she takes over Buffy, but this time structurally rather than corporeally as Buffy is told to leave by the Scoobies and the Slayers in training. Far from being an act of usurpation, there is still some doubt from Faith as to her legitimacy in this position of control. We are never allowed to forget what she has done and is capable of doing again, and one of the (many) indices for this is her coloring, which always seeps toward the evil end of the spectrum.

If the main characters exist in an aesthetic that is subtle, complex and multilayered in terms of the ways in which color acts as an index of moral capacity, the same, as has been said, is not true of the monsters. However, each monster, vampire or demon does contribute to the aesthetic sense of the show's engagement with ethical questions in a number of ways. Most obviously is the fact that not all monsters, demons and vampires are inevitably bad.[28] It is true that their bad aspects are always manifested with hideous visages or gruesome bodies, but the ability of the show to allow even this level of moral flexibility is impressive in what appeared to be simply a teen horror high school drama.

If we turn to the straightforwardly bad monsters first, we shall see that even here there are ethical questions that derive from the aesthetic, even if these are occasionally oblique or attenuated. An important fact about *Buffy*'s monsters is that there are so many of them. There are undoubted practical reasons for this from a production point of view, such as the desire to keep the audience interested, and a simple succession of vampires getting staked each week would become less than thrilling as a televisual spectacle.

This is not the whole story, though. Even within the different species of monster (demon, ghost, vampire, primals and so on) there is a surprising amount of differentiation. The vampires themselves, the show's main titular enemy, are often very different from one another in looks and characteristics. There are, of course, the common or garden-variety vampires who tend to lack motivation beyond being vampires, are often less than quick-witted and usually end up getting staked. These are the necessary opponents who provide the show with its fight scenes. Often they have only a peripheral relationship with the main story and the fight is there as much for its own sake as for any sense of the narrative or thematic progression.

These vampires are simply evil. They want to kill humans and feed but are lacking any grand design. However, their presence is essential. Buffy is a vampire Slayer; however much she may battle other forces, it is as a Slayer of vampires that her destiny has been designated. To that extent, the fights with vampires are a constant reminder of the show's premise. Additionally, they allow for exciting, well-choreographed demonstrations of Buffy's physical power, skill and strength. These sequences draw from a range of different fight skills, devised and executed by the stunt coordinator and the doubles. Jeff Pruitt, stunt coordinator for *Buffy* for the opening seasons, managed to bring not only a street-fighting aspect to the show (necessary for the rough and tumble urban feel of some of the dark alley fights) but also a martial arts aspect. Being the only U.S. stunt coordinator to have belonged to an Asian stunt team allows Pruitt (and hence the show) to have a feel that is different from most other television dramas. It also means that Whedon's well-known admiration for *The Matrix* and its martial arts–oriented fight sequences was allowed some outlet in the fighting area even before the climactic fight scene with Adam in "Primeval" (4.21).[29]

The vampires not only act as foils for the fighting, though; they carry their own set of aesthetic attributes. Primarily, their dispensability means that there is a guilt-free killing by Buffy each week.[30] Being murderous themselves and also not human means that Buffy is able to use violence (and the program is able to delight its viewers with the same) with little or no ethical dilemma in terms of the show's thesis. The fact that many of the fights are cut when shown on channels around the world that have misread *Buffy*'s demographic and show it at teatime, indicates that the violence is not without supposed ethical problems relating to viewer eligibility.

The vampires' status as expendable fight fodder is shown not only by their visages but also by their lack of speech. These creatures tend to have few if any words to say: they fight, they die and we are not encouraged to enter into their psychologies or motivations. As such, we are free to assume that they don't have any. This is an aesthetic decision — to provide dialogue, backstory, relationships would be to remove the vampires from the realm of objects to be dusted to something much more akin to humans, and one of Buffy's main ethical rules is that her version of justice has no place in the human world. Her dismay when she thought that she had killed her mother's boyfriend Ted was only vitiated when she discovered that he was a robot ("Ted" [2.11]). Faith's seeming refusal to acknowledge her guilt or responsibility when she kills Allan Finch, the deputy mayor, is another indication of her distance from Buffy's world of morality ("Bad Girls" [3.14]). There are some exceptions. In the episode "Conversations with Dead People" (7.7) Buffy chats with a vampire with whom she used to go to school when he was human. Holden Webster is charming, witty, thoughtful and he encourages Buffy to express some of her current despair. Her spiking of him seems rather more shocking than usual simply because we are able to know him. The fact that he is an evil vampire does, of course, temper this to an extent.

Most vampires do not have this level of engagement. They do, however, have a look. They can come in all sorts of clothes, ethnicities, be male or female but they do share the face. This face is largely influenced by the look of the vampires in *The Lost Boys*, the 1988 teen vampire movie that made a star of Kiefer Sutherland (whose father was, of course, Merrick in the film version of *Buffy the Vampire Slayer*). The "meaner"[31] vampire visage on *Buffy* provides a less campy feel but does place the vampires themselves in an aesthetic that is reasonably current, part of popular culture and comparatively untainted by previous incarnations.[32] Importantly, this is a specifically American vampire, derived from American culture and expressive of American ideas.[33]

It is interesting to note the differences between the *Lost Boys* American vampire look and the older, traditional European look of the vampires. The quintessential vampire is Dracula. Bram Stoker's 1897 novel forever placed the name at the forefront of vampire legends (though the history of both the real Dracula and the vampire myth itself have become deeply confused). It is noticeable that it is not until the fifth season of *Buffy* that he makes an appearance ("Buffy versus Dracula" [5.1]).

Unlike the typical *Buffy* vampire, Dracula has none of the usual facial disfigurements except for highly developed incisors. He is extremely pale skinned and has thick dark hair and wears a cape. In many respects he looks like a parody, the sort of figure that the would-be vampires in the episode "Lie to Me" (2.7) emulate. Indeed, Buffy is so non-plussed by his initial introduction that she comments: "And you're sure this isn't just some fan-boy thing? 'Cause I've fought more than a couple pimply, overweight vamps that called themselves Lestat," (5.1) thereby refusing both his actually being Dracula and sequestering him in a cultural heritage that is specifically American.[34] Xander likewise assumes that Dracula is a joke and mocks the vampire's *Sesame Street* accent. Dracula's power and sensuality derive from his ability to control minds rather than from strength alone. He expresses charm, intelligence and guile, as well as evil, but he knows Buffy and what she is in terms of her heritage, repeating almost word for word the warning from Tara in Buffy's dream in "Restless" (4.22): "You think you know ... what you are, what's to come. You haven't even begun" (5.1). Her Slayer traditions are older than her country, and his traditions are older also. The European vampire comes from a different place, with different sensibilities and possibilities. It is *Buffy's* skill that such an aesthetically different representation of the vampire could be placed so seamlessly in the program. Partly this is to do with the filmic heritage of Dracula[35] and the impossibility of playing too much with this, but it is also because, as with the general mixing up of aesthetically pregnant tropes, so too the entire undertaking allows for massive generic and artistic hybridization. This postmodern aspect of the show is firmly cemented when Buffy refuses to accept that Dracula is dead because she has seen too many films where he comes back to life. And in addition to this self-reflexive ironic comment concerning the series' own fictive status, Buffy (with the help of scriptwriter Marti Noxon) also pushes the postmodern button when she fuses the history, the aesthetic and the dusting of Dracula with contemporary culture speak and declares that Dracula has been "Eurotrashed" (5.1).

Dracula, then, allows the show to enhance its position as part of the postmodern pantheon of contemporary U.S. television. This has clear ethical implications that, as has been commented on by many writers, are often expressed in aesthetic terms. Dracula's appearance does not just invite question about the relationship of his particular aesthetic to his ethical reading but broadens the discussion out to a more general set of attributes that the show has.

A much earlier manifestation of the European vampire is the Master. His look is among the most terrifying and sinister that the series has offered, much more monster than human. The Master is not the sophisticate that Dracula is (though he is clever), he is, instead, an age-old emissary of pure evil whose sole purpose is to escape from the Hellmouth and destroy humanity. There is no mistaking him for a human, no transformation to be undergone: he is absolutely a vampire. This is primarily a function of his age. The capacity to stay alive (or undead, at least) for 600 years means that he has "become more demonic as time goes by."[36] Along with other vampires who achieve old age he has become more of what he is—a demon—and the humanity begins to fade. According to David Greenwalt, a producer-director and writer on *Buffy* and co-creator of *Angel*, this begins to become noticeable after a few hundred years.

Not only his age makes the Master necessarily European but also his name, which is Heinrich Joseph Nest. More European, however, is his aesthetic representation. Drawing heavily on the visual appearance of Count Orlok from the 1922 masterpiece by Friedrich Wilhelm Murnau, *Nosferatu*, the Master is an homage to Expressionist German filmmaking and the modernist tradition in the arts of which it was a part. The lavishly stark lighting, the rodentlike aspect of Max Schrek's makeup, and the psychological fury of Orlok borne of isolation and solitude are all present in Mark Metcalf's excellent performance, Todd McIntosh's and Jeri Baker's work on makeup and Joss Whedon's initial vision. Not only does the Master carry the weight of the first season in terms of the specific evil that the team must face (he actually kills Buffy), but he also carries a large part of the aesthetic sensibility of the show too. His lair is lit in cold blues, his clothes are black, his appearance and demeanor horrifying. The long talonlike fingernails make him seem almost birdlike at times and the studied calm of his brutality implies a rationality behind the apparently illogical world in which he lives. The heir of medieval and then Enlightenment Europe, he fuses the mythical and superstitious with the empirical and the scientific.[37] The age and weight of history are only part of the story, however. The Master, though European, has been in America long enough to realize its opportunities. For all that he pays a huge debt to Murnau and Schrek, one cannot avoid the sense of, as Golden et al. put it, "Clive Barker's *Hellraiser*, perhaps."[38] Indeed, he has adopted American culture (both in his attenuated resemblance to a bald version of Pinhead from Barker's movies) so much that in an alternative reality, where Buffy does not come to Sunnydale and his escape from the Hellmouth is achieved, he sets up a blood extraction factory along the lines of Ford's production line ("The Wish" [3.9]).

Whereas the purely European Dracula allows a certain expression of postmodern sensibilities in terms of aesthetics and ethics, the much older European but much more Americanized cultural hybrid, the Master, is an expression of American modernity and its subsequent postmodern turn in economic as well as artistic circles. And as he comments, the U.S.-led expansion of industry from the production line to mass production with all its socioeconomic and political effects is much more demonic than anything he could have dreamed up (3.9). The ways in which the show problematizes ideas concerning modernity and a concept of progress has been discussed elsewhere, but a more general point about what constitutes evil in the show is posed by the Master. He is evil, and through him production-line economics and the resultant alienation of labor is said to be evil: both inherent nature and cultural forces are conceptually liable to evil, which makes any specific claims about Evil's *being* very difficult (even its actions are highly debatable). Roz Kaveney glosses it thus:

> There is a neat joke across the series about the social construction versus essentialism debate — The Master is evil because he regards it as his ascetic religious duty to be so, the younger Darla and Angelus out of a selfish aristocratic hedonism, Spike purely because he is a predator; the precise form evil takes recapitulates medievalism, the ancien regime and cutthroat capitalism.[39]

And in each case the precise form evil takes is expressed through a precise aesthetic analogue or vehicle. When vampires are not caught in the dilemma of having souls, having chips in their brains or else being simply stupid fodder to allow the necessary (and wonderful) violence, they often act as ciphers through which a range of the show's themes— both plot-related and more abstract —can be articulated. Differing designs, lighting, makeup and so on do not only add diversity to the look of the show, though they do that too, they also provide the possibility for visual prompts to ask questions about, for example, the European and American dimensions of the show, the role of intertext, the self-reflexive turn, and the artistic tradition.

While it is at the level of light, color and makeup that most of the ethical aspects of *Buffy* are represented in aesthetic terms, the visual immediacy of these signs compels the audience to be much more careful in its initial readings than is ordinarily the case with television. By confusing many (though not all) of the expected connections between certain choices regarding lighting and costume, *Buffy* not only provides a more subtle and complex representational space for the expression of horror than is usual for the medium but it also asserts that the medium itself is more capable of eliciting complex and thoughtful responses to itself than is typically allowed. When Spike and Anya, both feeling wronged by Buffy and Xander respectively, seek comfort together, Anya drunkenly reminisces about Xander, especially, as she is wont to do, about his body. She wistfully remarks, "Then he was all bumpy in the right places and nice to me..." (6.18). *Buffy* may well still have the bumpy guys meeting bad ends, but the nature of the bumps themselves will have been called quite sharply into question.

Part II

Restless Traditions:
The Aesthetics of Involution
in *Buffy the Vampire Slayer*

◆ CHAPTER 5 ◆

The Aesthetics
of Involution

"I've got a theory"

May 23, 2000, saw the first airing of "Restless" (4.22), the finale of season 4. Along with a number of other episodes, "Restless" would assume for *Buffy* fans and critics a position of preeminence. While almost all episodes of the show display a quality of production, writing and acting that are exceptional, these particular episodes propel the possibilities of television drama. Apart from "Restless," episodes in this mold would include season 2's "Passion" (2.17); season 3's "The Wish" (3.9); season 4's "Hush" (4.10) and "Superstar" (4.17); season 5's "The Body" (5.16); season 6's "Tabula Rasa" (6.8), "Once More with Feeling" (6.7) and "Normal Again" (6.17); and season 7's "Storyteller" (7.16).[1] Each of these episodes, and others, will be engaged with at some point in this section, but all of them will be arrived at through the conduit of "Restless."

The reasons for this is that "Restless" falls just over halfway through the complete *Buffy* corpus. As such, it is, at the very least, a useful pragmatic decision to flow back and forth across the whole story from this point. But this itself implies something about both the program and my approach to reading it. While *Buffy* exists as a story spanning seven seasons and 144 episodes, and while this, clearly, invokes a conception of a narrative that begins at episode 1 and ends at episode 144, to contain *Buffy* solely within the straitjacket of a superficial linearity would be to deny it one of its greatest achievements: the aesthetics of involution.

This introduction will begin by offering a definition of "the aesthetics of involution." It will then move on to discuss some of the structural and formal features of "Restless" that will contribute to an overall sense of the analysis of the episode and its possibilities, as well as providing a small glossary of useful terms related to the study of narrative in classical, literary and film studies. Finally, it will present a brief reading of the opening scene that occurs before the dreams themselves start.

The extent to which *Buffy* plays with ideas of narrative can be seen to have implications beyond the immediately aesthetic, or even thematic, to much more general issues.[2] In many ways, this study of *Buffy* is also an attempt to recast television narrative, as exemplified by *Buffy*, with all its attendant aesthetic attributes, as a contribution to these more, seemingly abstract, points of inquiry. One of the reasons for this is the extent to which *Buffy* is so far in excess of many of the categories of classical narratology. This is in large part because narratology was at its inception a literary exercise, though it is still possible to see the ways in which its claims are transferable to films, one–off television shows and other media. It is far less capable of offering a theoretical model that will account for what *Buffy* is: a television serial. While any one scene in *Buffy*, or even a whole episode, may be amenable to narratological analysis (to very interesting ends), the relation between one episode and another is less easily accounted for, still less the relationship between one season and another.

There are two very obvious reasons why this is so. First, a television serial can develop much more slowly and over a much greater amount of time than a novel or even a film; second, the visual aspects of television do not open themselves up to the same sorts of narrative elucidation. How, for example, does the use of a lighting effect from an episode in one season that is repeated in an episode in another season work in terms of narrative? It does, I will argue, but in ways that literary and filmic narrative cannot emulate or mimic. In an environment where television criticism is still regarded primarily as a sociological rather than aesthetic venture (which is reserved for literature and certain films), it can be hard to assert that a television show is worthy of serious analysis as much for its aesthetic/production values as it is for its "themes" or sociological aspects.[3] The simple fact that *Buffy* is a television show means that there is an immediate snobbery in relation to its status as a worthy object of academic scrutiny. However, the question of its seriality, and the particular sorts of possibilities that the show explores with this, seems to insist on respectful serious thought. The question has been addressed by Philip Mikosz and Dana Och.[4] The predicament outlined by Mikosz and Och is that accounts of narrative drawn from literary and film studies do not really provide a vocabulary sufficient to the needs of televisual serial drama. They say that where such an account does exist, for example, in Umberto Eco's "Interpreting Serials" in *The Limits of Interpretation*, the arguments are wholly unable to account for the ways in which *Buffy* works. One that does work, I hope, is the concept of the aesthetics of involution.

I am indebted to Alfred Appel, Jr.'s introduction to, and annotations of, Vladimir Nabokov's *Lolita*[5] for revealing involution to me as a tool of criticism. While I have developed the term for my own uses, his work is a magnificent example of its potential. Appel's general argument concerning *Lolita* and his idea of involution is as follows. To read *Lolita* as the confessions of a murdering pedophile, recounted in prison over a certain number of days with the intention of explaining the motivation and history of his relationship with the young girl (in other words, to read it as a realist text), is to miss the point. While Nabokov goes to great lengths to give the impression of a realist discourse amenable to psychoanalytical interpretation, the text is not itself realist; it is a pastiche of realism.

The point of *Lolita*, for Appel, is its allusive, referential, artificial qualities. These exist as either complex relations with other literature (including his own) or else as self-contained, hermetic devices that circulate within the text itself. In the latter category would be the puns and coincidences, especially of number; in the former an enormous range of reference to literature and other cultural forms. At the heart of the novel, for Appel, is its relationship with Edgar Allan Poe's "Annabel Lee" and from this (though with other aspects interfering) grows all the rest. Appel says, "[T]he verbal *figurae* in *Lolita* limn the novel's involuted design and establish the basis of its artifice."[6] As I have mentioned in various ways in part I, *Buffy* plays with the codes and conventions of realism so that it can further explore the possibilities of its own artifice both in terms of the imagined world of Sunnydale and environs and also in terms of the production techniques employed to represent this world. Like *Lolita* in some ways, it provides the veneer of a realistic technique in order that this formal pastiche can elaborate and bolster the emotional, thematic and narrative concerns.

Additionally to Appel's use, I am drawing from a range of potential meanings for involution drawn from the *Oxford English Dictionary,* second edition, including "An involved or entangled condition [...] intricacy of construction or style" and "A rolling, curling or turning inwards." Together, these meanings, and other subsidiary ones, allow for an examination of *Buffy* that pays attention to specific moments within an episode, a particular episode, a relationship between episodes, a relationship between seasons, and also the inter-, intra- and paratextual elements.[7] Involution is, then, a necessarily relational term but one in which the relation between two or more points is not simply additive. A sixth meaning in the *OED* includes "the raising of a quantity to any power, positive, negative, fractional or imaginary." Cognizant of Alan Sokal's timely attack on badly used science and maths in bad theory, I will only allow for the metaphorical translation of the term from its arithmetic birthplace to my aesthetic adoption.[8] The fact that the word's own meanings seem to encourage a sense of the entangled, commingled, complex, even messy, provides a perfect opportunity for it as an aspect of engaging with a text (*Buffy*) that revels in its own textual excess, that seems to enjoy rewriting its own premises and dismantling the world it had created, that invites the audience to laugh at itself and the show, while being utterly serious in its commitment to a notion of art and artistry that pushes television to places it has not been before.

One may also wish to have in mind Jean-François Lyotard's notion of the "tensor sign" as presented in *Libidinal Economy*.[9] Lyotard's very difficult argument can best be presented via a small section of his book: "Intensity, the Name." Here Lyotard poses a common problem, which is that the name

> refers in principle to a single reference and does not appear to be exchangeable against other terms in the logico-linguistic structure: there is no intra-systemic equivalent of the proper name, it points towards the outside like a deictic, it has no connotations, or it is interminable.[10]

While I would be very keen to look at the importance of the name "Buffy" as a version of a tensor sign, this section is rather more concerned with a broader array of signs and signifying practices and the relationships between them. Luckily for me, then, Lyotard claims that names are not a privileged category of the tensorial sign but are a good example because a name, as tensorial sign, "covers a region of libidinal space open to the undefinability of energetic influxes, a region in flames."[11] A tensorial sign, by which is meant in principle *any* sign, refuses to be subordinated to a lack and, therefore, blocks its insertion into a system of replacements/equivalences whether these be in terms of absent signified or adjacent signifier. Importantly, there is no decision to be made between sign as semiotic unit and sign as tensor. The sign is both of these. The extent to which it acts as one or the other is an effect of the intensities that flow through it at any given instance. Or, in my phrase, "involution."

This notion of involution will tend to operate across episodes and seasons, but it has a certain purchase at the level of individual episodes insofar as these episodes themselves, even when they stand alone, operate as part of the structure of a season and have formal qualities that intimately tie them to this. If we think briefly about "Restless" in this regard, the discussion can then broaden out to a consideration of the ways in which the structure of episodes in and of themselves, and as parts of seasons, contributes to the involutional qualities of them.

Before "Restless" (4.22) aired it was already an anomaly. The three previous season finales all had the final episode be the climactic culmination, the end point, of the season's main story line. Season 1 ends with Buffy fighting and defeating the Master ("Prophecy Girl" [1.12]); season 2 ends with Buffy leaving Sunnydale after having killed Angel ("Becoming II" [2.22]); and season 3 ends with the killing of the mayor and the thwarting of his ascension ("Graduation Day II" [3.22]). Season 4 revolves around the Frankenstein monsteresque Adam and the secret government Initiative that had spawned him. The penultimate episode had the great battle leading to Adam's death and the supposed destruction of the Initiative's headquarters and laboratory ("Primeval" [4.21]). So, what would the finale be, and how should it be read? Would there be some additional strand that had appeared to be peripheral that would, in fact, mark the end of the story? If not, where should "the end" of the season be located? Would it simply be an afterthought, a curious addendum or, as Joss Whedon has called it, a "coda"?[12] The choice of a term usually associated with music implies the extent to which the seasons are planned in terms of emotional intensities, the rising and falling of the patterns of the shows having a metaphorical relationship with a sonata whose own sense of repeating phrases, returning to motifs and so on has its own involutional aspect.[13]

To a certain extent then, "Restless" already poses questions about narrative and seriality by subverting what had appeared to be a structural requirement of the show: the finale of a season as the end of that season's overarching storyline. Here, whatever was to happen, was clearly something other than that. Its opening certainly offers a sense of an ending, an "afterwards." We enter just as the Scoobies and Joyce are saying goodbye to Riley, apparently after a gathering at Buffy's house, seemingly not long after the events of the previous episode. Joyce goes to bed, leaving Buffy, Xander, Willow and Giles in the lounge preparing to watch videos for the rest of the night.

This little scene has echoes and presentiments of its own, before we engage with the main aspect of the story. The group left on their own at the end of the season is also the group that begins the entire series. The four of them, despite others becoming involved (Cordelia, Oz, Wesley, Angel, Tara) are the focus of the show and their fights and estrangements over the seasons so far, including this one, are here annulled as all others leave the kernel of the show to rest. However, the scene has a morbid prospective element to it too. The group gathered at Buffy's house, seemingly restful and happy as Joyce (as she does here) plays the caring, attentive and understanding mother, is also the organizing principle behind the most harrowing of *Buffy* episodes, "The Body" (5.16), which occurs in the next season. While "The Body" also has Tara, Anya and Dawn present, the familial structure of Joyce, Giles and the gang operates in an organizationally and emotionally similar fashion. Seriality, allied with technology such as DVDs, allows for these moments of stylistic or organizational similitude to be engaged with. The effect of this, or one of them, is to dissipate a linearity of reading. While story arcs and character development occur on an episode-by-episode basis, thereby maintaining the necessity of linear narrative in that respect, points of contact between episodes remote from one another (temporally, emotionally and so on) can be adduced (or more powerfully, simply exert their own force) in the act of rewatching. For me, at least, I cannot watch the opening of "Restless" (4.22) without "The Body" (5.16) being brought into critical focus. Similarly, the opening of "The Body" (5.16) always forces me back to "Restless" (4.22). This is not an act of narrative but an act of involution; the text folds back in on itself to occlude narrative patterns in order to invoke relationships that have no necessary causal pattern.

Even before this moment, however, the episode has already begun and its involutional aspect has been brought into view. The usual form for the beginning of an episode from about halfway through season 2 is a "previously on *Buffy the Vampire Slayer*" montage of clips from earlier shows that have an influence on the direction that the episode will take. This is then followed by the teaser, which varies in length but is usually fairly short and sets up an action that will reverberate after we have had the next section, the credits, and then (in America, anyway) the first commercial break. This pattern is not absolute and there are variations, but it is general. I would like to spend a little time thinking about each of these aspects first, before moving onto the episode itself.

The "previously on" section offers to *Buffy* and, in principle to all serial shows, the chance to fundamentally dismiss one of the abiding claims made about television serials. This has been posited most notably by Umberto Eco:

> [A] series works upon a fixed situation and a restricted number of fixed pivotal characters, around whom the secondary and changing ones turn [which gives] the impression that the new story is different from the preceding ones while in fact the narrative scheme does not change.[14]

And, additionally, for the viewer, the "recurrence of a narrative scheme that remains constant [...] responds to the infantile need of always hearing the same story, of being consoled by the return of 'The Identical,' superficially disguised."[15] In other words, seriality, for Eco, is a simple repetition of the same, a same that, moreover, makes no progress forward, keeping the characters and the viewer in a mythical (because, for Eco, de-historicized) present untainted by such concerns as demise or failure: the future is constantly deferred in a present that remains constant, informed by a secure and total past.

Buffy's past is not constant. Nor for that matter is its present at these moments. The voice that says "previously" is Anthony Stewart Head's. The viewer then is placed in a position of undecidability. Either he or she accepts the voice as the actor's in which case an attendant acceptance of the fictionality of the show is understood, as the character is recognized as being just that, and part of a fiction; or the voice is heard as Giles's, in which case the possibility that Giles is both a character *in* the show as well as a commentator on it *externally* is accepted. In either case, the show's constructedness and its artifice are highlighted and the sorts of questions relating to different levels of ontological negotiation discussed in part I are again rehearsed.

The montages that are introduced render the past of the show unstable. This is not to say that they destroy the past nor that the past of the show is somehow erased in the moment of its attenuated recapitulation. It is, however, to insist that these moments upset the narrativity of *Buffy*. Mikosz and Och claim that *Buffy* is not a narrative show at all. They write:

> *Buffy* the series, by contrast, although it partakes of elements of narrative, does not amount to a narration. Season by season, and even episode by episode, the series accumulates a multiple past, elements of oftentimes incongruous combinations. Moreover, the series seizes upon the clichés "Buffy" and "Vampire Slayer" and posits them as axioms, as simultaneous conditions that nonetheless retain their incommensurability (this is, after all Buffy's existential crisis!).[16]

I would dispute the general claim and maintain that each season does present an overarching narrative that, while being lost for episodes at a time in some instances, nevertheless does belong to the realm of narration. This is true even for the story (narration) from season 1 to season 7. It is, however, true, that *Buffy's* games with narrative present difficulties for narration that are brought into immediate focus by the "previously" sections. Before moving forward with this point, a small account of narrative as derived from structuralist theory and narratology might be helpful.

A (very limited) definition of narrative would be the one offered by Seymour Chapman in his 1963 *Theory of Literature*. This book, heavily influenced by structuralist theory, says, narrative has two parts: a story (histoire), the content or chain of events (actions happenings), plus what may be called existents (characters, items of setting): and a discourse (discours), that is, the expression, the means by which the content is communicated.[17]

In other words, there is a set of events (the story) and then the means by which those events are put together and represented to a reader (discourse) and the combination of these two elements makes the narrative. This distinction is rather easier to keep in mind if the terms used are story and plot. A basic story might be something like, "I woke up. I went to the window. I saw a wolf. I ran away." The plot aspect is the arrangement of the story in a fashion that is not simply its order of happening. So, for example, "I ran away after I had woken up, gone to the window and seen the wolf." This comparatively simple conceptualization is made much more specific and sophisticated by Chapman and the other great narratologists like Propp, Tomashevsky, Bakhtin, Genette and others through the analysis of a number of other aspects that contribute to each of these parts of the combination. While this is not going to be a narratological analysis in the sense implied from my referencing the writers above, there are some categories of explanation that classical narratology offers that will be useful to bear in mind during parts of this discussion. Readers who are either familiar with narratological theory, or those who are not interested in the finer points of the theory, should probably jump ahead a couple of pages as I am going to enumerate and briefly define some of the aspects from narratology that might be helpful in considering certain moments in *Buffy*. These are not at all sufficient for looking at the ways in *Buffy*'s aesthetics of involution operates, but they do provide a way into the more straightforward aspects of storytelling that the show deploys. This list owes a debt of gratitude to the list at the end of *The Narrative Reader*, edited by Martin McQuillan:

> *Act*— an event that is narrated and that brings about a state of change by an agent. ("Buffy sleeps with Angel" is an act; "it rained yesterday" is not.)
>
> *Actant*— a category of character (hero, sought-for person, dispatcher, helper, donor, villain/false hero) rather than a character itself. Buffy, the character, might, at different times be the hero or the helper, the sought-for person and so on. In *Buffy* the characters' inhabitations of any number of these actant positions provide much of the opportunity for drama, comedy and so on.
>
> *Action*— a series of connected events that have unity and purpose and (in many instances, at least) a beginning, middle and an end.

Anachrony— The placing of an event out of sequence in the telling or retelling of the story. The most obvious examples of this in *Buffy* are the flashbacks (analepsis) to Angel's life as a vampire.

Anterior narration— the narration of events that occur before the events happen. In *Buffy* there are the occasional prophetic dreams (such as those in "Restless") but it is with Doyle's and later Cordelia's visions on *Angel* that this is most prevalent.

Aporia— a situation where what makes a thing possible is also paradoxically what makes the thing impossible at the same time. This results in an impasse of interpretation or a moment of undecidability. The episode "Normal Again" (6.17) plays with this notion to some considerable effect as we are left not knowing whether Buffy is insane or not.[18]

Conative function— a narrative act that focuses on the narratee. Andrew's seeming address to viewers in "Storyteller" (7.16) is a complex example of this, as is Lorne's account of events in "Spin the Bottle" from *Angel* (*AtS* 4.6).

Defamiliarization— a technique by which the world and/or the artwork is "made strange" to heighten, among other things, the artistic effect. The lack of music in "The Body" (5.16) is, curiously, a prime example of this, though *Buffy* is constantly in the process of defamiliarizing, especially in terms of genre.[19]

End— this seemingly obvious term, which is little more than the last incident in a plot or sequence of actions, actually has the force of making all the rest of the narrative lead to that point and acts as a site of meaning for the whole. The end of the last season of *Buffy*, then, is the final shot of the group looking at the hole that used to be Sunnydale.

Extradiegetic— external to any diegesis (outside of the world or space of the narrative). Most often in *Buffy* this will be found in the music played over the top of a scene (as opposed to, for example, a band playing in The Bronze who are part of the scene and, therefore, part of the diegesis or *intradiegetic*).

Genre— a type or style of narrative. The question of what, if any, genre *Buffy* is will be part of this discussion.

Intertexts— one or more texts that are referenced or rewritten by another text and which provide, at least, some of the meaning of the latter text. The plethora of intertextual moments in *Buffy* will also be a part of this discussion.

Montage— the placing side by side in juxtaposition a sequence of noncontiguous events, which creates meaning. The "previously on..." sequences are a prime, though not only, example of this in *Buffy*— Andrew's reintroduction of Faith in "Dirty Girls" (7.18) is another example.

Teleology— the study of the end; the compulsion of a narrative toward its end point, which gives shape and coherence to the preceding events. Chapter 3 has a long discussion about teleology and its related, though different, concept eschatology.

The "previously" sections by virtue of their formal aspect as montages cannot operate as "actions" in the way described above as they derive their meaning through juxtaposition and not continuity. As a consequence, aspects that we might ordinarily associate with narrative as a linear concept are displaced. There is no teleology as such, no end point except the formal cessation of the clip, which may or may not have had a structural and thematic end. What we have instead is a set of scenes (or, more usually, partial scenes) spliced together in order so that the story to which they refer is brought back into the mind of the viewer. Each section of the montage, then, is synecdochic of a larger story. This juxtapositional synecdoche reassembles the narratives that have gone before. These scenes initially existed as a combination of story and plot but now are decontextualized and have no narrative power at all in their own terms.

What they do have, and are clearly intended to have, are a different sort of combinatorial capacity whose effect is to provide a specific context for the episode to come. This means that the immediate prehistory to an episode can be made up of excerpts from all and any parts of the existent history of *Buffy* which can be re-assembled such that these histories are foreshortened, contracted. The history that is alluded to from one excerpt is then placed in juxtaposition with a history that may have had no bearing on its own trajectory but now becomes enmeshed in a new revisioning of the past of the show in order that the future (the immediate episode and its aftermath) can be altered. The past becomes infinitely malleable, subject to any number of revisions, thereby opening up the possibility of any number of possible futures. Eco's assessment of the mythical fixed present built on an absolutely certain past denying the fear of futurity is significantly undermined, even just from the paratext of "previously."

The "previously" section on "Restless" (4.22) begins with a shot of Adam and Buffy's assertion that they shall stop him. Immediately this brings the Big Bad of the season to the fore and reminds us of his genealogy in terms of his monsterness. He is part human, part cyborg, a twentieth-century revision of Frankenstein's monster and as such is part of an ongoing dispute concerning the legitimate experiments of science.[20] The initial shot, then, provides a simple reminder of the narrative of the season and a reinforcement of the intertextual[21] links of the monster to Mary Shelley's text. The extent to which this might, in turn, broaden out to a much wider intertextual[22] relationship with Romanticism in general will be addressed later. One of the important aspects about involution as a strategy is that it is potentially endless both in terms of its intra- and paratextual elements, but especially of its intertextual relations. The relationship of a text to its intertext is never simple or singular. *Frankenstein* cannot have a relationship with *Buffy* that is linear, exclusive and hermetic. Even if a linear relationship were possible, *Frankenstein* would have other points of contact with other texts (therefore it is not exclusive), each of which has, theoretically, a relationship with *Buffy* (so it cannot be hermetic). Wilcox and Lavery draw on the work of Robert Stam to indicate the ways in which this is fundamental to a reading of *Buffy*:

> As any new-comer to the series quickly realizes, Buffy constantly and pervasively draws on its own past history, but it casts its nets widely beyond its own developing text. "Any text that has slept with another text," Robert Stam has noted, extending a central insight into STD prevention into the realm of film theory, "has necessarily slept with all the texts the other text has slept with" (202). [...] the series offers us humor that only the textually promiscuous are likely to get.[23]

It is not only the promiscuous nature of the text that is important for an involutional reading of *Buffy* but, to continue the sexualized imagery, the incestuous, the exogamous and the fetishistic. Adam takes us, promiscuously, to Mary Shelley's text and thence to Romanticism and the gothic. He moves us incestually as described below to other parts of *Buffy*. He demands exogamy by insisting on relations outside of our community not only via intertext, but also through the body of the actor George Hertzberg who brings in from the outside memories of him from his appearances in, for example, *3rd Rock from the Sun* and, more interestingly, *Home Improvement* where he appeared in an episode entitled "Desperately Seeking Willow," which returns us incestually to *Buffy* through the name Willow but also opens up through promiscuity the film *Desperately Seeking Susan* and its star Madonna and her gamut of possible meanings, the film's other star Rosanna Arquette, director Susan Seidelman, and so on. And he provides us with the fetishistic route by virtue of a supposed belief that he (or any other character, event, reference, allusion or whatever) might somehow provide us with the ability to control and stay the superabundance of meaning delivered at almost every moment of the show. The fetishist is always disappointed, of course.

    Intratextually (incestually) Adam as a monster and his relationship with Frankenstein does draw the character, and therefore this opening moment from the "Previously on..." montage, back to "Some Assembly

Required" (2.2) in which the brother of a disfigured school sports star tries to create a perfect girlfriend for his brother from the bodies of dead students. The fact that this episode has as "consulting producer" Howard Gordon, who is also a writer and producer of *The X-Files*, provides another intertextual link and involutional contortion.

The next scene in the "previously on..." section is a reprise of the spell undertaken in the previous episode where the four main characters joined in order to provide Buffy with the skill, strength, intelligence and heart of the whole group.[24] The viewer is not necessarily certain exactly what power has been invoked in order for the spell to work, but that it did and that Buffy defeated Adam is certain. "Primeval" (4.21) acts in some senses as a final episode in terms of the resolution of the story, so this episode (which begins by reminding us of that one) is re-framed as already strange. It is intriguing that a small clue as to the potential direction of "Restless" (4.22) was given in "Primeval" (4.21) by Spike referencing yet another English Victorian literary classic, *Alice's Adventures in Wonderland* by Lewis Carroll. While Buffy is no Alice, the surreal dream of Carroll's book has some resonance with what, we discover, is to come.[25]

The clearest intertext in the opening sequence is to *The Matrix*, the Wachowski brothers' groundbreaking, intelligent, cinematically startling 1999 sci-fi thriller. Whedon's admiration for this film is well known and the shot of the dissolving bullets being pulled out of the air and turned to doves is a clear homage. The fact that both the episode and the film engage with questions of "the human," though from significantly different positions, allows a depth of analysis and philosophical speculation to seep into the show by sheer virtue of the connection. This is one of the main strengths of involution: the contact between two points (whether intra- or intertextual) that magnifies the connotative and interpretive power of both.

The death of Adam that marks the last part of the "previously" montage much more simply tells the audience where the narrative has got to, before the opening credits occur. Even though this montage is nearly all located in the previous episode, and therefore has less revisionist possibility than other montages, it has redefined and refocused what the current episode regards as the most significant moment of the previous one.

The importance of this in terms of a notion of involution is that the program has a built-in structural feature that already provides elements of seasonal foreshortening and the juxtaposition of moments of it that might previously have had no obvious narrative relation to each other at all. These elements of the montage then usually move straight in to the teaser. Karen Sayer has pointed out how the teaser tends to work in contrast to the main action that will unfold later. Often this is a movement from light to darkness, or vice versa[26] or from domestic peace to some sort of violence. She continues:

> Even without a cut to violence, any happy moment in the teaser will inevitably be framed by the shows' [*Buffy* and *Angel*] credits, which recycle predominantly dark scenes overlain by sudden energetic bursts of action.[27]

The teaser, then, stands in dramatic juxtaposition to the initial montage (that reframes the past of *Buffy* to recontextualize the present) and with the opening credits.

"Restless" (4.22) has no teaser section. After the "previously" section we move straight to the credits and thence to the commercials. In itself this provides a moment of defamiliarization for anyone who has watched the show regularly. The already strong expectation of an unusual episode is augmented by this formal shift. This formal choice has the effect, by doing nothing, of furthering the audience's potential excitement or anxiety with respect to the episode (on a first viewing, in sequence, anyway). It is useful to note, however, that this aesthetic moment (the attributes of which work as I have described and are, therefore, properly part of the artistry of the show) comes about due to pragmatic requirements. There were such a lot of guest appearances on this episode that the contractual requirements regarding the placement of actor's names meant that a teaser before the credits was simply impossible.[28] An external, legal responsibility has an effect on a formal expectation that influences the viewer's response to the opening of an episode whose position within a seasonal structure is already curious. So, lacking a teaser, we head straight into the credits.[29]

These also offer a montage. This time, however, the clips can be from any previous season or the present or forthcoming one, though once chosen the credits remain the same throughout the season. In addition to the visual aspect of the credits, there is also the musical element and this has been discussed marvelously by Janet K. Halfyard. In her essay, Halfyard shows how *Buffy* plays with allusion (involution) even at the level of music and not just in relation to the horror tradition, but also with its own offshoot *Angel*. In terms of the horror tradition as it is presented to us via the music used in the credit sequences, she writes:

> Firstly, there is the instrument itself: we have the sound of an organ, accompanied by a wolf's howl, with a visual image of a flickering night sky overlaid with unintelligible archaic script: the associations with both the silent era and films such as *Nosferatu* and with the conventions of the Hammer House of Horror and horror in general are unmistakable.[30]

Halfyard then offers a brief history of the use of the organ in horror, from *The Phantom of the Opera*'s explicit diegetic use to "Dr. Jekyll playing the organ in *Dr. Jekyll and Mr. Hyde* (1932) and the sound of the organ becoming synonymous with Hammer Horror in the 1960s and 70s."[31] From this the turn to comedy and parody is noted in, for example, *Dracula: Dead and Loving It* (1996). *Buffy*, then opens with a musical trope that both pays homage to its filmic heritage at the same time it recognizes the potential for cliché that this invites. Involution takes us to the general trope and then to specific films, all of which inform and bleed into our reading of the present show. However, being *Buffy*, this already extravagant aesthetic turns the cliché in on itself, recognizes its own complicity in its perpetuation and radically shifts its sensibilities:

> It removes itself from the sphere of 1960s and 70s horror by replaying the same motif, the organ now supplanted by an aggressively strummed electric guitar, relocating itself in modern youth culture, relocating the series in an altogether different arena than that of both Hammer and its spoofs.[32]

The repetition of the motif means that, in addition to relocating (which it most certainly does), it nevertheless remains moored to its old reference: the aesthetic shift signifies its movement away from a particular tradition of horror while simultaneously insisting on a certain relationship with it, however ironic or iconoclastic. The juxtaposition of the two styles, related through the repeated motif, encourages an involutional set of readings via the filmic tradition and then appears to deny that very tradition at the moment of its invocation.

This process is compounded in the episode "Superstar" (4.17). As mentioned above, the credit sequence tends to provide a montage of shots from previous episodes and seasons as well as from the present season. This is played beneath the music with all its attendant involutional and ironic possibilities (as well as its sheer exuberance and strength). This episode is considered by Mikosz and Och in their discussion of seriality in *Buffy*. They first offer a description of Jonathan's usurpation of the credits:

> Here is Jonathan upstaging all of the usual suspects: shooting a crossbow; disarming a bomb; smiling back at Xander (Oh Xander you dawg!); some smarmy dude in a tux; secret agent-like in a tux with a gun; doing a kung-fu move; and, finally, walking in grim-reverse–Angelesque-slow-mo towards the camera, trench coat and all.[33]

Following on from this, they provide a wonderful cross-analysis of this with Jon Moritsugu's *Fame Whore* and a discussion of the generative power of cliché. The reimagined Jonathan and his many versions on the credit sequence draws attention to the images with which *Buffy* is working and, in so doing, cause a reappraisal of their supposed radicalism from a gendered viewpoint:

> He is one cliché, yet he — rather, his image (for he is nothing but an image: Adam recognizes this instantly, Buffy actually intuits it from the opening scenes) has proliferated to the degree that it has acquired a monopoly over all of the other images. This is why he can simultaneously be Michael Jordan, a swimsuit model, the inventor of the internet, the author of the book *Oh, Jonathan!*, Hugh Hefner, Frank Sinatra, Angel, James Bond, a hard-boiled detective type, a witty roué, friend and advisor to the traumatized and the lovelorn and the downtrodden, military tactical analyst, and so on, and so on. Jonathan literally becomes all things and everything to all people. He is not a superstar, he is THE super-duper-star.[34]

What Jonathan's alternative credits provide is a counterpoint to the credits' usual function. His pastiche version forces us though defamiliarization to recognize what the credits do. They assert certain sorts of attributes to each of the characters by choosing images from sections of seasons that best fit what we consider those characters to be. They are a moment of structural and formal stability that help (in a fashion similar to that mentioned by Eco, but much more precariously) to render known and safe the narrative space that we shall soon enter. In relation to "Superstar" (4.17), however, this supposed solace of the same is undermined, as McNeilly, Sylka and Fisher describe. They take the inevitably discursive nature of characters on television shows to be the source of a specific engagement with a more broadly conceived notion of identity as discourse, through the "Superstar" (4.17) episode:

> Near the middle of the episode, Adam sits before an array of surveillance monitors — like us, he watches the Buffyverse on t.v. — and points to the mediatized nature of Jonathan's magic, its mucked up reality effect: [...] Jonathan's image is rendered extensive by mass media; he is a superstar because he appears as the superhero — because he represents himself as a t.v. "star." [...] The unstable perfection of "Jonathan" comes to appear as a patchwork of deception that cannot resolve into a coherent character; that perfection, after all, is a discursive construct, rather than an ontological given.[35]

The opening sections to "Superstar" (4.17) have foregrounded to an exceptional degree the discursively constituted nature of the show, but in so doing have enabled questions about its ontological status to be asked. And we have not even got to the first commercial break yet. From "previously" to teaser, to credits to commercials, it is a surprisingly long journey before we get to the episode's first act. The commercials, clearly, provide an enormous level of possibility for recontextualizing and decontextualizing what has just gone. Lorne on *Angel* is given a marvelous moment in the excellent "Spin the Bottle" (*AtS* 4.6) where his recounting of the episode's story to the audience in his club, and thence to us, is punctuated, of course, by commercial breaks. After the third commercial break he simply comments (evidently not to the audience in the club, but to us, in a knowing metafictional moment), "Well, those were some exciting products. Am I right? Mmm. Let's all think about buying some of those" ("Spin the Bottle" [*AtS* 4.6]).

After the episode has finished its storytelling, there is still more that should properly be called a part of the world of the show, which would include the closing credits and the legal declaration of ownership of the program via the company logo. An excellent example of the ways in which involution can operate through paratext is given to us via the logo, the fabulous monster who goes "grr arrgh" at the end of, nearly, every episode. This will be discussed as part of chapter 8.

Bearing in mind all the questions already raised by the preliminary sections of the show, we can now begin an analysis of the opening scene of "Restless" (4.22). As mentioned above, we are in Buffy's house, saying goodbye to Riley and seeing Joyce go to bed while Buffy, Willow, Xander and Giles sit up to watch videos. By the time of the season's end, the franchising of *Buffy* was well underway, and the VHS box sets of earlier seasons were selling (outside of the United States first due to syndication issues). The fact that such an enormous number of fans would be sitting round having *Buffy* nights in a fashion much akin to our heroes in this episode is a gently affectionate form of the involutional. This is made much more emphatic when Xander places the first video in the player and the whole screen is taken up by the FBI warning against property theft and the enforcement of copyright law. The FBI aspect throws us back to the Initiative and the presence of government and conspiracy with which the season has partly dealt (which will also remind us of Marcie Ross in "Out of Mind Out of Sight" [1.11]); and the fact of the image at all means that we understand that we are watching a show that is also available on video and DVD and which is under the same protection and uses the same laws, signaled by the same warning of the same organization as that which we are currently watching. This moment opens up a possible mise en abyme that is significantly more pronounced when viewing the same scene on video or DVD.

The videos have been a source of concern to the group as Xander wants to watch *Apocalypse Now*, which Willow is concerned is too *Heart of Darkness*-ey. The constant threat of apocalypse is one with which the characters are always contending; the promise of an imminent demise as suggested by the film (especially as the previous episode saw the defeat of a potentially apocalypse-inducing machine) is a pleasingly subtle self-reflexive joke at the show's expense. However, the role and importance of both *Apocalypse Now* as a film and as Conrad's novella are much more central to some of the overarching concerns of the show: the battle between archaism and modernity, the construction of "the human" and the possibilities of narrative.[36]

Even before the dream sections, then, the episode has dealt with the allusive, referential, involuted games that are such a core element of the show's aesthetic. So pervasive is involution that to pretend to be able to enumerate even each single reference, let alone provide a critical assessment of the possible strands of these, is impossible. There will, inevitably, be many examples of the "attentive viewer"[37] who extrapolates his or her own involutional threads in directions that I have not followed or who disputes some of the connections I have made. This is to be welcomed; involution invites such multiple readings, such tangled critiques, and *Buffy* possibly more than any other television show revels also in its own multiplicity and variousness. Involution celebrates the multiplication of possibilities and, along with Xander, would seek to disavow the stringent reductionism of the critical equivalent of "tick-box" psychometrics who cannot allow deviation: "That would allow too many variables into their mushroom-head, number-crunching little world" ("What's My Line I" [2.9]).

♦ CHAPTER 6 ♦

Willow's Dream

"It's exactly like a Greek tragedy"

When Anya makes the comment that "it's exactly like a Greek tragedy" toward the end of Willow's dream, the, inevitably, gnomic comment provides two related observations about the concerns of the dream. One is to do with the notion of performance and identity[1]; the other relates to an initial sense of classicism, which draws together literature and spirituality. These two strands of the dream have a number of involutional aspects that shall be discussed shortly, and they also provide the thematic template that offers some sense of unitariness to Willow's experience.[2]

Performance dominates her dream. The opening shot frames the action in a televisual equivalent to the theatrical space of the proscenium arch stage. The lens operates as our fourth wall and the strong verticals at either side of the screen and the joining horizontal at the top provides the stagelike quality. The wide shot then slowly moves into a close-up of Willow and Tara in Tara's bedroom, thereby asserting the specifically film-oriented nature of the production, though maintaining the opening theatrical trait via the visual sign. At this point, the opening does not necessarily lead the viewer to imagine that the whole act will be so committed to the concept of performance, but by the simple and beautiful opening shot the televisual space folds into the possibility of theatre.

The highly stylized opening shot is followed by another of the cat, Miss Kitty Fantastico, playing with a ball of string. The couple had mentioned getting a cat in one of the most emotionally grueling *Buffy* episodes, "New Moon Rising" (4.19). For many fans, the decision of Willow to spurn

Oz in favor of Tara in that episode was a real shock, and this close-up of the cat (which makes her look extraordinarily malevolent) acts as a link back to this massively important moment, both for the characters and for plot development. The most important plot development for Willow in relation to Tara is, of course, her turn to the bad after Tara's killing and, rewatching the seasons on DVD, Miss Kitty's appearance in all her ferocity in this shot indicates an emotional prolepsis that is daunting.[3] The cat's first appearance is actually in "The Yoko Factor" (4.20) where she still does not have a name, a state of affairs that is paradoxically asserted here as Tara ponders why the cat has not given them her name and Willow asks if she means Miss Kitty.[4] Not only does Miss Kitty push us to the two previous episodes simply by virtue of her appearance, she also takes us to season 5's "Family" (5.6) in which Tara tells her cute anti-story about the cat of which Willow ruins the ending. Tara's status as a fully integrated member of the Scooby family is presented in this episode (5.6), which also has her biological family represented as both appalling misogynists and liars (pretending that Tara is a demon to continue the patriarchal structures of dominance in the family structure). This episode is important, too, as it shows how the group's continually shifting makeup and dynamic can accommodate Tara and the much newer addition Dawn, an addition that "Tara"[5] in Buffy's dream later in "Restless" (4.22) foretells. The final mention of the cat, which seeks to explain its sudden disappearance from the show, is Dawn's comment three seasons later in "End of Days" (7.21) that she does not leave the crossbow lying around anymore since the incident with Miss Kitty. This mention of crossbows itself involutes us to "What's My Line II" (2.10) in which Buffy warns Kendra not to pick up the crossbow, Kendra retorts that she is an expert in all weapons and then, of course, lets loose the bolt across the room: a brilliant bit of predictable humor. This episode cannot help but return us to Oz and Willow, with Oz's marvelous surreal monologue about cookie animals and their respective dress sense, a conversation included because Alyson Hannigan had a dream in which Seth Green said it to her. Buffy's own dream in "Surprise" (2.13) in which Willow says to her in French, "The hippo stole my pants" is a further involutional moment. So Miss Kitty starts us on an involutional trajectory that moves backwards to Oz episodes, forward to later mentions and then, from these, back again to other points of contact that, in this version at least, ends us back with Oz and his love affair with Willow, before invoking another dream episode that finally sends us once more to "Restless" (4.22).

The sheer aesthetic oddness of the Miss Kitty shot insists on her being given what is, in effect, an undue amount of consideration. This, though, is what propels the involutional possibility for the viewer with his or her memory of the previous episodes, with all their emotional rawness and pain. It also means that the future mentions or sights of the cat will inevitably produce a moment of recognition for this scene. In large part, that is what involution is as an internal mechanism: a moment of aesthetic intensity (by which could be meant any number of areas from dialogue to facial expression to camera work) that imparts the linking together of related aesthetic moments elsewhere with which there is not any necessary narrative connection. These moments then create a matrix of readings that coexist with the more usual episodic and or seasonal narrative. The potential number of these matrices is infinite and allows the production of a deep palimpsest, wherein the meanings generated are linear-syntactic and also involuted.

Involution at the external level operates slightly differently. Here, the sign that sparks the recognition need not be so aesthetically profound, though it can be. For Willow's dream, the first externally involutional moment is aesthetically striking. Tara and she are discussing naming, of the cat ostensibly, and we see a paint brush dipped into a glass inkwell. As the camera draws back from the close-up on their faces, we see Tara lying naked in bed, her back covered in marks that Willow is painting on to her. The scene is redolent with sensuality, especially given the sumptuous colors and deep tones.

Even for those who do not recognize the writing for what it is, the scene is likely to prompt a recognition of Peter Greenaway's 1997 masterpiece *The Pillow Book*. The central idea of this film is the search of the heroine Nagiko for a lover who can unite literature and sensuality by being a master calligrapher able to cover her body with signs that are both a story and an expression of love. The exoticism and eroticism of the story and its denouement toward a lesbian relationship has an obvious link to Tara and Willow, and the delightful direction by Greenaway, with his usual and wonderful experiments and formal innovations, has a clear link to Whedon as a program maker. The scene then is an integral moment in the dream sequence as well as an homage to another filmmaker and an intertextual marker for the exotic-erotic aspect of the dream. In "Restless" (4.22) the exoticism is less located in an Occidental thrill from the Orient,[6] and more expressed through the formal guise of the dream itself; a psychic estrangement equivalent to the cultural one proposed by Greenaway. The eroticism is in part created by the room's splendor but primarily through the intimate seeming foreplay of two lovers. The audience at this point, then, has been propelled back by internal involution to the passionate desolation of earlier episodes through the sign of Miss Kitty, and externally linked to another lesbian relationship that draws on calligraphic fetishism as a point of erotic manipulation. The ball of string being played with by Miss Kitty can be read as a visual prompt for the viewer to try and unravel the clues in the episode (its seemingly simply denotive function) but it also serves to augment the extratextual allusions that the writing on Tara's back represents.

Willow is writing a Sapphic ode. There is an unambiguous troping of the relationship as lesbian here simply by the use of Sappho. The erotically charged poetry of Sappho, often with its erotic object being a young woman, has made her an iconic figure of homosexuality. Her poetry has been translated over the last 2,500 years and each generation of poets has been able to reimagine the poetic world into which he or she is going to place Sappho. The poetry has survived all the vicissitudes of her image's own various incarnations. Greek comedies travestied her and invented the great tragic love affair with Phaon that led to her suicide; Ovid inadvertently seemed to undermine her worth when he wrote "Lesbia quid docuit Sappho, nisi amare, paellas?" (What did Sappho of Lesbos teach girls, except how to love?),[7] although the full context from which this quotation was excised was in fact offering her praise by comparison with other writers. If the classical world seemed to belittle her life, it nevertheless still admired her work, for the most part, and translations continued throughout the great period of English literary output from the Renaissance onwards. This translation work was, however, typically done by men, and those men, equally typically, tended to translate the work in such a way that the loved objects were men. The myth of Phaon was a useful tool in this regard and it was not until the very late nineteenth century and early twentieth centuries when women had greater access to an education that would allow them to learn ancient Greek that many women worked on Sappho's original poetic fragments. It was not until 1958 that the first collection of translated fragments by a woman, Mary Barnard, was published. These carry their own cultural and poetic signature, Barnard having been an heir to a certain modernist poetic practice and having corresponded with the great Ezra Pound whose encouragement to her from as early as 1934 to begin the translations implies some degree of the imagistic flavor that her work demonstrates.

As we are offered the Greek version on Tara's back, it is impossible to know exactly how Willow is envisioning the poem. Clever though she is, we have no reason to suppose that she is fluent in Greek (even if her dreaming self is able to capture the graphic exactness of the lettering) and the translation she would have in mind could be from any number of writers. What is indisputable, whatever the translation, is that the poem opens with an invocation of the goddess Aphrodite. It is, then, a poem and a prayer, or, more exactly, a song and a prayer as the lyric was a poem recited or sung to music. The additional aspect of the music (sadly, of course, lost forever) exerts a slightly stronger sense of ritual over the poem and its prayerlike qualities can be read as being very closely allied to another ritualistic goddess-invoking form: the magic spell. While Sappho is doubtless being used more as a marker of sexuality than of magic, it is noticeable that nearly all of Willow's spells that we hear her incant are prefaced by a supplication to a goddess. To that extent, this poem folds itself back into the text of *Buffy* as a point through which her spells can be traced.

Interestingly, Willow's first truly important spell and one of the most memorable insofar as it returns Angel's soul to him, invokes a "Lord" or male god, rather than a goddess ("Becoming II" [2.22]).[8] As the spells become stronger, and Willow's magical power increases, we see her use her magic against a god (the hyperfeminine but crazy Glory [5.13]), which is the first time we also see the destructive effects on Willow, with headaches, a nosebleed and her eyes turning black as they do throughout season 6's Bad Willow story. The destructive effects of the magic on others, rather than on Willow, is seen in "Something Blue" (4.9) where her feelings of despondence at Oz's leaving (mirrored of course in her feelings of grief at Tara's death two seasons later) cause her to cast spells that go disastrously wrong: Giles becomes blind; Xander becomes a "demon magnet" and Buffy and Spike are made to fall in love (thus foreshadowing Spike's infatuation of season 5, and their mutual if asymmetric passion in season 6). Bad Willow is first hinted at in "Bargaining I" (6.1) where she invokes Osiris in order to bring Buffy back to life. Season 7's reconstitution of Willow ultimately means that she no longer invokes the goddess for her spells, she actually seems to become one ("Chosen" [7.22]).[9]

In addition to opening as an invocation to the goddess, most translations of Sappho's poem also express an open admiration for Aphrodite's capacity at intrigue or guile. Ambrose Phillips [1671–1749] draws on the conventions of the late seventeenth and early eighteenth centuries to write:

> O *Venus*, Beauty of the Skies,
> To whom a thousand Temples rise
> Gayly false in gentle Smiles
> Full of love-perplexing Wiles...[10]

Not only does this provide a pleasing anachronistic link to both Sappho and Willow through the use of the word "gayly," it also asserts the guileful aspect of the goddess. So too, does John Addisson (1672–1719):

Many-Scepter'd Queen of Love,
Guile-enamoured Child of *Jove*[11]

and John Addington Symonds's (1840–1893) marvelous nineteenth-century
version:

Star-throned incorruptible Aphrodite,
Child of Zeus, wile-weaving, I supplicate thee.[12]

Whilst guile is a cherished attribute in much Greek literature, its apotheosis must surely be found in *The Odyssey* where Odysseus himself is a champion of deceit (most famously in his trick on the Cyclops),[13] but also with Penelope, who quite literally strings her suitors along for a decade. And that returns us to Miss Kitty via Sappho's translators, notably Symonds. Aphrodite is guileful, as was Penelope, and Penelope famously unwound her weaving every night, thereby "wile-weaving" in both literal and metaphorical senses. Sappho, too, is a wile weaver and Kitty invites us to weave her string, to make patterns and connections throughout this section of the dream. We, like Penelope, have to weave some sense out of the dream, which, if not exactly wile-weaving, is at least engaged in the dreamy pastime of deceiving to enlighten.

Guile is to be found too in the greatest Greek tragedy, *Oedipus Tyrannus*. The moment that Oedipus's parents attempted to defy the oracular prophecy of patricide and incest by killing their son, the inexorable suffering of Oedipus is inevitable.[14] Their deceit leads to the slow unraveling of his coming to a knowledge of his identity. Willow's journey in the dream, less tragic than that of Oedipus, revolves around a similar unmasking of a deception, but one, it would seem, initiated by the protagonist herself. The involutions from the calligraphy lead us to ancient Greece via a plethora of translations: back to a different literature through the auspices of Miss Kitty's string; out, by inference, to Anya's Greek tragedy; and thence back to the dream's theme and structure, to Willow, to the episode. Involution need not be so tightly structured or even almost-hermetic, but its capacity to extend and expand a single moment of the show to, in this case, three millennia of intertextual possibility is, to say the least, marvelous.

We then shift from the world of Greek literature and culture to that of a more contemporary version of America with the staging of dream Willow's *Death of a Salesman*. The internal involution here is pointed out by the character herself who, fearful of public performance, has already had nightmares about being made to take the lead in *Madama Butterfly* in "Nightmares" (1.10). "Nightmares" also has the literalization of Buffy's most intense fear, that of becoming a vampire, and the circulation of connections is made more intense by virtue of Buffy's costume for the production of *Salesman* which is that of a '20s "vamp" such as Louise Brooks. The specific reference to the Puccini opera that returns us to "Nightmares" invites us to remember too Willow's more general reluctance to undertake public performance. This is wonderfully expressed in "The Puppet Show" (1.9) in the formally unusual epilogue section where Xander, Buffy and Willow perform a dreadful version of *Oedipus* (involutions just keep on spreading) and the severely stage-frightened Willow runs from the stage, leaving Xander, Buffy and an empty space. The decision for "Puppet Show" to have the epilogue section means that the credits are played out against this, as opposed to the more usual Nerf Herder song. The only other episode that has not used the Nerf Herder track is "Once More with Feeling" (6.7) in which Tara discovers that Willow has been using magic on her to make her forget their quarrels so that Tara essentially becomes Willow's puppet, providing both formal and indirect thematic connections between the two seemingly utterly disparate episodes, which is one of involution's main attributes.

"Nightmares" (1.10), as well as being linked by virtue of Willow's performance anxiety (an anxiety that the entire dream is engaged with though at the level of the performance of identity on a day-to-day basis[15]), is also part of a group of episodes that relate to the totality of "Restless" (4.22) through their being partial dream episodes. In addition to "Nightmares," which is already curious as the events are not dreams as such but, rather, the manifest realization of dark fears, the dream episodes include "When She Was Bad" (2.1), "Anne" (3.1), "Dead Man's Party" (3.2), "Faith, Hope and Trick" (3.3), "Graduation Day II" (3.22), "Living Conditions" (4.2), "Hush" (4.10), "This Year's Girl" (4.15), and "Dead Things" (6.13). While each of these episodes will have other points of contact to "Restless" (4.22) and each other, the element of their dreamness unites them all in an involutional complex. Before returning to Miller's play, I would like to provide a brief account of how some of these episodes operate involutionally.

"When She Was Bad" (2.1) has Buffy having nightmares about the Master whom she is unable to believe is dead. This evidently returns us to season 1 in a reasonably straightforward manner, but other aspects of the episode are more complicated in their involutional twists. The first of these relates to the female vampire in the episode. Though never mentioned on-screen, her character name in the shooting script is Tara. A coincidence of naming that is not even explicit in the show, nevertheless, provides an involutional relationship between this and later episodes, not the least of which is "Restless" (4.22) wherein the character we know to be Tara occupies a number of roles that are not her (the mouthpiece for the First Slayer being the obvious example).

More obvious, perhaps, is Sarah Michelle Gellar's haircut. Noticeably shorter than in season 1 (though still blonde — see chapter 4), the actress had to have her hair cut short for her part in Wes Craven's *Scream 2*. As mentioned in chapter 1, the *Scream* films have a specific relationship with *Buffy* beyond Gellar's appearance, which is that the costume designer for *Scream* became the wardrobe mistress on *Buffy*. Here, a haircut provides the sign for the opening up of related but differing external involutional strands.

An internal connection between episodes, which is as much the accidental effect of production requirements as any sort of purposeful design,[16] occurs near the beginning of the episode. It is a shot of students walking in front of the school, and it is a reused piece of film from "Never Kill a Boy on the First Date" (1.5) and actually has Owen (Buffy's would-be love interest) walking away from camera. (This "production error" involution links this episode with "The Yoko Factor" [4.20] in which the group's arguments— that Tara and Willow are trying to escape by fleeing upstairs— are clearly taken from the episode "Pangs" [4.8], and thence to Willow's concerns over the Chumash, which forms a part of the discussion of chapter 1). Owen's love of poetry, especially Emily Dickinson, is oddly reprised in (2.1) to the extent that its title ("When She Was Bad") is taken from an almost exact contemporary of Dickinson, Henry Wadsworth Longfellow, and his nursery rhyme.[17]

One of the most sustained treatments of fairy tales occurs in "Hush" (4.10). This episode has been the object of more critical discussion than almost any other single *Buffy* episode. Apart from its staggering achievements of having 27½ minutes without dialogue, of being truly frightening, of propelling Buffy's and Riley's relationship to new areas, of being incredibly funny, of allowing overt thematic concerns to be intrinsic to the piece's formal design and vice versa, there are other reasons why "Hush" is important here. First is Buffy's dream, which provides the formal involutional link to "Restless" (4.22), and also serves to unite the themes of communication and Buffy's and Riley's love with the plot-line of the gentlemen (however obliquely through the child's rhyme). Additionally, it is the last time Olivia (Giles's British black girlfriend) appears, except for her dream manifestation in "Restless," thereby offering a clue to Giles's motivations in his dream. Of most pertinence here is the fact that it is the first appearance of Tara. That Amber Benson's first *Buffy* appearance should be in an episode with Lindsay Crouse, who plays Maggie Walsh, is involutionally pregnant as they also worked together in the

1995 film *Bye Bye Love* in which Benson was best friends with a character played by Eliza Dushku, who is, of course, Faith in *Buffy* and it is Tara who first realizes that "Buffy" is not in fact Buffy but Faith in "Who Are You?" (4.16). In the same episode, Buffy tries to convince Giles that she is Buffy (despite inhabiting Faith's body) by referring to a number of episodes from her life. One of these is to remind Giles that she knows that he had sex with her mother. This happened in the episode "Band Candy" (3.6), which has its own involutional trajectory, including the other episodes that include the marvelous character of Ethan Rayne and also the Jane Espenson scripted episodes (this being her first), which would include the other great fairy tale–one "Gingerbread" (3.11), which she co-wrote with Thania St. John. Also in "Band Candy" (3.6) (which we have arrived at via "Who Are You?" [4.16] and "Hush" [4.10]) Buffy makes the comment that she is sure that everyone is delighted to be going "all Willy Loman" at the prospect of selling the candy. This, of course, refers to Arthur Miller's *Death of a Salesman* and so brings us back to Willow's dream in "Restless" (4.22).

Externally, the reference to Miller's play sets up a number of correspondences and relations. The first is back to "Gingerbread" (3.11) where the burning of the witches refers in part to Miller's *The Crucible* and this in turn will bring the figure of Amy to many viewer's minds whose incarnation as a rat has, by "Restless" (4.22), been unresolved. Amy is de-ratted in "Smashed" (6.9) at the beginning of Willow's addiction to magic, an addiction that leads her into the role of the season's Big Bad where she is similar to her doppelganger from "The Wish" (3.9) and "Doppelgangland" (3.16),[18] which then circles back to other vamp doubles, such as Buffy's in "Nightmares" (1.10), and thence back to Buffy's '20s vamp costume here.

In terms of the play itself, however, there are features that serve to act as comments upon both this dream and the episode in general. A year after the play's first production, the psychoanalytical critic Daniel E. Schneider wrote of it:

> Willy Loman, exhausted salesman, does not go back to the past. The past, as in hallucination, comes back to him; not chronologically as in flashback, but dynamically with the inner logic of his erupting volcanic unconscious. In psychiatry we call this "the return of the repressed," when a mind breaks under the invasion of primitive impulses no longer capable of compromise with reality.[19]

This résumé could stand in, with slight modifications, for "Restless" (4.22). The analeptic and proleptic nature of the episode's structure encourages a reading that, at least, questions chronology, if it does not eschew it altogether. The "return of the repressed" in the episode is not, however, a neat and easy psychoanalytical rhetorical flourish. The First Slayer's presence is not symptomatic of neurosis for the characters, nor is it symbolical of anything else (sometimes a Slayer is only a Slayer). Rather, the First Slayer's return is a physically motivated "real" event whose causes and consequences are thoroughly material. One of the great joys of the episode is its refusal to pander to a casual psychoanalysis: the cheeseman's utter arbitrariness[20] may have structural, formal or thematic interest but acts as a delightful debunking of much psychoanalytical theory. However, the questions of chronology and flashback that the quotation mentions are obviously pertinent for Whedon's text. Similarly, the desire of Miller to move away from established forms of playwriting has a resonance with Whedon's attempts to push television into new areas. Miller said:

> *All My Sons* had exhausted my lifelong interest in the Greco-Ibsen form, in the particular manner in which I had come to think of it. Now more and more the simultaneity of ideas and feelings within me and the freedom with which they contradicted one another began to fascinate me.[21]

Buffy may well be less "contradictory" than Miller's texts (though still deeply complex and self-divided in its way), but the notion of simultaneity is one of its extraordinary achievements and is another way of figuring the notion of involution. Indeed, this expanding simultaneity is evidenced here as the Greco- reference and is an unintended but further example of how involution moves off in many unexpected directions but has a strange capacity for patterns, or what Julian Barnes described history as being: "strange links and impertinent connections."[22]

The play, however, is not Miller's; it is Willow's surreal dream version of a semi-surreal dream play taking place as part of a dream that will, in turn, bleed into the other characters' dreams. Its involutional property exists in relation to its fame as a name that can be attached to a bitter critique of a perceived mid-century failure of the American dream; an engagement with versions of modernity and its counterpoints of technological advance, institutional power, instrumental reason and denial of the irrational. The play then is an antecedent to *Buffy*, and its inclusion is as much an affirmation of a convoluted tradition as it is a simple formal tool for humor.

Though humor, indeed, there is. Riley's appearance as "cowboy guy" draws him into a pardoic relationship with Westerns and the myth of the American hero; Harmony's milkmaid works on a stereotype of pastoralism and simplicity, much undermined by her vampire visage; and Buffy's vampness draws a line from early-century filmic visions of femininity to a newly envisioned sexualization that disavows a too-easy recapitulation of the male gaze.[23] Giles's overbearing director-role introduces another involutional moment as his performance links neatly with that of another British actor made good in the United States: Jack Buchanan in *The Bandwagon*.[24] His overly jolly attitude masks a seeming sexism in his response to the people on stage. Harmony attempts to answer a question (correctly, as it happens) but Giles dismisses her response in favor of Riley's. As she is trying to have herself heard, vamp-faced Harmony stands behind Giles, hands on his shoulders and nibbles at his neck in a threatening sexual-comic fashion. What is elaborately confusing about this, is that it exactly mimics the action that Harmony had used on Spike when he was digging for the Gem of Amara ("The Harsh Light of Day" [4.3]). Apart from Harmony's desire to turn Antonio Banderas into a vampire (with the involutional extratextual joke that he already is one thanks to his role in Neil Jordan's 1994 film version of Anne Rice's *Interview with a Vampire*) she also wants Spike to kill Willow. She asks him to do this and to say it is because Willow was "messing with my sweet girl" (4.3). She then adds that he can bite her, and uses the mock-biting move, from exactly the same position behind Spike as she uses behind Giles. A scene of which Willow can have no knowledge, though she is implicated in it deeply, is reprised here in her dream.

If there is a meaning to be derived here (and the specific points of hermeneutic endeavor are constantly thwarted in the episode) then it is only through involution and noncontiguous relation and not through character analysis or narrative in any usually defined way. It is also curious that Harmony writes on Spike's back in a fashion akin to Willow's writing on Tara in her dream (though Willow's calligraphically delightful and culturally profound script rather beats Harmony's red-lipsticked "Spike Loves Harmony" [4.3]).

While Willow is nervous about the forthcoming production, the scene falls eerily silent except for some strangely loud footfalls. The use of silence as a method of estrangement is most notably deployed in "The Body" (5.16), an episode that, as has already been mentioned, has an involutional relationship with "Restless" (4.22). In a different context, but still pertinent here, Brian Wall and Michael Zryd make the following observation about "The Body" (5.16):

> This episode, though moored in the Real, uses stylistic elements of realism (long takes, dead time, and especially silence) that, in comparison to the regular style of the show, become defamiliarized in order to echo the dislocated and unmoored subjectivity of its mourning protagonists.[25]

For Wall and Zryd, realism here becomes itself a tool of defamiliarization. This is because they mistake the formal characteristics that we call realism with a complete and unadorned presentation of "the real," which is, in any case, impossible. As I mention elsewhere, realism is a technique whose aim is primarily to draw as little attention to itself as possible in order that the thing represented seems as ordinary as possible. "The Body" (5.16), by using techniques like the one-shot long-walk in real time made by the doctor toward the end of the episode, presents the real (in terms of duration) but the technique, by virtue of its formally alienating effect (that walk would normally be passed over in a second) is not realism. Notwithstanding that, the point is well made: viewers are dislocated from their expectations such that they, paradoxically, become more attached to the emotional reality being displayed. This is done to exceptional, indeed unique, lengths in "The Body" (5.16) but its usage in Willow's dream operates at a similar pitch. Already disoriented by the strangeness of what they are watching, viewers are further formally alienated in order that the character's own bewilderment is made paramount: formal innovation serves a deeper emotional resonance, in this case the expression of Willow's subjectivity.

Her movement out of the play is through sets of red curtains that are strongly reminiscent of *Twin Peaks*, which is, perhaps, one of the very few television shows that has ever attempted to be as adventurous with narrative and technique as *Buffy*. Whedon claims that the relation here is accidental and is meant to be much more literally a sign for sexuality and for the comfort and trust that might be thought to accrue from that with respect to her relationship with Tara.[26]

The simultaneity addressed in the earlier quotation from Miller is manifested in the dream with Buffy's spectacular monologue happening synchronously with the other action of Willow's dream. This monologue itself, apart from being a tour-de-force of writing and acting, makes good use of the Frasier lens to produce an extreme depth of focus on the tableau. While it does not have the same focus depth, the scene in "Pangs" (4.8) where a high shot from over Spike's seated frame draws Buffy and Giles into a deep elevated diagonal is compositionally strikingly similar to the one here and provides another involutional point of contact.

As Willow, mercifully for her, leaves the play behind (it has finished long ago) she is attacked by what we later realize is the First Slayer. Her rescuer is Buffy who brings her to the safety of the old high school. The return to the school from the first three seasons in this, the university-based fourth season, is an emotionally charged moment. Inevitably it invites the viewer to remember any number of scenes in the classrooms and, perhaps most strongly, the final destruction of the building in "Graduation Day II"

(3.22), as this would have been the last time we saw the building. That, in itself, will remind us of the Class Protector award given to Buffy by Jonathan in "The Prom" (3.20), which was destroyed by Sunday as a symbol of Buffy's maturation ("The Freshman" [4.1]), and this will probably also bring to mind two of the great Jonathan episodes, "Earshot" (3.18) and "Superstar" (4.17). "Graduation Day II" (3.22) contains another famous dream sequence where an injured Buffy and the comatose Faith seem to share a psychic manifestation, which includes Faith's gnomic, "Oh yeah. Miles to go— Little Ms. Muffet —counting down from 7–3–0" (3.22). The 7–3–0 part of this will be addressed in Buffy's dream, but the "miles to go" reference to Robert Frost's "Stopping by Woods on a Snowy Evening" reprises the exact same reference that was used by Buffy in "The Prom" (3.20), in which she received her award.

Buffy protects and saves and, in Willow's dream, the Class Protector once again saves Willow from physical harm but draws her back into a place of early worry and anxiety. The questions of identity and performance that have dogged her dream from the initial framing shot, are now made clear as the dream Willow has to confront the possibility that the newly confident, rather chic Wiccan is just a disguise covering over the still shy and geeky girl that we first met in "Welcome to the Hellmouth" (1.1). This is made clear by Buffy's stripping Willow of her clothes and leaving her in an outfit very similar to that from the first episode with a hair style and makeup to match. I have discussed Willow's narrative progress in chapter 4, but this moment is of a different order.

Willow from season 1 (or more specifically, episode 1[27]) is here represented by the sleeping Willow of "Restless" (4.22) as the eidolon[28] of her dream. There are close enough similarities between the costumes of episode 1 Willow and dream Willow to make the relationship specific, but the alterations allow us to also recognize difference. Dream Willow is therefore a partial return to episode 1 Willow but is not a simple return to the same. Between the sleeping Willow having the dream and the Willow of episode 1 there stands a superabundance of change of which eidolon Willow stands as a figure.[29] The Willow in the dream who moves from Tara, to Xander and Oz, from university back to high school via a strange desert-moment, who has Greek at her fingertips and still reads *The Lion, the Witch and the Wardrobe*, who relies on Buffy to save her but who is then revealed as a fraud by Buffy, seems to imply a fraught journey from one Willow to another, the latter one being in some sense the Willow of full signification, complete to this point (a completeness marked, in part, by the very fact of her striving to recognize herself). However, it is evidently not true to suppose that Willow is anything like a fully signified character, and this is for two reasons. First, when viewing the episode contemporaneously with its first airing, the audience knew that at least one more season was to come and could, therefore, reasonably assume that Willow would grow and change again. When seeing the episode from the perspective of the show's ending, we are aware of three whole seasons of development, thereby having seen her changes. So, from this point of view there is a future Willow that renders present Willow unfinished. Second, even had this been the final episode of *Buffy*, we could not have believed Willow to be a complete representation of herself for an almost opposed reason: even by this point, she has an excess of signification, a superabundance of meanings and possibilities that have been invested in her, none of which is recuperable within a clear narrativity that would see this or any moment as the full expression of her identity. And this is due, in large part, to the aesthetics of involution with which the show operates.

The name "Willow" clearly identifies the character played by the actress Alyson Hannigan and who we recognize visually by that mundane but vital point. The bodily fact of representation, and the changing of that body through makeup, costume and so on, offers us the chance to see the development of her in purely visual terms. These terms are involuted in this episode by contracting the space of representational growth that covers 78 episodes and occluding the points between. Or, rather, the points between are compressed into a single superabundance of signification that bursts out at the point of involutional contact. Willow may be seeking to find her identity, to unpack her performativity, but the audience is forced to recognize the sheer profusions of Willows, each related to the other but inassimilable into a neatly packaged, unifying entity. Jess Battis makes a similar point when he writes:

> Throughout the seven seasons, Willow has occupied many personas: shy academic; computer expert; budding witch ("budding" being a signifier commonly ascribed to Willow's magical studies, which holds all kinds of double-voiced meaning when connected to her name) [...] ingénue; agent of the apocalypse; and, finally, a guilt-stricken, "reformed" addict.[30]

An unassuming point about the character's superabundance, and the impossibility of locating her neatly under the sign of her name, is the fact that the name itself is so fractured, being broken down into constituent parts for nicknames, and being eschewed altogether at points in favor of other designators attributable to the same person. Tzvetan Todorov in his often stunning *Genres in Discourse* posits what he sees as an irresolvable problem for representation in what may be loosely termed experimental texts. He invites the reader to

imagine that, in a text, the same character is mentioned in turn by different names: at one point he is called "John," at another "Peter," or he is
referred to as "the man with black hair" and then "the man with blue
eyes," [...] the text will be representatively undecidable.[31]

Todorov is asking about the same subject referred to by different
names. For Todorov, his many-named and many-referenced character leads
to the text being representatively undecidable. Without going into too much
detail about Todorov's thesis, the reason for this undecidability is that the
work of construction undertaken by the reader (or in this case, viewer) is
disturbed, or thwarted, by the inability to construct a character from the
information given in the text. There is too much conflicting information
with regard to the supposed subject being represented, and representation
qua construction cannot occur.

My contention with relation to *Buffy* is that an aesthetics of involution plays with the recognition of the representational awkwardness of
naming (a problem less pronounced on film than in novels due simply to
the visual prompt, but still a prominent concern here) but without its
being a cause for such hermeneutic despair. Involution presupposes that
a single instance is always open to an internal or external point of contact
(or many such points) so that every signifying unit of an episode is both
part of the closed system of the episode's structure and equally part of the
open system of audio-visual circulation mentioned in chapter 5. Any sign
then (the name Willow or the body on-screen who we recognize as that
character) signifies as part of the episode's syntax. Any sign is also subject
to increased stresses or intensities and at these moments it signifies both
episode-syntactically and involutionally, across episodes and across other
cultural forms.

Willow is named, as mentioned, with a variety of different cognomens
throughout *Buffy*. The most memorable in terms of its direct relation to
the question of Willow's identity and our understanding of her as a multiple, excessive character comes in "New Moon Rising" (4.19). Willow is
trying to explain to Buffy about her relationship with Tara, and Buffy is
clearly uncomfortable with the knowledge:

> BUFFY: Oh. Um ... well ... that's great. You know, I mean, I think Tara's
> a, a really great girl, Will.
> WILLOW: She is. And ... there's something between us. It — it wasn't
> something I was looking for. It's just powerful. And it's totally different
> from what Oz and I have.
> BUFFY: Well, there you go, I mean, you know, you have to— you have to
> follow your heart, Will. And that's what's important, Will.
> WILLOW: Why do you keep saying my name like that?

BUFFY: Like what, Will?
WILLOW: Are you freaked?
BUFFY: What? No, Will, d — No. No, absolutely no to that question.
(Willow looks skeptical.) [4.19]

Buffy's attempt to use the familiar nickname Will over-emphasizes the close friendship she and Willow have to the extent that the act of naming estranges the one from the other. Willow recognizes the name, and presumably realizes its connotations of friendship, but it also serves to try and bind Willow into a version of her that Buffy wants to control. In his extraordinary introduction to *Bleak House*, J. Hillis Miller provides a number of ways of thinking about naming that have a peculiar resonance here. A general point he makes about names is that all "proper names [...] are metaphors. They alienate the person named from his unspeakable individuality and assimilate him into a system of language."[32] Following on from this, the notion of the relationship between a name and the thing named is broached in terms of the ways in which overt fictionality is a method of "demystifying the belief, affirmed in Plato's *Cratylus*, that the right name gives the essence of a thing."[33] This refers us back to the start of Willow's dream where Miss Kitty's naming is of such seeming import, and also forward to Buffy's dream where Riley and Adam are busy "giving names to things." In the context of Buffy's overuse of Willow's nickname, Hillis Miller's general observations regarding nicknames assume a very precise and emphatic power: "To give someone a nickname is to force on him a metaphorical translation and to appropriate him especially to oneself."[34] Buffy's over-eager usage of the diminutive of Willow's name makes explicit the sense in which Willow has a fixed meaning for Buffy, which can be asserted and maintained through the process of naming. Willow's recognition of the nature of this process indicates the extent to which the question of her identity as a construct that can be largely determined by linguistic colonization is disturbing for her. As it is for us. The character of Willow across the seven seasons is nicknamed (sometimes affectionately, oftentimes not) with a range of phrases and words. These are, obviously, intended to demonstrate the speaker's attitude to Willow and, through this, to assert Willow as a type of person either in the structural sense of locating her in a relationship of friendship or hostility, or in the sense of a category of individual. Thus Willow is constructed as weak, needy or childlike; powerful and godlike; dangerous and bad; clever but nerdy; clever and helpful; sexually desirable; unappealing; and enjoyable to be around. These categorizations stem from what Hillis Miller calls "nominal displacements," the effect of which, he contends, "is to mime in the permutations of language that movement within the social system which prevents each person from being himself and puts him beside himself into some other role."[35] Willow is striving to find herself, especially in this dream, but our reminder of the many and various Willows we have met, simply through nominal displacement, which finds its visual equivalent in the stark contrast between the costumes of the dreamer and the dreamed here demonstrates how impossible this search will be.

For the viewer, it is not only the various Willows we are asked to compartmentalize that makes the question of her identity awkward, but the other manifestations that share something of her physicality but are not Willow. If the linguistic aspect provides a cross-referential interpretive dance between and across episodes and seasons, the physically changing Willow does the same thing visually. I have discussed this in chapter 4.

By invoking the image of early Willow, then, "Restless" (4.22) draws attention to the involutional possibility of signs. We do not, here, simply have the implication of non-narrative points of connection, the connection is made explicit, and with it the whole retinue of involutional possibilities. If we take just one instance of the involutional possibility at a specific level, as opposed to the general points made just above, the extent of this moment's intensity can be seen. That our movement between the two Willows (that of episode 1.1 and that of "Restless") is sparked by dream Willow and her clothes makes it likely that clothing would be a point of involutional connection. In "Welcome to the Hellmouth" (1.1), Willow's vampire-paramour is identified as such by a caustic and belligerent Buffy due to the state of his dress which is somewhat unfashionable:

> GILES: It's dated?
> BUFFY: It's carbon dated. Trust me, only someone living underground
> for ten years would think that was still the look [1.1].

The humor here and its specific object of vampire fashion connects to other episodes where the undead's dress sense is the motor for the comedy. Angel's particular brand of attire is lovingly mocked in a self-conscious moment in "Lie to Me" (2.7) when he berates the vampire wanna-bes for having no idea about vampiric lifestyles or dress codes at which point a young aspirant dressed exactly like Angel walks past. This episode also introduces us to Chantarelle whose desire to become one of the "Old Ones" is somewhat dampened by her confrontation with Spike and his gang. Chantarelle disappears seemingly for good, until Buffy, who has run away, finds her again, now called Lily, and helps rescue her. This episode ("Anne" [3.1]) sees both Lily/Chantarelle and Buffy, who has called herself Anne, striving to discover their identities. The fact the Buffy is now called Anne

Summers cannot but provide a culturally specific smirk from British viewers who will be aware that her attempt to redefine herself through naming has meant that she now occupies a nominal space shared with a famous chain of high street adult stores. Buffy succeeds in reestablishing a semblance of self and returns home and Lily, who now calls *her*self Anne, then appears in *Angel* as a worker with young runaways ("Blood Money" [*AtS* 2.12]). The emphasis on names and naming central to this little circuit leads us straight back, once again, to Willow's dream. However, the clothes aspect still provides other links. Angel's particular brand of sartorial elegance causes a jealous Riley to grimly recognize the general level of allure that the soul-cursed vampire exudes in "The Yoko Factor" (4.19). Believing Angel to have been turned evil again and, therefore, believing further that Angel and Buffy have slept together, Riley is relieved but surprised to discover that this is not the case:

> RILEY: Seriously? That's a good day? Well, there you go. Even when he's good, he's all "Mr. Billowy-Coat, King-of-Pain," and girls really... [4.19].

This explicit union of attire, attitude and heroism is wonderfully parodied by Spike in a crossover episode on *Angel*, "In the Dark" (*AtS* 1.3). Arriving in L.A. to seek out the gem of Amara, Spike watches Angel save a young woman in a dark alley. Providing his own voice-over for the action unfolding below, he impersonates the woman's thanks by saying, "How can I thank you, you mysterious, black-clad hunk of a night thing" and then Angel's response to her seeming advance:

> No, not the hair! Never the hair! [...] Say no more. Evil's still afoot! And I'm almost out of that nancy-boy hair gel that I like so much. Quickly, to the Angel-mobile, away! [AtS 1.3].

Even more episodes are connected by the question of vampire dress, all of which have been spawned for this involutionary circuit by Willow's dress in episode 1. Season 5 sees Spike and his own billowy coat explained in "Fool for Love" (5.7) as the trophy he took from the second Slayer he killed in a New York City subway in 1977. This then lurches us forward to season 7 where we discover in "First Date" (7.14) that Principal Wood's mother was a Slayer and that she was the one from whom Spike stole the coat, thereby ensuring Wood's antipathy toward Spike.

All of these episodes, and others too, are joined by their involutionary connection. Their thematic equivalence to Willow's dream enables the texture of the dream to be deepened through the emotional montage created by the circulation of correspondences. A final one of these occurs as

Willow begins to read aloud her book report on *The Lion, The Witch and The Wardrobe* whose story of four children discovering a hidden mystical world and saving the day has obvious echoes. As she starts, though, her friends all turn on her and Xander, bored and mean, simply says, "Oh, who cares?" The look of utter hurt on Willow's face cannot help but draw the images of hurt–Willow from a number of episodes into this signifying moment, intensifying its power beyond the confines of the specific representational instant. The look of devastation when primal-infected Xander in "The Pack" (1.6) ridicules her in front of his new friends is one of the most heartrending single looks of the entire run of the show. The fact, once again, that it is Xander who is able to wound so intensely increases further the overflowing signifying moment of the dream. A similarly searing encounter for Willow, and us, is from season 2's "Innocence" (2.14) when she discovers Xander's and Cordelia's tryst. Her pain is excruciating to see, made the more so in some ways by her brave attempt at mordant humor:

> WILLOW: I knew it! I knew it! Well, not "knew it" in the sense of having the slightest idea, but I knew there was something I didn't know. You two were fighting way too much. It's not natural!
> XANDER: I know it's weird...
> WILLOW: Weird? It's against all laws of God and Man! It's Cordelia! Remember? The, the "We Hate Cordelia" club, of which you are the treasurer.
> XANDER: Look, I was gonna tell you.
> WILLOW: Gee, what stopped you? Could it be shame?
> XANDER: All right, let's overreact, shall we?
> WILLOW: But I'm...
> XANDER: Willow, we were just kissing. It doesn't mean that much.
> WILLOW: No. It just means that you'd rather be with someone you hate than be with me [2.14].

And now, in her dream, he mocks her with her ex-lover and present lover sitting right there and doing nothing to help her. This vulnerable, hurt Willow, who is scared about who she is and how she is viewed is far removed from the Willow of later seasons and the circulation of signs of poignancy that the eidolon has prompted also suggests this change, most especially the face of grief transmuted to rage after Tara's shooting. No longer the little girl who responds to hurt with self-doubt and tears or simple petulance as when Buffy in "Fear Itself" (4.4) describes Willow's spells as "only fifty-fifty" and Willow responds with the gloriously inept "Oh, yeah? Well, so's your face"; she is now capable of exteriorizing her pain and using it to great harm, or, ultimately, harnessing that energy and becoming a goddess (though not Greek) herself ("Chosen" [7.22]).

Willow's dream acts as a coda to a character's development over the four seasons to this stage, or as a punctuation point for the entire duration of the show. Its thematic concerns with Willow's malleable identity engage in a complex cross-fertilization with the show's questions concerning its own identity. This generically hybridized text destabilizes any conceptualization of it in genre terms and its identity as an aesthetic construct is constantly put into question. The dream's foregrounding of both identity and involution as production and hermeneutic activities is another demonstration of the extent to which this subtle and multifaceted show extends the aesthetic possibilities of television while still managing to produce high-quality popular entertainment week after week. And it is with television that we shall now turn to Xander's dream.

CHAPTER 7

Xander's Dream

"It's all about the journey, isn't it?"

Xander's dream begins where Willow's has left off. He believes himself to be awake and he, Giles and Buffy are sitting watching a version of *Apocalypse Now* as Willow struggles for life. Buffy comments that Willow is a big faker, thereby providing a thematic commentary on Willow's dream in Xander's. This implies that these two dreams, at least, should be read as related and sequentially connected. The connection between the dreams continues at a formal level as the actor in Xander's dream–*Apocalypse Now* is wooden, and the script awful so that the production of *Death of a Salesman* in Willow's dream, and particularly Riley's appearance as stereotype and ham, is brought back into focus.

The point of connection is important as it becomes clear to the viewer who, on a first watching, may well be rather confused, that he or she is involved in a journey that includes all the characters, however oddly. While the viewer's journey will have to wait for the episode's end to make some sort of sense (a sense that is likely to be a minimal episodic-syntactic one with the dream's presence explained, rather than a hermeneutic one as the dream's meaning is still somewhat a mystery), Xander's own sense of journey is more immediate. Giles provides a prospective commentary on the dream to come by saying, in relation to *Apocalypse Now*, that "it's all about the journey, isn't it?" which is evidently true of Xander's unconscious expression.

As shall become clear by its end, Xander's dream concerns itself with the continuing sense of failure and frustration that he feels.[1] Unlike his friends, he has not gone to the university, he has little sense of purpose, no obvious future and still lives in his parents' basement, a basement to which he returns throughout his dream in a nightmare vision of repetition, entrapment and stasis. It is then, a sort of emotional echo of "The Zeppo" (3.13), where he feels redundant, undervalued and lost. In "The Zeppo" we see him accidentally embroiled in a gang of reanimated corpses for whom he becomes the unwilling leader. Against this, the rest of the Scoobies are averting another apocalypse but, as Steve Wilson has pointed out, the subplot assumes dominance over the narrative in a manner akin to Tom Stoppard's *Rosencrantz and Guildenstern Are Dead*.[2] Not only does the subplot here assume dominance, but in so doing it offers the writers and producers a chance to mock some of the standard tropes of the main show itself. One of the ways in which this happens has been described by McNeilly et al. They say:

> When Xander walks in on Angel and Buffy, the romantic mood-music abruptly fades and they glare at him; his presence essentially breaks the frame, and reminds us that this is a *Buffy* cliché, with Angel and Buffy playing the same roles and spouting the same dialogue they do on the verge of every cosmic catastrophe. Xander backs off, and the romance resumes, but as viewers our attention has been redirected, and fractured. We recognize the ways our expectations have been controlled by the convention of generic television.[3]

Genre television lives by its adherence to convention, and *Buffy* is no different except that its adherence is to a number of genres that become commingled and undifferentiated, producing a new genre that is not a genre at all. Involution is part of this commingling process, an aspect of the interpenetration of genres, of the mixing of styles, of references, of allusions and points of contact. To actively seek (and then accidentally allow) non-narrative involutional connections as well as narrative ones, the show amplifies the viewer's awareness of its indebtedness to genre at the same time it demonstrates its removal far beyond its confines. The external involutional possibilities in "The Zeppo" (3.13) are great, but I want to concentrate on the internal ones for the moment. Most clearly is the enormous monster that we catch sight of coming out of the Hellmouth that Buffy and the rest are trying to kill as Xander is busy fighting the zombies. This is the same monster as that in "Prophecy Girl" (1.12), which attempted to escape as part of the Master's release. It was Xander who saved Buffy's life at this point, a fact that makes his continuing sense of isolation or worthlessness within the group especially saddening. The importance of Xander is recognized on a number of occasions by the group, but it is season

7, as the series is winding to its end, that the most marvelous expression of it is given to us. In "Potential" (7.12), having seen Dawn think that she was a potential Slayer and then find that she is not, Xander commends her grace in accepting her position and comments on his own position and experience:

> XANDER: They'll never know how tough it is, Dawnie, to be the one who isn't chosen. To live so near to the spotlight and never step in it. But I know. I see more than anybody realizes because nobody's watching me. I saw you last night. I see you working here today. You're not special. You're extraordinary.
> DAWN: Maybe that's your power.
> XANDER: What?
> DAWN: Seeing. Knowing.
> XANDER: Maybe it is. Maybe I should get a cape.
> DAWN: Cape is good [7.12].[4]

The inevitable sense of undercutting, the ironic suggestion that he find a hero costume is symptomatic of Xander and of his journey: quiet, unassuming but always, as shown in "Primeval" (4.21), the heart. This quiet strength and courage is demonstrated in "The Zeppo" (3.13) by his being able to remain calm in the face of imminent death as he forces the zombie, by simply refusing to panic or flee, to defuse the bomb that has been planted beneath the school. This clearly has prospective irony as the school will be destroyed later in season 3, but it also foreshadows the closing sequence of "Touched" (7.20) and the opening sequence of "End of Days" (7.21), where Faith uncovers a bomb that is counting down in its red numbered display — that time, however, leading to an explosion. That it should be Faith who is so obviously structurally located in a position Xander occupied four seasons previously is no accident. In the same episode that Xander proves beyond doubt to himself that he is capable of acts of heroism that need no audience (the Scoobies, we assume, never find out about his deeds), he also loses his virginity to Faith in circumstances very far from romantic. Faith's discovery of the bomb reminds us of this relationship between the two, provides Faith and Xander with a moment of plot-derived doubling, and also leads to an ironic joke concerning the fact that The First appears as the mayor from season 3 and calls Faith a "firecracker" (7.20). Apart from the rather stretched humor of her then having to escape an exploding bomb, the name is the same that the mayor used for her in "Graduation Day II" (3.22), the episode in which Xander's impeding of the destruction of the high school in "The Zeppo" (3.13) becomes rather overshadowed by its devastation at the hands of Buffy and her killing of the newly ascended mayor-monster.

The emotional echo that Xander's dream resonates with in relation to "The Zeppo" (3.13) (feelings of alienation from his friends, a certain purposelessness) is complemented by the rather more specific fact of his disappointment with his home situation that we see articulated in "Amends" (3.10). Here, the relationship of his parents is such that he chooses to sleep outside in a sleeping bag on Christmas Eve, rather than have to cope with his mother and father's fights. The continuing efforts to escape this situation are clear in the structure of return to the basement in "Restless" (4.22), and the need to escape is made manifest in "Amends" (3.10) where the miracle of snow at Christmas to save Angel's life simply makes Xander cold and wet.[5] This episode has another point of contact with "Restless" (4.22) insofar as Oz and Willow attempt a reconciliation but Willow's rather excessive desire to seek forgiveness leads her to try and seduce Oz in dazzlingly rococo style. Oz is left a little bewildered and comments, "You ever have that dream where you're in a play, and it's the middle of the play and you really don't know your lines, and you kinda don't know the plot?" (3.10). This refers back to "Nightmares" (1.10) and "The Puppet Show" (1.9), and forward, of course, to Willow's dream version of *Death of a Salesman* that has just preceded. Xander's fear of his life's potential for failure expressed in his dream looks forward too, to his final decision not to marry Anya ("Hell's Bells" [6.16]): a state of affairs that sends her back into the demon fold and, thence, to a number of memorable episodes from her, especially "Selfless" (7.5).

But Xander's dream starts watching a video and thinking about eating popcorn, surreally flavored as "new car smell," which once again tends toward ideas of travel and escape, ideas Xander failed to achieve in his far from new car between seasons 3 and 4. He recounts his attempt to drive across all 50 states, and the ignominious disappointment that was derived from the engine falling out ("The Freshman" [4.1]). He goes upstairs and finds himself dreaming of seducing or being seduced by Joyce, all resplendent in the great romantic trope of the red dress, which, while having a long and pervasive cultural history, cannot help but return the viewer to Whedon's favorite movie, *The Matrix,* and "the woman in red" in that film. Whether or not Chris deBurgh's hit of the 1980s ("Lady in Red") is also a purposeful intertext is another question; its inclusion as a point of involutional contact is, however unwanted, undeniable. A more obvious point of contact is *The Graduate,* Mike Nichols's 1967 hit with Dustin Hoffman. That film's tagline — "This is Benjamin. He's a little worried about his future"— is marvelously transposed onto Xander through the allusion. The fact that it is a 1967 movie is also resonant, given that year's growing unrest with regard to the war in Vietnam and the presence there until 1969, of the war correspondent Michael Herr whose memories of his experiences became the basis for his book *Dispatches*, first published in the 1970s and then, famously, used for parts of Martin Sheen's character's narration in Coppola's monumental *Apocalypse Now*, based on Conrad's *Heart of Darkness*, the place to which Xander, metaphorically, continually returns.

His encounter with Joyce, with its strange slow motions and odd dubbing, is a formal link with Steven Soderbergh's 1999 film *The Limey*, the editing style of which, with its off-center framing and cutting and dialogue where there is no dialogue, had appealed to Whedon.[6] Xander leaves Joyce[7] to go to the bathroom where he finds himself being watched and scrutinized by the Initiative soldiers and scientists before the first of his accidental entries back to his basement with the foreboding rattling of the door upstairs. This moves swiftly to an outdoors scene where Xander sees Buffy in a sandbox[8] while Spike and Giles are playing on swings. Spike's costume for this (deer-stalker hat, plaid suit and so on) are all reprised in the excellent "Tabula Rasa" (6.8). This episode, which is also of importance for Giles's dream, has a number of involutional contacts for Xander. After the gang loses their memories as a result of Willow's spell, Anya and Giles think that they are married and have a row about Giles leaving. Anya conjures a spell that inadvertently produces scores of rabbits. We know of her fear of bunnies from "Fear Itself" (4.4), which is also one of the earliest episodes where Anya's feelings for Xander become apparent. This is another of the episodes in which Xander's anxieties regarding his position in the group are paramount and he becomes, effectively, invisible to the group. This, then, of course invokes Macie from "Out of Mind, Out of Sight" (1.10) and the slapped girl in (7.16). Interestingly, Xander's fear of invisibility closely relates to the quality about him that is so admired by Dawn: his vision and capacity to know and see things. His eventual semi-blinding by Caleb in "Dirty Girls" (7.18) ties together this strand of Xander's journey in a graphically and morbidly ironic fashion. As early as "Dead Man's Party" (3.2) Xander's eventual eye loss has been mooted. Buffy, returning from her exile as Anne, believes she has spotted a potentially bad person but it is just Xander patrolling. Buffy responds: "Didn't anyone ever warn you about playing with pointy sticks? It's all fun and games until somebody loses an eye" (3.2). Much later, Xander is dressed as a pirate in The Magic Box in an attempt to entice customers in "All the Way" (6.6), and his costume has him resplendent with eye-patch, an accessory that he has to wear for real after the encounter with Caleb (7.18). The pirate's uniform itself is a recursive sign back to "Halloween" (2. 6) where Xander's seeming nemesis Larry is dressed as a pirate, and Xander, newly incarnated as a soldier, punches him, providing the amnesiac-inhabited

Xander with a sense of closure for that episode's mini-journey. The soldier motif, however, will keep on occurring, especially in its parodic form in the dream in "Restless" (4.22).[9]

Back at the sandbox, Xander is talking to Buffy who is massively overexposed due to the whited-out sky and the wide-angled lens used for shooting. This, and the sudden flash-cut to the desert reminds us of the same level of brightness and cutting technique in Willow's dream and lends a foreshadowing power to a similar level of exposure as Buffy steps out of her back door in "The Body" (5.16). Buffy's comment that she is ahead of Xander again brings the notion of journeying, and of Xander's not being timely, to the front, and her additional comment "big brother" not only locates Xander's relationship with her in his mind but also invokes Orwell's novel.[10] In the context of a season that has introduced a covert military organization whose surveillance methods are reminiscent of totalitarian regimes, this serves to add another layer of paranoia and concern to an already disorienting experience for the viewer. The gnomic reference by Buffy to a shark that is, as Xander additionally comments, "with feet ... and much less fins" has its payoff also in "Tabula Rasa" (6.8) where the literalization of metaphor that had been such a staple of entire episodes in season 1 is rendered at the level of character with the loan shark being quite literally a shark with feet.

After this exchange we see Xander working in and then driving an ice-cream van, which relates to his experience in "Where the Wild Things Are" (4.18) and prefigures his movement from job to job in the next couple of seasons, though also has parallels with Buffy's own sojourn in the world of service industries in "Doublemeat Palace" (6.12) and beyond. Anya's comment that she is considering returning to vengeance is a foreshadowing of events from "Hell's Bells" (6.16) onwards and reaches some sort of conclusion in "Selfless" (7.5). "Hell's Bells" (6.16) is related to this particular strain of involution as it is the one and only time we actually meet Uncle Rory who is the man who lent Xander the car that causes him such trouble in "The Zeppo" (3.13). During this sequence the clearly imposed green screen of his supposed driving and the poor dubbing are again tribute to some of Soderbergh's techniques.

The next part of Xander's dream is a clear expression of young male sexual fantasies as he watches Willow and Tara, both dressed in sexually alluring clothes, engage in lesbian sex, while Anya encourages him to join in. This scene connects explicitly with the opening scene of "Dirty Girls" (7.18). In this episode, it appears as though Xander, the heart of the household (even to the extent of literally keeping it physically together through his workmanship) is trying to comfort one of the young potentials. The opportunity for older man seducing young woman is evident and when the girl coyly remarks that she could die without ever having been with a man the viewer is encouraged to ponder Xander's moral resolve. Once a second potential appears and the two of them offer to have sex with each other in front of Xander it becomes apparent that Xander is dreaming a rather more specifically pornographic fantasy than the equivalent scene in "Restless" (4.22). The long shot through the newly opened door to a slow-motion pillow fight between the rest of the potentials shifts the emotional tone from the overtly sexualized to the pseudo-parodic. These two dreams unite the episodes closely.[11] Xander's continual fear that he is not central to the Scoobies' needs has been somewhat allayed in season 7 by his role as moral center, and this episode (7.18) marks the collapse of the integrity of the household through his blinding by Caleb, a blinding that is the result of Buffy's rash decision to attack the preacher despite warnings that it is likely to be a trap. Xander has delivered his rallying speech to the potentials, persuading them of Buffy's merits and her attributes of courage, valor and sincerity, but he, despite being the one who sees, has not accounted for her genuine lack of judgment.

"Dirty Girls" (7.18), apart from Xander's pornographic desires, is important involutionally, too, for its purposeful titular allusion to the episode "Bad Girls" (3.14). The former sees the final corruption of Faith through her murder of the deputy mayor. Her own down spiral and later attempt to seek redemption leads to her eventual incarceration, an incarceration that has come to an end on the previous few *Angel* episodes and allows for her reentry into *Buffy*. "Bad Girls" (3.14) has Xander increasingly nervous about his having had sex with Faith, and his eye twitches every time her name is mentioned; the coincidence in relation to his eventual eye loss seems, at least, strong. Faith's reentry into *Buffy* clearly requires some backstory for newer viewers and so Andrew, in a delightful repetition of his actions in "Storyteller" (7.16) provides the potentials with a narration of her life, which is accompanied by a montage of previous scenes that include Faith. The involutional aspect here is, inevitably, immense, but it is the shot of her killing the deputy mayor that has most resonance for this circulation as this takes us back to "Bad Girls" (3.14), thence to "Dirty Girls" (7.18) and, finally, spirals us back to "Restless" (4.22).

One of the important events in "Bad Girls" (3.14) is the appearance of the new Watcher, Wesley. While his role in Buffy is essentially comic foil and counterpoint to Giles, his arc in *Angel* has resonance with Xander's "Restless" (4.22) dream insofar as Wesley, arguably more than any other character, has a storyline that is quintessentially katabatic.

Rachel Falconer in *Hell in Contemporary Literature* provides a wonderful critical engagement with katabatic literature, which is literature that concerns itself with "the *journey* through Hell, the idea of the transformative passage, the destruction and re-birth of the self through an encounter with the absolute Other."[12] The structure of this narrative has clear antecedents in Odysseus's descent in *The Odyssey*, followed by Aeneas's version of the same in *The Aeneid*.[13] It recurs throughout literature and finds an appalling political-social expression in Conrad's *Heart of Darkness*. Wesley's journey into despair and his slow attempt at recuperation follow the general pattern where, in a typically early twenty-first-century move, the Other is himself. Conrad's book will be dealt with at some length shortly, but one of its most famous moments is, of course, the lie to the Intended. After Marlow's horrifying journey and meeting with the crazed Kurtz, he meets Kurtz's fiancée and has a decision to make. He can either tell her the truth about what Kurtz has become, or he can allow the memory of the man he once was and, as is well known, he chooses the latter. Hiding "The horror! The horror!"[14] behind the pretense that Kurtz's last words were his betrothed's name, Marlow fears heavenly wrath, but the emotional rightness of his action seems to outweigh any overarching moral query, or even more local obligation to Kurtz.

Wesley, too, having journeyed into darkness chooses a lie from his Intended. Fred, with whom he had been becoming increasingly close, has been killed and her body inhabited by an ancient god, Illyria, who has the ability to resume Fred's shape if she chooses. In the very last episode of *Angel* ("Not Fade Away" [*AtS* 5.22]), the group has been sent by Angel to enjoy themselves for the afternoon as the fight may well be their last one. While the others go off to their various pursuits (Spike memorably choosing to attend a performance poetry club to recite the "Cecily" poem first encountered in "Fool for Love" [5.7]), Wesley stays in the offices with Illyria. Confused as to his motives, Illyria has to have it explained to her by Wesley that he has no special place he would like to be or special person he would like to be with since Fred is dead. Illyria offers to assume her shape but Wesley adamantly refuses to accept the illusion of Fred over the fact of her absence, saying "I won't accept a lie." Later, after being mortally wounded and nearing death, Illyria finds Wesley and the following exchange occurs:

> ILLYRIA: Would you like me to lie to you now?
> WESLEY: Yes. Thank you. Yes.
> WESLEY: Hello there.
> FRED: Oh, Wesley. My Wesley.
> WESLEY: Fred. I've missed you.

> FRED: It's gonna be OK. It won't hurt much longer, and then you'll be
> where I am. We'll be together.
> WESLEY: I — I love you.
> FRED: I love you. My love. Oh, my love.
> (Wesley dies.) [*AtS* 5.22].

Apart from being one of the most heart-wrenching moments in any tele-vision show, let alone simply *Buffy* and *Angel*, due in large part to the exceptionally understated and emotionally compelling acting performances, the choice of the emotionally sincere lie over the morally sincere truth locates the culmination of Wesley's journey into his heart of darkness structurally and emotionally adjacent to Marlow's.

The next allusion in "Restless" (4.22) to *Apocalypse Now* and then, via intertext, to *Heart of Darkness* is with Xander's arrival in the school corridor, which is lit in a pale sickly green with purple and mauve light-ing in the distance. Whedon states that this is another homage to *The Limey* but also to Coppola's film.[15] Xander meets Giles in the hallway but cannot understand Giles as he is speaking French. The dubbed element of Giles's foray into French is overdubbed by Diego Gutierrez who subsequently went on to write season 6's "Normal Again" (6.17). This episode has clear affinities to the *Deep Space Nine* episode "Far Beyond the Stars" (*DS9* 6.13) in which Captain Sisko imagines that he is a writer of science fiction in the 1950s who is hallucinating the existence of Deep Space Nine and all its characters, including Quark, the Ferenghi bar manager played by Armin Shimmerman.

Joss Whedon asserts that when Xander is picked up by the soldiers from the initiative, this moves into an attempted shot-for-shot copy of *Apocalypse Now*.[16] At this moment Coppola's filmic version of Conrad's novel frames the dream by virtue of its being the video that the group is watching at the dream's opening, ordering the imagery of the continual return to Xander's basement, and now by Xander himself occupying the role of Martin Sheen's character on his way to discover Kurtz, here played by Armin Shimmerman, previously, of course, Principal Snyder.[17] It is noticeable that Snyder already has a relationship with *Apocalypse Now* due to his paraphrase of one of the film's most memorable lines, spoken by the character of Lieutenant Colonel Bill Kilgore, played by Robert Duvall. His "I love the smell of napalm in the morning" is translated by Principal Sny-der into "I love the smell of desperate librarian in the morning" in "Help-less" (3.12).

If we consider the full extent of involutional possibility and the mise en abyme into which we have potentially fallen, the episode's reach becomes extraordinary. We recognize the filmic allusion to *Apocalypse Now* and, therefore, also have the video version from the very opening of the episode (and therefore the "normal" Buffyverse), as well as the bad video version from the start of Xander's dream. By virtue of the real film, though, Marlon Brando and Martin Sheen will loom large in the palimpsest being created. These two actors could veer us off into any number of directions but even *The West Wing* for Sheen and *The Godfather* for Brando as texts will seep into this episode ("any text that has slept with another text has necessarily slept with all the other texts that text has slept with"[18]) and extend the emotional and hermeneutic reach considerably. Xander occupies a structural similarity with Willard and therefore with the actor who played him. But Xander is not Willard, he is Xander's dream image with all of the involutional possibility already seen there. Similarly, the person occupying the Kurtz role is not Kurtz (or Brando) rather he is an eidolon of Snyder — not Snyder himself — played by an actor who is best known for his portrayal of an alien in a different series. The fact that the Star Trek brand is so pervasive makes the connection almost impossible not to impose, especially as three years later, in one of Xander's most important episodes (if not his most important one), the already mentioned "Dirty Girls" (7.18), Faith's reintroduction via Andrew's montage has her fighting a Vulcan drawn directly (though clearly and funnily erroneously) from the Star Trek world. An accident of casting unites with a deep cultural knowledge to foreshadow a recursive involution between two episodes that have little narrative connection but intensely important character and emotional resonance.

While this may be true, it ignores the fact that the Kurtz played by Brando and then reproduced by Xander in the guise of Principal Snyder is not the Kurtz of Conrad's book. The figure of Kurtz is ever-mutating but nevertheless solidly fixed insofar as Coppola retained the name and emotional resonance as well as an aspect of his cultural critique, and Whedon retains the physicality and mise-en-scène such that there can be no ambiguity with regard to the significance of the power of the figure. Why, though, should *Heart of Darkness*, especially the name of Kurtz, figure so strongly? I have already addressed this briefly, but I want now to provide an extension of those ideas.

The Buffyverse, as I have mentioned throughout this book, is, in part, concerned with the consequences of the juxtaposition of a post–Enlightenment tradition with that of a pre–Enlightenment one. This can be articulated in an academic shorthand as discussion regarding modernity. Whether it is in relation to questions of identity and ethnicity, ethical choices, moral frameworks, narrative, history, or art (that is, questions of aesthetics and culture), *Buffy* presents us with complex responses to complex questions and, much to its credit, the responses are themselves multi-layered and often contradictory, or at least not uniform. A great many literary texts of the modernist period engage with similar questions. Indeed, one need only look at *The Waste Land, Ulysses* or *Mrs. Dalloway* to see modernity turned inside out, and it is clear that these texts can also be read alongside *Buffy* in its entirety or with individual episodes. Rhonda Wilcox has written an excellent essay "T.S. Eliot Comes to Television: *Buffy's* 'Restless'"[19] in which she draws out some of the structural and thematic linkages between Eliot's text and Whedon's. It is difficult to imagine a more perfect example of comparative media analysis. *Heart of Darkness* explicitly manifests a relation to modernity that is both aesthetically challenging and morally outraged from a political perspective, especially as to the question of what constitutes the human, and this, it seems to me, is part of its strength in the context of *Buffy* and especially of Xander as he is the only character who remains singularly human in the sense of having no obvious extra- or superhuman qualities. The notion of what exactly the human is in terms of the Buffyverse is still moot.

By the time of the publication of *Heart of Darkness*,[20] Conrad was already recognized as a writer of significance and innovation. His 1902 novella secured both of these reputations. Not yet furnished with a vocabulary to use for a text of this sort, many critics found it difficult to locate the work. A few years after its publication, Conrad wrote a letter to Richard Curle saying, "That, I suspect, has been the difficulty the critics felt in classifying it as romantic or realist."[21] Neither realist nor romantic, *Heart of Darkness* was not yet modernist either, although Eliot's famous use of "Mr. Kurtz — He dead" at the opening of "The Hollow Men,"[22] two years after the above letter, places it inevitably in the context of early modernism as well. Different from *Buffy*, then, but similar to it, Conrad's text somewhat stupefied critics and readers alike as it was neither generic enough to be one thing nor experimental enough to be another.

The bland desire to locate and reduce a text to a moment or a group is one that irked Conrad during his lifetime. Not only critics, but also writers, felt the scorn of Conrad if they succumbed to what he regarded as creative dishonesty:

> Liberty of imagination should be the most precious possession of a novelist. To try voluntarily to discover the fettering dogmas of some romantic, realist or naturalistic creed in the free work of its own inspiration, is a trick worthy of human perverseness which, after inventing an absurdity, endeavours to find for it a pedigree of distinguished ancestors. It is a weakness of inferior minds, when it is not the cunning device of those, uncertain of their talent, would see to add lustre to it by the authority of

a school. Such for instance are the high priests who have proclaimed Stendhal for a prophet of Naturalism. But Stendhal himself would have accepted no limitation of his freedom. Stendhal's mind was of the first order. His spirit above must be raging with a peculiarly Stendhalesque scorn and indignation. For the truth is that more than one kind of intellectual cowardice hides behind literary formulas. And Stendhal was preeminently courageous. He wrote his two great novels, which so few people have read, in a spirit of fearless liberty.[23]

It is difficult to imagine Joss Whedon expressing himself in such arch terms, but the generic malleability of *Buffy*, its constant efforts to elude categorization or stagnation all imply a similar sense of artistic freedom and discontent with dogma. In a different context, Jean-François Lyotard has attempted to suggest that postmodernism has something to do with writing outside of what might be considered preexisting, "safe" modes of discourse. Perhaps one of his most pithy descriptions is this one: "The artist and writer therefore work without rules, and in order to establish the rules for what *will have been made*."[24] In other words, only after the text has been finished can anyone try to decide what the rules of its composition were (the opposite of, as a crude example, genre fiction).

Heart of Darkness is the site of a violent disruption. Its generic volatility marks a literary expression of modernity's sense of crisis in a different but related way to *Buffy* itself. The tale is located in modernity by Marlow. The narrative of modernity in which he finds himself is one of colonial expansion: a narrative that promises us, the heirs of the Enlightenment, emancipation from ignorance and freedom for humanity. This idea is summarized by Lyotard in the following way:

> This idea (of freedom, "enlightenment," socialism, etc.) has legitimating value because it is universal. It guides every human reality. It gives modernity its characteristic mode: the project.[25]

The projects of this supposedly universal emancipation, whatever may have been the financial and military rewards, were often camouflaged in the foliage of philosophical justification, subtly sheltered in the rhetorics of redemption and holy salvation. Marlow's account opens with an appeal to this idea:

> The conquest of the earth, which mostly means taking it away from those who have a different complexion or slightly flatter noses than ourselves, is not a pretty thing when you look into it too much. What redeems it is the idea only. An idea at the back of it, not a sentimental pretence but an idea; and an unselfish belief in the idea — something you can set up, and bow down before, and offer sacrifice to....[26]

Marlow attempts to reclaim some benefit, some sense of worthiness, from the colonial project (an important aspect of the movement of modernity) by an insistence on the idea and a belief in the idea. The idea, powerful enough to produce supplication in its adherents, is left rather vague in terms of its specific promises and desires. However, it would seem reasonable to assume that the idea would include such notions as the spreading of western civilization in order to produce a shared commonwealth of all humanity, free and equal and laying claim to a universal and common justice: the putative narrative of modernity. This same narrative is one that *Buffy* constantly interrogates, though perhaps rather less radically than some commentators would like to assert.[27]

So, in response to the question about Marlow's relation to modernity, we have to recognize at least two options that the text supports. A reading of the previously quoted passage tends to falter between these options. The eulogizing, semi-devotional aspect of the language bespeaks a strength of faith in the idea that seems powerful and sincere, yet this strength is unable to sustain itself, is unable to allow the idea to reach fruition. The supplicant before the idea reaches a point of incapacity and the speech falters, falls away into the flabby instability of the ellipsis ("[...] offer sacrifice to ..."). The original narrator tells us starkly that "He broke off." Both belief in and doubt about the idea are seen.

Whatever else may have prompted Marlow's hesitation toward the idea, it is certainly the case that his confrontation with Kurtz has played a significant role. More especially, in this argument, it is Kurtz's writings as much as his actions that so disarm and disorient Marlow. If Kurtz, as he was before we see him, is in some ways representative of a type of Enlightenment benefactor, spreading wealth and civilization in equal measure, then the Kurtz we finally see appears to be an awful perversion of this, a horrific victim of some preternatural force. This is clearly different from Xander's Kurtz. Snyder was always a figure of ridicule or resentment for the other characters, though his position as high school principal does locate him structurally, if not emotionally or intellectually, in the domain of educational enlightenment, which is one of the obvious legacies of modernity.

Marlow's Kurtz occupies in his writing a classic colonialist position. His "Suppression of Savage Customs" betrays a particular mindset in its title, and the opening line is presented as if for assent from the reader: "By the simple exercise of our will we can exert a power for good practically unbounded."[28] The idea is here in all its power of benevolence: the expansion of Europe will lead to the spread of good across the globe. Underpinning this idea, however, there is another one, equally as strong and equally as important to modernity's eschatology and the colonial enterprise. This idea is that there is a "we" that is identifiable with a particular group (the colonizers), but which is theoretically capable of expanding to include all of humanity in its universal and universalizable progress. "We," however, implies a "them" who are not human, who fail to meet the requirements of what modernity determines the human to be. Marlow himself, despite his horror at the treatment of the natives, cannot escape this aspect of modernity's claim to shape how the world is seen. Describing the journey upriver and the things he saw, he mentions seeing the natives: "No, they were not inhuman. Well, you know the worst of it — this suspicion of their not being inhuman."[29] Snyder-as-Kurtz has no such qualms about his position in respect to the students over whom he has control, calling Xander a mongrel and "mulch," which echoes his comment in "The Puppet Show" (1.9) about the subhuman aspect of students. Involutionally, Buffy's eventual job as school counselor, a role that Snyder has been sneeringly referring to, begins in "Lessons" (7.1) and draws yet another strand in. This is compounded if we remember that the performance in the epilogue to "The Puppet Show" (1.9) has Xander, Willow and Buffy performing *Oedipus Tyrannus*, and the desire Xander feels for Buffy is there metatextually related to Freud's psychoanalytical-cum-counseling concept. A curious possibility of incest arises; a possibility tangentially offered in Buffy's calling Xander "big brother" in his dream. Snyder's concerns are, perhaps, less abstruse. Differentiating himself from the more liberally minded Principal Flutie, he observes to Giles:

> I know Principal Flutie would have said, "Kids need understanding. Kids are human beings." That's the kind of woolly-headed liberal thinking that leads to being eaten [1.9].

Snyder is emphatic about a hierarchy of being with humanity at its peak, and children clambering to aspire to *become* human, a position that is a clear heir of the paternalist colonial position as expressed by Conrad's Kurtz, where the natives were regarded as children. What is terrifying to Marlow is that the "we" of the human might have to include this thing that seems to be so alien, so Other.

Kurtz's document evidently assumes the possibility of this unity, of the natives suppressing their customs and adopting those of the colonizers as part of a first step toward homogeneity. However, despite its "magnificent peroration," its "exotic immensity ruled by august Benevolence," its "unbounded power of eloquence," Kurtz's writing cannot equal the task asked of it. Kurtz cannot overcome the failure of the "we." His, and by extension European modernity's, notion of a common, abstract, universal humanity cannot assimilate or integrate the natives. While Kurtz's document is not as explicit as my argument is claiming, the native peoples whom he encounters have sets of customs, arrangements of belief, conceptions of time, relations with the environment that are alien to those of the European colonizers. As, of course, were those of the indigenous peoples to the new Americans of the western expansion, as have been those of Jews and as are, though rather less problematically in many ways, those of vampires and demons. The chapter on ethnicity deals in large part with *Buffy*'s efforts to confront some of these continuing aspects of postcolonial life.

If the natives are to be regarded as human by Marlow it is not because they share these trappings of culture but rather because they are the primitive versions of what humanity will become. His account of them ("stripped of [their] cloak of time"[30]) allows them to be like "us" because "we" were once like them. Historicity promises that they will progress to where we are now, but in the meantime the deep core of nature (as might have been fantasized by Rousseau) is what provides Marlow with his allowance of sameness. This is a sameness that insists on difference, however: we are better (further along the narrative) than they are (this is much like Snyder's view of students).

For Kurtz, this alien nature is not negotiable, not exchangeable in some sort of cultural economy that would trade aspects of each for the other in an accumulation of human capital. The methods of appropriation and expropriation are not and cannot be commutable, unless by extreme measures. This level of irreducible otherness is not just a phrase easily ignored in favor of a more humane, more human, attempt at exchange.

Kurtz's attempt to represent the natives to himself, to produce an image, takes the form of his tract, which presents an image assimilable to the western imagination. However, the limit point of this method of representation occurs at the moment when the writer has to try to think beyond the representation, beyond the image, and to engage with the beings, the discrete identities, in front of him who do not necessarily abide by the same discursive strictures that the language of anthropological analysis might be thought to provide. In a clearly different but analogous way, Buffy's first realization of Angel as a specific individual, and not just a representative of a genus, allows her movement beyond the "demonological" generalizations (and casual moral allowance of the killing of the inhuman qua inhuman). Despite his most strenuous efforts, Kurtz is unable to turn the "non-we" of the "savages" into the "we" of colonial subjects, of the extended European family of modernity. There is only one course of action left open to him. In a scrawled note, apparently to himself, in the text of "The Suppression of Savage Customs," Kurtz has left the message of modernity to the "non-we" peoples it believed it was engaging with. He writes, simply, "Exterminate all the brutes!" The non-we are no longer allowed into the world of the we, of the human. Instead, their difference will be maintained by the reassertion of that other axis of modernity's endeavor: the insistent hierarchization of the West as the only true humans (and by virtue of that fact, the only humans per se), and the relegation of difference to being subhuman, to being brutes. The painfully easy nomination of "brute" leads effortlessly to the appeal to destruction, extermination. The Watchers' Council's edict to kill all vampires operates in a similarly brutal and obtuse fashion, and it is arguable that the Old World Council's confrontation with New World sensibilities precipitates a breach in its colonialist positioning, though it is far from clear that the seeming movement beyond modernity's models that this implies is at all true of other facets of Buffy or, indeed, *Buffy*.

Xander's Kurtz has none of the moral strength attributed to either Conrad's or Coppola's, and his attacks on Xander (wonderfully played with a sinister calm and deliberateness) only carry the force of the previous argument through their involutional circulations. But the involution is there, and the interstitial critique of modernity and colonization that seeps in provides Xander's dream with a political force that is deeply felt for being quietly expressed.

As Xander moves out of the dream-set of *Apocalypse Now* (though helicopter sounds continue) he enters Giles's house where he finds himself ignored by the gang, thereby returning us to "The Zeppo" (3.13) and "Nightmares" (1.10) as well as propelling us forward to episodes like "Dirty Girls" (7.18). The fabulous combination of entrances and exits from one location to the next is partly a consequence of the fact that soundstage three, where the episode was being filmed, is set up with all the interiors next to one another so it was simply a question of following Xander from one set to another and having the random dream-logic allow these spatial incongruities to make sense. To say "simply" is to massively underestimate the awkwardness of filming such a long sequence. The Steadicam operator and the actor have to be cued to perfection, and the choice of lens makes all the difference in terms of breadth and depth of vision. Whedon chose a 17 lens in order to show a wide-enough angle of vision without it turning into a "special effects dream shot" and in doing this was inspired by similar scenes from Kubrick's *Eyes Wide Shut*.[31] Whedon's admiration of Kubrick's work provides another involutional contact point, especially as Kubrick's *The Shining* is referenced by Jonathan in "Normal Again," (6.17) which, as has already been mentioned, was written by Diego Gutierrez, the man who does the voice-over for Giles's French in Xander's dream just before Xander is taken off to see Kurtz-Snyder. Jonathan's "I'm going all Jack Torrance here, you know" (6.17) is perhaps rather less in keeping with *The Shining*'s brooding terror than Xander's borrowing of a line when he is playing with the extremely disquieting (but, as it happens, down on the side of good) puppet Sid in "The Puppet Show" (1.9). Xander has him say "Red rum. Red rum," thereby offering a powerful allusion to Kubrick's work.

There are other intriguing involutional moments that derive from "The Puppet Show" (1.9). Cordelia's efforts in the talent show are blisteringly lacking. She chooses to sing "The Greatest Love of All" (written by Linda Creed and Michael Masser and made a huge hit by Whitney Houston in 1986). Six seasons, or over 127 episodes, later, and on a different show, she is being read by the empath Lorne and chooses this song to sing again ("Slouching Toward Bethlehem" [*AtS* 4.4]). Once again, the utter care and commitment to character and audience that the *Buffy* and *Angel* writers have is witnessed. The second involutional point is Buffy's embarrassed claim that she thinks Sid was in her room. So aware of the ridiculousness of the claim is she, that she tells everyone to look at her as though she were wearing a bunny suit. Three seasons later, in "Fear Itself" (4.4), Anya's foolishness and fear are represented by her wearing of a bunny costume. This fear is reprised in "Once More with Feeling" (6.7), "Tabula Rasa" (6.8) and "Selfless" (7.5). That Halfrek (Anya's vengeance demon friend in "Selfless") is the incarnation of Cecily, Spike's love object when he is William the bloody awful poet, who we see in "Fool for Love" (5.7), and that the poem he writes for her in that episode is the poem he reads before the final big battle in *Angel* ("Not Fade Away" [*AtS* 5.22]) provides another set of involutional, cross-series links. Additionally in "The Puppet Show" (1.9) Xander calls Willow "Red" (a term usually used by Faith or Spike), which acts as an involutional spur to Willow's change to the bad in "Seeing Red" (6.19) and Xander's eventual saving of Willow and the world in "Grave" (6.22). In this episode Willow forces Giles to unwillingly defy gravity by holding him on the ceiling with a spell, thereby bringing to ironic fruition Giles's comment in Xander's dream in "Restless" (4.22) that "a Watcher scoffs at gravity," said while he is on the swings next to deer-stalkered Spike, thus setting us off in the direction of "Tabula Rasa" (6.8) again.

Xander's final return to the basement has his father come down the stairs chastising him for upsetting his mother. The family catastrophe that is Xander's life has an impact throughout the series but the fact that his father's image asserts Xander's blame for his mother's tears is prophetic insofar as Xander's absconding before his wedding to Anya in "Hell's Bells" (6.16) does lead to his mother crying. This rather more literal-narrative use of involution brings us to the end of dream–Xander's journey, as his father mutates into the monster and rips out his heart, thus closing the dream. The dream itself is partly a metaphor for Xander's continuing efforts to find a role for himself in the Scooby Gang and in his life. These efforts afford the viewer narrative, symbolic and involutional hermeneutic journeys of their own, journeys that range across terrain as seemingly far apart as Xander's sexual fantasies and questions of the condition of contemporary modernity. The production strategies that allow such a comprehensive set of connotations once again remind us of the show's remarkable capacity to provide a visualization of the aesthetics of culture.

CHAPTER 8

Giles's Dream

"There's a great deal going on. And all at once"

Giles's dream opens in a fashion that is structurally dissimilar to Xander's whose is, in essence, a segue from Willow's dream to the extent that all the characters are back in the living room watching the videos. Willow's dream itself is contextualized by the living room, although hers begins elsewhere; and Buffy's has a brief shot of Buffy lying on the sofa in the living room before moving to the bedroom. Giles's is the only one that is absolutely divorced from the immediate context of the other dreamers. Not only are he and Buffy in his own, very bare, apartment, which has only a single chair on which Buffy sits, the opening fade locates the dream's beginning in an aesthetic that is clearly aged: the silent movies of the '20s and early '30s. This spatial and stylistic differentiation provides the visual key for the dream's general concerns, which include Giles's inner tension with regard to the life he has chosen (British Watcher working in the United States away from home and with little life outside of Buffy), set against other possibilities, most notably the possibility of a sexual partnership and the potential of children, though also the simple expression of his own sense of identity detached from his position as Watcher.

The opening shot of the watch swinging hypnotically across his chest locates his position as Watcher (through the visual pun on his title: "watch" = "Watcher") centrally in the dream but also invokes a broader conception of time that the style of the shot complements. Buffy laughs (apparently thanks to Joss Whedon's comedic exploits behind the camera[1]) and her happy but contorted face sets off an immediate involutional chain. Sarah

Michelle Gellar's willingness to have her notional beauty disfigured or mocked on the show is one of its strengths. There is never any sense that the characters will be safe or always seen in their best light. Whatever else the actors' contracts may offer or demand, they seemingly do not have a clause that protects their characters from various forms of ridicule. The two scenes that are most prominent in this respect come from "Who Are You?" (4.16) and "Life Serial" (6.5). In the former, Faith-in-Buffy is parodying Buffy's goodness, mock-rebuking herself for doing "wrong." All the while, still getting used to being in Buffy's body, she is contorting her face, prodding herself, stretching her cheeks, pulling at the sides of her eyes: she is using and deforming Buffy's physicality to augment her own sense of achievement at switching bodies, and Gellar performs the scene excellently. The notion of body switching is, of course, a staple of science fiction and has been used to great effect in series as diverse as *The X-Files* and *Star Trek*. It has been used before in *Buffy*, too, in "The Witch" (1.3) where Amy Madison is forced to switch bodies by her mother. Amy's long-enduring metamorphosis into a rat, initiated in "Gingerbread" (3.11), briefly reversed in "Something Blue" (4.9) and finally resolved to very bad ends in "Smashed" (6.9) is of a different order, though it does provide Amy with a unique point of contact with Buffy, who was also made into a rat by Amy during a love-spell-gone-wrong performed by Xander, with Amy's help, in "Bewitched, Bothered and Bewildered" (2.16).

The fact that at the opening of Giles's dream we are encouraged to read dream–Buffy's facial contortions in a way that returns us to Faith-in-Buffy indicates that the involutional journey (that can appear to be little more than a formal trick) is also thematically related to what will unfold in Giles's dream, which is a sense of duality predicated on duty (being the Watcher) superseding desire (wishing to have a life of his own). This, then allows us to move forward to the second involutional point of contact, which is Buffy's staggeringly funny drunk scene with Spike in "Life Serial" (6.5), where her tough-girl persona, exemplified by swigging Spike's whiskey straight from the bottle, produces a physiognomic reaction of utter disgust accompanied by a verbal sound best rendered as "blaaah" but wonderfully extended and played for full comic effect. Here, the duty-bound but confused Watcher's dream links through facial expression to an aspect of Buffy (in this case, desire — and the future expectation of desire through Spike) that complements his state. "Life Serial" (6.5) is also, of course, the episode in which the paternal Giles and the Watcher Giles coincide once again as he gives Buffy a check for $10,000 to help toward her financial plight.

In the dream, after the laugh from Buffy, we have a quick cut to a fun fair in which a childlike Buffy in pigtails is excitedly running to a game booth, followed by Giles and his sometime girlfriend, Olivia, who is pushing an empty pram. Whatever the potential symbolism of the empty pram, the appearance of Olivia produces two involutional trajectories. The first is to her first appearance, which was in "The Freshman" (4.1); the second was in "Hush" (4.10). "The Freshman" (4.1) clearly returns us to the start of this season and so provides a neat hermetic sense, which is true of both this episode and the season as a whole. Alongside this, though, the reference back to the first episode of this season pushes us beyond the confines of the 22 episodes both back and forth. Olivia calls Giles "Ripper," which, perhaps unintentionally, places her in the context of Giles's only other significant love interest, Jenny Calendar, whose own introduction to the Ripper side of Giles results in her being inhabited by the demon Eyghon in "The Dark Age" (2.8). Any allusion or reference to Jenny Calendar is always going to propel one to Jenny's death and, as a consequence of this, to her appearance as the First Evil in "Amends" (3.10), which will then take us to season 7 and all that happens there. It will also invite us to remember Drusilla's mesmerizing of Giles to make him believe that he is speaking to Jenny so that she, Angel and (so she thinks) Spike can perform the necessary ritual in "Becoming II" (2.22). Another foreshadowing that happens in "The Freshman" (4.1) is Joyce's death, when Buffy comments that the cost of all her books will shock her mother and she hopes it will be a "funny aneurysm," a desire that is cruelly undermined in "The Body" (5.16).

A notable feature of "The Freshman" (4.1) is that it is the first time that *Angel* airs immediately afterward as part of his spin-off series. The introduction of Riley Finn at this juncture as the man who will replace Angel as Buffy's boyfriend is also important. This becomes increasingly pronounced as the season progresses and is brought to a head, in terms of the discovery of each other's secret lives, in "Hush" (4.10), which is Olivia's only other appearance before her dream-image in "Restless" (4.22). "Hush" (4.10), apart from the Olivia presence, is also related to "Restless" (4.22) by virtue of the dream sequence that opens it. What is, in some senses, little more than a postadolescent sexual fantasy becomes prophetic when Buffy in the dream hears the nursery rhyme that introduces us, somewhat obliquely, to the horrifying presence of the Gentlemen of the episode. These monsters pay a huge debt to *Nosferatu*, which is itself another return to the Master of season 1. Other allusive aspects of the Gentlemen would take us to Mr. Burns from *The Simpsons* and also Pinhead from Clive Barker's *Hellraiser*. The score by Chris Beck owes a debt to Danny Elfman whose music has been used by, among others, the *Buffy* movie, to which he contributed the song "We Close Our Eyes," and by Tim Burton, whose cinematic style complements the curiously affecting, whimsical spookiness of Elfman's "Pogo" (postmodern gothic) musical sensibilities. The score also contributes to the visual appeal of the Gentlemen.

Olivia's eventual decision that Giles's life is too worrying for her to be a part of at the end of "Hush" (4.10) makes her appearance here a perfect choice in terms of the dream's theme of Giles's choices and regrets, and her presence makes these regrets more urgent and real by virtue of the involutional circulation she prompts. The questions pertaining to ideas of communication in "Hush" (4.10), exemplified by the requirements of paralinguistics after the removal of sound by the Gentlemen, is introduced in a number of ways.[2] Arguably the most memorable visual moment is Giles's lecture, given with a flip chart and a soundtrack. The flip chart has a variety of drawings of the Gentlemen and their actions and culminates in a sketch of Buffy, which she feels rather overemphasizes the size of her hips. Her earlier attempt to mime staking has been misconstrued by Xander as a sign of masturbation and the comedic value of the scene is remarkable. It has its own involutional aspect when it is reprised in season 7, though the graphic nature of Giles's drawings proves rather too much for the new Chinese arrival who is left traumatized and tearful ("Dirty Girls" [7.18]). This moment with the flipchart is wonderfully parodied by Andrew in "Storyteller" (7.16), where a whiteboard is used to describe the Über-vamps.

The soundtrack used by Giles in "Hush" (4.10) has a different sort of involutional momentum. The song played is Saint-Saëns' *Danse Macabre*. In itself this seems to be a perfectly good choice of music with the late Romantic gothic sensibilities working in perfect unison with the overall sensation produced by the Gentlemen. It is interesting, however, that the same music was used as the theme tune to the British comedy-drama-detective show *Jonathan Creek* for which Anthony Stewart Head was cast in the pilot as Jonathan's boss. Head did not take the role, coming back to the United States to film season 2 of *Buffy* but, of course, he finally returned to the United Kingdom during the filming of season 6. At this stage (season 6), Giles's sense of impotence after Buffy's death has clarified the concerns that are being expressed in his dream in "Restless" (4.22). He finally has the chance, if that is the correct term, to try and find a life for himself that is outside of the Council and away from his duties as a Watcher.

His departure from the show, and from the core of the Scoobies, is marked by an involutionally arresting event in the opening episode of season 6, "Bargaining I" (6.1), where, at one point, Willow returns to the Magic Box after collecting ingredients for a spell. Xander, Tara and Anya are there waiting for her return and they eventually cast a spell to revive Buffy who had died at the end of season 5. Anya discovers a note from Giles saying that he is leaving Sunnydale, and the group, along with Dawn, rush to the airport to see him off, with a banner and some presents. One of the presents is a small finger-monster that Tara gives to Giles accompanied by a little "grr arrgh" noise.

Willow's return to the Magic Box[3] that begins the sequence is preceded by her killing a deer as part of a spell. The allusion to *Bambi* is inescapable as is the sense of lost innocence, which is derived both from the Disney film and from the lack of sentimentality here as opposed to Willow's horror at the thought that horses might get hurt in a deadly chase in "Spiral" (5.20). The unsentimental pragmatism of Willow is, in part, a necessary character development and is, therefore, part of the simple economy of a linear-sequential narrative. It also, however, acts in an involutional way. It does this partly through the introjection of *Bambi* into the storyscape of the show with all the attendant cultural extrapolations and personal nightmares that this might invoke (which themselves extend beyond the film to a host of *Bambi*-centered productions such as the Sex Pistols' "Who Killed Bambi," a reference that, though not obvious or immediate, curls back into *Buffy* via the figure of Spike and his punk demeanor). It also does it by the foreshortening of Willow's character. We are forced to see the change not only from the "don't hurt the horsies" Willow of "Spiral" (5.20) but also from Willow's character as a version of "Welcome to the Hellmouth" (1.1) Willow and all the ones in between. These include, of course, Vamp Willow of "The Wish" (3.9) and "Doppelgangland" (3.16), which foreshadows the Willow who will unravel throughout season 6 as well as teasingly indicates Willow's later sexuality. This is not just a case of character development (Vamp Willow is, after all, a different character); rather, it is an involutional moment of the same sign being inhabited by a superabundance of signification that is in excess of the simple narrative requirements. This superabundance makes the involution monstrous as the sign of "Willow" is interpenetrated by competing, even contradictory, signifying practices and discursive regimes. The extent to which *Buffy* is not only a show that deals in monsters but also actively seeks an aesthetic that is itself monstrous is one of the many facets of its ever-astounding aesthetic engagement in cultural practices.

Similar examples of the monstrous aesthetics of involution just in this two-and-a-half-minute section include, though are far from being limited to, the following. The chiming of the bell above the door of the Magic Box is an aural sign of entry and is; a sign repeated numerous times in seasons 5 and 6, most notably in "Life Serial" (6.5),[4] which is *Buffy*'s pastiche of *Groundhog Day*. It also acts as the sound signal for Spike's dramatic and frantically funny entrance in his deer-stalker hat and tweeds in "Tabula Rasa" (6.8), a tragic and comic episode that is called to mind here and that itself, as has been mentioned, offers intratextual threads back to "Restless" (4.22). The fact that each one of these episodes branches off themselves in an equally astonishing, self-referential, recontextualizing, narrative foreshortening, raised-to-the-power-of, cumulative number of ways is simply one example of its aesthetics of involution.

Xander's question about "*vino de madre*" in "Bargaining I" (6.1) offers another set of ways of thinking about *Buffy* and the program's own reflections upon itself. Here, the translation as "blood of the mother" returns us back to *Bambi* in a darkly ironic fashion (and, arguably the entire Disney oeuvre, franchise and cultural impact — McCarthy *witch*-hunt and all). It also simultaneously invokes Buffy's mother and potentially even Buffy herself. Also, the program's constant use of, and games with languages (commonplace, slang, archaic, made-up) is here manifest.[5] One phrase is itself monstrous to the extent that it interpenetrates and pollutes intra- and extratextual references, thus creating an involuted relation of excess.

Willow's comment about "kinda black market stuff" foreshadows her growing addiction to and misuse of magic in this series (and the rather blunt and dull drugs allegory that went along with this), which culminates in her murder of Warren in "Villains" (6.20) and her eventual recuperation back with Giles in England ("Lessons" [7.1]). It also introduces, if obliquely, the season's growing interest in the financial lives of the characters and the season ends up with Buffy's job at the Doublemeat Palace. Anya's capacity to be calmed through money reminds us of her eulogizing of capitalism and the American way ("Tough Love" [5.19]) and acts as a funny critique and artful celebration of capitalism and the American way, which is a point that I shall return to shortly. Also, it evokes (once again) Arthur Miller's *Death of a Salesman*, which, of course, finds its own surreal take on America being made more surreal in Willow's dream in "Restless" (4.22).[6]

The fact that Xander, Willow, Anya and Tara are sitting in the Magic Box while Xander shuffles a deck of cards and Tara says "better we stay together" presents an allusion to "Primeval" (4.21) where Willow has the cards and the togetherness is an effort to forge a Slayer from each of their attributes (though Tara, of course, is absent then). Here, as we discover, there is a similar effort to forge (or revivify) a Slayer from their combined talents. The difference here is that Giles is being excluded and the magic is dark, thus allowing both retrospective connection and prospective difference. A different version of this level of interconnectedness and involuted circulation comes from Tara's remark that she does not have butterflies in her stomach but "bats." The irresistible (if not very funny) pun on vampire bats is one that Xander does not give in to, having already used it in "Out of Mind, Out of Sight" (1.11), the penultimate episode of season 1, which finds its ghostly comic reprise in "The Storyteller" (7.16) where the girl who is about to disappear is slapped around the face by Buffy.

At the airport we see the typically British Giles, wonderfully described by Howard Hampton as "wearing his English reserve as a coat of armor against his own pagan nature."[7] The gift giving plays, once again, with the delightful juxtapositions between Britain and America and, also, the variegations of Britishness with which the show has operated. But, finally, we get to Tara's "grr argh" puppet show. On the one hand this is just a moving and amusing goodbye present that is both a warm farewell and a bathetic gesture toward Giles and the program. On the other hand, though, it is an unexpected transposition of a paratext into the main text. The paratext is, we know, the logo for Mutant Enemy, the production company responsible for making *Buffy*. This logo is, moreover, a trademark, a sign of legal ownership. Tara's present then operates as an aspect of the narrative but also forces the discourses of U.S. law and property into the show in a relation of monstrous involution. The fact that this episode was the first one aired on the UPN network after *Buffy*'s move from the WB could indicate that the show's makers were keen to assert their ownership of the show for any new viewers.[8] By so clearly imposing their trademark into the show at a moment of intense emotional impact, this is achieved. It is achieved, once again, by the show's continued adherence to an aesthetic of involution. By interpenetrating the fictional world of the show and the legal-discursive world of the production company the barriers between the fictional and the real become, however briefly, warped. This is similar to the introjection of authors into their work as in Julian Barnes's appearance in *A History of the World in 10½ Chapters*[9] or Paul Auster in *New York Trilogy*,[10] but there is a substantial difference. For a start, a production company is not an author and the legal relationships between author and text and production company and text operate in different ways. The mention of Marti Noxon's or David Fury's name in the episode would have drawn the author into the text in a very different way than the Mutant Enemy logo. In part this is because of the way that Joss Whedon *is* Mutant Enemy for many *Buffy* fans.[11] While he is the creator of the show and, of course, the film, Joss Whedon is not its author (at least not always). Or if he is, then he is in a way very different from how we conceptualize the author of a literary fiction. Tara's "grr argh" brings into play all of these questions and relationships.

Of course, the clashing of the text and its paratexts via the logo is something that *Buffy* has already played with. To that extent, Tara's gift not only swells the monstrous by virtue of the superimposition of the real onto the fictional, creating something that is both and neither, but it is also a perfect example of involution. The monster on her finger and her little monster-voice bring to mind the trademark, which by implication carries the discourses of ownership, law, authorship and so on. It also acts as an involuted point of contact between this and other episodes where the show has impinged on the logo (rather than paratext infiltrating text, text has bled out onto paratext). Examples of this would include the logo wearing a little graduation cap at the end of "Graduation Day Part II" (3.22). This episode also has the reference by dream–Faith to 7–3–0, creating one further inter-, intra- and paratextual circulation of involutional possibilities. Previously in season 3, the show airing just pre–Christmas, "Amends" (3.10), the logo ends with wearing a little Santa cap. This episode has a curious prospective importance as it is the episode in which the First Evil is presented, the entity that causes such damage and eventually destroys Sunnydale in season 7. The episode's witty but important insistence through Xander of the commercialization of Christmas provides an interesting tension with the seeming commercialization (or, at least, emphatic product placement) in "Bargaining I" (6.1). A very sweet logo change occurred at the end of season 2's finale episode, "Becoming II" (2.22) where the trauma of the episode leads the logo to forego its usual "grr arrgh" in favor of "oooh, I need a hug." Here the paratext acts almost as a commentary on the main text. And, again, in "Once More with Feeling" (6.7) the logo sings at the end. After Andrew's extraordinary performance as the storyteller (7.16), with his and the rest of the geeks' appearances as deeply silly and very colorful pastoral gods frolicking and singing "we are gods," the logo at the end of the episode sings "We are as gods," though whether as sincere expression of greatness or ironic commentary is difficult to discern. The logo at the close of "Chosen" (7.22) turns to the audience and takes a bow, much like a conductor at the end of a concert: the auteur mutely receiving the applause of the worldwide audience.

Buffy in Giles's dream in "Restless" (involution will always lead you back, if you want it to) can only hope for his applause or approbation, and it is not forthcoming. She throws a big yellow balloon at a puppet vampire but from Giles there will be "no treats" (4.22). She buys herself some cotton candy and it covers her face in a fashion that prefigures her curious makeup in her own dream but which also prompts a dual recognition form Giles, played out over some more misdubbing. He asserts "I know you" twice. This refers in part to his growing awareness about the First Slayer but also implies a recognition of what Buffy is destined to be as a fully fledged Slayer. As we discover in Buffy's dream and have iterated in "Buffy versus Dracula" (5.1), there is a lot more about Buffy's role that she has to learn. It seems that this will lead her more and more to alienation, loneliness and a simple sense of killing. However, Giles's dawning understanding as expressed through his "I know you" comment, which implies his comprehension of her singularity and its burden, is undermined in the series climax "Chosen" (7.22). Here, the sense of the Slayer as alone is radically reoriented. Giles's understanding then, is somewhat askew — a state of affairs that is evident throughout his dream. Although he seems determined, he also lacks a certain direction.

He is prepared in his dream-state to tell Olivia to keep out of his business, which is "the blood of the lamb" but he is also busy — "I have a great deal to do" — a state of affairs made clear later in the section in the Bronze where he discovers that "there's a great deal going on. And all at once." His confusion, both personal and intellectual, is manifested stylistically in the crypt through the wonderful use of visual irony. The world of the film is divided quite clearly into black and white, but Giles's moral and emotional world is far less easily dichotomized.

Spike, in his black and white section (itself a stylistic reminder of the dream's silent movie-esque opening shot), is only, according to Giles, a "sideshow freak." His filmic representation in black and white and his character's presentation of iconic poses allow the sense of an easily comprehended moral universe where ethical choices are either/or, and character is reduced to simplistic and simplified posturing. However, Spike, albeit unwillingly, is a member of the team. His danger is neutered but his actions (as seen in "The Yoko Factor" [4.19]) can still lead to difficulty for the Scoobies. Spike cannot be just an evil vampire, though he is still that; nor can he be just a member of the group, though he is that too. The seemingly straightforward iconographic simplification of Spike here acts, in fact, as a marvelously weighted visual juxtaposition to his increasingly complex and subtle modulations in terms of ethical analysis and emotional inclusion; this nexus of concerns will deepen over the next three seasons.[12] It is, curiously, Spike in the dream who offers Giles the point of it all — "You've got to make your mind up, Rupes" — but his monochromatic simplicity is countermanded by some of the poses he strikes. The flamboyant crucifix he makes at the end of his stint for the cameras is clearly reminiscent of a whole slew of Christian iconography, but this also impels us to read his development as a growing hero-figure, which will be made manifest in season 7, especially and, emotionally resonantly, in "Beneath You" (7.2). Here, after a vicious fight with Buffy, the newly ensouled, clearly mad,

Spike, seeking redemption and love falls exhausted onto a large crucifix, over which he drapes himself as his body burns and he pleads, quietly, to Buffy, "Can we rest now? Buffy, can we rest?" (7.2).[13] The Big Bad of season 2, the irritation of season 4, the failed rescuer of season 5, the sadomasochistic lover of season 6, is here a shell, emptied of his energy and power. The black and white evil-doer of the '20s movies, with which Giles's dream stylistically opens, gives visual and proleptic counterweight to Giles's lie to Buffy in "Lie to Me" (2.7):

> The good guys are always stalwart and true, the bad guys are easily distinguished by their pointy horns or black hats, and, uh, we always defeat them and save the day. No one ever dies, and everybody lives happily ever after [2.7].

That Spike should have his katabatic journey *after* he gets his soul,[14] and that a vampire should assume the role of savior expresses a marvelously subversive relationship with Christianity, yet one that nevertheless adopts its narrative structures. The morally ambiguous nature of Giles is also alluded to in a foreshadowing when he says to Spike, "I still think Buffy should have killed you," which is a sentiment he acts upon three seasons later in "Lies My Parents Told Me" (7.17). The title of the episode has clear implications for "Restless" (4.22). Giles's sense of surrogate fatherhood toward Buffy (complicated by his role as teacher and Watcher) is an integral part of this dream and his whole relationship with her. It comes to an end after he joins with Principal Wood in an effort to kill Spike. Buffy calmly tells Giles, "No. I think you've taught me everything I need to know" (7.17). The young girl of Giles's dream has grown up and away from him, and it is he and not she who is alone.

Giles's moral ambiguity, which is alluded to in the dream via the visual ironization of black and white, is also evident in "The Gift" (5.22). Having formed attachments to Ben who, we have discovered, is the human in whom Glory, the mad god and Big Bad of the season, has decided to live, Buffy is unable to kill him when the opportunity arises. Giles, despite the fact of Ben being human and largely innocent of Glory's crimes, chooses to kill him:

> GILES: Can you move?
> BEN: Need a ... a minute. She could've killed me.
> GILES: No she couldn't. Never. And sooner or later Glory will re-emerge, and ... make Buffy pay for that mercy. And the world with her. Buffy even knows that ... and still she couldn't take a human life. She's a hero, you see. She's not like us.

> BEN: Us?
> (Giles suffocates Ben.) [5.22].

This murder is necessary for purely utilitarian reasons: if Glory comes back, she will wreak vengeance on Buffy and the whole battle will have to be fought again. Also, though, it is necessary to protect the integrity of Buffy whose self-imposed moral structures (unlike Faith) will not allow her to kill a human, whatever the necessity. Once again, Giles's moral position is different from many of the rest of the characters, and once again we see the extent to which the easy dichotomies already refused in *Buffy* become incomparably more awkward when faced by Giles.[15]

    The moral questions for Giles (what his life ought to have been, what to do with the life he has, what his future life ought to be — all framed as moral problems as much as, if not more than, psychological ones) are involutionally magnified via the startling stylistic choices in this part of his dream. Spike's positioning in the stark world of black and white also has repercussions for him, one of which also relates to "The Gift" (5.22). After Buffy sacrifices herself to save Dawn, the shot of Spike collapsing in a distraught heap at the foot of the tower from which she has jumped illustrates the genuine sense of grief he feels, a grief that testifies to the growth he has undergone. Once Buffy is revived in "Bargaining I and II" (6.1 and 6.2) it is a responsible, penitent Spike whom she encounters, one whose notion of making a promise, and of having failed to keep that promise, is a torture:

> But I want you to know I did save you. Not when it counted, of course, but ... after that. Every night after that. I'd see it all again ... do something different. Faster or more clever, you know? Dozens of times, lots of different ways ... Every night I save you [6.3].

We have already seen the potential of Spike to act self-sacrificingly in "Intervention" (5.18) where he endures all of Glory's homicidal and sadistic tortures in order to protect Dawn's secret that she is the Key. Having nothing to gain, and believing the person to whom he is speaking to be the Buffybot, he is simple and honest in his declaration of good faith. Giles's dream offers an eidolon whose capacity for dissimulation means that Giles can have him affecting the iconographic representation of sacrifice and faithfulness, but Spike himself is able to move beyond the simulacrum to the truth of what those words mean. As Buffy puts it in "Intervention" (5.18), "What you did for Dawn and me, that was real," which is also a comment reflecting back on Spike's relationship with the unreal Buffybot.[16] This relationship gets significantly reprised itself in season 6, but the comment here also represents a reflection on duality and doubleness. Spike may well be like a son to the Giles within Xander's dream, but he is also an inverted double of Angel and these two curious alignments with supposedly good characters produce an even greater sense of moral ambivalence in the show, one that Giles himself is representing in his dream.

As he passes through the crypt into the Bronze, the sense of Giles's personal dilemma becomes even more apparent. He is in an environment that we know from "Welcome to the Hellmouth" (1.1) he finds odious at best, and yet in his dream it is the space in which he is most capable of engaging with those he needs to. The presence of Xander and Willow at the Bronze in his dream is curious. They are both sporting the wounds they have suffered from the First Slayer, and yet they are articulate and seemingly safe. It is unlikely that they are actually in Giles's dream as themselves as neither mentions it, so one would have to assume that Giles has somehow intuited their danger as he sleeps in the living room and has, then, introduced them unwittingly.

This strange interpolation of them into his dream is presumably one of the many things that is going on all at once. Xander's unusually literal unpicking of his metaphor that he will soon be pushing up daisies indicates the extreme difference of Giles from him: Xander is able, even in his terminal state, to understand the significance of things, however brutally banal that understanding might be; Giles is striving toward an answer but is surrounded by too much detail, which he is incapable of fully deciphering. Behind him, Anya is beginning her joke. The joke, which we never fully hear, operates in two distinct ways. On the one hand, the very precise manner of Anya's conclusion and her explanation of where the humor resides is another example of clear comprehension (even if we, like Giles, are left somewhat baffled). On the other, the joke being pared down and opened up as it is, with each aspect being described and then presented ("Wait, there's, there's a duck"; "See, it was the duck, and not the man, who spoke"), is an exercise in formal analysis of sorts. By being asked to engage so actively not only in the joke's enunciation but also in its structure and the formal qualities of its exposition, the audience in the Bronze and the audience watching the episode are reminded of both the hermeneutic difficulty of the episode and the episode's formal inventiveness.[17] This almost anti-humor is one of Anya's most lovable attributes and is excellently played with in "Selfless" (7.5). While still Aud, the eighth-century Nordic wife of Olaf, Anya is approached by the vengeance demon D'Hoffryn and she explains her plight to him. Explaining that she is regarded as odd (and the pun on her names is just one more small example of the show's enduring delight) she says that people do not talk to her, "Except to say that your questions are irksome, and perhaps you should take your furs and your literal interpretations to the other side of the river" (7.7).

Anya's joke plays out against Giles's confusion and Willow's leveling of blame. She, like Spike, tells Giles he has to focus. Her rebuking of him, in a manner familiar to *Buffy* fans because it is how he has often spoken to Buffy, is perfectly timed to happen just seconds before one of the great moments of self-ironic writing on any television show. From the moment in the very first episode where he lectures Buffy on who she is, Giles has always been the exposition character. It is a testament to the writers and the actor that he never became dull while doing it (unlike Buffy herself in season 7 whose lectures to the static potentials very quickly degenerated into tedium, and required Jane Espenson to parody them in "Storyteller" [7.16]).[18] Giles has always been capable of explaining the monsters and threats without irritating the audience.[19] The opportunity to celebrate this by having him sing the exposition here was a master stroke. It is also an ingenious compression of the dream's theme into a single moment. Here, the involution (that is, the circulation of a number of different intensities through a single sign) happens within the structure of the episode itself. Giles's singing of the exposition elides the Watcher Giles and the independent Giles such that both are able to occupy one position, though that position is fraught.

Giles's singing inevitably has an involutional lead to "Once More with Feeling" (6.7), but before that, there are other directions in which this section can take us. It is music, more than anything else, that has been used as a sign of the other, independent, Giles. As S. Renee Dechert puts it, "[P]erhaps no character is more clearly defined (and developed) via music than Giles."[20] Despite assuming an air of aged disquiet in the Bronze in (1.1), Giles is clearly a fan of music and a number of references and episodes toy with this part of his personality.

The first instance where his love of music is clearly identified, and this is explicitly located as an aspect of a very different Giles from the one we have come to know, is "Band Candy" (3.6). In this episode, which features the wonderful character of Ethan Rayne, who is also present in "Halloween" (2.6), "The Dark Age" (2.8) and "A New Man" (4.12), the adults of Sunnydale are returned to a teenaged state after eating candy. Giles reverts to his pre–Watcher persona, all attitude and violence, replete with a more common accent and a vicious edge. The character as played by Anthony Stewart Head bears a passing resemblance to another thuggish character, interestingly called Rupert, in *A Prayer for the Dying*, a film produced in 1987 and directed by Mike Hodges, and also played by Anthony Stuart Head who appears to have partly reprised him in "Band Candy" (3.6). Here, the context is far removed from the terrorism of the mid–1980s IRA, though still particularly unpleasant (there is an attempt to harvest all the babies from a local maternity wing), and Giles, or Ripper as his character at this point should more properly be called, is unable to solve the problem. Instead he has a brief, but carnal, affair with Joyce, Buffy's mother, and Joyce commends his record collection. We see the pair of them listening, as only teenagers brought up in the age of vinyl could, to Cream's "Tales of Brave Ulysses." The choice of song is intriguing as its obvious antecedent shows the journey of Odysseus and the concurrent maturation of Tele-mechus, and it is tempting to see that coupling concertinaed into the character of Giles, with the episode offering an attenuated (and oddly reversed) coming-of-age tale.

The song appears again, in very different circumstances, in "Forever" (5.17), the episode after Joyce's death in "The Body" (5.16). "The Body" itself references "Band Candy" (3.6) in the teaser where all the gang and Joyce are having a lovely meal, and Joyce and Giles are contemplating drinking more wine, to which Buffy mockingly responds that she is happy so long as they stay away from the band candy. This itself is not just a reference to that episode but also to "Earshot" (3.18) where Buffy, as part of her unwished-for telepathic powers, overthinks her mother remembering her tryst with Giles. Buffy is significantly unimpressed. In "Forever" (5.17), Giles stands next to the record player, glass of wine in hand and desolately mourns Joyce to the song that had been theirs for a small period.

Giles's love of music is, then, placed in a discursive regime that is exceptional to the rest of his life and is bound up with other questions of desire and sexuality, or else to aspects of his personality that have been subdued by his being the Watcher. The discovery by Giles of Jenny Calendar's death is played out against the backdrop of *La Bohème*, so that the interrelationship of music, sexuality and thwarted aspirations are all linked.[21] "The Freshman" (4.1), which is the first episode in which Giles is not only not the Watcher but has also lost his job as librarian due to the destruction of the school, has Buffy entering his home. In the background is playing David Bowie's magisterial song "Memory of a Free Festival." Again the choice of music is instructive. First, it indicates strongly Giles's preference for late 1960s and early 1970s intelligent rock. Second, David Bowie as an icon of the refusal to be aesthetically reduced to a single genre or even medium is something that has obvious connections with Joss Whedon and the artistic decisions he chooses to make. Thirdly, the song, from 1969, has a resonance for Giles insofar as it is likely to be near to the time of his youth, and is a song that, itself, is a celebration but also a mourning for a time passed (even though the time was simply the previous summer). The song, not unusually for Bowie, is also a yoking together of music and sexuality; the lyric that refers to kissing "a lot of people that day" is in part an homage to a general notion of love but also has clear implications for an innocent promiscuity, a promiscuity that *Buffy* is happy to undertake textually. As it plays, Buffy sees not Giles but Olivia. She is evidently there for reasons other than simply conversation and is unabashed about it being so. Buffy is less sanguine, and Giles is embarrassed. Buffy is revolted — "you're very, very old and it's gross" — but Giles's point is not so much about his sexuality per se and more about his not being allowed a "private life" (4.22). The appearance of Olivia in his dream as an emblem not just of the wish for that life but of the specific role that Buffy has had in denying him that is beautifully set up here.

Once again, though, it is music that acts as the dominant sign for the context of Giles's life separate from the rest of the Scooby Gang. This separateness is made a little less distinct in "The Harsh Light of Day" (4.3), during which Oz, like Joyce before him, displays significant thrill at Giles's record collection. Oz is not typically given to outbursts of emotion, a trait wonderfully captured in the *Angel* episode "In the Dark" (*AtS* 1.3) when Oz goes to L.A. to give Angel the ring of Amara. Their first meeting, in front of Cordelia and Doyle, is this:

> ANGEL: Oz.
> OZ: Hey.
> ANGEL: Nice surprise.
> OZ: Thanks.
> ANGEL: Staying long?
> OZ: Few days.
> DOYLE: Are they always like this?
> OZ: No, we're usually laconic [*AtS* 1.3].

Contrast that with his almost ebullient comment to Giles after seeing his collection: "OK, either I'm borrowing all your albums, or I'm moving in" (4.3). One of the things that has acted as a sign of Giles's private life is now the object of Oz's admiration. The record that he holds up as a particularly excellent one is The Velvet Underground's *Loaded*, which takes us back to David Bowie (as I'm sure both Giles and the writer Jane Espenson are aware) not only because Bowie was a huge fan of the group and got Lou Reed his first appearance in the United Kingdom and produced Reed's 1973 masterpiece *Transformer* but also because Bowie played the group's manager and artistic mentor, Andy Warhol, in the 1996 film *Basquiat*, directed by Julian Schnabel. Nothing comes of this potential crossing-over of Giles's private life into the domain of the rest of the Scoobies, and he actively tries to insist on the maintenance of this distance in "Where the Wild Things Are" (4.18). This episode sees Giles declining an invitation to a party because he has a "meeting of grown ups" that "couldn't possibly be of interest to you lot" at the Espresso Pump coffee house. His determination to keep a section of his life free from involvement with Buffy and her friends, which comes to its emotional climax in "Restless" (4.22) and thence is actualized in "Bargaining I" (6.1) is here clearly articulated.

It transpires that, once again, it is music that is the specific activity that contextualizes this distance. Unable to rescue Buffy from her marathon and deadly sex session with Riley, and in need of Giles's help, Willow, Anya, Xander and Tara go to the Espresso Pump and we see a look of comic brilliance on Willow's face as she disbelievingly watches Giles performing on guitar and singing. Her comment that she remembers why she had a crush on him is beyond Xander's capacity to understand, which is another (if only trifling and silly) expression of the group's general refusal to allow Giles a life that is not rigidly demarcated within the preestablished discourses of Watcher-Librarian-Mentor-Guide.[22]

The song that Giles sings is The Who's "Behind Blue Eyes." What becomes clear to anyone who did not know it is that Anthony Stewart Head is a very good singer. His role as Frank N. Furter in *The Rocky Horror Picture Show*, the Richard O'Brien musical, which he performed in 1990 and 1995, is regarded very highly by aficionados of that show, and his own recording career has been irregularly successful, with his collaborative album, *Music For Elevators* (2001 with George Sarah) being a big Internet sales success. (Buffy's caustic enjoinder to "do the Time Warp again" in the previously mentioned "Band Candy" [3.6] where Giles's record collection is first introduced, is a delightful little in-joke-cum-involutional-thread from writer Jane Espenson.) The bringing into the world of *Buffy* the talents of the actor, which will be known to a large portion of the audience, is another example of the show's involutional strategies. The parody-gothic horror of *Rocky Horror* has a tone more akin to *Buffy* the movie than the television series, but the link is still there, especially with Stewart Head's involvement with both. The particular brand of transgressive sexuality that is celebrated in the musical also has its own expression in *Buffy*, especially in season 6's sadomasochistic relationship between Buffy and Spike, which results in Spike's sleeping with Anya, an event that is loosely foreshadowed in "Where the Wild Things Are" (4.18) when Spike and Anya comfort each other's wounded pride with drink.

Unaware, of course, of what is to come, Giles is singing a song by The Who. The song is open to interpretation in and of itself, but it is of note that, after a couple of lines have been talked over by the gang, we return to him as he sings "But my dreams, they aren't as empty as my conscience seems to be"; the proleptic shift to "Restless" (4.22) seems unavoidable. The evocative quality of Head's voice lends a poignancy to the lyrics that serve then as a reflection on the episode's partial concern with his seeming effort to find a role for himself. We have yet to see the full extent of the emptiness that the gradual splintering of the group leaves Giles feeling (and the various sorts of manifestations of this, which include guilt, or "conscience") but it is brought home drastically in "The Yoko Factor" (4.20).

In an episode whose entire theme is written beneath the title of one of music's most famous antagonisms,[23] it is not perhaps surprising to find the character most evidently located within the discourse of music as an expression of self[24] being goaded into suspicion immediately after a musical moment that I shall explain presently, especially one that is deeply moving. We have a shot of Giles sitting in his house, playing guitar and singing Lynyrd Skynyrd's 1973 masterpiece "Freebird." As we move from the exterior to the interior (from a public space to a private one), Giles sings the opening of the song.

At this point he is interrupted by Spike, an event of such apparent shock to Giles that he screeches very high (pre-echoing Spike's similar noise as he falls off the counter in "Tabula Rasa" [6.8]), and Spike is then able to subtly play on Giles's sense of his superfluity to the group, especially to Buffy. The song here acts in a much more overt way than "Behind Blue Eyes" as a commentary on Giles by Giles. His resignation and desire for departure expressed, by virtue of the song, almost as a lover's lament to Buffy is deeply affecting and once again unites the complex emotions that relate to his uncertainty about his role within the context of music.

This uncertainty, which marks the tenor of his dream, is beautifully weighted in his exposition song in "Restless" (4.22), from which and to which most of the instances mentioned above will circulate. They will also, of course, circulate to "Once More with Feeling" (6.7), the eagerly awaited, massively enjoyed and subsequently favorite episode of many a *Buffy* fan. In relation to Giles, it is again the sense of his need to leave that is paramount. Not that he feels excluded from the group necessarily, but he believes that Buffy's recuperation will be hindered by his continuing presence and her reliance on him. This was a necessary plot development as Stewart Head had obligations in the United Kingdom that meant that he could no longer act as a regular on the show. Not only the Scoobies but also the audience and the writers felt his absence keenly and his departure signals a shift in the dynamic of the group and the program that was rarely for the better.[25]

The involutional drift from "Restless" (4.22) to "Once More with Feeling" (6.7) is not only signaled through Giles's song, but Giles's comments in Willow's dream concerning *Death of a Salesman* and his injunction to have "energy, energy, energy, especially in the musical numbers" also leads inevitably forward to season 6, episode 7. Apart from the fact that this episode is a musical and, therefore, achieves the monumental feat of translating one of the most expensive and production-heavy genres from cinema onto the small screen, there are a number of important plot features: Tara discovers Willow's memory spell, thus instigating their breakup, and the subsequently horrifying storyline for Willow; the group learn that Buffy was in a heavenly dimension and not in hell at all; Spike and Buffy kiss; and Giles determines to leave for England.[26]

Everything about this episode is exceptional, even to the time it ran, which was nearly eight minutes longer than a usual *Buffy* episode, much, as it transpires, to Whedon's ire as he had not wanted it to be unique in that fashion.[27] The network advertised it more heavily than usual and it was the first and (at the time of writing) only episode to have its own DVD release and script book to itself.[28] It is also the only episode of season 6 that Joss Whedon wrote or directed, and he did both, with the music written by himself and the show's major composer Christophe Beck, who plays the piano in Giles's singing exposition in "Restless" (4.22). Whedon was also busy with *Angel* and *Firefly*, which makes season 6 unique as no other season has fewer credited contributions from the executive producer. Its self-referentiality and range of external homages and pastiches are remarkable, so much so in fact that *Time* voted the episode one of the top ten TV highlights of 2001.

The clearest and most obvious involutional moment with regard to Giles's singing is the first group song, which begins with Giles offering yet another exposition in "I've got a theory" but quickly dispels his thoughts (with a facial gesture and verbal exhalation that reminds us of Buffy in "Life Serial" [6.5]) as others offer their ideas, ideas that circle back to "Nightmares" (1.10), when Willow sings of some kid dreaming "and we're all stuck inside his wacky Broadway nightmare" (accompanied by a tiny, unwilling and prefect little flapper-style hand movement), and "Fear Itself" (4.4), when Anya iterates her fear of bunnies. His next song is the most compelling in terms of his realization that he has to leave Buffy to face her future. It alludes, lyrically, to Giles's speech at the end of "Lie to Me" (2.7) in which Giles has presented the generic stereotypes of good and evil and the aesthetic qualities inherent to both. He typifies the good guys as stalwart and true; here he wishes he could be her "stalwart / standing fast" and, in addition to this, recognizes that what he has said constitutes a lie

to her: "I know I said that / I'd be standing by your side / but I...." The
emotional intensity of the song, sung over the slow-motion pictures of
Buffy training and undermined in beautiful fashion by Buffy's cute concern that the training session may turn into a montage from an '80s movie,
provides a delightful coming together of Giles's anxieties as seen in "Restless" (4.22): the paternal care he has for Buffy, her casual-seeming but
absolute trust in him, and the show's continuous refusal to allow one emotional tone to dominate, even for a moment.

Giles's next song, sung as a semi-mutually-exclusive duet with Tara,
acts as a literal reprise of "Standing in Your Way" but also as an allusive
reprise of his singing "Freebird" with, here, the inevitability of his leaving
substituting for the potential expressed in the Skynyrd lyrics. Although he
wishes he could stay, the fact of the matter, confirmed in a different context by Tara's using the same words to sing to Willow, is that "I must do
what I must do," which is to leave.

The simple fact that Giles sings the exposition in "Restless" (4.22)
embroils it in a vast involutional nexus of related scenes, but the content of
the exposition also has certain ramifications, which will be discussed more
in the next chapter. However, the description of the First Slayer as a "primal evil" presses back to the episode "The Pack" (1.6) with its transpossessed
hyena-people called "primals" and forward to season 7 where the First Evil's
reign of terror also leads to Buffy's discovery that her ancestor was created
by the transplanting of a demon spirit into the First Slayer ("Get It Done"
[7.15]) and, therefore, that the First Slayer is, in part, part primal evil.

Giles's dream, ostensibly, concerns itself with his own uncertainty
about his role throughout the season and is played out against a scenery
that propels us back and forth across the other seasons. This movement
infuses certain parts of the dream with a specific intensity that augments
the dream's concerns and also allows the ever-developing character of Giles
to be recognized in his richness and depth. This, in turn, foregrounds his
and the show's emphases on questions of identity and belonging; responsibility, duty and individual choice; and the cultural practices that support or hinder these things. The very particular emphasis on Giles's music
also demonstrates the extent to which aesthetic expression as cultural practice is every bit as much a constituent of notions of personality as its formal quality as a work of art. The two interrelate so that Giles's playing the
guitar is an expression of aesthetic desire, a cultural practice, a character
trait and, through involution, a formal sign allowing the influx of other
discourses, each of which is also a representation of the aesthetics of culture, which, recursively, is an expression of aesthetic desire and so on. It
is truly a dream, and a show, with so much going on, and all at once.

◆ CHAPTER 9 ◆

Buffy's Dream

"You think you know what you are?"

This book has attempted to address the thematic and artistic diversity of *Buffy*. By identifying broad thematic concerns and their representation in part I, and then by locating the argument more firmly at the level of character development as articulated through a range of aesthetic devices in part II, I hope that this diversity, this aesthetic and cultural heterogeneity, has been shown. However, and without wishing to undermine what has gone before, there is one clear way in which *Buffy the Vampire Slayer* is always and inevitably homogenized, and this is via Buffy herself. Whatever ethical choice has to be made; no matter what questions pertaining to knowledge are asked; irrespective of the historical frameworks deployed; implicated in all debates surrounding ethnicity and identity: there is always Buffy. This obvious, but important, point is central not only to the show but to this chapter, too. Like the other chapters concerned with specific characters, this chapter will use the aesthetics of involution to move back and forth across episodes and seasons to demonstrate the symbiotic relationship between theme and style and to show the inextricable links between these and characterization. And, where the other similar chapters have occasionally detoured into more general areas of inquiry that are not directly related to the involutional analysis, the Buffy chapter will do this even more.

As with the other dreams, Buffy's dream is largely concerned with her identity and the different ways in which she tries to cope with the demands placed on her. Unlike the other characters, the specific event she has to cope with is being the Slayer. The opening shot of her dream brings this fact very starkly into the foreground. As with Willow's and Xander's, her dream starts in the living room and she is asleep on the sofa. This brief, but thematically central, image provides much of the impetus for the rest of the dream and of this chapter.

As we see her lying there, our attention is drawn to the scar on her forehead. This immediately places her dream image at a moment in time when the strains of her being the Slayer have forced a sense of rift between her and her friends. "The Yoko Factor" (4.19), in which she received this scar, is an episode that works with an ever-present aspect of Buffy's existence, which is her separateness from others. This was first introduced at the very opening of the series, where Buffy tells Xander that he cannot join her searching for his friend Jessie. Starkly and without apology, she asserts: "There's no 'we,' okay. I'm the Slayer, and you're not" (1.2). While this causes Xander to immediately feel a slight to his masculinity, the point is true; irrespective of the sex of the person who is not the Slayer, he or she is always not the Slayer and the Slayer always is. The fluctuating dynamic that derives from this is one of the main motors of the rhythms of the seasons. At some stage in all seasons, Buffy becomes alienated from her friends. The specific causes of the particular sense of isolation will differ, and will be resolved, but the general category of difference cannot be so easily overcome. Her death and resurrection at the end of season 1 is probably the least alienated at the end of a season that she ever is. Season 2 sees her kill Angel, get expelled from school and forced out of her home, and leave Sunnydale for we know not where. Her return in season 3 is far from harmonious and much of the season is an effort for her to regain the trust of her friends, which is not helped by her harboring the re-arrived Angel. Even at the season's close, after her efforts have been rewarded in the very touching presentation of the Class Protector award, she is adrift from her friends as Angel disappears from her life and from the show. Season 5 ends with the ultimate act of alienation when Buffy dies, again, this time in an act of self-sacrificing nobility that is also a suicide. Once more her return is a difficult, even tragic, affair and the ramifications are desperate with respect to Willow's eventual turn to the bad, and the physical distantiation of Buffy from the rest of the group, except for Dawn, at the season's end. And season 7 has her with her friends; victorious after defeating the First; a member of the newly numerous Slayers in the world; but quiet, and reflective, distant from the conversation around her with just a small smile to signify something new.

Her dream's opening in "Restless" (4.22), with its physical sign of this separation, is a motif of Buffy's constant and unchanging difference from others. It is interesting that the scar on the forehead is also the sign used by Bram Stoker to mark Mina out as having been tainted by the demon while she waits for her husband, van Helsing and the rest to try and save her.[1] Buffy, unlike Mina, cannot rely on others to redeem her state, because it is she whom they rely on. Like Mina, though, the outward show of difference at the opening of her dream also acts as a sign of having been tainted by a demon, as we discover in "Get It Done" (7.15). Although we do not know it yet, the moment of coming together that happens in "Primeval" (4.21), a moment of clear physical, symbolic and spiritual union for the previously segregated Scoobies, is precisely the event that triggers the season finale's affirmation of her strangeness and implacable uniqueness. By summoning the power of the First Slayer (even if they did not know that was exactly what they were doing), Buffy's brief and intense union has simply deepened her recognition of her aloneness. That her first image should be a sign of this is not just a conceit of the dream but a fact of Buffy's being.

The next brief section is so overladen with involutional aspect that it is almost impossible to distinguish them all. The first one I wish to look at is Anya's presence; the second, the appearance of the First Slayer; the third, the reference to Faith; and finally, the gnomic allusion to Dawn.

Anya's comment off-screen as Buffy wakes up in the bed in her dorm room, with the scar gone, is replete with possibility. Its first involutional strand is to "Welcome to the Hellmouth" (1.1) where Luke intones the incantation: "The sleeper will awake." While this is directed at the Master, and his coming escape, its uttering in that episode reminds us of the first shot of Buffy (the *very* first shot of Buffy in the whole series), which is of her dreaming. Dreams in Buffy are central to her being, acting in almost oracular fashion at times or simply as expressions of desire, fear or remorse at others. Nevertheless, she is, and has been from the beginning, deeply associated with dreams and, therefore, sleep. And this is potentially dangerous. The demand of "Anya" that Buffy wake up foreshadows Willow's attempt to rescue Buffy from her catatonic state in "The Weight of the World" (5.21). In this episode, a massively demoralized Buffy is finally unable to bear her responsibilities anymore, especially as she feels that she has failed to protect Dawn. Willow uses a spell to enter her mind and there encounters present-day Buffy and a much, much younger Buffy. Young Buffy welcomes home her mother and father and the new baby Dawn and asks if she can look after her. While Buffy is working through her psychodrama, Glory is in the world and her plans for getting home and, thereby causing interdimensional chaos, are moving forward unabated. The risks of a distracted Slayer are unambiguous. The motif of potential calamity striking while Buffy is otherwise engaged has been seen before in a variety of contexts. Whatever its cause (magic in "The Witch" [1.3], alcohol in "Beer Bad" [4.5], possessed sex in "Where the Wild Things Are" [4.18], body switching in "Who Are You?" [4.16]) we are encouraged to be wary of an unfocused Slayer.

The fact that it is Anya who initiates this set of involutions is especially important as it is through her agency that the full realization of what a world where Buffy is not fully aware and not even around to do her job in the first place would be like. Anya's granting of Cordelia's desires in "The Wish" (3.9), which precipitates a world where Buffy never came to Sunnydale, is an emphatic demonstration of the importance of our main character. More than this, though, is the fact that not only do we see a Sunnydale without Buffy but we see a Buffy without Sunnydale. Arriving from Cleveland, where she has been doing her best to secure the Hellmouth there, Buffy in this version lacks in everything that makes her such a marvelous heroic figure. The Buffy of our usual Buffyverse, for all her sense of alienation and separateness, nevertheless, has a mother and is part of a set of friends who provide a genuine sense of community and support: she has been allowed to develop the humanity of herself, the Buffy-part of who she is. This strong sense of her humanity is that which distinguishes her from the other two Slayers that we come to know: Kendra and Faith.[2] For the time being it is necessary to note that Buffy in effect negotiates a difficult process of identity by avoiding both Kendra's rigid, rule-bound impersonal mode of slaying, and Faith's libidinal, overly individuated, unrestrained version. The Buffy of "The Wish" (3.9) is a devastatingly nihilistic hybrid of the two: utterly compelled by the simple vocation of killing vampires with absolutely no greater sense of her mission, she is unable to recognize the reason for Giles's desire to reverse the spell that has produced this world. The death of this Buffy in battle is a bleak outcome to a life lived without all the advantages that "our" Buffy has. For all the psychological anguish that Buffy suffers, she is still Buffy, at least as much as she is the Slayer. However, she is still the Slayer, equally as much as she is Buffy, which is where her problems start.

Anya urges Buffy to wake up again and we see a brief, but startling, shot of what we recognize to be the monster from the previous three dreams, and, after Giles's dream, we intuit it is the First Slayer. The clear sets of oppositions that are being set up encourage us to differentiate Buffy from the First Slayer. Buffy, for a start, is white, and the First Slayer is black; Buffy is sleeping here and the monster is aggressively awake; Buffy is lying on her back, the First Slayer is hanging from the ceiling; Buffy is talking in a quiet dozy voice, the First Slayer is snarling animalistically. Each of these differences opens up a significant space between the two, especially with regard to a recognizable sense of the monstrous in the First Slayer, as opposed to the All-American girl image into which Buffy is being discursively and representationally written.[3] Later in the dream, Buffy asserts to Riley and not–Adam that "we are not demons." This is said as the First Slayer is in frame with, and behind, her, and the clear identification with the First Slayer is unambiguous; that Buffy has, equally as unambiguously, mistaken her nature as nondemonic will become apparent as the remaining seasons unfold. It is, it would appear, Buffy's humanity that is the major point of contrast between the two. As we shall see through the next three seasons, this is an aspect of her that is far more complicated than might previously have been imagined. Though it would be untrue to say that we have not seen the potentially monstrous, or demonic, side of Buffy before. This has been typically implied through certain narrative ploys, rather than explicitly asserted, but it has been present. Firstly, there was the manifestation in "Nightmares" (1.10) of Buffy as a vampire. This is evidently meant to demonstrate the fear that Buffy has of being turned into that which she is supposed to kill, but the fact of the vampire being a demon lodged in a human body is a teasing (if unintended) presentiment of what we discover about her as a Slayer.[4] Second, as mentioned above, is the image of Buffy excluded from the bonds of family and friends as the single-minded killer devoid of future or faith in "The Wish" (3.9). These early indications of other aspects of Buffy are now played out in a number of ways.

Some of these ways refer directly to the First Slayer. As Buffy's dream unfolds, the significance of the First Slayer becomes clearer. Partly it is obvious that the power of the Slayer has been affronted by the enjoining spell undertaken to defeat Adam in "Primeval" (4.21). This, itself, is indicative of the extent to which the simple fact of being a Slayer is intrinsically singular; any attempt to work collaboratively, socially, is an insult to the very nature of Slayerdom. Once again, the realization of Buffy's uniqueness, of her inevitable, natural isolation is enforced. However, what is less clear, at this point, is the reason or purpose of this isolation. While there are pragmatic issues that would readily lend themselves to the acceptance of Buffy ordinarily trying to keep her identity secret, these are hardly sufficient to explain the ferocious refusal to allow her collaboration. These issues have been articulated a number of times in the show and generally refer to safety. Buffy does not want to endanger her family or friends by exposing them to the dangers with which she alone is equipped to deal. Her reluctance to let Xander search for Jessie in (1.2); her decision not to date Owen because of his seeming overenthusiasm for danger and inability to act rationally ("Never Kill a Boy on the First Date" [1.5])[5] and her ongoing duplicity in relation to her mother are all examples of this. Her comment to Owen in (1.5) that she almost feels like a girl is one of the earliest points of pathos that her struggle elicits and it is expressly defined in terms of her own identification as a person, specifically a girl with all of the attendant concepts of fun, friends and flirtation that go along with that.

It is, though, the deeper, archaic reason for her singularity that the First Slayer begins to show Buffy. In the dream, speaking initially through the figure of Tara, and later in her own, rather gruff, voice, the First Slayer insists that there are "no friends, just the kill," and "I am destruction. Absolute. Alone" (4.21). The First Slayer and, by implication, all Slayers, are forces of destruction, working alone with the sole purpose of killing, of bringing death. Buffy rejects this assessment in the dream but the extent to which she, or the audience, believes her assertion of difference is dubious. While Buffy has friends and is not alone and, therefore, differs from the First Slayer in that respect (at least, in part), it is not necessarily the case that she differs from her in terms of being a force for destruction, a being designed to kill.

In a moment of aesthetic brilliance that is so commonplace in *Buffy* that it is easy to overlook, this apparently unambiguous assertion of the Slayer's role as killer is wonderfully complicated in season 5's "Intervention" (5.18). Aside from a number of memorable moments such as Giles's dance with the gourd and the Buffybot's mispronunciation of Giles's name, this episode sees the return of the First Slayer. Except that it does not. As Buffy enters her spiritual journey, in the same desert in which she meets the First Slayer in "Restless" (4.22) she sits by a fire, across from which she sees what she takes to be the same person. It is not her, however; it is the spirit guide who has adopted the form of the First Slayer.

There is a complex unlayering to undertake here. In "Restless" (4.22), Buffy dreams. In this dream a representation of herself meets with a representation of the First Slayer. The First Slayer is, herself, initially represented in terms of speech by an image of Tara. This image, which is similar to but clearly different from the images in Xander's and Willow's dreams, talks on behalf of the First Slayer and her message is that Buffy brings death and has to be alone. The same image of Tara (or, at least an image of Tara in the same dream, whether she is representing the same character of the First Slayer is impossible to discern) tells Buffy that there is a lot more that she has to learn about herself. This learning begins in "Buffy versus Dracula" (5.1) with Dracula using almost exactly the same wording to Buffy that the image of Tara used. So a dream image that acts on behalf of another dream image tells Buffy's version of herself in the dream something that is repeated by the great iconic vampire dream-weaver Dracula. He himself is mistaken for a false representation by Buffy and Xander,[6] and dismissed by Spike as a mere purveyor of "showy gypsy stuff" (5.1). Showy gypsy stuff, however, is precisely what Miss Calendar and her clan used to re-ensoul Angel as we discovered in season 2.

The cross-referencing and involutional contacts serve to undermine our trust in what we are told by these characters who are increasingly removed from any sense of authenticity. When Buffy meets what she believes to be the First Slayer again, we discover that this time it is the image of the First Slayer that is being used by the guide. Once more there is a tension between the physicality of a character and that character's actual identity. From the mouth of the image of the character who has told Buffy that she is destruction and alone, she now hears that she should "Love. Give. Forgive" (5.18). Moreover it is love that will bring her to her gift. The image of the First Slayer, then, proposes two seemingly antithetical ideas: that Buffy is alone and her job is destruction; and that Buffy is full of love. In other words, Buffy is both potentially monstrous and full of humanity.

The unequivocal knowledge that Buffy, and all Slayers, exist in the liminal space of the demon-human is presented in "Get It Done" (7.15). Once again we meet the First Slayer in a dream that Buffy has, and later we discover her history. This, itself, is manifested curiously. During one of the scenes in "Restless" (4.22), Buffy is in an office with Riley and the man that used to be Adam. The image of the human beneath the beast that is Adam is offset by the image of the beast in the human as Buffy covers her face with the mudlike substance that has been in her bag. This is the same substance as was seen in Giles's dream and which prompted Giles's initial suspicion about the presence of the First Slayer. The negative image used here is partly a production requirement because the mud looked too much like an expensive face mask,[7] but it provides a wonderful visualization of the theme of Buffy's dual existence. Importantly, the bag from which she takes the mud in the dream is given to her in "Get It Done" (7.15) by Principal Wood. It was his mother's, and apparently it should have been passed down to the next Slayer. This extraordinary involutional moment (a rather innocuous bag from season 4 being the heirloom of a Slayer killed by Spike — which we are shown in season 5's "Fool for Love" [5.7] — actually being given by the dead Slayer's child to the current Slayer in season 7) links the setting up of Buffy's fears regarding her humanity with the culminating point of this part of her search three years later.

Such a remarkably slow-burning story, which is so central to the mythology of the Slayer and our understanding of Buffy, would, one would have thought, find its resolution in an extraordinary moment of battle or other high-intensity action. *Buffy* never ever gives the audience what it expects. Having had episodes that have veered between musicals and silent movies, it is perhaps only fitting that one of the central components of the series should be represented via a puppet show. The thematic element of this is reasonably straightforward insofar as the ever-present debate between the free will of the characters and their submission to fate is concerned. The especially important effect of this conflict for Buffy has been noted elsewhere, but her fulfillment and denial of the prophecy regarding her death in "Prophecy Girl" (1.12) is a particularly good example. That "Prophecy Girl" (1.12) also shows us a terrified young girl, sixteen and desperate not to die, means that, as ever, the metaphysical and thematic aspects are always located firmly in the emotional effects on the characters and our responses to them. *Angel* takes the tension between free will and fate (of our being part of a cosmic puppet show) even further with the clear intervention of the Powers that Be and their knowledge of the future, but a future that, while known, is still changeable — indeed, the very reason for sending the fragmentary visions at all is so that Angel and company can change them.[8] And, although not related to questions of fate per se, the puppet show component of "Get It Done" (7.15) finds its hilarious reprise in *Angel*'s "Smile Time" (*AtS* [5.14]) in which Angel is transformed into a *Puppets*-style figure who sports the best brooding, overdeveloped eyebrow ridge ever seen on television.

For Buffy, the puppet show that comes out of the bag given to her by Principal Wood is the story of the First Slayer. It acts as an elaboration of Giles's discussion of the history of the world in season 1. As the story unfolds, and the puppet figures' shadows grow, the sound effects intensify, and Dawn's narration comes to a halt, and we know that a girl was chained by unknown men in order to fight demons. The action produces a vortex and Buffy steps through to meet the Shadow Men. The desert in which she finds herself is the same as that in which she was for her spirit guide journey where she met the form of the First Slayer and it is also the same desert as that which she is in for her dream meeting in "Restless" (4.22). The lighting is extremely high, with the lens set very fast, which provides not only a link in terms of place but also of style and aesthetics, as the same lens type (or one very near to it) was used in the previous episodes, too. She is told that the first girl to become a Slayer was forcibly given a demon heart to give her the power. Buffy finds herself chained (just as in her dream the First Slayer was chained above her) and she realizes the spiritual rape that she is about to undergo. Apart from the potential violation and pain, her most urgent and immediate reason for resisting the same fate as happened to the First Slayer is that it will make her "less human" (7.15).

She rejects the possibility of more power and chooses to fight the First Evil with the same level of humanity that she has always had, refusing the cost to her being if she allowed the demon part of her to become any more prominent.[9] Like Angel, Spike, Oz, Willow and Anya, Buffy has to continually negotiate the parameters of her humanity and her inhuman parts. The same is also true of Dawn, whom I shall discuss later. However, still in the same episode (7.15), another of the specific concerns regarding Buffy's humanity, and the terrifying slide toward nihilism that this produced, is alluded to. Worried that Buffy might be stuck in the portal, Willow decides to try and rescue her. She uses a spell that momentarily produces the physical transformations seen in season 6's "Bad Willow" and also draws some of the life out of Kennedy. Xander steps in to protect, though it appears the spell is successful. Buffy thanks Willow for bringing her back "again" (7.15). This evidently refers to Willow's spell that brought Buffy back after her death in season 5. The effects of magic on Willow have been discussed earlier, but the impact on Buffy and also our understanding of Buffy and her humanity are even more astonishing.

The specific peculiarity of Buffy (that she is part-demon, part-human and the Slayer) is compounded throughout the seasons by her being made even more peculiar. The most important of these additional peculiarities is that she has died twice (as she tells us in a gorgeous moment of pathos and bathos in "Once More with Feeling" [6.7]). The first time, her resuscitation at Xander's hands is relatively immediate and the fact of her revival is unimportant in large measure except that it triggers Kendra and demonstrates the flexibility of prophecies. Her second death, however, is very different and its narrative and thematic possibilities are much more closely dealt with.

Her death, first of all, is at her own hands and is the apotheosis of her mission as Slayer. She saves the world from certain devastation, primarily as a way to safeguard her sister. The humanity of her actions belie the supernatural, demonic attributes that allow her to do it at all. The episode was, of course, a season finale and, more than that, was also potentially going to be the last episode of *Buffy* ever. Joss Whedon has said that this meant that he was able to try and resolve the show, to draw together its themes and provide closure to the whole 100-episode corpus.[10] This is begun in the show's "previously" section, which has at least one image from each of the preceding 99 episodes.[11] Buffy's death, then, is a conclusion. The production team knew by the point of its filming that UPN had bought the franchise and that there would be at least another season, but as a story *Buffy* could have ended here.

It did not, and this created a clear problem for the writers about how to bring Buffy back. Their decision was to have Willow, Xander, Tara and Anya perform a resurrection spell, with their motivation being that Buffy was probably trapped in a hell dimension and it was their duty to rescue her. While the mechanism for reviving Buffy strikes me as a little too easy,[12] its ramifications allow two separate aspects of Buffy's relationship to humanity to be investigated. The first of these is the group's use of the Buffybot; the second is Buffy's response to being back.

The Buffybot, of course, had first made its appearance in "Intervention" (5.18) and is designed by Warren Meers, who we first met in "I Was Made to Love You" (5.15) in which he had made a robot girlfriend for himself. He goes on to become one of the troika in season 6, eventually killed by the rampaging Willow. Warren's robot is not the first on *Buffy* and its use here is illustrative of the ways in which the show is able to mine its own narrative and mythology.[13] The first robot is the ancient demon Moloch who, after being released from a book via the Internet, becomes a robot in "I Robot, You Jane" (1.8). This episode is also one of the most explicit in terms of considerations regarding modes of information storage and dissemination, which is a continual adjunct to more specific questions concerning knowledge and its relation to identity. After this, we have Ted, from the episode of the same name (2.11). The growing powers of Buffy are examined here both in terms of her superhuman sensitivity (she senses something is wrong with Ted before she can know it) and in terms of her ethical considerations. Believing she has killed Ted (whom she does not like, but who is nevertheless a human to her), she is distraught. Once his being a robot is discovered, this becomes no longer an issue. However, it is a clear circumscription of her powers that she articulates, one with which Faith in the next season has no such problem. Buffy's (and *Buffy*'s) increasingly sophisticated engagement with the performative aspect ethnic identity that is discussed in chapter 2 is also developed as a consequence of this episode and her response to the destruction of the robot. The fact of its being seemingly nonsentient provides a puzzling addition to questions pertaining to the performance of identity and ideas of the simulacrum.

The robot girlfriend in (5.15) has little that she can offer in the way of horror or surprise. Indeed, the discovery is dealt with almost perfunctorily:

> BUFFY: So, what do you guys think she is? I mean, this may sound nuts, but I kinda got the impression that she was a —
> TARA: Robot.
> [Everyone nods in complete agreement.]
> XANDER: Oh yeah, robot.
> BUFFY: Yeah, I was gonna say robot [5.15].

The questions that she poses, then, are much more concerned with notions of legitimate sexuality, identity, authenticity and so on. As becomes clear with the Buffybot made by Warren, the Buffybot is there for similar reasons for Spike to try and find an outlet for his continuing fascination with Buffy.

Spike has been seeking a simulacra Buffy for a while. He has had Harmony dress up and act like Buffy ("Crush" [5.14]), has stolen her clothes ("Shadow" [5.8]) and has dressed a mannequin like Buffy, ironically enough in "The Replacement" (5.3), and now he forces Warren to make the robot like Buffy. It looks identical to Buffy, sounds like her, is strong like her but, unlike her, is utterly pliable to Spike's (or, given the right programming) anybody's will. This deeply biddable Buffy is, in many ways, an amplification and parody of her humanity. She is eager to please, willing to accede to commands and utterly incapable of doing anything without being told to. The combined effect of submissive toy-cum-child is an obvious effect of Spike's fetishistic desires, but this also presents him with a dilemma: while he can rehearse his desires with the Buffybot, he cannot achieve them because for that he would actually need the Slayer herself. As Melissa M. Milavec and Sharon M. Kaye state:

> Yet Spike does not love the Buffybot. Realizing that Buffy's feelings cannot be programmed, Spike, like Warren, concludes that "a robot is predictable, boring."[14]

However difficult it might be to identify Buffy exactly in terms of who she is, she is still unique.

The Scooby Gang finds this too. They use the previously discarded and deeply damaged Buffybot — her own "sacrifice" in the season finale being a neat echo of Buffy's real one — to stand in for Buffy in order to maintain the sense that there is a Slayer patrolling. They, like Spike, have particular aspects of Buffy that they want the Buffybot to replicate. Less perverse than Spike, they nevertheless find the same frustrations. In a scene that demonstrates the wonderful versatility of Sarah Michelle Gellar (which is always evident, but here, through her own pastiching of her character, manifestly excellent), the Buffybot attempts to slay like Buffy. While the killing is comparatively easy (which is to say, the mechanics of slaying are imitable) the being Buffy is much harder. Willow's efforts to provide the robot with a sense of Buffy's personality comes back in a hail of gibberish as the robot attempts a pun, which comes out as "That'll put marzipan in your pie plate, Bingo" (6.1). Tara ruefully expresses the truth of the situation when she says, "The only really real Buffy is really Buffy" (6.1).

This, though, begs the question of who, or what, is really Buffy. The mechanical simulacrum is clearly not and can never be. The show affirms time and again the processes of *becoming* rather than the state of *being* an individual,[15] but it is still emphatic in its assertion of individuality and uniqueness. Buffy's uniqueness is not in doubt after the Buffybot, but her identity still is. Her reanimation does nothing to assuage any of the concerns relating to her. We see her corpse in the coffin as the gang desperately tries to complete the spell while being attacked by demon bikers (in what is, frankly, a rather silly and, thankfully, short-lived arc). Her corpse's slow coming to life is a horrible image and as she attempts to smash through the coffin and drag herself from the grave the visual cues resolutely remind us of the vampire–Buffy from "Nightmares" (1.10) and, thence, sustain the iconographic as well as narrative-based avowals of her demonic traits.

As we discover, she was not in a hell dimension at all but in a heavenly one and her coming back to earth causes a sense of displacement that is almost unbearable. The seemingly loveless sexual relation she has with Spike provides a physical outlet that affords her some brief sense of contact and belonging. Its sheer desperation, however, provokes in her a realization of her own nihilism elsewhere and her inability to engage with humanity precipitates one of the most demoralizing seasons ever. It takes one demon to force her to be honest with her friends about where she has been (the song-and-dance demon Sweet in "Once More with Feeling" [6.7]) and another, Spike, in the same episode to stop her form committing suicide-by-dance. Tellingly, it is he who first knows of her plight and he who provides the reason for her continuing to struggle. While it is, in part, a simple declaration of the importance of life, irrespective of its pain ("Life's not a song / Life isn't bliss / life is just this / it is living" [6.7]) it is also a specific appeal to her humanity through the negative invocation of his own inhumanity by virtue of being a vampire ("You have to go on living / So one of us is living" [6.7]).

What differentiates the demon from the human, what makes Buffy more human than demon, is that she is living. This is a complicated notion. Despite concerns later in the season that are subsequently dismissed — that she has come back "wrong"— it is clear that Buffy is regarded as living (human) in a way that Spike is not. What this poses as a philosophical conundrum relates in large part to the way in which the Buffyverse figures the soul as a marker of humanity. This has been discussed in earlier chapters. For the time being, I would like to engage with this question from a different perspective. Spike's comment, while relating to demon-human differences (differences that are central to our understanding of Buffy, especially as season 7 heads toward its resolution), also invokes a more specifically human consideration. If season 1 can be read as a "metaphor-per-episode" season, then season 6 in its totality is also a metaphor, just a rather more extended one. The main question of season 6, which is asked primarily of Buffy, but has strong resonance with Willow and with Spike, is: why live at all when death is an option? Buffy during this season is brought back from the dead, has a violent and empty affair with Spike, loses Giles, sees her best friend have her lover murdered, is shot herself, is raped, sees the same best friend decline into a sociopathic monster, and is estranged from everyone, including her sister, is unable to pay for the house and is still recovering from the death of her mother. Additionally, her other best friend walks out on his wedding and she has enforced hallucinations wherein she is the victim of an especially virulent schizophrenic condition.

When she eventually has to act to try and stop Willow, it is not surprising that Willow is scornful in the extreme of the claims made for life by Buffy:

> You're trying to sell me on the world. The one where you lie to your friends when you're not trying to kill them and you screw a vampire just to feel, and insane asylums are the comfy alternative. This world? Buffy, it's me! I know you were happier in the ground — hanging with the worms. The only time you were ever at peace in your whole life is when you were dead. Until Willow brought you back [6.21].

Willow attempts to justify her own violent nihilism by recourse to Buffy's recent biography. And Buffy herself, in the next episode, indicates that Willow's assessment is not so very wrong. After Giles's staggeringly heroic return (one of the few occasions when I have actually cheered a moment on television) he and Buffy are catching up. We hear snippets, and the full extent of the season's dreadful decline is apparent. The pair laugh hysterically to overcome the sheer scale of disaster and then the following dialogue takes place:

> BUFFY: I guess ... I wasn't ready before. It took a long time for that feeling to go away ... the feeling that I wasn't really here. It was like ... when I clawed my way out of that grave, I left something behind. Part of me. I just ... I don't understand ... why I'm back.
> GILES: You have a calling.
> BUFFY: But it was my time, Giles. Someone would have taken my place. So why? [6.22].

Buffy feels herself to be less than before she died and, moreover, believes that her being back at all is a mistake. Giles is unable to provide a satisfactory reason and she is left with the interrogative hanging. The question of her purpose, which, though awkward and difficult, has at least defined her being in some measure and offered her a particular notion of worth and even destiny, is now less secure. Still the Slayer, but unsure of her role or reason, Buffy's predicament in season 6 is to attempt a reconciliation of her demon and human parts that also has to be aware of more common existential dilemmas. Her dying words to Dawn from season 5 ("The hardest thing in this world is to live in it" [5.22]) are repeated back to her by Dawn not long after Spike's uncompromising wisdom in (6.7). Her decision to refuse the extra power from the Shadow Men, and then to deny her own uniqueness for a greater good of commonality and more widely disseminated power by giving the potentials the attributes of full Slayers via Willow's spell, indicates that she has learned this lesson. Her learning to be a Slayer, on her own terms and outside of the Council or providential dictate, is demonstrated in less ebullient fashion in "Lies My Parents Told Me" (7.17) when, feeling betrayed by everyone, she tells Giles that he has taught her everything she needs to know. While the context is clearly one of anger and hurt, the maturation of the girl of season 1 to the young woman of now who can leave her "father" behind is also the maturation of the Slayer whose need for a mentor has now passed. The learning is, as ever, painful, but it is profound. And in discovering that maturation to full independence can then lead to the delegation of power and responsibility, she has unequivocally denied the First Slayer's command in "Restless" (4.22), to which I will now return.

After Anya's demand that Buffy wake up, we have a cut to Buffy's room in her mother's house and then a cut to her standing in the doorway looking at the crumpled sheets and saying that she and Faith have just made the bed. The involutional quality of this comment is quite remarkable. It refers to "This Year's Girl" (4.15) and especially the dream that Faith has while she is in a coma and in which she and Buffy are making the said bed, before Buffy stabs her in the stomach. A dream induced by the spirit of the First Slayer draws on a dream by another character. The sense that Buffy and Faith are united at a deep psychic level by virtue of their both being Slayers is unmistakable. This is particularly true if one starts from Faith's dream and sees its own point of contact with her previous dream in "Graduation Day II" (3.22). In this dream she utters the famous riddle "Oh yeah miles to go. Little Miss Muffet, counting down from 7–3–0." This dream, which is shared with Buffy who is also unconscious and in the next room, acts as a curious prophecy for the coming of Dawn and as a portent for Buffy's death. Little Miss Muffet, as we shall shortly see, is Buffy's sister, and the 7–3–0 supposedly represents the number of days until Buffy's death. Later in Buffy's dream in "Restless" (4.22), still by the bed, the clock says 7:30 and Tara (or her image) tells Buffy that the clock is wrong. As it would have had to have said 3:65 it was probably a wiser choice to maintain the inscrutability of the initial "clue."

However much the numerology is important, it is the clear connection between Buffy and Faith that is most arresting. They share dreams, reference each other's dreams and seem to occupy a position of prophetic insight that belies the specificity of Buffy in favor of a commonality of Slayers. While the pair are linked in these ways, and involutionally in others, they are also importantly different. I have discussed Faith elsewhere in terms of her similarities and differences to Buffy,[16] but an additional point to make relates very specifically to their relationship with each other.

When Faith kills the deputy mayor, Buffy is unable to understand the seeming refusal by Faith to feel remorse or admit that she has done wrong. *Buffy*'s code does not allow people to kill humans without some form of punishment. It is one of the ongoing points of contention, however, that there is such a disparity between the ways in which this is addressed. Faith is put in prison for her crimes while Willow goes on a sort of spiritual retreat and Andrew is kept as a houseguest-cum-prisoner-cum-joke. Whatever the final punishment, the prohibition is clear and each character, in one way or another, has breached it. Buffy has already shown her dread of killing a human in "Ted" (2.11) and also in "Dead Things" (6.13) where she is made to believe that she is responsible for Katrina's death, though Katrina has in fact been murdered by Warren. This prompts her to attempt to confess to the police (once again asserting the show's commitment, however attenuated, to a state law that rather undercuts claims to its uncomplicated anarchism[17]) but then choose not to. Her outrage at what appears to be the killing of children by a human in "Gingerbread" (3.11) invites her query as to whether there may be a loophole in the interdiction against killing people at all, but it is maintained.

All this is important because Buffy is perfectly willing to kill Faith. We have seen Faith's lack of remorse and Buffy's efforts to convince her of the wrongness of her acts, but after Faith nearly succeeds in killing Angel, Buffy's ethical decision shifts. Faith, in order to deflect Buffy's attention from the forthcoming ascension of the mayor, poisons Angel. The antidote to this is the blood of a Slayer. Ultimately, Buffy offers herself to Angel, in order to save him, and the plan works. However, before this moment of pathos, sacrifice and love, Buffy has been prepared to kill Faith. Xander recognizes the potential consequences for Buffy when he tells her that he doesn't want to lose her (3.21), but she is adamant. Already having resigned from the Watchers' Council and, therefore, placed herself outside of their specific laws and structures, she is now in a position of operating only from her own sense of right. The Council's uncompromising refusal to help Angel provides both the narrative prompt to allow her to resign (or to graduate, as she puts it) and a thematic marker against which we can judge Buffy's actions. No longer subject to the Council's laws, Buffy is free to try to save a vampire and to kill a Slayer. The rather stark inversion of the expected moral order is made more problematic by the questions it raises about Buffy's actions and, equally, about her and Faith's status as people.

For Buffy to be able to kill Faith one of two things has to be true: either the prohibition against killing humans does not extend to Faith because her being a Slayer also means she is inhuman, or Buffy is no longer prepared to accept the restriction imposed on her of not being allowed to kill people. Both of these could be true, of course, but at least one has to be.

Whichever of the propositions is true, a significant shift in the Buffy-verse occurs at this point. If Buffy feels free to kill people, then any sort of metaphysically oriented morality on which her ethical choices can be based must be rendered obsolete. The decision to kill or not to kill is no longer part of an absolute injunction; rather it is a utilitarian or pragmatic ethical decision made on a case-by-case basis and whose legitimacy or otherwise has to be calculated in terms of eventual benefit. Saving Angel, with all the possible good he may do, is more important than killing Faith: indeed, Faith's death is a cost that is necessary and Buffy justifies it in these terms, as well as by invoking ethical contiguity: "as justice goes, it's not un-poetic, don't you think?" (6.21). While we have seen pragmatic ethical decisions before (most notably, perhaps in her decision to work with Spike to avert the awakening of Acathla [2.22]) these have primarily been under the clear aegis of a universal moral code that has always defended the notion of the sanctity of human life.

And that brings us to the other possibility. If Buffy is still operating under the categorical injunction not to kill people, then it must be the case that Faith is not human. At no point up until now has there ever been the suggestion that the Slayer is anything other than human, except insofar as she is superhuman. The category of the superhuman, while obviously indicating some aspect of the Slayer that is beyond normal human scope, has not been used in *Buffy* to indicate a difference in kind, only in degree. In season 7, the assumed nature of the Slayer's superiority in terms of strength, speed, agility and so on is explicitly refused any translation into the moral or ethical domain. In "Empty Places" (7.19), Anya accepts Buffy's physical attributes but still avers that this does not make Buffy better than the rest of them, simply luckier (which seven seasons' experience might dispute). Even then, if there is a categorical difference between Slayers and other humans it is typically supposed to be in terms of superiority (physical if not moral) and not in terms of an ontological degradation. Monsters are always degraded beings, either physically or morally or both. So the willingness of Buffy to kill Faith, if it is taken to mean that Faith is not human, strongly implies that Faith's not being human is in some measure commensurate with her being subhuman. If this is true for Faith, it has to be true for Buffy and the discovery that the Slayer has, in part, demon heritage would support this reading.

Faith and Buffy, while very different in many ways, share something profoundly important. Either they share an ethical system that (though more pronounced in Faith is also evident in Buffy) allows pragmatism to override any supposed absolute morality (an absolute morality that in other respects the Buffyverse maintains, however awkwardly) or they share an ontology that renders them unhuman.

Buffy's "doubles" in the show (Faith, the Buffybot, vampire Buffy) all tend to offer us glimpses of the unhuman Buffy, to hint at the possibility that the demon is as important, as integral to her, as her humanity.[18] And when shorn of her identity as a Slayer at all, in "Normal Again" (6.17), what we see is an evacuated person, someone who is incapable, scared and fragile. While we might all love Buffy, and it is as Buffy that we watch her mature, find and lose love and so on, it is the Slayer that is her core.

However, such an analysis is inevitably likely to falter. While her willingness to kill Faith might imply, and the Shadow Men finally reveal, that Buffy is to some degree inhuman, she as a young woman (and *Buffy* as a show) constantly confronts, challenges, inquires into and celebrates an idea of humanity, especially a humanity that is constantly becoming. Each of the characters is constantly in the process of becoming themselves, of developing their humanity; a static individual, one who believes he has become, such as Principal Snyder, is seen to be laughable or dangerous.[19] The main focus of the process is obviously Buffy, but Angel and Spike, Willow, Anya, Tara, even Giles and Xander are never completed as individuals. Perhaps, though, the clearest presentation of humanity-as-becoming, and the concomitant refusal of essentialist ontologies is through Dawn.

Dream-image Tara's comment to dream–Buffy that she be back before dawn is an oblique reference to the character who will be a regular in seasons 5 through 7. As such, it is the only part of the whole of "Restless" (4.22) that is closed off to a backward involutional reading as there is, quite literally, no point of contact with the character before this time. Even here, the reference is only meaningful after we have been introduced to Dawn in the surprise ending to "Buffy versus Dracula" (5.1) with Buffy moaning to her mother about having to take Dawn out with her. Until that point, the mention of "dawn" appears to be a nonsequitur, possibly alluding to something, possibly not.

This particular joy of *Buffy*— that it almost never takes the easy route and it expects its audience to wrestle with thematic, aesthetic and plot complexities— is manifested here. Discussion boards on the Internet were rife with speculation about Dawn. I remember writing with my wife and friends on the Internet after having watched the episode in a baffled silence, punctuated with occasional assurances to each other that we were *sure* that there had never been a reference to Buffy having a sister. The program writers kept the audience in this situation of un-knowing for five episodes. When the explanation finally arrived it did little to assuage the confusion, simply proffering more questions and, once again, recontextualizing the entire Buffyverse. This time, the recontextualization did not pertain to the rather abstruse nature of ethical decision making but to the rather more blatant fact of the whole series' history to this point.

To have introduced a character who is supposed to have such an intimate connection to Buffy and her mother, and, by extension, to all of Buffy's friends, and then to tell us that she is really a magical ball of energy that acts as a key to an interdimensional portal and that she must be hidden and protected from a god from another dimension, and that, to achieve this, a group of monks cast a spell to make her assume human form and superimposed her existence on the memories of everyone with whom she is connected, is an exceptional undertaking. It bespeaks a level of confidence in the strength of the show and its audience that it could be undertaken at all, and for it to be achieved so seamlessly is extraordinary. That it managed to avoid the crass ineptitude of an "and it was all a dream" interpolation such as that provided by the writers of *Dallas* with the return of the Bobby Ewing character after Patrick Duffy decided he wanted to come back to that show after a season is to be applauded.

Yet it does provide problems. From this point on, the characters inhabit a world different from that remembered by the audience. Dawn's existence in each of the characters' memories (even though they discover that they are false, they cannot erase them, and do not seem to want to) means that in each of the episodes we have seen up until this point, Dawn has been present for them, though she is resolutely absent for us. While it is likely that Dawn would have been as ignorant of Buffy's activities as her mother was until the end of season 2, and would not, therefore have known about or witnessed, for example, Buffy's death, many of the familial and emotional repercussions she would have been present for: Buffy's leaving home, the destruction of the high school, Oz's band, Angel as boyfriend if not as vampire with a soul, and all the rest. For the characters, these events now include Dawn and any reference to them has to include her, too, even if only as an emotional echo. While the Buffyverse has changed and expanded in a variety of ways, nothing has been as dramatic in terms of the audience's relationship with it.

The ever-changing constitution of the Buffyverse provides the show with an aesthetic analogue for the characters' own sets of transformations and developments. Neither the aesthetic construct itself nor the characters in it are afforded the lazy luxury of completeness; both are constantly becoming. With Dawn, these complementary attributes are utterly fused.

While the audience strives to understand Dawn's place in the Buffyverse, Dawn strives to understand her place in the world. This is cast in terms and preoccupations associated with early teenagerhood. She has opinions about all of Buffy's friends and about Buffy herself. Knowing Buffy is a Slayer only makes Dawn even more acutely aware of her own seeming lack of autonomy and importance, and her lament that no one knows her or understands her is equally as applicable to the audience's sense of her as it is to her own sense of self. And it is precisely the notion of self that Dawn's character most intensely interrogates.

As Buffy's little sister and Joyce's youngest child, Dawn's role in the show is, partially, to allow a sense of family that it has never had before. We have seen Buffy struggling with her mother in the way that teenagers can, but now we have a working, if slightly dysfunctional, family unit that is fully open with each other in a way that Buffy was not earlier. The Scooby Gang "family" fractures in season 4 with Giles losing his job, Xander not going to college, Willow hiding her sexuality and Buffy being rather at a loss. While there is an effort to reinstitute it in season 5 ("Family" [5.6] being the strongest affirmation of friendship-as-family so far), the decision to relocate family in its more traditional environment is important.[20]

Its importance lies partly in plot terms (after Joyce's death the specific emotional resonance that Buffy has can be transferred onto Dawn) but also thematically. Buffy's continuing engagements with her own identity, especially the question of the conflict between the supernatural and the human, is intensified with Dawn, and the show is able to express a range of ideas through this one developing storyline. After her discovery that she is the key, one of Dawn's arcs is as a metaphor for adoption, specifically adoptees who ascertain their status when they are past infancy. Dawn's sense of bewilderment at being the key is compounded by her sense of betrayal at not having been told before.

The figure through which her discovery is made is Spike. He too is unaware of her being the key and the discovery for both of them is traumatic: for Dawn because of what it means for her; for Spike because Buffy, with whom he is increasingly in love, claims that he is responsible. Spike's refusal to allow Buffy to escape the obligations she has had to Dawn in telling her is one of the many ways in which the relationship between Spike and Buffy further complicates any simple notion of good and bad with, here, Buffy's mendacity and unfair accusations being juxtaposed with a certain integrity shown by Spike.

Once in possession of the fact that she is the key, Dawn's response is a complete questioning of everything she thought she knew. Her anguished question to Buffy and Joyce, "Am I anything?" ("Blood Ties" [5.13]) places her search for self firmly in an existential context and from this devastating position of doubt with regard to her being she has to try and create anew a sense of personhood, a process of becoming that is in many ways as heroic as anything seen on the show (which is not to deny that she is also an extremely irritating teenager at times, too). Given the fact that *Buffy* is primarily a show about a vampire Slayer it is not surprising in some senses that one of the efforts made by Buffy to assure Dawn that she is very much a part of the family should be via blood. However, the confirmation of kinship through blood lines, though expressed literally by Buffy, can only be a metaphor. While Buffy is right to say of the blood that is coming from Dawn's wounded hand that it is Summers' blood, this is a legal-cultural rather than a biological truth. The point, of course, is that it is unimportant. The importance for Dawn is that she can attempt to build for herself a context in which she makes sense, and that context, as it always has been experientially, if not actually, is as Buffy's sister and Joyce's daughter.

She does not have much time in which to become used to being Joyce's daughter after finding out the truth about herself. From "Blood Ties" (5.13), when Dawn discovers her history, to "I Was Made to Love You" (5.15), when Joyce dies, is only two episodes. Michelle Trachtenberg's performance in "The Body" (5.16) at the point where Buffy tells her of her mother's death is, like the entire cast's, extraordinary. The physicality of her grief and the shattering collapse that it induces are extremely well played by Trachtenberg and this allows (along with her qualities elsewhere in the season) the attempt made by Dawn to resurrect her mother in "Forever" (5.17) a poignancy and pathos that is at times unbearable. Through her grief and her misguided attempt to bring her mother back, Dawn is reconciled to her humanity and to Buffy. In the final scene of this episode, Dawn accuses Buffy of not caring or of wishing Dawn were not there. Buffy, trying to convince Dawn to end the spell, as ghoulish shadows of the presumably zombielike creature that has been summoned approach the house, finally collapses herself. Her grief, her anguish, her distress and fear are palpable and as the door knocks it is Buffy who runs to open it, to welcome her "mommy" back while Dawn exhibits her strength and love by ceasing the spell, dispelling the zombie and holding Buffy, trying to calm and soothe her. It is a traumatic scene, wonderfully acted, and one that provides Dawn with a sense of purpose, with a role. The use of the term "mommy" has its own specific and heartrending involutional circuit. First used by Buffy on the discovery of her mother's body in "I Was Made to Love You" (5.15), reprised in the following episode's "mom, mom ... mommy" (5.16), it is repeated two seasons later by the devastated Dawn when the First Evil assumes Joyce's form in "Conversations with Dead People" (7.7). This episode is itself unique in being the only one that uses the technique of superscripting the date and time of the action. The date and time ("November 12, 2002; 8:01 P.M.") are exactly synchronous with the date and time of the episode's first airing in America. A technique that is a clear sign of the show's constructedness is attempting to force a direct equivalence between its world and the world of the viewer. This tense struggle between the desire to assert a specific realism via an overtly aesthetic gesture is compounded by the episode also having its title displayed. The giving of a title is an emphatic index of its fictionality (or, at least, it is a paratextual marker of the processes of construction) and one that clearly mitigates against the claims for the particular realism it strives to achieve. The fact that this also provides an involutional link back to "Once More with Feeling" (6.7) (self-conscious, artificial, aestheticized television at its most pronounced and glorious[21]), by virtue of that episode's emblazoning of its title, seems to reinforce this aesthetic tension. That "Conversations with Dead People" (7.7) is so profoundly concerned with questions of the authentic versus the counterfeit, simulacra versus the real, means that this aesthetic antagonism provides a supreme and subtle metatextual commentary on its own action.

Beyond her mystical beginnings Dawn, like Xander, has little to offer in specific supernatural abilities; the purpose, or role, that Dawn has discovered is unspectacular. She is, however, and again like Xander, selfless and courageous (when she is not being self-absorbed and a teenager) and the pair of them have a moment for quiet mutual expressions of respect and love in "Potential" (7.12).[22] They are not the special ones, the superheroes; they are never in the spotlight and, for that reason alone, theirs is the hardest job of all. *Buffy*, through Buffy, can applaud a new notion of female heroism, can challenge gender stereotyping through the figure of a sexy, smart, powerful woman; through Xander and Dawn it can interrogate the specific existential requirements of the rest of us, the quiet core whose endeavor to create a viable process of becoming is all the more remarkable because it is so little noted or taken account of. If Faith represents the potential other side of Buffy as the Slayer, Dawn represents the other side of Buffy as the person.

It is the tension between these two sides that Buffy has to endure and that is such a prominent focus of her dream in "Restless" (4.22). Having finally moved out of the different bedrooms of its opening, we now find Buffy in the school. We have seen in "The Freshman" (4.1) that Buffy positions herself as Buffy in the context of high school, that the move to the university has been difficult for her and she is uncertain about who she is in simple human terms. It takes Xander (himself adrift and alienated) to affirm her status as hero in order to comfort her. That she finds comfort in her role as Xander's hero, as the Slayer (4.1), rather than fully confronting her concerns about her Buffyness, is an interesting example of the potential succor that her position as Slayer can bring. This is explored later between Xander and Dawn. While high school is one context of familiarity and reassurance, her mother is another. Both are elided in the dream. Obscurely, she sees her mother living in a wall. The sense of dirt and containment may well be an involutional prelude to Joyce's death, and there is a potential reading of it as symbolic of mother-daughter estrangement, but it also returns us to Buffy's talking to her mother through the hole in the door in "School Hard" (2.3), an episode that is memorable for first introducing us to Spike and Drusilla, an introduction that ends with Joyce saving Buffy by smashing Spike over the head with a fire axe. This is referenced with a moment of comic genius in "Becoming II" (2.22) when Joyce learns of Buffy's true calling, and Spike reminds her, in a scene of wonderfully observed social awkwardness that leads to excruciating embarrassment, that she has met him before and that an axe was involved. The surprising level of civility and good grace shown by Joyce to Spike is one of the reasons for his genuine sadness at her death, which is a further involutional link from Buffy's dream-image of her mother in the wall to Joyce's burial.

Death, bereavement and sorrow are constant companions in *Buffy* in one way or another, and the dream-scene in which she speaks to Riley and the man who became Adam is abounding in allusions to them. The simple presence of the not–Adam is a narrative reminder of the deaths that he or the Initiative have caused. Beyond this, though, are hints and teasers for what is to come. Buffy's surprise that Riley is back and his claim that he never left foreshadow his eventual leaving in "Into the Woods" (5.10). This episode is dedicated to the real death of the leadman on *Buffy* for seasons 1 and 2, Gustav Gustafson, reputedly a good friend of Sarah Michelle Gellar's. As leadman, Gustavson's enormous contribution to set construction and dressing is integral to any assessment of the first two seasons in terms of their look and overall feel.

Riley's trip to the vampire brothel in "Into the Woods" (5.10), where he allows himself to be fed from in order to appear more exciting or dangerous, portends the theme of addiction and non-normative sexuality that will be explored further in season 6. His departure at the episode's end seems to be the culmination of Buffy's prophetic, if confused, exclamation in her dream. The too-strong hug given by Buffy to the doctor for successfully performing the operation on her mother in the same episode (5.10) inevitably leads to "The Body" (5.16), while also looking forward to a similarly overzealous show of affection to Giles when he returns in "Flooded" (6.4). The rearrival of Giles logically reminds us of his departure in the season 6 opener — the two-hour special "Bargaining I and II"— which was used by UPN as part of its heavy promotion of the show. This opener itself is alluded to in "Restless" (4.22) as Riley gleefully proclaims his plans for world domination via "coffeemakers that think" (4.22) while the Buffybot is described in (6.1) as the "descendant of a toaster-oven." The absurdist kitchen appliance reference has rarely been better utilized, though it has got a curious, if peripheral, role in the Buffyverse. The post–Oz Willow is called a "brave little toaster" (4.9) by Xander (so the kitchen appliance motif is also part of the involutional matrix, referring as this does to the ever-so cute animation from 1987); and Fred's anti-demon contraption in *AtS* (3.5) is finally recognized as being "not a toaster" by Gunn.

Riley's deeply self-impressed image as a James Bond–esque figure in "Restless" (4.22) is marvelously captured by the shot through the glass table from underneath with the image of the gun lying on its top. Buffy herself has been seduced by the potentially useful nature of guns, especially when working for the Initiative. While seeking a method for killing Adam, she is eager for Xander to fix the blaster that Maggie Walsh had given to her. This had been purposefully broken and Buffy wants it fixed. Willow appears skeptical and Buffy retorts that just because it is not in the Slayer's handbook it does not exclude it from use ("This Year's Girl" [4.15]). The Slayer's handbook has been mentioned on a number of occasions. Giles is excited to discover that Kendra has read it (2.10) though had previously said there was no instruction manual (1.5), and its occasional mentioning thereafter is as much a parodic expression of disdain for an overtly instrumentalist object in such a mystical context, as it is an expression of an actual manual. Buffy's desire for the blaster acts as a connection (however unwelcome) to Maggie Walsh. It is perhaps one of the great understated moments of irony in the show that the great psychologist should be the one who, through her duplicity and scheming, allows Buffy one of the most forceful declarations of her identity as a Slayer. It is an unintended consequence of her plan to kill Buffy, but the Slayer really does seem to have a moment of realization about herself, a psychological breakthrough, when she announces, "you really don't know what a Slayer is. Trust me when I say you're gonna find out" (4.13).

The fact that it is a gun (however space-age) that is nearly the cause of Buffy's demise reminds us (and her) of her more general dislike (even abhorrence) of guns. The shot of the gun through the glass table links to this and, among many others, to "The Harvest" (1.2), where Buffy refuses the possibility of police involvement because they would only come with guns; "Seeing Red" (6.19), where Warren's killing of Tara with a gun precipitates the devastation of Willow (and where, also, Spike ironically declares to Dawn "Ain't love grand," which is the same phrase he uses to Riley in relation to their mutual affection for Buffy in "Into the Woods" [5.10]); and guns are also given short shrift in "Flooded" (6.4), where Buffy prefers her powers to the security guard's weapon.

And it is her powers and the apprehension these cause in the effort to identify herself as both Buffy and the Slayer that the dream (and the entire show) continues to investigate. As she approaches the final fight with the First Slayer, ready to proclaim her distinctive quality, there is a shot of her looking into the desert. The desert (with all its symbolic attributes and sublime invocation) is a recurring theme in the episode. Its most curious manifestation is its diminished representative in Xander's dream. Reduced and contained, the desert-as-sandbox houses Buffy and we have a shot of her face. The lighting is stark, overexposed and we see her forehead shine a little as she appears tired, almost ill. The shot lasts only a moment but in it we see all the strain and fear of being a Slayer. The shot is a reprise of a very similar use of lighting on Buffy during her fight with Angelus in "Becoming II" (2.22) in which her isolation and aloneness is used by the vampire to try and demean her but leads instead to her assertion of self-reliance and individual capacity. The shot is further reprised in "The Body" (5.16), an episode in which Buffy's Slayerhood is almost entirely unimportant except for a brief fight at the end. After having been sick from the shock of seeing her mother dead on the couch, Buffy steps outside and we see her look into the middle distance at the normalcy of the world. The lighting on her face, her expression, the same sense of formal alienation felt by the viewer, the framing of each shot: all of these things bring the Slayer and the girl together. One shot has her as quintessential Slayer (2.22), one as absolute human (5.16) and one caught between the two (4.22): all are moments of unusual, even extreme, emotionality. Involution is able to provide an overwhelming fusion of the two aspects of Buffy, and the unremitting pain of Buffy as both girl and Slayer is written on her face through the production values of each shot. We see both versions of her, are asked to feel deeply for both versions of her, and are still, like she is, unsure of who she is.

Buffy never quite knows who she is or what is to come and neither do we. The show places its main character in a position of constant uncertainty, of perpetual becoming. Our last image of her, standing with her friends, looking back at the destroyed Sunnydale, is of a quietly thoughtful woman (7.22). She has transformed cosmic law by making more Slayers; she has saved the world (again); she has friends and she has powerful new allies; she has overcome the death of her mother, the arrival of a mystical sister, the departure of her real and her surrogate fathers; she has had heartbreak; she has died twice; and for the entire last scene she is quiet. She thinks and she does not act. When asked what is going to happen now she simply smiles. She is as enigmatic as ever. Buffy continues to become.

Conclusion

"I'd call that a radical interpretation of the text"

There is a danger inherent in any sort of cultural criticism, which is that the critic overstates the importance of a particular example or undervalues the significance of another. As David Lavery points out, *Buffy* criticism seems especially prone to both sorts of antagonism. If the difficulty of taking a television program seriously at all were not bad enough, one called *Buffy the Vampire Slayer* being posited as a genuine and important contribution to debates concerning culture and aesthetics is likely to produce splenetic outbursts that verge on the incontinent. Lavery writes, in response to one branch of hostile receptions of *Buffy* criticism, "We are, it seems, not serious enough, not sufficiently aware of the modes of production of *BtVS*. Our objectivity is so deficient we cannot take back our projections from a series which has inexplicably mesmerized us."[1] Equally, however, and from a different perspective, to dare to write on *Buffy* at all is seen as an act of critical vampirism, sucking the life out of a vivid and delightful show in order to maintain the derelict career of a pseudo-academic stuck inside the crumbling carapace of a nearly dead, wholly unfeeling, body.

Put differently, *Buffy* criticism cannot be "real" because it is too influenced by fandom; or else it is so lacking in the required celebratory gestures of fandom that it is not "true" to the show. In addition to this, the ongoing critical divide between scholars who study "Culture" and scholars who partake of cultural studies means that one group refuses television anything but the most banal aesthetic possibility, while the other rejects

208

aesthetics all together, as it conjures up images of elitism and hierarchies of taste that immediately appear to propose antipathetic political agendas.

Both positions (perhaps a little simplified by me here) are clearly stupid. Even if no other television show attempted to provide interesting, challenging and inventive aesthetics, then the presence of *Buffy* alone would still deny the general observations peddled by the "Culture" lobby; and if every show capitulated to a dominant culture's preferred aesthetic and its ideological ramifications, force-feeding a public that it had created with the detritus of a decadent and lame late-capitalist credo, then *Buffy*'s staggering refusal to do so would indicate that such a wholesale rejection of a potentially invigorating aspect of cultural studies was an act of profound myopia.

And many other shows do offer points of cultural insight and challenge, and many shows do expand and delight in the enormous aesthetic openness of television. One need only think of contemporary dramas like *The West Wing*, *The Lyon's Den*, *The Shield*, *24*; of British comedies like *Little Britain*, *The Office*, *The Green Wing* or *The Fast Show*; as well as series and individual shows that have always pushed the potential of television such as *Star Trek*, *The X-Files*, *Twin Peaks*, *The Singing Detective*, *Z-Cars*, *Cathy Come Home*, *Boys From the Blackstuff*, *Seinfeld*, *Brasseye*, and a host of others. Even if much television drama and comedy is less impressive than this, there is no reason to assume that it is inevitably degraded: most novels fail to be anywhere near as interesting in terms of what novels can do as these shows are in terms of the possibility of TV; few films achieve the heights of *Citizen Kane* or *The Lord of the Rings* trilogy; plastic arts can boast only a limited number of important contributions. And if this sounds like the reintroduction of a hierarchy of taste, a use of the aesthetic and cultural choices made by a show as a marker of quality, then it is unapologetically so. Some television is better than others, just as some novels, films, paintings, sculptures and photographs are; just as some football teams are.

And *Buffy* is among the best of the best. It looks at the culture that has helped to produce it and it reflects critically on it. It does not do this through a blunt "look at this issue, isn't it important" mechanistic, socially engaged instrumentalism (though it can, and is the worse for it when it does as with Willow's addiction to magic). Instead, it asks its characters, and its viewers, to assume a longer vision, to track questions of knowledge, of ethnicity, of history and of ethics (among others) and to participate in the awkward, politically contradictory, socially messy, culturally fraught, personally painful effects of these questions. And it does this by choosing, carefully, critically, knowingly, aesthetic styles that complement or stand in juxtaposition to these ideas. The aesthetic and the cultural interpenetrate with the material quality of the one challenging or supporting the material influence of the other.

Jean-François Lyotard, back in 1989, at a panel held by the Institute of Contemporary Arts, warned against what he saw as a certain utopianism being claimed for popular culture in general and television in particular. He said,

> I believe that the only line to follow is to produce programmes for TV, or whatever, which produce in the viewer or the client in general an effect of uncertainty and trouble. It seems to me that the thing to aim at is a certain sort of feeling or sentiment. You can't introduce concepts, you can't produce argumentation. This type of media isn't the place for that, but you can produce a feeling of disturbance, in the hope that this disturbance will be followed by reflection.[2]

Buffy does introduce concepts and argumentation, because it uses the season structure as the formal conduit through which sustained narratives can function (already an important aesthetic decision), but more importantly it produces the feeling of disturbance demanded by Lyotard. And, in turn, as demonstrated by websites, chat forums, conferences, collected academic essays, all sorts of guides and reflections, and monographs such as this one, reflection occurs.

Buffy demands reflection. Even at its most conservative (the disappearance and silencing of the Chumash in "Pangs" [4.8]); at its most unambiguously emotional in "The Body" (5.16); when seemingly constrained by enforced didacticism "Beer Bad" (4.5); when potentially mired in mere formalism "Restless" (4.22), the show never fails to be complex, to demand of its audience a reflective as well as sensuous response. Indeed, the reflective and the sensuous are aspects of each other, inseparable in the experience of *Buffy*'s aesthetics. The reflective requirement is demonstrated at a very simple level by the fact that the show is bounded by two questions: "Are you sure this is a good idea?" ("Welcome to the Hellmouth" [1.1]) and "What are we going to do now?" ("Chosen" [7.22]). The reflections required of the characters at this point are additionally layered for the audience who is also embroiled in the aesthetic quality of scenes, which have been discussed in this book. And these aesthetics, as I have tried to show, are the necessary condition of a relation to culture, a culture (in all its various manifestations and meanings) that *Buffy* continually critiques and questions.

Rarely has a television show had such a seemingly silly-sounding name as *Buffy the Vampire Slayer*. Never has a show taken so seriously, nor had as much fun in doing so, the possibilities of television as the site for a thoroughgoing examination of an aesthetics of culture. Though Andrew may have had other things in mind in "Storyteller" (7.16), his assessment is absolutely true: *Buffy*, in ways that are already becoming apparent and in many which remain to be seen, is spectacularly, wonderfully, culturally and aesthetically "a legacy for future generations."

Episode Listing

The list is organized by the following pattern:

Title / season and episode number / production number / first U.S. airdate / writer(s) / director(s)

Season 1

1. Welcome to the Hellmouth / 1.1 / 4V01 / 10 March 1997 / Joss Whedon / Charles Martin Smith

2. The Harvest / 1.2 / 4V02 / 10 March 1997 / Joss Whedon / John T. Kretschmer

3. The Witch / 1.3 / 4V03 / 17 March 1997 / Dana Reston / Stephen Cragg

4. Teacher's Pet / 1.4 / 4V04 / 25 March 1997 / David Greenwalt / Bruce Seth Green

5. Never Kill a Boy on the First Date / 1.5 / 4V05 / 31 March 1997 / Rob Des Hotel and Dean Batali / David Semel

6. The Pack / 1.6 / 4V06 / 7 April 1997 / Matt Kiene and Joe Reinkemeyer / Bruce Seth Green

7. Angel / 1.7 / 4V07 / 14 April 1997 / David Greenwalt / Scott Brazil

8. I Robot, You Jane / 1.8 / 4V08 / 28 April 1997 / Ashley Gable and Thomas A. Swyden / Stephen Posey

9. The Puppet Show / 1.9 / 4V09 / 5 May 1997 / Dean Batali and Rob Des Hotel / Ellen S. Pressman

10. Nightmares / 1.10 / 4V10 / 12 May 1997 / David Greenwalt / Bruce Seth Green

11. Out of Mind, Out of Sight / 1.11 / 4V11 / 19 May 1997 / Ashley Gable and Thomas A. Swyden / Reza Badiyi

12. Prophecy Girl / 1.12 / 4V12 / 2 June 1997 / Joss Whedon / Joss Whedon

Season 2

13. When She Was Bad / 2.1 / 5V01 / 15 Sept. 1997 / Joss Whedon / Joss Whedon

14. Some Assembly Required / 2.2 / 5V02 / 22 Sept. 1997 / Ty King / Bruce Seth Green

15. School Hard / 2.3 / 5V03 / 29 Sept. 1997 / David Greenwalt / John T. Kretschmer

16. Inca Mummy Girl / 2.4 / 5V04 / 6 Oct. 1997 / Matt Kiene and Joe Reinke-meyer / Ellen S. Pressman

17. Reptile Boy / 2.5 / 5V05 / 13 Oct. 1997 / David Greenwalt / David Green-walt

18. Halloween / 2.6 / 5V06 / 27 Oct. 1997 / Carl Ellsworth / Bruce Seth Green

19. Lie to Me / 2.7 / 5V07 / 3 Nov. 1997 / Joss Whedon / Joss Whedon

20. The Dark Age / 2.8 / 5V08 / 10 Nov. 1997 / Dean Batali and Rob Des Hotel / Bruce Seth Green

21. What's My Line I / 2.9 / 5V09 / 17 Nov. 1997 / Howard Gordon and Marti Noxon / David Solomon

22. What's My Line II / 2.10 / 5V10 / 24 Nov. 1997 / Marti Noxon / David Semel

23. Ted / 2.11 / 5V11 / 8 Dec. 1997 / David Greenwalt and Joss Whedon / Bruce Seth Green

24. Bad Eggs / 2.12 / 5V12 / 15 Dec. 1997 / Marti Noxon / David Greenwalt

25. Surprise / 2.13 / 5V13 / 19 Jan. 1998 / Marti Noxon / Michael Lange

26. Innocence / 2.14 / 5V14 / 20 Jan. 1998 / Joss Whedon / Joss Whedon

27. Phases / 2.15 / 5V15 / 27 Jan. 1998 / Rob Des Hotel and Dean Batali / Bruce Seth Green

28. Bewitched, Bothered and Bewildered / 2.16 / 5V16 / 10 Feb. 1998 / Marti Noxon / James A. Contner

29. Passion / 2.17 / 5V17 / 24 Feb. 1998 / Ty King / Michael Gershman

30. Killed by Death / 2.18 / 5V18 / 3 March 1998 / Rob Des Hotel and Dean Batali / Deran Serafian

31. I Only Have Eyes for You / 2.19 / 5V19 / 28 April 1998 / Marti Noxon / James Whitmore, Jr.

32. Go Fish / 2.20 / 5V20 / 5 May 1998 / David Fury and Elon Hampton / David Semel

33. Becoming I / 2.21 / 5V21 / 12 May 1998 / Joss Whedon / Joss Whedon

34. Becoming II / 2.22 /5V22 / 19 May 1998 / Joss Whedon / Joss Whedon

Season 3

35. Anne / 3.1 / 3ABB01 / 29 Sept. 1998 / Joss Whedon / Joss Whedon

36. Dead Man's Party / 3.2 / 3ABB02 / 6 Oct. 1998 / Marti Noxon / James Whitmore, Jr.

37. Faith, Hope and Trick / 3.3 / 3ABB03 / 13 Oct. 1998 / David Greenwalt / James A. Contner

38. Beauty and the Beasts / 3.4 / 3ABB04 / 20 Oct. 1998 / Marti Noxon / James Whitmore, Jr.

39. Homecoming / 3.5 / 3ABB05 / 3 Nov. 1998 / David Greenwalt / David Greenwalt

40. Band Candy / 3.6 / 3ABB06 / 10 Nov. 1998 / Jane Espenson / Michael Lange

41. Revelations / 3.7 / 3ABB07 / 17 Nov. 1998 / Douglas Petrie / James A. Contner

42. Lover's Walk / 3.8 / 3ABB08 / 1 Dec. 1998 / Dan Vebber / David Semel

43. The Wish / 3.9 / 3ABB09 / 8 Dec. 1998 / Marti Noxon / David Greenwalt

44. Amends / 3.10 / 3ABB10 / 15 Dec. 1998 / Joss Whedon / Joss Whedon

45. Gingerbread / 3.11 / 3ABB11 / 12 Jan. 1999 / Thania St. John and Jane Espenson / James Whitmore, Jr.

46. Helpless / 3.12 / 3ABB12 / 19 Jan. 1999 / David Fury / James A. Contner

47. The Zeppo / 3.13 / 3ABB13 / 26 Jan. 1999 / Dan Vebber / James Whitmore, Jr.

48. Bad Girls / 3.14 / 3ABB14 / 9 Feb. 1999 / Douglas Petrie / Michael Lange

49. Consequences / 3.15 / 3ABB15 / 16 Feb. 1999 / Marti Noxon / Michale Gersham

50. Doppelgangland / 3.16 / 3ABB16 / 23 Feb. 1999 / Joss Whedon / Joss Whedon

51. Enemies / 3.17 / 3ABB17 / 16 March 1999 / Douglas Petrie / David Grossman

52. Earshot / 3.18 / 3ABB18 / 21 Sept. 1999 / Jane Espenson / Regis Kimble

53. Choices / 3.19 / 3ABB19 / 4 May 1999 / David Fury / James A. Contner

54. The Prom / 3.20 / 3ABB20 / 11 May 1999 / Marti Noxon / David Solomon

55. Graduation Day I / 3.21 / 3ABB21 / 18 March 1999 / Joss Whedon / Joss Whedon

56. Graduation Day II / 3.22 / 3ABB22 / 13 July 1999 / Joss Whedon / Joss Whedon

Season 4

57. The Freshman / 4.1 / 4ABB01 / 5 Oct. 1999 / Joss Whedon / Joss Whedon

58. Living Conditions / 4.2 / 4ABB02 / 12 Oct. 1999 / Marti Noxon / David Grossman

59. The Harsh Light of Day / 4.3 / 4ABB03 / 19 Oct. 1999 / Jane Espenson / James A. Contner

60. Fear Itself / 4.4 / 4ABB04 / 26 Oct. 1999 / David Fury / Tucker Gates

61. Beer Bad / 4.5 / 4ABB05 / 2 Nov. 1999 / Tracey Forbes / David Solomon

62. Wild at Heart / 4.6 / 4ABB06 / 9 Nov. 1999 / Marti Noxon / David Grossman

63. The Initiative / 4.7 / 4ABB07 / 16 Nov. 1999 / Douglas Petrie / James A. Contner

64. Pangs / 4.8 / 4ABB08 / 19 Oct. 1999 / Jane Espenson / Michael Lange

65. Something Blue / 4.9 / 4ABB09 / 30 Nov. 1999 / Tracey Forbes / Nick Marck

66. Hush / 4.10 / 4ABB10 / 3 Nov. 1999 / Joss Whedon / Joss Whedon

67. Doomed / 4.11 / 4ABB11 / 18 Jan. 2000 / Marti Noxon, David Fury and Jane Espenson / James A. Contner

68. A New Man / 4.12 / 4ABB12 / 25 Jan. 2000 / Jane Espenson / Michael Gershman

69. The I in Team / 4.13 / 4ABB13 / 8 Feb. 2000 / David Fury / James A. Contner

70. Goodbye Iowa / 4.14 / 4ABB14 / 15 Feb. 2000 / Marti Noxon / David Solomon

71. This Year's Girl / 4.15 / 4ABB15 / 22 Feb. 2000 / Douglas Petrie / Michael Gershman

72. Who Are You? / 4.16 / 4ABB16 / 29 Feb. 2000 / Joss Whedon / Joss Whedon

73. Superstar / 4.17 / 4ABB17 / 5 April 2000 / Jane Espenson / David Grossman

74. Where the Wild Things Are / 4.18 / 4ABB18 / 25 April 2000 / Tracey Forbes / David Solomon

75. A New Moon Rising / 4.19 / 4ABB19 / 2 May 2000 / Marti Noxon / James A. Contner

76. The Yoko Factor / 4.20 / 4ABB20 / 9 May 2000 / Douglas Petrie / David Grossman

77. Primeval / 4.21 / 4ABB21 / 16 May 2000 / David Fury / James A. Contner

78. Restless / 4.22 / 4ABB22 / 23 May 2000 / Joss Whedon / Joss Whedon

Season 5

79. Buffy versus Dracula / 5.1 / 5ABB01 / 26 Sept. 2000 / Marti Noxon / David Solomon

80. Real Me / 5.2 / 5ABB02 / 3 Oct. 2000 / David Fury / David Grossman

81. The Replacement / 5.3 / 5ABB03 / 10 Oct. 2000 / Jane Espenson / James A. Contner

82. Out of My Mind / 5.4 / 5ABB04 / 17 Oct. 2000 / Rebecca Rand Kirshner / David Grossman

83. No Place Like Home / 5.5 / 5ABB05 / 24 Oct. 2000 / Douglas Petrie / David Solomon

84. Family / 5.6 / 5ABB06 / 7 Nov. 2000 / Joss Whedon / Joss Whedon

85. Fool for Love / 5.7 / 5ABB07 / 14 Nov. 2000 / Douglas Petrie / Nick Marck

86. Shadow / 5.8 / 5ABB08 / 21 Nov. 2000 / David Fury / Daniel Attias

87. Listening to Fear / 5.9 / 5ABB09 / 28 Nov. 2000 / Jane Espenson / David Solomon

88. Into the Woods / 5.10 / 5ABB10 / 19 Dec. 2000 / Marti Noxon / Marti Noxon

89. Triangle / 5.11 / 5ABB11 / 9 Jan. 2001 / Jane Espenson / Christopher Hibler

90. Checkpoint / 5.12 / 5ABB12 / 23 Jan. 2001 / Douglas Petrie and Jane Espenson / Nick Marck

91. Blood Ties / 5.13 / 5ABB13 / 6 Feb. 2001 / Steven S. DeKnight / Michael Gershman

92. Crush / 5.14 / 5ABB14 / 13 Feb. 2001 / David Fury / Daniel Attias

93. I Was Made to Love You / 5.15 / 5ABB15 / 20 Feb. 2001 / Jane Espenson / James A. Contner

94. The Body / 5.16 / 5AB16 / 20 Feb. 2001 / Joss Whedon / Joss Whedon

95. Forever / 5.17 / 5ABB17 / 17 April 2001 / Marti Noxon / Marti Noxon

96. Intervention / 5.18 / 5ABB18 / 24 April 2001 / Jane Espenson / Michael Gershman

97. Tough Love / 5.19 / 5ABB19 / 1 May 2001 / Rebecca Rand Kirshner / David Grossman

98. Spiral / 5.20 / 5ABB20 / 8 May 2001 / Steven S. DeKnight / James A. Contner

99. The Weight of the World / 5.21 / 5ABB21 / 15 May 2001 / Douglas Petrie / David Solomon

100. The Gift / 5.22 / 5ABB22 / 22 May 2001 / Joss Whedon / Joss Whedon

Season 6

101. Bargaining I / 6.1 / 6ABB01 / 2 Oct. 2001 / Marti Noxon and David Fury / David Grossman

102. Bargaining II / 6.2 / 6ABB02 / 2 Oct. 2001 / Marti Noxon and David Fury / David Grossman

103. After Life / 6.3 / 6ABB03 / 9 Oct. 2001 / Jane Espenson / David Solomon

104. Flooded / 6.4 / 6ABB04 / 16 Oct. 2001 / Douglas Petrie and Jane Espenson / Douglas Petrie

105. Life Serial / 6.5 / 6ABB05 / 23 Oct. 2001 / David Fury and Jane Espenson / Nick Marck

106. All the Way / 6.6 / 6ABB06 / 30 Oct. 2001 / Steven S. DeKnight / David Solomon

107. Once More with Feeling / 6.7 / 6ABB07 / 6 Nov. 2001 / Joss Whedon / Joss Whedon

108. Tabula Rasa / 6.8 / 6ABB08 / 13 Nov. 2001 / Rebecca Rand Kirshner / David Grossman

109. Smashed / 6.9 / 6ABB09 / 20 Nov. 2001 / Drew Z. Greenberg / Turi Meyer

110. Wrecked / 6.10 / 6ABB10 / 27 Nov. 2001 / Marti Noxon / David Solomon

111. Gone / 6.11 / 6ABB11 / 8 Jan. 2002 / David Fury / David Fury

112. Doublemeat Palace / 6.12 / 6ABB12 / 29 Jan. 2002 / Jane Espenson / Nick Marck

113. Dead Things / 6.13 / 6ABB13 / 5 Feb. 2002 / Steven S. DeKnight / James S. Contner

114. Older and Far Away / 6.14 / 6ABB14 / 12 Feb. 2002 / Drew Z. Greenberg / Michael Gershman

115. As You Were / 6.15 / 6ABB15 / 26 Feb. 2002 / Douglas Petrie / Douglas Petrie

116. Hell's Bells / 6.16 /6ABB16 / 5 March 2002 / Rebecca Rand Kirshner / David Solomon

117. Normal Again / 6.17 / 6ABB17 / 12 March 2002 / Diego Gutierrez / Rick Rosenthal

118. Entropy / 6.18 / 6ABB18 / 30 April 2002 / Drew Z. Greenberg / James A. Contner

119. Seeing Red / 6.19 / 6ABB19 / 7 May 2002 / Steven S. DeKnight / Michael Gershman

120. Villains / 6.20 / 6ABB20 / 14 May 2002 / Marti Noxon / David Solomon

121. Two to Go / 6.21 / 6ABB21 / 21 May 2002 / Douglas Petrie / Bill Norton

122. Grave / 6.22 / 6ABB22 / 21 May 2002 / David Fury / James A. Contner

Season 7

123. Lessons / 7.1 / 7ABB01 / 24 Sept. 2002 / Joss Whedon / David Solomon

124. Beneath You / 7.2 / 7ABB02 / 1 Oct. 2002 / Doug Petrie / Nick Marck

125. Same Time, Same Place / 7.3 / 7ABB03 / 8 Oct. 2002 / Jane Espenson / James A. Contner

126. Help / 7.4 / 7ABB04 / 15 Oct. 2002 / Rebecca Rand Kirshner / Rick Rosenthal

127. Selfless / 7.5 / 7ABB05 / 22 Oct. 2002 / Drew Goddard / David Solomon

128. Him / 7.6 / 7ABB06 / 5 Nov. 2002 / Drew Z. Greenberg / Michael Gershman

129. Conversations with Dead People / 7.7 / 7ABB07 / 12 Nov. 2002 / Jane Espenson and Drew Goddard / Nick Marck

130. Sleeper / 7.8 / 7ABB08 / 19 Nov. 2002 / David Fury and Jane Espenson / Alan J. Levi

131. Never Leave Me / 7.9 / 7ABB09 / 26 Nov. 2002 / Drew Goddard / David Solomon

132. Bring on the Night / 7.10 / 7ABB10 / 17 Dec. 2002 / Marti Noxon and Doug Petrie / David Grossman

133. Showtime / 7.11 / 7ABB11 / 17 Jan. 2003 / David Fury / Michael Grossman

134. Potential / 7.12 / 7ABB12 / 21 Jan. 2003 / Rebecca Rand Kirshner / James A. Contner

135. The Killer in Me / 7.13 / 7ABB13 / 4 Feb. 2003 / Drew Z. Greenberg / David Solomon

136. First Date / 7.14 / 7ABB14 / 11 Feb. 2003 / Jane Espenson / David Grossman

137. Get It Done / 7.15 / 7ABB15 / 18 Feb. 2003 / Doug Petrie / Doug Petrie

138. Storyteller / 7.16 / 7ABB16 / 25 Feb. 2003 / Jane Espenson / Martia Grabiak

139. Lies My Parents Told Me / 7.17 / 7ABB17 / 25 March 2003 / David Fury and Drew Goddard / David Fury

140. Dirty Girls / 7.18 / 7ABB18 / 22 April 2003 / Drew Goddard / Michael Gershman

141. Empty Places / 7.19 / 7ABB19 / 29 April 2003 / Drew Z. Greenberg / James A. Contner

142. Touched / 7.20 / 7ABB20 / 6 May 2003 / Rebecca Rand Kirshner / Marti Noxon and James A. Contner

143. End of Days / 7.21 / 7ABB21 / 13 May 2003 / Marti Noxon / Marti Noxon

144. Chosen / 7.22 / 7ABB22 / 20 May 2003 / Joss Whedon / Joss Whedon

Notes

Introduction

1. The WB seemed to find the name awkward, suggesting that "Joss Whedon rename it with some kind of pun such as *She Slays Me!* Later, the network marketed the show — without telling Whedon — to affiliates as just *Slayer*." Lawrence Miles, Lars Peterson and Christa Dickson, *Dusted*, p. 29.

2. Contemporary American culture is itself a clearly rather broad term. Much of the discussion in this book is predicated on an understanding of contemporary America as part of the ongoing development of modernity (a term itself that will be much questioned and analyzed throughout the chapters) and of *Buffy* as an explicit engagement with the same phenomenon. The particular example offered by Brian Wall and Michael Zryd is symptomatic of a more general undertaking. They say, "Buffy and Angel's skirmishes with supernatural creatures are battles with the very logic of modernity." "Vampire Dialectics" in Kaveney, *Reading the Vampire Slayer*, p. 76.

3. Umberto Eco, "Reflections on *The Name of the Rose*." *Encounter*, LXIV (April 1985): 7–19.

4. It is not only the antipathy to television as an example of popular culture that demands to be taken seriously that needs to be addressed. Within television criticism there is a canon of the serious and the rest is regarded as largely worthless: "While they [colleagues] no longer raise an eyebrow about *The X-Files*, I get blank and some-times open-mouthed stares when I announce — without embarrassment —*Buffy the Vampire Slayer, Angel, Roswell* on the WB." Richard Campbell with Caitlin Campbell, "Demons, Aliens, Teens and Television" in *Slayage*, number 2 (March 2001). Here, of course, it is not only the presumption that the type of show is already known and deemed inferior, but the network itself is taken to be an example of diminished quality.

5. Jean-François Lyotard, "Answering the Question: What Is Postmodernism?" in Lyotard, *The Postmodern Condition*, p. 82.

6. This is not to imply that genre television is itself degraded. As Giada da Ross passionately argues, "a genre is not good or bad as such, but becomes one or the other on the basis of its use. A genre is as good as you make it to be in the correctness of the single experience." "When, Where and How Much Is *Buffy* a Soap Opera?" in *Slayage*, numbers 13 and 14 (October 2004).

7. One of the best ways of signaling *Buffy's* manipulation of genre can be seen in two types of critical responses to the notion of the gothic. The first type can be represented by the following, primarily literary, study that details the significance of the gothic in its more traditionally understood engagement with culture: "We now realise that quandaries about class conflicts and economic changes, uneasiness over shifting family arrangements and sexual boundaries, and versions of the 'other' which establish racial and cultural distinctions when traditional economic divisions are being

challenged, are projected (or *retro*jected) together into frightening 'gothic' spectres and monsters." Jerrold E. Hogle, "Stoker's Counterfeit Gothic: *Dracula* and Theatricality at the Dawn of Simulation" in Hughes and Smith, *Bram Stoker: History, Psychoanalysis and the Gothic*, p. 206. The second type recognizes the significance of this style of analysis but indicates the ways in which *Buffy* plays with the standard tropes, at least as they are viewed by critics. Boyd Tonkin says, "*Buffy* breaks away from the Gothic tradition with which it so deliriously plays. It masks, or allegorizes, few of its abiding themes. To take the most glaring example, vampires can hardly function as merely an erotic, Freudian 'return of the repressed' in a context that foregrounds sexual desire in such an endearingly matter-of-fact way." "Entropy as Demon" in Kaveney, *Reading the Vampire Slayer*, p. 49. In a similar vein, Robert A. Davis states, "In this respect, as in others, *Buffy* lays claim to the status of a genuinely late, postmodern gothic. [...] Paying homage to the genre does not preclude questioning it and the meanings with which it is currently invested. Indeed a sincere engagement with the artifice of the gothic appears to demand such questioning." "*Buffy the Vampire Slayer* and the Pedagogy of Fear" in *Slayage*, number 3 (June 2001).

8. This dehistoricization, which is also an aesthetic condition and one which operates similarly to Lyotard's notion of the eclectic as mentioned above, is described by Fredric Jameson in relation to architecture: "This situation evidently determines what the architecture historians call 'historicism,' namely the random cannibalization of all the styles of the past, the play of random stylistic allusion. [...] This omnipresence of pastiche is, however, not incompatible with a certain humor (nor is it innocent of all passion) or at least with addiction — with a whole historically original consumers' appetite for a world transformed into sheer images of itself and for pseudo-events and 'spectacles.'" *Postmodernism, or the Cultural Logic of Late Capitalism*, p. 67.

9. It is a point of fact that the gothic as a literary genre appears as an aspect of modernity and that, in part, it is a response to the claims of scientific inquiry to rationalize the supernatural explanations of phenomena for which there had been no other explanatory model during the early modern period. The most explicit expression of this comes, predictably, from Stoker's *Dracula*, where on page 36 Jonathan Harker writes, "the old centuries [...] have powers of their own that mere 'modernity' cannot kill." Harker's assertion of the continuing powers of the old centuries, of the centuries of the premodern, establishes a particular relationship between his narrative and a conception of cultural understanding. The famous move by Stoker of the Castle of Dracula from Styria to Transylvania marks, as has been observed, a specific politicization of *Dracula*, by making concerns about the "Eastern Question" an atmospheric centerpiece of his tale. The contemporary political worries of the day, allied with their attendant fears of "reverse colonization" and the location of these ideas within an explicitly marked "modernity," provide the novel with an attitude to culture that takes the gothic out of the simply sensational and into the profoundly critical.

While modernity for Harker would not have had the plethora of philosophical meanings as it would have today in the light of the debates surrounding modernity and its relationship with postmodernity, it nevertheless means more than just "contemporary." The whole gamut of technological, industrial, political, colonial and sexual questions that are now unambiguously part of the study of the culture of modernity are present in Harker's use, and the explicit juxtaposition of these with the premodern version of engaging with questions of identity, knowledge, ethical decision making, and the general categories of historical movement, insists upon the novel being read as a critique of the culture of modernity.

10. *Buffy*'s own penchant for pastiche and delight in the allusive places it in a general aesthetic economy that can be considered postmodern, but its choices are far from random, and if "historicism" is that which marks the "depthless" aspect of the postmodern in Jameson's, and other's, eyes, the specific historicity of *Buffy* allows it a genuine engagement with the past while retaining the aesthetic tools predominant in the present.

11. Joss Whedon quoted in Gabrielle Moss, "From the Valley to the Hellmouth: Buffy's Transition from Film to Television" in *Slayage*, number 2 (March 2001).

12. Moss, "From the Valley."

13. *Ibid.*

14. See Wendy A. F. G. Stengel, "Synergy and Smut: The Brand in Official and Unofficial *Buffy the Vampire Slayer* Communities of Interest" in *Slayage*, number 4 (December 2001), for a fascinating account of the ways in which *Buffy* circulates across an enormous range of cultural spaces. See also Scott R. Olsen, *Hollywood Planet: Global Media and the Competitive Advantage of Narrative Transparency*, for a wonderful examination of different methods of merchandising and fan involvement more generally.

15. Raymond Williams, *Keywords*, p. 87.

16. Homi Bhaba, *The Location of Culture*, p. 19.

17. Terry Eagleton, *The Ideology of the Aesthetic*, p. 9.

18. Georg Hegel, *Introductory Lectures on Aesthetics*, trans. Bernard Bosanquet, p. 3.

19. See *Slayage*, numbers 13 and 14 (October 2004).

20. "Joss Whedon [...] except for writing earlier shows like *Roseanne* and *Parenthood*, had no prior hands-on experience with making TV." David Lavery, "Emotional Resonance and Rocket Launchers: Joss Whedon's Commentaries on the *Buffy the Vampire Slayer* DVDs" in *Slayage*, number 6 (January 2001).

21. The extent to which competing cultural forces can serve to compromise aesthetic choices is discussed by Judith L. Tabron in "Girl on Girl Politics: Willow/Tara and New Approaches to Media Fandom" in *Slayage*, numbers 13 and 14 (October 2004). She, like many, is concerned that the gay relationship between Willow and Tara ends with Tara's pointless death. Unconvinced by reasons offered by the program makers for the decision to kill Tara, Tabron asserts that economic factors relating to a desire to raise the Nielson ratings in order to be able to gain higher advertising revenue, as well as a general disquiet among advertisers due to the fact of the relationship at all, influenced the choice. The "positive" aesthetic choice is therefore seen as part of a culture of liberal values; the "negative" aesthetic as the material culture of capitalist instrumentalism. The figures following Tara's death and Willow's homicidal turn are interesting insofar as the episodes following the death of Tara until the end of the season all ranked 75th out of

100, as opposed to 93rd for the episode in which Tara dies. This means that the Nielson share increased from 2.7 for the episode in which she dies to 3.2, 3.3 and 3.3 respectively for the season's last three episodes. Whether Tabron is right or not, the argument is illustrative of the inevitable relationship between cultures and aesthetic decisions, whether these are seen as positive, negative, accidental, arbitrary or dialectical.

Chapter 1

1. Jean-François Lyotard, *The Postmodern Condition*, trans. Geoff Bennington and Brian Massumi, p. 19.

2. *The Oxford English Dictionary*, 2nd ed. vol. X, p. 219.

3. This link is enforced when, in a discussion concerning Giles's function as expositor in the show, Kevin McNeilly, Christina Sylka and Susan R. Fisher make the following point: "Giles mediates, discursively, between Buffy and her world. After we learn of his past as 'Ripper' his role becomes increasingly spell-caster [...] But 'spell' in the context of *Buffy* has another, more literal, meaning: *spel* in Old English refers not to magic but to narrative — a story, a telling [...] Library work provides and shapes the narrative line of each episode, the path to follow." "Kiss the Librarian, But Close the Hellmouth: It's Like a Whole Big Sucking Thing" in *Slayage*, number 2 (March 2001).

4. A much fuller assessment of Buffy will be offered in chapter 9.

5. Warping genre for comedic or any other effect clearly necessitates that the audience is aware of genre in the first place and is able to read its subversion accordingly. A notion of a televisual competence not entirely dissimilar to that suggested by Jonathan Culler for literary competence in *Structuralist Poetics: Structuralism, Linguistics and the Study of Literature* would be a useful adjunct to this idea, and is clearly essential for the "external" aspects of the involutional readings that will be offered in later chapters.

6. This claim is described in a different context by Gregory Waller who suggests that 'the bloody confrontation between man and monster is linked with questions about the role of faith and the status of science in

the modern world — in the broadest sense, with the relationship between civilization and the primitive." *The Living and the Undead: From Stoker's "Dracula" to Romero's "Dawn of the Dead,"* p. 22.

7. For a discussion of the importance of secrecy in relation to eschatology and eschatology's presence in *Buffy*, see chapter 3.

8. See Tzevtan Todorov's seminal essay "The Typology of Detective Fiction" in his *The Poetics of Prose*, pp. 42–52 for an account of the different narrative forms and functions of these two genres.

9. Anthony Bradney, "I Made a Promise to a Lady: Law and Love in *BtVS*' in *Slayage*, number 10 (November 2003).

10. Lawrence Miles, Lars Peterson and Christa Dickson. The ever iconoclastic writers of *Dusted*, do not agree with this claim, proposing that (1.1) does "a particularly bad job of hiding Angel's big secret," continuing that the revelation was far from shocking as the audience had "taken [it] for granted from the beginning" (p. 9).

11. The extent to which nihilism is regarded as an evil in itself, thereby making Buffy an instrument of evil at times like this, is addressed by Brian Wall and Michael Zryd in "Vampire Dialectics: Knowledge, Institutions and Labour." They write, "The villains in *Buffy* and *Angel* have totalizing and apocalyptic goals, especially nihilism, the desire for nothingness." In Kaveney, *Reading the Vampire Slayer*, p. 56.

12. Alison Lee, *Realism and Power*, p. 12.

13. *Ibid.*

14. *Ibid.*, p. 13.

15. *Ibid.*, p. 14.

16. Linda Hutcheon, *The Politics of Postmodernism*, p. 3.

17. *Ibid.*

18. Greg Erickson describes the psychiatrist's comments as "a meta-critical and postmodern comment on the discontinuities of the show itself in season six." "The (A)Theology of *Buffy*" in *Slayage*, numbers 13 and 14 (October 2004).

19. See chapter 4 for a short discussion about the costumes in *Buffy*.

20. See chapter 2 for a discussion of the "American-ness" of *Buffy*.

21. Sue Turnbull, "Not Just Another *Buffy* Paper: Towards an Aesthetics of Television" in *Slayage*, numbers 13 and 14 (October 2004).

22. Kevin McNeilly, Christina Sylka, and Susan R. Fisher, "Kiss the Librarian, But Close the Hellmouth: It's Like a Whole Big Sucking Thing" in *Slayage*, number 2 (March 2001).

23. See Rhonda V. Wilcox's "There Will Never Be a Very Special *Buffy*: *Buffy* and the Monsters of Teen Life" in *Slayage*, number 2 (March 2001).

24. Westerfeld in Yeffeth, *Seven Seasons of "Buffy,"* pp. 30–40.

25. In ed. Glenn Yeffeth, *Seven Seasons of "Buffy,"* pp. 176–87. Carter makes the following point in order to allow altered responses to the existent reality (such as in "Superstar" or "Normal Again") the same status as a truly "alternative" reality: "The audience, standing outside the *Buffy*verse, is aware of both realities, old and new. To the characters, though, the old reality does not exist and never existed [...] As far as any practical effects are concerned, the world as they perceive it in the present and remember it in the past is the only reality" (pp. 178–79).

26. The ability of the rules of the Buffyverse to shift and expand can be seen in a variety of ways, most important perhaps in terms of the lore regarding the Slayer. The co-authors of *Dusted* assert that the expansion of Slayer lore with the introduction of Kendra is that which "grants the series a *mythology*," (p. 56). I would say it extends the mythological reach of the show, which has already been instituted by Marcie's story, if mythology here is taken to mean the deep reservoir of the external into which the series can continually delve.

27. The importance of the structure of the show, including advertising breaks, closing credits, trademark logos and so on, will be the focus of chapter 5.

28. At the risk of substituting the fan for the critic, my response to seeing this for the first time was utterly thrilled confusion. I knew that the program would have some sort of explanation at some point, but I was happy to revel in my bewilderment.

29. This point will be developed in part II.

30. *Buffy*'s remodeling of the gothic along postmodern lines has been wonderfully described by Robert A. Davis. His magisterial essay, *"Buffy the Vampire Slayer* and the Pedagogy of Fear" in *Slayage*, number 3 (June 2001), locates *Buffy* in the context of the postmodern gothic. He says, "The best storylines of the series succeed in dramatizing the ambiguities of the postmodern

gothic, showing how the gothic tradition now struggles to make its fundamental insights meaningful to a culture desensitized by the horrors of its own sense of history, and frequently distanced from the conventional sources of fear by its scientific rationalism and finely tuned capacity for irony."

31. The role of Dawn will be addressed in chapter 9.

32. Michel Foucault, *Madness and Civilization*, trans. Richard Howard, p. x.

33. The extent to which the institutional power of the school is subverted by Buffy's, Giles's and the gang's use of it is questioned (along with other supposed subversions of institutional power in the show) by Martin Buinicki and Anthony Enns in "Buffy the Vampire Disciplinarian: Institutional Excess and the New Economy of Power" in *Slayage*, number 4 (December 2001). They write: "Therefore, these apparent subversions of institutional power merely signal a resistance to the excessive use of power, to outdated institutional models rather than to institutional power in general."

34. The most famous "closed" library in contemporary culture is probably that of Jorge's library in Umberto Eco's *The Name of the Rose*. Jorge's desire to retain control over the dissemination of knowledge has strong parallels with Giles's role.

35. The failed detective Sergeant Cuff in *The Moonstone* offers a marvelous early critique of the limits of both detective fiction and the detective process it employed.

36. McNeilly et al., "Kiss the Librarian, But Close the Hellmouth."

37. *Buffy*'s hesitant engagement with popular culture, both in terms of its products and its material processes, is discussed in Sue Turnbull's fabulous essay "Not Just Another *Buffy* Paper." Thinking of Andrew's love of television particularly, she writes "that Andrew the TV fan is routinely portrayed as comic provokes the niggling possibility that the creators of this series can't help but construct fandom for popular culture as somehow inherently 'funny.'"

38. Michelle Callander, "Bram Stoker's *Buffy*: Traditional Gothic and Contemporary Culture" in *Slayage*, number 3 (June 2001).

39. Toby Daspit, "Buffy Goes to College, Adam Murders to Dissect: Education and Knowledge in Postmodernity" in ed. South, *"Buffy the Vampire Slayer" and Philosophy*, p. 121.

40. See chapter 3 for a discussion of modernity and history.

41. A similar sense of the rational deployed in order to control and understand the irrational is the Mothers Opposed to the Occult (MOO) group in "Gingerbread" (3.11). Rob Breton and Lindsay McMaster suggest that Buffy's defeat of them is also a defeat of rationalism at the hands of something more archaic, even anarchic: "Buffy's ad hoc tactics threaten not the purpose of MOO but their governing strategy, which would establish a predictable, systematic world order to control it." "Dissing the Age of MOO: Initiatives, Alternatives and Rationality" in *Slayage*, number 1 (January 2001).

42. Examples of this would be any number of Cordelia's and Doyle's visions, Wesley's seeming misinterpretation of the prophecy regarding Connor, and, most important, the prophecy concerning the status of Angel should he ever achieve salvation.

43. The show's willingness to present *any* form of claim to absolute knowledge as suspect, be it rational, scientific, mystical or magical implies that it is as much, if not more, the extent of knowledge's claims rather than its mode that is most important. Brian Wall and Michael Zryd have some concerns about the actual mode, especially to the extent that the show might be promoting the mystical over the rational: "[such categories of the supernatural] are easily understood as remnants of quasi-religious pre–Enlightenment mythology functioning ideologically to reinstate metaphysical categories: a regressive return to magical thinking." "Vampire Dialectics" in Kaveney, *Reading the Vampire Slayer*, p. 63.

Chapter 2

1. Charlaine Harris, "A Reflection on Ugliness" in Yeffeth, *Seven Seasons of "Buffy,"* p. 116.

2. Lawrence Miles, Lars Peterson and Christa Dickson worry that even with such a major figure, the representation of his ethnicity (especially when he uses terms like "my people") "once again makes all foreigners (this time Irish) sound like quaint storybook tribesmen." *Dusted*, p. 64.

3. As Kent A. Ono has indicated: "the marginalization of vampires on the show takes the place of racial marginalization in

the world outside the show." "To Be a Vampire in *Buffy the Vampire Slayer*: Race and (Other) Socially Marginalized Positions on Horror TV" in Helford, *Gender in the New Universe of Science Fiction and Fantasy Television*, p. 172.

4. Julie Rivkin and Michael Ryan, "English Without Shadows" in Rivkin and Ryan, *Literary Theory: An Anthology*, p. 855.

5. Greg Erickson's excellent essay "Religion Freaky or a 'Bunch of Men Who Died?': The (A)Theology of *Buffy*" in *Slayage*, numbers 13 and 14 (October 2004), makes the following crucial point, among others, with regard to any supposed grounding of identity through the concept of a soul: "On *Buffy*, it is not the presence of a soul that separates humans from vampires (Angel, a vampire *with* a soul is still not human), but it *is* the lack of a soul that seems to make a vampire evil." Martin Buinicki and Anthony Enns make an even more striking point when they try to demonstrate how the soul is itself a disciplinary category wherein, "Buffy's exercise of disciplinary power actually rehearses the process by which souls are produced and sustained." "Buffy the Vampire Disciplinarian: Institutional Excess and the New Economy of Power," *Slayage*, number 4 (December 2001).

6. Luke Owen Pike, *The English and Their Origin: A Prologue to Authentic English History,* quoted in Patrick Brantlinger, "The Rule of Darkness" in Rivkin and Ryan, *Literary Theory: An Anthology*, p. 857.

7. The utterly coincidental fact that Pike happens to be the name of Buffy's mortal love interest in the original movie could be argued as one of the moments of involution that I discuss in part II of this book, though I would be hesitant to push this particular claim.

8. Robert Knox, quoted in Rivkin and Ryan, *Literary Theory: An Anthology*, p. 85.

9. The Chumash tribe and *Buffy*'s representation of U.S history with regard to indigenous peoples will be discussed in chapter 3.

10. Lyotard has used this phrase in a variety of books and essays, but the first and, therefore, most cited is from *The Postmodern Condition: A Report on Knowledge*, trans. Bennington and Massumi.

11. Lyotard, "A Postmodern Fable" in *Postmodern Fables*, trans. Van Den Abbeele, p. 96.

12. I discuss this further in chapter 3.

13. Lyotard, "A Postmodern Fable," p. 96.

14. *Ibid.*, p. 97.

15. Lyotard, "Apostil on Narratives" in *The Postmodern Explained to Children*, trans. Pefanis and Thomas, pp. 29–30.

16. Lyotard, "Postscript to Terror and the Sublime" in *The Postmodern Explained to Children*, trans. Pefanis and Thomas, p. 84.

17. The danger of trying to reduce *Buffy* to a simple expression of sociologically required representations is addressed by Boyd Tonkin in his "Entropy as Demon: Buffy in Southern California" in Kaveney, *Reading the Vampire Slayer*. He states "though *Buffy* can indeed be read in the light of an underlying social truth, it is also a clever and knowing enough enterprise to be able to mock [...] its own more pedestrian analysts" (p. 47).

18. *Buffy the Vampire Slayer: The Script Book, Season One, Vol. One*, p. 7.

19. I am very grateful to David Lavery for sending me his "Fatal Environment: *Buffy the Vampire Slayer* and American Culture," which he presented at the *Staking a Claim* conference held in Adelaide, Australia, July 2003.

20. Boyd Tonkin, "Entropy as Demon: Buffy in Southern California" in Kaveney, *Reading the Vampire Slayer*, pp. 37–52.

21. The character of Charles Gunn in *Angel* is interestingly critiqued from the position of ethnicity in Naomi Alderman and Annette Seidel-Arpaci, "Imaginary Parasites-Sites of the Soul: Vampires and Representations of 'Blackness' and 'Jewishness' in the *Buffy/Angel*verse" in *Slayage*, number 10 (November 2003).

22. In terms of identity, it is important to remember (and this will form a substantial part of chapter 9) that Buffy's own position as human is far from secure. The extent to which she is herself demonic or monstrous (whether through performance or nature) is mentioned by Christopher Golden, Stephen R. Bissette and Thomas E. Sniegoski in *Buffy the Vampire Slayer: The Monster Book* where they say, "By extension [to Willow, Amy, Tara etc.] our definition also encompasses the Slayer. As we stated at the outset, based on those parameters Buffy herself readily fits the bill [of monster]" (p. 360).

23. Bill Readings, "Pagans, Perverts or

Primitives? Experimental Justice in the Empire of Capital" in Benjamin, *Judging Lyotard*, p. 86.

24. Anthony Bradney, "I Made a Promise to a Lady: Law and Love in *BtVS*," in *Slayage*, number 10 (November 2003).

25. As Hilary M. Leon asserts in "Why We Love the Monsters: How Anita Blake Vampire Hunter, and Buffy the Vampire Slayer Wound up Dating the Enemy" in *Slayage*, number 1 (January 2001), it is true that "in Buffy's world, Angel is introduced as the single exception to Giles's vampire law." And it is equally true that Joss Whedon has made his feelings clear about what a vampire is, as the following quotation from Michelle Callander's "Bram Stoker's *Buffy*: Traditional Gothic and Contemporary Culture" in *Slayage*, number 3 (June 2001) attests: "a vampire is not a person. It's a monster that looks like a person." But Buffy's refusal to allow the Council's law to include Angel also, of necessity, refuses its applicability more generally.

26. The episode "Hero" (*Ats* 1.9) offers a version of differing ethnicities through the rather grim storyline of an attempt at ethnic cleansing within the demon world.

27. As Mary Alice Money suggests: "Increasingly, the heroes begin to recognize the Other figure as an individual person instead of reacting to the figure as merely an unchanging member of a certain race, gender, or culture." "The Undemonizing of Supporting Characters in *Buffy*" in Wilcox and Lavery, *Fighting the Forces*, p. 107.

28. Rob Breton and Lindsey McMaster, "Dissing the Age of MOO: Initiatives, Alternatives, and Rationalism," in *Slayage*, number 1 (January 2001).

29. Aimee Fifarek, "Mind and Heart with Spirit Joined: The Buffyverse as an Information System," in *Slayage*, number 3 (June 2001). Additionally, the dehumanizing aspect of ontological discrimination that can be seen to have justified Nazi actions during Hitler's rule are provided with a broader (though no less dreadful) set of applications when Spike ponders the Initiative and asks a fellow inmate in their lab who these people are: "The government? Nazis? A major cosmetics company?" "The Initiative" (4.7).

30. Alderman and Seidel-Arpaci, "Imaginary Para-Sites of the Soul: Vampires and Representations of 'Blackness' and 'Jewishness' in the *Buffy / Angel*verse" in *Slayage*, number 10 (November 2003).

31. *Ibid.*

32. *Ibid.*

33. Mary Alice Money appears to adhere to a much more liberal notion of ethnic inclusion when, in discussing the ways in which peripheral character become less and less demonic, she asserts, "in these rehabilitated humans and demons, the main characters and the audience confront the Other: the marginalized figures who are worthy of inclusion, the nonhumans who are people after all, the strangers who become us." "The Undemonization of Supporting Characters in *Buffy*" in Wilcox and Lavery, *Fighting the Forces*, p. 98.

34. Jean François Lyotard, "Heidegger and 'the jews,'" in Readings, *Political Writings*, p. 141.

35. Jean François Lyotard, "Heidegger and 'the jews,'" p. 144. Lyotard's notion of screen memory is taken from Freud's. The latter's conjecture about the individual's relationship to memory, especially in terms of amnesia, is that "what is important remains in the memory. But through the processes, already familiar to you, of condensation and more especially of displacement, what is important in memory is replaced by something else which appears unimportant." (Sigmund Freud, "The Archaic Features and Infantilism of Dreams," in Strachey and Richards, trans. Strachey, *Introductory Lectures on Psychoanalysis: Penguin Freud Library* vol. 1, p. 237. This notion is then used by Freud in part 1(C) section 3 of "Moses and Monotheism" to draw an analogy between the trauma suffered by an individual, which might be responsible for amnesia, and the trauma of a nation (or tribe) and its collective amnesiac condition and concomitant substitutive memory.

36. David Carroll, "Foreword: The Memory of Devastation and the Responsibilities of Thought: 'And let's not talk about that,'" in Jean-François Lyotard, *Heidegger and 'the jews,"* pp. xi–xii.

37. Lynne Edwards, "Slaying in Black and White" in Wilcox and Lavery, *Fighting the Forces*, p. 95.

38. *Ibid.*, p. 94.

39. *Ibid.*, p. 96.

40. For an excellent discussion of *Buffy*'s comedy see Steve Wilson's "Laugh, Spawn of Hell, Laugh" in Kaveney, *Reading the Vampire Slayer*, pp. 78–97.

41. Rob Francis's "London Calling: *Buffy* from a British Perspective," in Ruditis, *The*

Watcher's Guide, vol. 3, pp. 255–64, is an appealing and sympathetic view of the program from my side of the Atlantic.

42. See chapter 3 for a discussion of the importance of European history in *Buffy* and chapter 4 for some of the ways in which the European vampire myth and the U.S. (mainly Hollywood) reworkings of this myth are brought together in the show.

43. Vladimir Nabokov was irritated that his novel was reduced by some critics to a tale of brash, crude, young America being debauched by the sophisticated but depraved and perverse Europe (Nabokov, "On a book entitled *Lolita,*" in Appel, Jr., *The Annotated Lolita,* p. 314).

44. The delightfully caustic observations in *Dusted* with respect to *Buffy*'s treatment of the British is always amusing and I would recommend anyone interested in this to read them. They allow Giles a sense of realism because he enjoys Bovril but dismiss some of his language because no one on Earth, let alone in England talks that way. In fact, this is not true. Many of the more precious phrases Giles uses are still reasonably common, although in admittedly restricted and rarefied contexts. It is not unusual, for example, for me to say "frightfully," though I accept that the places where I would say this are becoming increasingly hard to find.

45. Giles's history and the conflict between his role as Watcher and his potential for a life of his own away from this responsibility will be discussed in greater detail in chapter 8.

46. For a number of discussions relating to questions of masculinity in *Buffy*, please see Stevie Simkin's two essays in *Slayage,* numbers 11 and 12 (April 2004). These are "You Hold Your Gun Like a Sissy Girl: Firearms and Anxious Masculinity in *BtVS*" and "Who Died and Made You John Wayne: Anxious Masculinity in *Buffy the Vampire Slayer.*" Also see Lorna Jowett's "New Men: Playing the Sensitive Lad" in *Slayage,* numbers 13 and 14 (October 2004).

47. The show's plundering of generic possibility only lightly alludes to the mafia movie and Western here. However, the payoff (and *Buffy* almost never seems to use an allusion lightly, there is always some later restatement or revision) comes, for the mafia movie homage, in the parodic figure of the loan-shark mobster in "Tabula Rasa" (6.8) as well as in many *Angel* episodes where su-

pernatural and human versions of organized crime are included. The Western motif gets its reprise in season five where the Western itself is fused with a medieval quest through the Knights of Byzantium and a bizarre take on the road-movie-family-holiday genre with the battered RV in "Spiral" (5.20).

48. A brief discussion of Giles's relation to language as a medium of political rebellion will be undertaken in chapter 3.

49. A further consideration of Spike's "punk" persona will be presented in chapter 4.

50. "Restless" (4.22) will be at the center of discussion in part II of this book.

51. It is not just Giles's language that marks differentiation, whether through ethnicity or age. As Rhonda Wilcox has pointed out in "There Will Never Be a Very Special *Buffy*: *Buffy* and the Monsters of Teen Life" in *Slayage,* number 2 (March 2001), language differentiation operates in a number of ways: "The striking differentiation of the teen language in *Buffy* has often been commented on. The language of the teens starkly contrasts with that of the adults. This linguistic separateness emphasizes the lack of communication between the generations, as does the series' use of the symbolism of monsters to represent social problems."

52. The extent to which it is more usual for performativity to be discussed in relation to sexuality and gender, than in relation to ethnicity, is a disappointment, though its work in these areas has produced some fine analyses. Among those who have used a notion of performativity in relation to sexuality in *Buffy* is Laura Diehl. Her essay "Why Drusilla's More Interesting Than Buffy," in *Slayage,* numbers 13 and 14 (October 2004), indicates how the general theory applies: "Monsters such as Drusilla and Darla hold discourse at a distance, turning misogynist narratives into excessive performances that destabilize, disempower and recirculate their meanings."

53. This is an accusation that is, for the most part, unfair; the description of him sounding "like a vampire David Bowie" (whose own verbal performance of Englishness is staggeringly polymorphous) is nearer the mark and is made by Lawrence Miles, Lars Peterson and Christa Dickson in *Dusted,* p. 42.

54. The BBC's choices with regard to editing and scheduling have been discussed by,

among others, Annette Hill and Ian Calcutt in "Vampire Hunters: The Scheduling and Reception of *Buffy the Vampire Slayer* and *Angel* in the UK," in *Intensities: The Journal of Cult Media*, issue 1; Vivien Burr, "*Buffy* vs. the BBC: Moral Questions and How to Avoid Them," in *Slayage*, number 8 (March 2003); and Kevin Andrew Murphy in "Unseen Horrors and Shadowy Manipulations" in Yeffeth, *Seven Seasons of "Buffy,"* pp. 138–51.

Chapter 3

1. In saying this, I am not denying its generally religious nor specifically Christian aspects. Rather I am locating my argument in line with the excellent essay written by Greg Erickson, "Religion Freaky or a 'Bunch of Men Who Died?': The (A)Theology of *Buffy*," in *Slayage*, numbers 13 and 14 (October 2004). This sophisticated and careful essay covers a range of areas and it is unfair to reduce it to its concluding sentence, but it is such an apt sentence, I cannot avoid it: "*Buffy the Vampire Slayer* expresses neither an absolute certainty nor a total abyss, but, as a postmodern atheology, finds in the death of its gods not despair but opportunity."

2. David Lavery, "Apocalyptic Apocalypses: Narrative Eschatology in *Buffy the Vampire Slayer*," in *Slayage*, number 9 (August 2003).

3. While this is true of each of the seasons' Big Bads, it is also necessary to note, as Boyd Tonkin does that "on reflection, *Buffy*'s bestiary of the underworld is memorable less for its heavyweight apocalyptic talent than for its capacity to generate interminable, medium-level annoyance." "Entropy as Demon: *Buffy* in Southern California" in Kaveney, *Reading the Vampire Slayer*, p. 43.

4. At the time of writing, this paper is unpublished and I am indebted to Professor Lavery for allowing me to use it.

5. Roz Kaveney, "Introduction" in Kaveney, *Reading the Vampire Slayer*, p. 4.

6. This "normal" aesthetic mode for *Buffy* both in terms of what is represented and in the filmic strategies deployed in order to provide a consistent and recognizable Sunnydale style is discussed in Sue Turnbull's essay "Not Just Another *Buffy* Paper: Towards an Aesthetics of Television"

in *Slayage*, numbers 13 and 14 (October 2004). In connection to the episode "Storyteller" (7.9) and its differing aesthetic choices, Turnbull makes the following observation: "What is interesting is that the *Buffy* 'standard' can contain, mock and mimic both the film and the video, using each style quite precisely in order to say important things about character and plot [...] [T]elevisual style is intrinsic to that of storytelling."

7. Bruce McClelland goes so far as to claim that here "then is why Buffy is chosen: in the movie more than in the TV show, she is the archetype of the postmodern, the perfect embodiment of the slick democratizing values which would be undercut by any admission of what had been displaced to make way for post-capitalism." "By Whose Authority? The Magical Tradition, Violence and the Legitimation of the Vampire Slayer" in *Slayage*, number 1 (January 2001).

8. See Francis Fukuyama's controversial expression of the inevitable and triumphal ascendancy of liberal capitalism in his *The End of History and the Last Man* for an example of this contemporary pseudo-eschatological approach to history and U.S. culture.

9. Among the many books written on this subject, the following provide a pleasing array of styles and approaches. The full citations are to be found in the bibliography: *Dracula: Prince of Many Faces. His Life and Times* by Radu R. Florescu and Raymond T. McNally; *In Search of Dracula: The History of Dracula and Vampires* by Raymond T. McNally and Radu Florescu; *Vlad the Impaler: In Search of the Real Dracula* by M. J. Trow; *Vlad III Dracula: The Life and Times of the Historical Dracula* by Kurt W. Treptow.

10. See Jonathan Riley-Smith's wonderfully readable and informative *Oxford History of the Crusades* for a very good history of this part of European and Arabic history.

11. Tom Shippey, "Editorial Note," in Shippey and Arnold, *Studies in Medievalism*, volume XII, p. 2.

12. Nikolas A. Haydock, "Arthurian Melodrama, Chaucerian Spectacle, and the Waywardness of Cinematic Pastiche in *First Knight* and *A Knight's Tale*" in Shippey and Arnold, *Studies in Medievalism*, volume XII, p. 5.

13. The specifically nineteenth-century aspect of William, and the extent to which

this is influenced by (or can be read against) a set of literary histories, is discussed by Claire Fossey in her "Never Hurt the Feelings of a Brutal Killer: Spike and the Underground Man," in *Slayage,* number 8, March 2003.

14. Tertullian, *De praescriptione haereticorum,* xii c.203.

15. St. Cyril, *Catechetical Lectures,* I xii.

16. Gore Vidal's *Julian* provides a fascinating fictional account of the tensions between early Christian and continuing pagan religions in post-conversion Roman culture.

17. I Thess. 4:16–17.

18. Matt. 25:31–46.

19. Luke 21:18–19.

20. Rom. 8:18–25.

21. 1 John 2:20–21.

22. 2 Peter 3:16.

23. 2 Peter 2:10–12.

24. Colossians 3:11.

25. References to a Christianized worldview, for example, are observable not only in mainland Europe but also in the Saga cycles from Iceland.

26. Jean-François Lyotard, "A Postmodern Fable" in Lyotard, *Postmodern Fables,* p. 97.

27. Mark Dery, *The Pyrotechnic Insanitorium: American Culture on the Brink,* p. 57.

28. Catherine Siemann, "Darkness Falls on the Endless Summer" in ed. Wilcox and Lavery, *Fighting the Forces,* p. 121.

29. *Ibid.*

30. Kevin Andrew Murphy writes an excellent defense of this episode in his wonderful and provocative essay "Unseen Horrors and Shadowy Manipulations," in ed. Yeffeth, *Seven Seasons of "Buffy,"* pp. 137–51. Berating a number of instruments of censorship, whether state sponsored or privately instituted, and ranging in his ire from the BBC to online lesbian communities angry at Tara's death (for an equally excellent response to that, see Judith L. Tabron's "Girl on Girl Politics: Willow/Tara and New Approaches to Media Fandom" in *Slayage*). Murphy encourages us to reread "Beer Bad" as a "hilarious parody" of what happens when an "independent-minded crew of writers are ordered to write an anti-drug and -alcohol propaganda" (p. 143).

31. Tanya Kryzwinska, "Hubble-Bubble, Herbs and Grimoires" in ed. Wilcox and Lavery, *Fighting the Forces,* p. 180.

32. See chapter 1 for a discussion of fate in *Buffy.*

33. It is, of course, worth noting that postmodern individualism is a surprisingly homogenized ideal, driven by capital and the requirements of the market. As Robert A. Davis cuttingly declares, "within the terms of her own narratives, the anarchy Buffy most consistently contains is the threat of genuinely radical alternatives to the largely docile and normative teen culture she and her friends embody." "*Buffy the Vampire Slayer* and the Pedagogy of Fear" in *Slayage,* number 3 (June 2001).

34. Jean-François Lyotard, "A Postmodern Fable," in Lyotard, *Postmodern Fables,* p. 97.

35. The extraordinary fun that the writers have with invoking and then undermining many of the tropes of popular culture, fantasy, horror and science fiction is discussed in Roz Kaveney in her introduction to *Reading the Vampire Slayer,* p. 27. Commenting on the episode "The Replacement" (5.3) and its use of the "evil double" figure that appears to be stalking Xander, she says that when "both Xanders laughingly reference the parallel episode of *Star Trek*—"kill us both Spock"—it is an acknowledgment that they and we have been misled by a stock trope of popular culture—not every double is a shadow double."

36. Vampires in *Buffy* are typically much less seduced by the potential benefits of technological advance and scientific rationalism and are much more enamoured of arcane ritual and the structures of belief that support this, which leads to Spike's famous clarion call of anarchistic turmoil in (2.3) where he demands less ritual and more fun. Using this as her article title, Stacey Abbott remarks: "In the end, it is her [Buffy's] embodiment of the 'now' that gives her an edge against the vampires with whom she does battle and the Council for whom she works, for her actions consistently undermine their expectations and confuse their tradition-bound perception." "A Little Less Ritual and a Lot More Fun: The Modern Vampire in *Buffy the Vampire Slayer*" in *Slayage,* number 3 (June 2001).

37. Probably the most famous debates concerning these issues are those that occurred between Jürgen Habermas and Jean-François Lyotard over a number of years.

38. Buffy has used the word "Indian" slightly earlier from which we can infer either a lapse in writing or a subtle linguistic

expression of Buffy's rather ad hoc response to the whole affair.

39. The surprising number of jokes related to kitchen appliances is briefly mentioned in chapter 9.

40. See the discussion relating to Willow's Jewishness in chapter 2.

41. Quoted in Helen Hunt Jackson, *A Century of Dishonor: A Sketch of the United States Government's Dealings with Some of the Indian Tribes*, p. 21.

42. *Ibid.*, p. 189.

43. Considering the teleological aspects of *Buffy* and its relation with certain philosophical conceptions in season 7 of the series, James South writes: "I think the ultimate lesson of the season is a destruction of Buffy's Slayer story and, by extension, a recognition that teleological stories can be more destructive in their way than the kind of evil they try to contain." "On the Philosophical Consistency of Season Seven: Or, 'It's Not About Right, Not About Wrong ...'" in *Slayage*, numbers 13 and 14 (October 2004).

Chapter 4

1. Frances Early, "Staking Her Claim: Buffy the Vampire Slayer as Transgressive Woman Warrior" in *Slayage*, number 6 (September 2002), previously published in *The Journal of Popular Culture*, vol. 35, no. 3 (Winter 2001), pp. 11–27.

2. Camille Bacon-Smith, "The Color of the Dark" in *Slayage*, number 8 (March 2003).

3. Charlaine Harris, "A Reflection on Ugliness" in Yeffeth, *Seven Seasons of "Buffy,"* pp. 116–20.

4. Scott R. Stroud, "A Kantian Analysis of Moral Judgment in *Buffy the Vampire Slayer*" in South, *"Buffy the Vampire Slayer" and Philosophy*, p. 194.

5. Greg Foster, "Faith and Plato: 'You're nothing! Disgusting, Murderous Bitch'" in South, *"Buffy the Vampire Slayer" and Philosophy*, p. 19.

6. Richard Greene and Wayne Yuen are more convinced of a set of determinable moral principles within which the characters of *Buffy* have to operate and they enumerate them in "Why We Can't Spike Spike: Moral Themes in *Buffy the Vampire Slayer*" in *Slayage*, number 2 (March 2001). Their list is as follows: "(1) Do not harm those

who typically do not pose a threat to human beings. (2) One ought to stop (either by killing or incapacitating) all non-humans who typically can or will harm other human beings. (3) Do not harm those who pose no immediate threat. (4) No harm should be done to those who don't harm human beings. (5) Unless there is some urgent or pressing matter, fairness should be taken into account. (6) Those that do harm humans but can be controlled should be controlled. (7) When the benefits of a good opportunity outweigh the risks of a dangerous situation, the good should be attempted."

7. Brian Wall and Michael Zryd, "Vampire Dialectics" in Kaveney, *Reading the Vampire Slayer*, p. 59.

8. Jean-François Lyotard, "Answer to the Question: What Is Postmodernism?" in Pefanis and Thomas, *The Postmodern Explained to Children: Correspondence 1982–1985*, trans. Don Barry et al., p. 24.

9. The school is Torrance High School, located at 2200 West Carson Street, Torrance, California, 90501.

10. The episode's opening provides a montage drawn mainly from the original movie of armies of vampires, which is used to show Buffy having nightmares. This locates her as the Slayer and demonstrates at the outset that she is not necessarily entirely comfortable with this role.

11. In Christopher Golden and Nancy Holder, *The Watcher's Guide*, vol. 1, p. 274.

12. The increasing fame of Sarah Michelle Gellar, and her attendant sexualization through, for example, magazines aimed at young men has led Sherryl Vint to wonder whether the openness of the text, its susceptibility to "producerly" readings in which the viewer is able to invoke a whole range of images external to the show in order to inform their understanding of the show, is detrimental rather than enabling: "Do the sexualised readings of Buffy/Sarah Michelle Gellar in magazines directed at male fans undo the powerful feminist role model offered by the primary text? Is the openness to producerly readings a liability rather than a strength for the show?" "Killing Us Softly? A Feminist Search for the 'Real' Buffy" in *Slayage*, number 5 (May 2002).

13. DVD commentary to "Welcome to the Hellmouth" (1.1).

14. The brooding noir hero that we see in *Buffy* becomes increasingly dark in *Angel*, and the complexity of his moral position is,

similarly, increased until he willingly sacrifices innocents for the greater good (see *AtS* 5.21–5.22).

15. The fish monsters, or more properly boys who become fish monsters after being forced to take steroids by their swim team coach, are from "Go Fish" (2.20), which is among the most dismal episodes in the *Buffy* catalogue but does have two redeeming features: first, Jonathan is mentioned by name onscreen for the first time, and second, the "Into every generation..." tag line appears for the very last time. Additionally, Buffy's inability to find a boyfriend who is not a monster in some form or another (and therefore *Buffy*'s ongoing rehearsal of the fear of youthful sexuality) is once again brought to the fore. Other episodes where Buffy's paramour is monstrous include "I Was Made to Love You" (5.15), "The Harsh Light of Day" (4.3), "Innocence" (2.14) and "Reptile Boy" (2.7), among others.

16. Olaf makes his first appearance in "Triangle" (5.11). This seemingly inconsequential episode becomes much more significant at the season's finale when the hammer that Olaf leaves behind becomes one of the important weapons used to defeat Glory. The attention to plotting and the sophistication of the narrative aside, the ethical meaning of the hammer shifts remarkably between the two episodes. Even at the level of a prop, the writers are able to provide subtle ethical points through their aesthetic.

17. The woman herself (the stand-in teacher from "Teacher's Pet" [1.4]) is not ugly, but the insectlike creature she becomes most definitely is ugly. Evil can hide behind beauty, but its true form, its real shape is nearly always repellent.

18. The ethical dimension of *Buffy* took a rather more practical turn with this episode. The WB decided not to show it in its proposed slot because the line "Who hasn't idly thought about taking out the whole place with a semi-automatic" was deemed inappropriate in the wake of the Columbine school shootings.

19. Dawn makes the point clear when she claims in "Blood Ties" (5.13) that Buffy is only upset because she has to fight someone prettier than she is. Buffy's retort is that Glory is evil, powerful and in no way prettier than she is.

20. For discussions concerning the nature of masculinity in *Buffy* see Stevie Simkin's two articles in *Slayage*, numbers 11 and 12 (April 2004): "You Hold Your Gun Like a Sissy Girl: Firearms and Anxious Masculinity in *BtVS*" and "Who Died and Made You John Wayne? Anxious Masculinity in *Buffy the Vampire Slayer*." See also Lorna Jowett, "New Men: Playing the Sensitive Lad" in *Slayage*, numbers 13 and 14 (October 2004).

21. James B. South, "My God, It's Like a Greek Tragedy: Willow Rosenberg and Human Irrationality" in South, *"Buffy the Vampire Slayer" and Philosophy*, pp. 131–46.

22. We have also seen the physically disabling effects on Willow of attempting high-level magic in her spell to make Glory disappear in "Blood Ties" (5.13). This causes her to have headaches and a nosebleed, in addition to her eyes turning black.

23. Laura Diehl writes wonderfully about Drusilla from the point of view of queer criticism in the fabulous essay "Why Drusilla's More Interesting Than Buffy" in *Slayage*, numbers 13 and 14 (October 2004).

24. Though Spike in his human incarnation as William, the would-be poet, does have simply blonde hair. For Delores J. Nurss this suggests that "Spike particularly reflects Buffy — he forces her to confront the fact that she is as much of a killer as he is, however much of a good guy she tries to be." Quoted in Rhonda V. Wilcox, "Every Night I Save You: Buffy, Spike, Sex and Redemption" in *Slayage*, number 5 (May 2002).

25. The move from season 2's evil but comic disruptor figure to season 4's comic hero to season 5's would-be savior figure to season 6's curious savior-cum-rapist to season 7's actual savior figure marks a trajectory that Michelle Boyette, following Wylie Sypher, reads as the move from the "azalon" to the "eiron." These terms, drawn from Sypher's "Appendix" to *Comedy*, locate Spike as a part of a tradition of comedic characters who nevertheless move well beyond the usually allowed scope of these tropes. The specifically comedic reading of Spike (which could never be undertaken for Angel, who, though occasionally funny is not a comic character) demonstrates another way in which the aesthetic choices regarding character are already imbued with certain ethical possibilities that, once more, the *Buffy* team are able to manipulate and undermine.

26. This will be discussed at greater length in chapter 9.

27. Ian Shuttleworth makes mention of the Faith-Buffy switch in "They Always Mistake Me for the Character I Play!" This essay, which is a glorious paean to the power of the acting performances in *Buffy* and *Angel*, addresses the extent to which the actresses' skills are central to the scriptwriters' wishes insofar as metamorphoses are concerned. The metamorphosis (whether a body swap, a vampire double, or the simple growth through time) of a character always has ethical implications and, here, the precise aesthetic function of fine acting is to accommodate that ethical probing (p. 213).

28. See chapter 2 for a discussion of this.

29. In this episode, Whedon attempted to reproduce something of the effect of the seemingly impossible super-slow-motion tracking shots used in *The Matrix* (achieved by having scores of single-shot cameras synchronized to split-second perfection and then editing together these images into the continuous stream we see in the film). And his show succeeded, even if he did not actually direct the episode (4.21): the slowing down and capturing of Adam's bullets by Buffy and her transforming them into doves is one of the most visually memorable moments in any episode. (Though, to my mind, rather less brilliant than the astonishing timing of the arrival of the fire trucks into shot on the word "fire" during the song "Walk Through the Fire" in "Once More with Feeling" [6.7]).

30. See Mimi Marinucci, "Feminism and the Ethics of Violence: Why Buffy Kicks Ass" in South, *"Buffy the Vampire Slayer" and Philosophy*, pp. 61–75.

31. Golden et al., *The Monster Book*, p. 94.

32. Although he locates the vampire representations in a primarily literary context, Bruce McClelland also highlights their comparatively modern antecedents: "The imagery of the vampire that pervades *BtVS* [...] is a blend of borrowed literary (essentially post–Stoker and significantly post–Rice) conceptions." "By Whose Authority: The Magical Tradition, Violence and the Legitimation of the Vampire Slayer" in *Slayage*, number 1 (January 2001).

33. Stacey Abbott would argue this point, claiming instead that "Joss Whedon's vampires seem to mark a return to a premodern representation of the vampire." "A Little Less Ritual and a Lot More Fun: The Modern Vampire in *Buffy the Vampire Slayer*" in *Slayage*, number 3 (June 2001).

34. Lestat, of course, being the famous vampire from the Anne Rice series of novels. The extent to which one may wish to claim a specifically Louisianan tradition, rather than a generally American one, is a matter for literary historians to dispute.

35. The University of Mississippi Film Studies department website (http://www. olemiss.edu/courses/engl205/draculafilm. html) has a comprehensive annotated filmography related to Dracula movies, from which the following is excerpted: *Nosferatu, Eine Symphonie des Grayens* (The Undead, a Symphony of Horror) (1922), directed by F. W. Murnau — a silent classic of the German expressionist cinema, believed to be the first vampire film, based loosely on Bram Stoker's novel; *Nosferatu, Phantom der Nacht* (The Undead, Phantom of the Night) (1979), directed by Werner Herzog — German remake of the original vampire film, starring Klaus Kinski; *Dracula* (1931), directed by Tod Browning and starring Bela Lugosi, classic by Universal Studios, also responsible for the famous Frankenstein movies of the 1930s and '40s, based on the Deane/Balderston play, the film transforms Dracula into a type of suave, continental lover; *Horror of Dracula* (1958), directed by Terence Fisher, starring Christopher Lee (Dracula) and Peter Cushing (Van Helsing), the first of the Hammer horror series of Dracula films, loosely based on Stoker's novel; *El Conde Dracula* (1970), Spanish version directed by Jesus Franco and based fairly closely on Stoker's novel, stars Christopher Lee (Dracula), Franco portrays the Dracula story as a confrontation between youth and age; *Love at First Bite* (1972), stars George Hamilton (Dracula), parody of the Dracula legend, Dracula enters the disco age to pursue the reincarnation of his lost love; *Dracula* (1973), made-for-television movie directed by Dan Curtis, starring Jack Palance (Dracula) and Nigel Davenport (Van Helsing), gives more sympathetic portrayal of Dracula as a noble warrior yearning for his lost love; *Dracula* (1977), BBC/PBS miniseries directed by Philip Saville and starring Louis Jourdan, more faithful to Stoker's novel than previous versions, filmed on location at Whitby; *Dracula* (1979), directed by John Badham and starring Frank Langella (Dracula), Laurence Olivier (Van Helsing), and Kate Nelligan (Lucy): set at the beginning of the twentieth century, Dracula is portrayed as

a romantic, dashing hero/villain, Lucy is a sexually liberated woman who is Dracula's perfect mate; *Bram Stoker's Dracula* (1992), directed by Francis Ford Coppola and starring Gary Oldman (Dracula), Winona Ryder (Mina), and Anthony Hopkins (Van Helsing): very faithful to the novel, except for the inclusion of a love story between Dracula and Mina, Mina is the reincarnation of Dracula's lost love, the love story transforms Dracula from the Satanic to the Byronic hero type; *Dracula, Dead and Loving It* (1997), parody of Dracula written and directed by Mel Brooks (*Young Frankenstein*) and stars Leslie Nielsen (Dracula) and Mel Brooks (Van Helsing), lacks the brilliance of Brooks's attempt at the Frankenstein legend.

36. Golden et al., *The Monster Book,* p. 93.

37. He is no less complex at the level of linguistic representation as Holly Chandler indicates: "he combines the stylized diction of the traditional supervillain with an ironic awareness of the modern world." "Slaying the Patriarchy: Transfusions of the Vampire Metaphor in *Buffy the Vampire Slayer*" in *Slayage* number 9 (August 2003).

38. Golden et al., *The Monster Book,* p. 117.

39. Kaveney, "Introduction," *Reading the Vampire Slayer,* p. 9.

Chapter 5

1. The GEOS guide lists the following as the top ten episodes as voted on by fans: 10th "Selfless" (7.5), 9th "Innocence II" (2.14), 8th "Fool for Love" (5.7), 7th "Becoming I" (2.21), 6th "Conversations with Dead People" (7.7), 5th "The Body" (5.16), 4th "The Gift" (5.22), 3rd "Becoming II" (2.22), 2nd "Hush" (4.10) and 1st "Once More with Feeling" (6.7). "Restless" is counted as 30th. http://www. geos.tv/index. php/index/buf, accessed July 25, 2004 (the list is open to change, though the favorite five have remained in place since the time of my initial check).

2. See, for example, the relationships between narrative and history and narrative and knowledge in chapters 1 and 3.

3. Sue Turnbull provides an excellent palliative to this in the previously quoted "Not Just Another *Buffy* Paper: Towards an Aesthetics of Television," in *Slayage,* numbers 13 and 14 (October 2004).

4. Philip Mikosz and Dana C. Och,

"Previously on *Buffy the Vampire Slayer*..." in *Slayage,* number 5 (May 2002).

5. Alfred Appel, Jr., "Introduction" in Appel Jr., *The Annotated Lolita,* pp. i–xlix.

6. Appel, Jr., "Introduction" *Annotated Lolita,* p. lvi.

7. Intertexts are those text from the "outside" of the show that are drawn into it by reference, allusion, quotation, parody, pastiche or any other formal device (drawn from literature, television, film, but also including food stuffs, brand names, sports, and other cultural artifacts that become textualized in the show); intratexts are the allusions and references made in one episode to another episode and these include obvious aspects such as plot development and character growth but also visual styles, camera angles, lighting techniques and so on). I use paratexts in the way described by Umberto Eco to include "the whole series of messages that accompany and help explain a given text; messages such as advertisements, jacket copy, titles, subtitles, introduction, reviews and so on" (*Six Walks in the Fictional Woods,* pp. 144–45). Donald Keller goes on to say, "In a television programme such as *Buffy,* paratext would include the intoned 'In every generation [...]' that appeared before early episodes, 'Previously on [...]' reminders of past episodes, commercials with previews of future episodes and so on." "Spirit Guides and Shadow Selves" in Wilcox and Lavery, *Fighting the Forces,* p. 176.

8. See Alan Sokal and Jean Bricmont, *Intellectual Impostures: Postmodern Philosophers' Abuse of Science.*

9. Jean-François Lyotard, *Libidinal Economy,* trans. Grant.

10. *Ibid.,* p. 55.

11. *Ibid.,* p. 56.

12. Joss Whedon's DVD commentary to "Restless" (4.22).

13. Roz Kaveney's Introduction in *Reading the Vampire Slayer* says *Buffy the Vampire Slayer* has "a structural pattern as coherent as the statement, development, second statement, recapitulations and coda of the sonata form" (p. 12).

14. Umberto Eco, *The Limits of Interpretation,* p. 86.

15. *Ibid.,* p. 87.

16. Mikosz and Och, "Previously on *Buffy the Vampire Slayer*...."

17. Quoted in Walder, *Literature and the Modern World,* pp. 106–07.

18. See chapter 1 for a further discussion of this episode.

19. Defamiliarization as a literary concept outlined three *devices* that could be used to make the work unfamiliar. These were (1) Canonization of the junior branch — taking a "degraded" genre (ballad, detective story, etc.) and working it into a more elevated genre thereby, upsetting expected formulations: defamiliarizing genre. *Buffy* constantly interjects generic instability not only by including degraded (or for that matter seemingly elevated) genres but also by the surprising juxtapositions between and within scenes; (2) *Syuzhet* and *Fabula*— the relationship between plot and story. The story would be "a" then "b" then "c" then "d" then "e." The plot (the order in which the story is recounted in the text) might be "d" then "a" then "b" then "e" then "c": defamiliarizing sequence and causality. This aspect of formalism developed into the structural/narratological enterprises of Gennette who spent his life finding increasingly sophisticated ways of describing all the possible variations of plot structure (analepsis [flashbacks] and prolepsis [flashforwards] being the two most common); (3) *Skaz*— the differing relationships between narrator and narrated. Famous examples of especially complex relationships are in *Wuthering Heights*, *The Canterbury Tales* and *Bleak House*. Not only is this in whole books, however, but in moments within books where the narrative voice seems to be displaced or disrupts the narration up to that point. This happen in nearly all novels at some point, and in *Buffy* it happens with the changing point of view from which a scene is shot.

20. The immediate involutional thread to *Frankenstein* provides one extension of the show's hermeneutic possibilities, and the invocation of the debates on science that Shelley's novel and *Buffy* engage in extend this formal aspect to a broader notion of cultural critique: the aesthetics of culture.

21. Intertexts are part of the process of involution (internal involution not being an intertext as such but an intratext, if one accepts the entire corpus as a single entity comprised of many parts, like a multi-chaptered or multi-volumed book). Though the terminology is different, Robert A. Davis's article "*Buffy the Vampire Slayer* and the Pedagogy of Fear" makes the point with its usual elegance: "The intertextual echoes

and allusion have also a serious purpose, as the conflicts they provoke are skilfully used by the writers to deepen and elucidate the show's underpinning mythology and to authenticate its ambitiously conceived inflection of literary vampirism." In *Slayage*, number 3 (June 2001).

22. While intertexts certainly do operate as involutional markers, they also have other functions. As Rhonda V. Wilcox notes in her discussion of language on the show, many of the references (in addition to involutional properties) operate as demarcations of cultural positioning, with the youthful characters creating a linguistic community from which the adult members are excluded by virtue of their failure to recognize the allusions to, for example, popular culture. "There Will Never Be a Very Special *Buffy*: *Buffy* and the Monsters of Teen Life" in *Slayage*, number 2 (March 2001).

23. Rhonda V. Wilcox and David Lavery, "Introduction" to *Fighting the Forces*, p. xxiv.

24. Aimee Fifarek provides a probably unintentional account of how the enjoining spell is itself involutional. She writes, "for a brief time, the Slayer is no longer 'one girl in all the world'— she is a network, a continuum of Slayers." "Mind and Heart with Spirit Joined: The Buffyverse as an Information System" in *Slayage*, number 3 (June 2001). The extent to which this foreshadows the unleashing of a network of Slayers in (7.22) indicates its involutional power.

25. Talking to Adam about their plan to lure Buffy into the Initiative's headquarters, Spike says, "Alice heads back down the rabbit hole": the allusion to Carroll's 1865 text is clear, the involutional link to (4.22) rather less so, perhaps.

26. See chapter 4 for a discussion of light and dark in *Buffy*.

27. Karen Sayer, "It Wasn't Our World Anymore — They Made It Theirs: Reading Space and Place" in Kaveney, *Reading the Vampire Slayer*, p. 103.

28. Joss Whedon's DVD commentary for "Restless" (4.22).

29. The accidental or purely pragmatic nature of some of the aesthetic decisions is commented upon by Kaveney in relation to an aspect of involution: "[while] the show's use of foreshadowing and echo [...] have been largely opportunist improvisations [they] have emotional and metaphysical

resonance." In "Introduction" to *Reading the Vampire Slayer*, p. 33.

30. Janet K. Halfyard, "Love, Death, Curses and Reverses (in F Minor): Music, Gender and Identity in *Buffy the Vampire Slayer* and *Angel*" in *Slayage*, number 4 (December 2001).

31. *Ibid*.

32. *Ibid*.

33. Mikosz and Och, "Previously on *Buffy the Vampire Slayer...*"

34. *Ibid*.

35. Kevin McNeilly, Christina Sylka, and Susan R. Fisher, "Kiss the Librarian, But Close the Hellmouth: It's Like a Whole Big Kissing Thing" in *Slayage*, number 2 (March 2001).

36. See chapter 7 for a much fuller account of *Heart of Darkness* and its relationship with *Buffy*.

37. Elizabeth Rambo, "Lessons for Season Seven of *Buffy the Vampire Slayer*" in *Slayage*, numbers 11 and 12 (April 2004).

Chapter 6

1. See chapter 2 for an extended discussion of the notion of performance as an aspect of ethnicity. In relation to Willow, the more usual idea, from a theoretical perspective, is to discuss her sexuality as an aspect of performativity, rather than her Jewishness. The fact that her Jewishness is not referenced at all in this dream would indicate that it is her sexuality that is the more dominant theme, though, as the dream unfolds, we discover that a more fundamental notion of identity is being interrogated: that of her self-image as a fraud.

2. More than the other dreams, Willow's has a narrative logic and consistency that is almost "normal." Although her ability to dream of events occurring simultaneously about which she can have no experiential knowledge (even within the curious confines of dream logic) makes this narrativity rather more complex.

3. The fact that Willow in "New Moon Rising" (4.19) asks if the cat will be a "familiar" suggests an extra level of potential malevolence.

4. In terms of internal points of contact, some of which are accidental but no less profound for that, Joss Whedon says on the DVD commentary that a fan pointed out that this scene sees naming as an act of waiting, allowing the thing to be named to offer you its name, whereas later Adam and Riley are engaged in giving things names — the potential for gendered readings of this is one that Whedon seems very keen to uphold.

5. The appearance of the character "Tara" in Buffy's dream is, of course, the conduit through which the First Slayer is able to communicate and as such is not Tara. The fact that each character's appearance in each of the dreams is not a character appearance so much as the image of that character as presented by the dreamer's mind is of great interest in a psychological reading of the dream (and influences the limits of interpretation) but it is of less importance as an aspect of the aesthetics of involution with which this section is working.

6. The extent to which Greenaway's work falls prey to a certain Orientalism in its negative sense is a point of conjecture. Edward Said's seminal work on the subject, *Orientalism* (and his almost single-handed invention of postcolonial studies that clearly influences my methodology in chapter 2), introduces the idea of Orientalism like this:

> Unlike the Americans, the French and British — less so the Germans, Russians, Spanish, Portuguese, Italians, and Swiss — have had a long tradition of what I shall be calling Orientalism, a way of coming to terms with the Orient that is based on the Orient's special place in European Western Experience. The Orient is not only adjacent to Europe; it is also the place of Europe's greatest and richest and oldest colonies, the source of its civilizations and languages, its cultural contestant, and one of its deepest and most recurring images of the Other. In addition, the Orient has helped to define Europe (or the West) as its contrasting image, idea, personality, experience. Yet none of this Orient is merely imaginative. The Orient is an integral part of European material civilization and culture. Orientalism expresses and represents that part culturally and even ideologically as a mode of discourse with supporting institutions, vocabulary, scholarship, imagery, doctrines, even colonial bureaucracies and colonial styles" [p. 5].

The recourse to a Greek cultural mode of exoticism in Willow's dream verges toward a similar idea of Orientalism, though, as Said indicates, the U.S. relation to Orientalism is markedly different to the European one.

7. Quoted in Jay and Lewis, *Sappho Through English Poetry*, p. 17.

8. The much vaunted value of friendship in *Buffy* is here rather undermined. Willow's spell, though successful, is the last tragic act to befall Buffy who now has to kill the man she loves rather than his vampiric avatar Angelus in order to save the world. Xander's lie to Buffy, which comes across to her as an assertion of support, allied with Willow's tragic success, leaves her alone, and she leaves Sunnydale. (For a subtle demarcation of the bounds of friendship and individualism in *Buffy*, see Jana Riess's chapter "The Power of Friendship" in her book *What Would Buffy Do?*, pp. 53–64.)

9. J. Lawton Winslade is concerned about some of the presentation of witchcraft in *Buffy* and, especially, about the use of the goddess motif: "The problem here is that these Greek goddesses, while strongly part of contemporary Wiccan practice, are also the goddesses most often mentioned in materials on the late medieval witch-trials, thus preserving the unfortunate Satanic connection. In fact, not until we hear about the mysterious Powers That Be and the *Xena*-esque 'oracles' in the *Angel* series, do we have any evidence that there are anything but chthonic entities in the *Buffy* mythos." "Teen Witches, Wiccans, and 'Wanna-Blessed-Be's: Pop Culture Magic in *Buffy the Vampire Slayer*" in *Slayage*, number 1 (January 2001).

10. Ambrose Phillips, "An Hymn to Venus," ll. 1–4, in Jay and Lewis, *Sappho Through English Poetry*, p. 38.

11. John Addisson, "An Hymn to Venus," ll. 1–2, in Jay and Lewis, *Sappho Through English Poetry*, p. 41.

12. John Addington Symonds, "Hymn to Aphrodite," ll. 1–2 in Jay and Lewis, *Sappho Through English Poetry*, p. 54.

13. Odysseus claims to be called Nobody so that when the Cyclops screams for help he can only declaim that "Nobody's killing me now," thereby allowing Odysseus to escape. See Homer, *The Odyssey*, trans. Robert Fagles, Book 9, esp. ll. 404–470.

14. The myth of Oedipus was already old by the time that Sophocles wrote his extraordinary plays on the subject. Present in *The Odyssey* in Book 11, where it is the mythic embellishment of a preexisting folktale, Sophocles chooses to leave out Apollo's warning to Laius that any son that he fathers will kill him. The reason for this is that Laius had broken one of the central injunctions of early Hellenistic culture which was to show *xenia* or guest-friendship: he had carried off his host's son while seeking refuge.

15. The performative notion of identity that I discussed in chapter 2 does not just assume an effort of the will to forge an identity from an empty canvas of possibility. Preexisting narratives and structures of expression are culturally determined in a number of ways through a variety of mainly aesthetic channels. It appears as though Willow, at the opening of the series, is being circumscribed by one such cultural expression as outlined by Angela McRobbie, who is quoted in an essay by Gina Wisker. Willow subscribes to a type of figure prevalent in late nineteenth- and early twentieth-century literature for girls, the "action-girl" stories. In these stories, the action-girl needed as a friend and counterbalance the "non-character, the friendly, open, fun-loving, 'ordinary' girl (who may perhaps be slightly scatty or absentminded). She is remarkable in being normal and things tend to happen to her, rather than at her instigation. Frequently she figures in stories focusing on the supernatural." "Vampires and School Girls: High School High Jinks on the Hellmouth" in *Slayage*, number 2 (March 2001). Willow's growth as a character, then, is as much as anything a refusal to be determined by these overarching narrative possibilities. Part of her sense that she is a fraud can be ascribed to the difficulty inherent in shifting stories, in rejecting a narrative that seemed to be definitional of her. Creating (performing) a new narrative (or series of narratives) is a complex and fraught business.

16. See note 29 in chapter 5.

17. *Buffy*'s use of nursery rhyme is discussed by Sarah E. Skwire in "Whose Side Are You On, Anyway? Children, Adults and the Use of Fairy Tales in *Buffy*" in Wilcox and Lavery, *Fighting the Forces*, pp. 195–206.

18. In this episode (3.16), Vamp Willow is seen to kill a student called Sandy (and we later infer, to have sired her). Sandy appears again briefly in "Family" (5.6) and then again as one of the "blood whores" who Riley visits in "Into the Woods" (5.10),

the episode that sees his final break-up with Buffy. As Roz Kaveney says, "only a show so aware of its fan base could possibly get away with continuity points that subtle." "Introduction" to *Reading the Vampire Slayer*, p. 36.

19. Daniel E. Schneider, *The Psychoanalyst and the Artist*, p. 67.

20. Joss Whedon's DVD commentary to "Restless" (4.22).

21. Quoted in Stephen Unwin with Carole Waddis, *A Pocket Guide to 20th Century Drama*, p. 124.

22. Julian Barnes, *A History of the World in 10½ Chapters*, p. 226.

23. See Anne Millard Daugherty's "Just a Girl" for a discussion of how *Buffy* plays with the construction of the male gaze in Kaveney, *Reading the Vampire Slayer*, pp. 149–53.

24. Joss Whedon makes this link explicit in the DVD commentary.

25. Brian Wall and Michael Zryd, "Vampire Dialectics: Knowledge, Institutions and Labor" in Kaveney, *Reading the Vampire Slayer*, p. 68.

26. Joss Whedon's, DVD commentary to "Restless" (4.22).

27. The studio decided that Willow was just too geeky-looking and insisted that her costume be changed for the second episode, though the emotional characteristics implied by her initial costume remain fairly constant throughout the first season; a set of characteristics that the audience and the production crew all felt a nostalgic yearning for in the representation of "Restless" (4.22) (Joss Whedon's, audio commentary on the DVD).

28. Drawn from Plato's famous assertion that the things we see on earth are simply representations of their pure identities in the upper reaches, the use of the term eidolon here is intended to convey the important fact that what we see in the dreams are not the characters but representations of them. In some cases the eidolon appears to be closely related to its progenitive identity (as with Willow's versions of herself in the dream) but other eidolons are more awkward, such as the different versions of Tara in the dreams, and this becomes especially problematic when the Tara eidolon becomes the voice of the First Slayer. The First Slayer herself is also awkward as she has to be dead so what we and the characters see is an eidolon of a spirit, or an image of an

image. This does little to help any hermeneutic endeavor in relation to the episode.

29. Here the images of the two Willows allow us to see each as a "double" of the other. Doubles also occur at the level of alternative-reality versions of the characters and as doppelgangers (Vamp Willow in [3.9] and [3.16]; second Xander in "The Replacement" [5.3], for example). However, characters also act as doubles of each other, as Roz Kaveney describes: "Characters are alternative versions of each other — Buffy and Cordelia (Buffy before her powers), Buffy and Faith (Buffy without family or friends) — or recapitulate aspects of each other's careers — Angel and Faith. Angel and Spike are not only related through their ties to Drusilla and to Buffy, but by being respectively dark and blonde and by being originally called Liam and William. One of the reasons why the poet William becomes the streetfighter Spike is because the roisterer Liam has become the moody, sadistic aesthete and the role of the family intellectual is taken." "Introduction" to *Reading the Vampire Slayer*, p. 9.

30. Jess Battis, "She's Not All Grown Yet: Willow as Hybrid/Hero in *Buffy the Vampire Slayer*" in *Slayage*, number 8 (March 2003).

31. Tzvetan Todorov, *Genres of Discourse*, p. 48.

32. J. Hillis Miller, "Introduction" to *Bleak House*, p. 22.

33. *Ibid.*, p. 23.

34. *Ibid.*, p. 24.

35. *Ibid.*, p. 23.

Chapter 7

1. Roz Kaveney provides a brief and general overview of "Restless" (4.22) in terms of each dream's purpose: "Willow is confronted with issues around her identity and sexuality; Xander with his failure to find a productive adult role; Giles with the contradiction between his parental relationship with Buffy and his need for self-expression; and Buffy with deep questions about the nature of her Slayer powers." In *Reading the Vampire Slayer*, p. 23.

2. Steve Wilson, "Laugh, Spawn of Hell, Laugh" in Kaveney, *Reading the Vampire Slayer*, p. 90.

3. Kevin McNeilly, Christina Sylka, and Susan R. Fisher, "Kiss the Librarian, But

Close the Hellmouth: It's Like a Whole Big Sucking Thing" in *Slayage*, number 2 (March 2001).

4. This speech, according to Joss Whedon, effectively means "You're the writer, not the star" and adds that he "couldn't have made [Xander] more of a writer's proxy than that." Quoted in Lawrence Miles et al, *Dusted*, p.286. The reference to the cape would seem to imply Superman, which takes us back to "The Zeppo" (3.13) as there Xander mockingly refers to himself as Jimmy Olsen, the would-be reporter who always feels left out.

5. This episode, with its introduction of The First Evil, its extraordinary cinematic quality and affectionate homage to *It's a Wonderful Life* remains one of the best episodes of *Buffy*. In terms of its involutional qualities (beyond Capra's 1946 icon), there is a moment when the First Evil who is appearing in the guise of Jenny Calendar (already taking us to "Passion" [2.17]) says that Angel "will be dead by sunrise." This, as any horror fan will know, is a quotation from Sam Raimi's groundbreaking 1981 movie *The Evil Dead*. In 2004, Sarah Michelle Gellar was the star of *The Grudge* whose executive producer is also Sam Raimi. If the Raimi connection with *Xena Warrior Princess* is introduced as well, then the involutional becomes even more intriguing. In "Halloween" (2.6), Buffy is temporarily disempowered by virtue of being turned into that which she is wearing (like everyone else in Sunnydale in costumes). She has on an eighteenth-century lady's dress and exhibits a version of femininity that is weak, passive and ineffectual. Willow comments, "Couldn't she have dressed like *Xena*?" And the compliment is repaid in *Xena* in the episode "The Play's the Thing" (*Xena* 4.17) in which two theater critics discuss the opening of "Buffus, The Bacchae Slayer."

6. Joss Whedon's, DVD commentary for "Restless" (4.22). The very neat uses to which Soderbergh puts the careers of his two main actors (Terence Stamp and Peter Fonda) is wonderfully involutional. In one scene we have a flashback to Stamp's character when he was younger, which is, in fact a shot from the 1967 (again) movie *Poor Cow*, which was Ken Loach's first feature film, though he had been made famous by the extraordinarily daring *Cathy Come Home*, produced for television in 1966, which allowed Loach to go on to inspire genre tel-

evision with the surprisingly gritty realism of *Z-Cars*, the BBC police show which ran from 1962–1978. And when Peter Fonda's character is first shown we have a song that tells us he is an "easy rider with a curse" which clearly brings the Fonda-Hopper collaboration of *Easy Rider* in 1969 to the fore, while also having, one would imagine, an unexpected synchronicity for Whedon whose vampire with a curse springs readily to mind.

7. The role of Joyce is central to the dynamic of Buffy for the first four and a half seasons. Often thought of as naïve but caring by critics, she has an awkward relationship with *Buffy*. Daniel A. Clark and P. Andrew Miller assert that she lacks relevance, which is evidenced by the fact that "prior to her illness and surprising death in season five, she has never made opening credit status; that is, the actress (Kristine Sutherland) who played her (and played her well) has never been featured in the show's opening credits." "Buffy, the Scooby Gang and Monstrous Authority: BtVS and the Subversion of Authority" in *Slayage*, number 3 (June 2001).

8. For a discussion of this shot and its importance for a reading of Buffy's tensions with regard to her human and her demon aspects, see chapter 9.

9. A further involutional link to soldiering from "All the Way" (6.6) is Xander's comment, after all the gang are exhausted from their day's work in costume, "Store. Go. Boom." This is an allusion to Willow's phrase "Tomb. Go. Boom" in "Shadow" (5.8) where she is referring to Riley's macho-soldier tactics in blowing up a nest of vampires.

10. George Orwell, *1984*.

11. Xander's very strong interest in sex would provide a whole other set of episode relations but one that is of relevance here by virtue of also being a dream image of his sexuality is taken from "Teacher's Pet" (1.4) (where his virginity is made clear by virtue of the fact that the praying mantis woman only chooses virgin males). At the opening of the episode, Xander is dreaming of heroism and stardom as he fights vampires while playing his guitar in front of an adoring Buffy. He wakes up to be told that he has drool on him.

12. Rachel Falconer, *Hell in Contemporary Literature*, p. 28.

13. A perhaps unexpected intertextual

relationship with *The Aeneid* is established to brilliant effect by C. W. Marshall in "Aeneas the Vampire Slayer: A Roman Model for Why Giles Kills Ben" in *Slayage*, number 9 (August 2003). As the title indicates, the essay is primarily concerned with Giles's killing of Ben (the human host of the malevolent God and Big Bad of season 5) in "The Gift" (5.22). The significant question (how "innocent" is Ben, and what, therefore, are the moral implications of killing him?) is asked by Xander, and asked in such a way as to provide a comparison with the other innocent figure whom the Knights of Byzantium want to kill — Dawn: "What about Ben? He can be killed, right? I mean, I know he's an innocent, but, you know, not, like 'Dawn' innocent. We could kill a ... a regular guy ... God" (5.22). Giles's own descent into a moral mire at this point, provides a grim recapitulation of Wesley's decline, which we have arrived at involutionally via Xander.

14. Joseph Conrad, *Heart of Darkness*, p. 87.

15. Whedon's DVD commentary for "Restless" (4.22).

16. *Ibid.*

17. The question about how the eidolon functions (see the discussion of Willow's dream) is made very difficult here. Xander's self-image in the dream is an eidolon, and is one that itself mutates — Buffy's helpmate, Anya's lover, Tara and Willow's sexual fantasy, lost soul and so on. The appearance of the Kurtz figure is, one would assume, meant to be an eidolon of Principal Snyder. It, however, is informed and recast in the light of a film character, himself played by a real actor (hence Snyder-Kurtz also being inhabited by Brando). This image is, in turn, framed within a broader conceived notion of the eidolon, which is the film *Apocalypse Now*, but this has been transmogrified by Xander's earlier terrible dream version. As mentioned in relation to Willow's dream, trying to unpick any substantive hermeneutic possibility from this difficult set of representations, eidolons and images is almost impossible.

18. See chapter 5, note 23.

19. *Slayage*, number 7 (December 2002).

20. It had been published in serialized form as "The Heart of Darkness" in 1899 in *Blackwood's Magazine*. The text was then revised and included in *Youth: A Narrative; and Two other Stories* published by Blackwood in 1902.

21. Joseph Conrad in Miriam Allott, *Novelists on the Novel*, pp. 132–33.

22. T. S. Eliot, "The Hollow Men" in *Collected Poems 1909–1962*, pp. 87–92.

23. Joseph Conrad, "Books" (1905) in *Notes on Life and Letters*, pp. 6–10.

24. Jean-François Lyotard, "Answer to the Question: What Is Postmodernism?" in Pefanis and Thomas, *The Postmodern Explained to Children*, p. 24.

25. Jean-François Lyotard, "Apostil on Narratives" in Pefanis and Thomas, *The Postmodern Explained to Children*, p. 31.

26. Joseph Conrad, *Heart of Darkness*, p. 10.

27. Jeffrey L. Pasley's excellent essay "Old Familiar Vampires: The Politics of the Buffyverse" in South, *"Buffy the Vampire Slayer" and Philosophy*, pp. 254–68, presents (from a different perspective) an overview of the show's troubled negotiation with late capitalism and the industries and histories that support it, while still recognizing the essentially liberal, rather than radical, accommodations made by the program.

28. Joseph Conrad, *Heart of Darkness*, p. 50.

29. *Ibid.*, p. 37.

30. *Ibid.*, p. 38.

31. Joss Whedon's DVD commentary for "Restless" (4.22).

Chapter 8

1. Joss Whedon's DVD commentary to "Restless" (4.22).

2. One of the best-ever essays on any aspect of *Buffy* is by Alice Jenkins and Susan Stuart, "Extending Your Mind: Non-Standard Perlocutionary Acts in 'Hush'" in *Slayage*, number 9 (August 2003). This article uses speech act theory to both read the episode and provide subtle and enriching thematic observations and concerns. An original, lively and utterly compelling piece of criticism.

3. The Magic Box, for Brian Wall and Michael Zryd, is a signal of a particular movement of Giles's that has seen him transmute from librarian–Watcher into small businessman. Locating this development in the context of economic history and, therefore, in the context of both European modernity and U.S. postmodern models of economics, they say, "The 'evolution' of

Giles's role from guild master to small businessman evokes in miniature another, broader narrative: the history of capitalism itself. Specifically, Giles's coding as *British* points to a larger historical narrative of economic transformation." "Vampire Dialectics" in Kaveney, *Reading the Vampire Slayer*, p. 74.

4. Lawrence Miles et al. aver that this episode can be read as a self-conscious critique of *Buffy* by *Buffy*. Talking of the tests that the geeks put Buffy through (the geeks standing in for "nit-picky fans"), they say: "The first test sees her slip through her college day at high speed, in much the same way that a TV show skips through the boring bits; her second involves a token monster-fight; her third teaches her the lesson of 'always giving the customers (i.e., the viewers) what they want'; and Warren complains that her life has no focus, in a way that suggests he's *really* criticizing the characterization." *Dusted*, p. 227.

5. Undeniably the most comprehensive treatment of language in *Buffy* is Michael Adams's *Slayer Slang: A "Buffy the Vampire Slayer" Lexicon*.

6. See chapter 6 for a discussion of this.

7. Howard Hampton, "American Demons: *Buffy* Amok in D. H. Lawrence's World," *Village Voice Literary Supplement*, 20 May 2003.

8. See Keith Topping's "Changing Channels" in his *Slayer: The Next Generation*, pp. 22–26, for a brief but highly readable and very informative discussion of the move from the WB to UPN.

9. See Julian Barnes, *A History of the World in 10 1/2 Chapters*, p. 168, where the narrator asserts that the reader will be asking whether it is the author Julian Barnes who is writing this section.

10. In the first of Paul Auster's *New York Trilogy* novels, *City of Glass*, the detective Quinn assumes the name of "Paul Auster" in his investigation.

11. See, for example, David Lavery, "Afterword: The Genius of Joss Whedon" in Wilcox and Lavery, *Fighting the Forces*, pp 251–56; David Lavery, "Emotional Resonance and Rocket Launchers: Joss Whedon's Commentaries on the *Buffy the Vampire Slayer* DVDs" in *Slayage*, number 6 (September 2002); David Lavery, "A Religion in Narrative: Joss Whedon and Television Creativity" in *Slayage*, number 7 (December 2002); and Emily Nussbaum,

"Must See Metaphysics," *New York Times*, 22 September 2002.

12. Michelle Boyette describes Spike up to about this point in the following way: "A figure of modern amorality and random evil, he has, however, by degrees, become a figure of fun, a buffoon, and is now becoming a comic hero, or anti-hero." "The Comic Anti-Hero in *Buffy the Vampire Slayer*, or Silly Villain: Spike Is For Kicks" in *Slayage*, number 4 (December 2001).

13. The role and function of the crucifix, as well as holy water and the other paraphernalia that in Stoker and earlier vampire traditions had been the source of mortal dread for vampires, is discussed by a number of critics of the show. Its clear failure to invoke such deeply rooted spiritual disgust and loathing (predicated on its imminent death-inducement) is made clear by the Master as early as season 1. It is most pithily described in a critical context by Stacey Abbott who investigates the move from premodern to modern and postmodern visions of the vampire and says that these objects, but especially the crucifix, "simply [have] a physical effect upon him [a vampire] like an allergy." "A Little Less Ritual and a Lot More Fun: The Modern Vampire in *Buffy the Vampire Slayer*" in *Slayage*, number 3 (June 2001).

14. For Brian Wall and Michael Zryd, Spike's getting a soul is one of the show's strongest claims for a strongly materialist, as opposed to metaphysical, notion of ethics: "[Spike has] *cultivated* a soul, suggesting a materialist rather than metaphysical conception of human ethics: his goodness is built, not given." "Vampire Dialectics" in Kaveney, *Reading the Vampire Slayer*, p. 63.

15. A literary forerunner, who has a similar decision to make, is Aeneas, who is forced, according to Virgil's *Aeneid*, to kill Turnus. C. W. Marshall writes with exquisite balance in his article that articulates this relationship most explicitly: "we should expect Giles to have read the *Aeneid* in Latin. Not only does the poem remain fundamental text in Latin pedagogy in England, but in addition the depiction of the Underworld in *Aeneid* 6 may be imagined to be a basic component of Giles's training as a Watcher, alongside other works of Latin epic [...] The connection I am suggesting instead operates for the modern audience of both works, whereby the knowl-

edge of one enriches and amplifies the ethical context of the other." "Aeneas the Vampire Slayer: A Roman Model for Why Giles Kills Ben" in *Slayage*, number 9 (August 2003).

Marshall's claim would seem to be validated in "A New World" (*AtS* 3.20) where the ostracized Wesley is given a copy of Dante's *Inferno*, which he has already read in the "original Tuscan," indicating both a deep knowledge of all facets of occult-oriented literature, even such commonplace classics, as well as (as we know) an enviably polyglot capacity.

16. The role of the Buffybot will be discussed in chapter 9.

17. The extent to which Anya's joke might be labeled postmodern is something that may be determined by reading N. J. C. Vasantkumar's essay "Postmodernism and Jokes" in ed. Arthur Asa Berger, *The Postmodern Presence*, pp. 212–38; see also Matthew Pearson's "Vic Reeves and Postmodern Comedy" in ed. Steven Earnshaw, *Postmodern Surroundings*, pp. 193–201.

18. While showing the presumed viewer of his video around the house, Andrew happens across Buffy giving yet another speech to the Potentials. He speaks for each of us when he says, "Honestly, gentle viewers, these motivating speeches of hers tend to get a little long. I'll take you back in there in a little while but in the in-between-time, I thought you might want to know a little about me, your humble host" (7.16).

19. In a marvelous tribute to Giles as a character and to the *Buffy* team for having made him a librarian, GraceAnne A. De-Candido writes, "Giles believes that what he needs to know for Buffy's sake lies in his many volumes at home and at work. Giles also makes the necessary leap of faith common to all good librarians: he bridges the chasm between the information as it lives in the text and the transfer of that information into a form the Slayerettes and Buffy [and the audience] can actually use. Sometimes that means literal translation, other times it means recasting what he reads into stories, tag lines, or aphorisms that make sense to the teens he serves." "A Bibliographic Good vs. Evil in *Buffy the Vampire Slayer*" in *American Libraries* 30.8 (September 1999), p. 46.

20. S. Renee Dechert, "My Boyfriend's in a Band" in Wilcox and Lavery, *Fighting the Forces*, p. 221.

21. See chapter 1 for a discussion of this scene.

22. Giles's roles as mentor, guide and teacher are discussed as part of Jana Riess's chapter "Obey Your Teacher, Except When He's Wrong: Spiritual Mentors on the Path to Maturity" in her book *What Would Buffy Do?*, pp. 65–78.

23. The splitting of The Beatles was due, in part, to the band's growing unease with John Lennon's and Yoko Ono's relationship. The band's last performance on January 30th, 1969, is in the same year as Bowie's first hit, "Space Oddity" taken from the same album that spawned "Memory of a Free Festival," which is listened to by Giles in "The Freshman" (4.1). Bowie and Lennon went on to record the massive hit "Fame," which comes from the album *Young Americans*, which itself provides a preemptive critique of Buffy's relationship with history as mentioned in chapter 3.

24. While it is true that Oz also loves music and is in a band, his character is not defined in such explicit terms through music. It is also worth noting that Giles was in a band in his Ripper days, as we see in "Band Candy" (3.6), where a photograph of Anthony Stewart Head's head is placed on a picture of Sid Vicious, the infamous punk star on whom Spike was, at least partially, based, thereby providing a further involutional link between him and Giles.

25. Marti Noxon admits as much in the DVD commentary to "Bargaining I" (6.1).

26. An aspect of the plot that Lawrence Miles, Lars Peterson and Christa Dickson are concerned with, and with good reason in terms of the show's continuing struggle to present plausible consequences for ethically bad or dubious actions, is Xander's seeming lack of remorse or punishment for having brought the song demon Sweet to Sunnydale in the first place, especially as the demon's presence causes the deaths of a number of Sunnydale citizens. *Dusted*, p. 232.

27. Joss Whedon's DVD commentary for "Once More with Feeling" (6.7).

28. There has been a move to provide compilation DVDs that deal with particular characters' arcs, but these are collections of episodes and seem to be a rather cynical marketing maneuver, offering little that a fan would not already have.

Chapter 9

1. This particular sign of a link between Buffy and Mina is part of a broader set of correspondences, according to Michelle Callander. She writes, "In *Buffy*'s Scooby Gang, there are similar roles [to those found in *Dracula*]. Van Helsing becomes Giles, learned in the occult and father figure of the group. As we've seen, Buffy shares some characteristics with Mina, particularly her insight and her telepathic link with the vampire; in other ways, Mina becomes Willow, a compiler of data who combines modern technology (the Internet) with supernatural power (Wicca incantation). Xander, like Jonathan [Harker] is physically inept [...] but, along with Willow, he is able to research and compile case histories of demons and vampires." "Bram Stoker's *Buffy*: Traditional Gothic and Contemporary Culture" in *Slayage*, number 3 (June 2001).

2. For a discussion of Kendra's character, see chapter 2. Faith will be discussed in more detail in the current chapter.

3. A very neat and well-argued sense of Buffy as an all–American girl is provided by Catherine Siemann who suggests that an unlikely but profoundly important intertext, at least in terms of the discursive and representational economy of the all–American girl, is the mid-century sitcom *Gidget* in "Darkness Falls on the Endless Summer: Buffy as Gidget for the Fin de Siècle" in Wilcox and Lavery, *Fighting the Forces*, pp. 120–32.

4. It also acts as a precursor to "Bargaining I" in which Buffy's fear from "Nightmares" (1.10), of being buried alive in a grave and then having to crawl out of it after being reanimated as a vampire, comes partially true insofar as she has to fight her way out of a grave having been reanimated as a very frightened Buffy.

5. Jana Riess indicates the way in which Buffy's refusal to date Owen is an early act of self-sacrifice, foregoing her desire for normalcy in order to accept (if not exactly embrace) her destiny. To that extent, even a fairly simple episode encourages us to view Buffy's decisions within the broader contexts of fate and individuality, ethical choices, responsibility and desire, and so on. *What Would Buffy Do?*, p. 5.

6. See chapter 4 for a discussion about Dracula's representation and a broader engagement with the various representations of the vampire figure in *Buffy*.

7. Joss Whedon's DVD commentary to "Restless" (4.22).

8. What is probably the finest example of *Angel*'s representation of the battle between free will and fate, between puppets and their masters, is in *AtS*, season 4. The complexity of the narrative is almost impossible to present straightforwardly but in the overall story arc would have to be included (from previous seasons as well as this one): Fred's return from the alternative dimension of Pylea; Gunn's killing of his newly vamped sister and joining forces with Angel; Angel and Darla having sex and thereby producing the impossible baby, Connor; Cordelia's ascension to a Power that Be (is? are?); and the demon Skip's appearance as a seeming good-guy. Cordelia is now having her own mystical baby (which is apparently going to be evil); she and Connor are together and everyone is unsure what is to come. Into this brilliant, complex, sophisticated and wonderful story (not only in terms of narrative but because of its thematic magnificence too) comes Skip again. He tells how everything has been set up so that Cordelia can have this baby:

> SKIP: You really think it stops with her, amigo? Do you have any concept of how many lines have to intersect in order for a thing like this to play out? How many events have to be nudged in just the right direction? [to Lorne] Leaving Pylea. [to Gunn] Your sister. [to Fred] Opening the wrong book. [to Wesley] Sleeping with the enemy. Gosh, I love a story with scope.
>
> GUNN: No way. We make our own choices.
>
> SKIP: Yeah, sure. A cheese sandwich here, when to floss ... but the big stuff, like two vampires squeezing out a kid?

The affirmation of a fatalistic universe is strong, but so too is the self-conscious joke with regard to the Buffyverse itself inevitably being the fatalistic toy of the writers and producers, with the characters obviously subject to their whims and desires. In a manner similar to Luigi Pirandello's *Six Characters in Search of an Author* or, more presciently, *Henry IV*, the characters recognize (or we at least recognize about them) the distance between the aesthetic and the cultural. What Skip says is absolutely true *of* the show but may be less true *in* the show. Gunn is certainly not going to let a pesky thing like fate override his own sense of individual worth and the possibility of free will:

> GUNN: Then we'll kick it over and start a new game. Look, monochrome can yap all he wants about no-name's cosmic plan but here's a little something I picked up rubbin' mojos these past couple of years: the final score can't be rigged. I don't care how many players you grease, that last shot always comes up a question mark. But here's the thing — you never know when you're taking it. It could be when you're duking it out with the legion of doom or just crossing the street deciding where to have brunch. So you just treat it all like it was up to you, the world in the balance, 'cause you never know when it is.

9. Importantly for Rob Breton and Lindsay McMaster, Buffy's rejection of the claims of the First Slayer (Buffy had not yet met the Shadow Men, but the argument holds good for them too) is achieved "without referring to the grammar or sober sanctimoniousness of rationalism" in "Dissing the Age of MOO: Initiatives, Alternatives and Rationality" in *Slayage*, number 1 (January 2001). So Buffy does not embrace rationalism as opposed to irrationalism, but humanity as opposed to demonness, a set of pairings that disavows the too-easy yoking of one to another.

10. Joss Whedon's DVD commentary to "Chosen" (7.22).

11. For a discussion of the "previously" section, please see chapter 5.

12. This is a sentiment shared by the writer, Marti Noxon, who says on her DVD commentary to the episode that she feels that neither they nor the characters had to work hard enough to bring Buffy back.

13. The mining of the show's mythology often serves to destabilize it, and a whole other book could be written on seeming inconsistencies of the mythos. However, for Brian Wall and Michael Zryd, "the very lack of mythological coherence on the show points to a diverse and mixed universe in which multiple and shifting regimes of knowledge are always aligned with salutarily multiple and shifting ethical domains." "Vampire Dialectics" in Kaveney, *Reading the Vampire Slayer*, p. 63. As the title of their

essay implies, Wall and Zryd offer and discover a materialist *Buffy* and so would inevitably eschew any metaphysical assertions, a position to which I am very sympathetic.

14. Melissa M. Milavec and Sharon M. Kaye, "A Slayer's Solution to Aristotle's Love Paradox" in South, "*Buffy the Vampire Slayer" and Philosophy*, p. 176.

15. See chapter 2 for a discussion of the notion of becoming, especially as it relates to an idea of the performative.

16. See chapter 4.

17. Even the most explicit expression of the anarchistic strain in *Buffy* (Riley's assertion to an officer that "I'm an anarchist" in "New Moon Rising" [4.19]) is little more than a repudiation of the particular military hierarchy that he has invested himself in, and its substitution for a different form of organizational control as part of the Scooby Gang. That the one is state sponsored and the other is seemingly independent of an overarching structure of control does imply the Scoobies' anarchistic sensibilities, but this is, in the show, heavily tempered by both metaphysical and material structures of control and containment that supervene any strong claim to their being simply anarchist. Riley's eventual return to the military means, for him as a character anyway, the anarchist impulse is swiftly reoriented to a more state-driven conception of belonging.

18. A different way of thinking about the notion of doubling is provided by Roz Kaveney and focuses on the extent to which the actors chosen for particular roles (and passed over for others) can have an influence in terms of how we view the show: "It is interesting to note that both Julie Benz (Darla) and Charisma Carpenter (Cordelia) auditioned for the role of Buffy, given that both Darla and Cordelia are in some sense shadow doubles of Buffy and, in *Angel*, of each other. Cordelia is the person Buffy was before her powers; Darla the rival Angel killed for her who perpetually casts a shadow on her relationship with him." In *Reading the Vampire Slayer*, p. 35.

19. The slow recovery of Faith (her moral rehabilitation) is one such example of the continuing notion of becoming, of the refusal of the static. It is also another example of the katabatic journey discussed in chapter 7, and one that, for Rhonda Wilcox, has a direct analogy with one of the earliest

of these types of tales, Virgil's *Aeneid*, itself, of course, a revisiting of *The Odyssey*'s Book 11. Wilcox says: "In Faith, Buffy has battled the dark side of herself, and they have yet to come to a resolution — though, interestingly, Buffy's shadow Faith has taken Angel as her Vergilian guide through hell in her search for atonement on his eponymous series." "Every Night I Save You: Buffy, Spike, Sex and Redemption" in *Slayage*, number 5 (May 2002).

20. Reid B. Locklin asserts that Buffy's sacrifice at the end of the season (5.22) "is also a dramatic embodiment of a family ideal that does not neglect the common good, an ideal of a family founded, not primarily on blood, self-interest or patriarchal control, but instead on love, mutual responsibility and a mission to serve and save others in need." "*Buffy the Vampire Slayer* and the Domestic Church: Revisioning the Family and the Common Good" in *Slayage*, number 6 (November 2002).

21. The, comparatively rare, critical dissension from this view, is chastized by Lawrence Miles, Lars Peterson and Christa Dickson who write, "Some critics have attacked the fairly run-of-the-mill plot, claiming that without the songs it'd just be an ordinary *Buffy* episode — which is about as sensible as saying that 'Hush' would be ordinary if people talked a lot or that 'The Wish' would be ordinary without a parallel universe. The songs are a form of structure and storytelling in themselves. Here the script and the music, the characterization and the orchestration, are all part of the same process. It's *about* the characters, so much so that it becomes a celebration of everything the series has built over the previous five years." In *Dusted*, p. 233.

22. See chapter 7 for a discussion of this.

Conclusion

1. David Lavery, "I Wrote My Thesis on You!: *Buffy* Studies as an Academic Cult" in *Slayage*, numbers 13 and 14, October 2004.

2. Jean-François Lyotard, "Brief Reflections of Popular Culture" in Appignanesi, *Postmodernism*, pp. 181–82.

Bibliography

Abbott, Stacey. "A Little Less Ritual and a Lot More Fun: The Modern Vampire in *Buffy the Vampire Slayer.*" *Slayage: The Online International Journal of Buffy Studies*, number 3 (June 2001), http://www.slayage.tv/essays/slayage3/sabbott.htm.

Aberdein, Andrew. "Balderdash and Chicanery: Science and Beyond." In Buffy the Vampire Slayer *and Philosophy*, ed. South, pp. 79–90.

Adams, Michael. *Slayer Slang: A* Buffy the Vampire Slayer *Lexicon*. Oxford: Oxford University Press, 2003.

Alderman, Naomi, and Annette Seidel-Arpaci. "Imaginary Para-Sites of the Soul: Vampires and Representations of 'Blackness' and 'Jewishness' in the *Buffy/Angel*verse." *Slayage*, number 10 (November 2003), http;//slayage.tv.essays.slayage10/Alderman_&_Seidel-Arpaci.htm.

Alessio, Dominic. "Things are Different Now?: A Postcolonial Analysis of *Buffy the Vampire Slayer.*" *The European Legacy* 6.6 (2001): 731–40.

Allott, Miriam. *Novelists on the Novel*. London: Routledge and Kegan Paul, 1959.

Almond, Brenda (ed.). *Introducing Applied Ethics*. Oxford: Blackwell, 1995.

_____. "Liberty or Community: Defining the Post-Marxist Agenda." In *Introducing Applied Ethics*, ed. Almond, pp. 247–59.

Anderson, Wendy Love. "Prophecy Girl and the Powers That Be: The Philosophy of Religion in the Buffyverse." In Buffy the Vampire Slayer *and Philosophy*, ed. South, pp. 212–26.

Anolik, Ruth Bienstock, and Douglas L. Howard. *The Gothic Other: Racial and Social Constructions of the Literary Imagination*. Jefferson, N.C.: McFarland, 2004.

Appignanesi, Lisa (ed.). *Postmodernism: ICA Documents*. London: Free Association Books, 1989.

Arata, Stephen D. "The Occidental Tourist: *Dracula* and the Anxiety of Reverse Colonization." In *The Nineteenth Century Novel*, ed. Regan, pp. 458–64.

Auerbach, Nina. *Our Vampires, Ourselves*. Chicago: University of Chicago Press, 1995.

Auster, Paul. *The New York Trilogy*. London: Faber and Faber, 1992.

Bacon-Smith, Camille. "The Color of the Dark." *Slayage: The Online International Journal of Buffy Studies*, number 8 (March 2003), http://www.slayage.tv/essays/slayage8/bacon-smith.htm.

_____. *Enterprising Women: Television Fandom and the Creation of Popular Myth*. Philadelphia: University of Pennsylvania Press, 1992.

Bakhtin, Mikhail M. *Rabelais and His World*. Trans. Helene Iswolsky. Cambridge: MIT Press, 1968.

Banes, Sally. "Introduction to *Terpsichore in Sneakers*." In *Postmodernism*, ed. Docherty, pp. 157–71.

Barnes, Julian. *A History of the World in 10½ Chapters*. London: Jonathan Cape, 1989.

Barthes, Roland. *Image Music Text*. Trans. Stephen Heath. London: Fontana, 1977.

_____. *Mythologies*. Trans. Annette Lavers. London: Jonathan Cape, 1972.

Battis, Jess. "She's Not All Grown Yet: Willow as Hybrid/Hero in *Buffy the Vampire Slayer*." *Slayage: The Online International Journal of Buffy Studies*, number 8 (March 2003), http://www.slayage.tv/essays/slayage8/battis.htm.

Baudrillard, Jean. *The Illusion of the End*. Trans. Chris Turner. Cambridge: Polity Press, 1994.

_____. "The Masses: The Implosion of the Social in the Media." In *Jean Baudrillard: Selected Writings*, ed. and trans. Mark Poster (Cambridge: Polity Press, 1988), pp. 207–19.

Belsey, Andrew. "Ethics, Law and the Quality of the Media." In *Introducing Applied Ethics*, ed. Almond, pp. 89–103.

Benjamin, Walter. "Theses on the Philosophy of History." In *Literature in the Modern World*, ed. Walder, pp. 362–65.

Bennett, Jane. "How Is It, Then, That We Still Remain Barbarians?: Foucault, Schiller, and the Aestheticization of Ethics." *Political Theory* 24 (1996): 653–672.

Berg, Jonathan. "How Could an Ethics Depend on Religion?" In *A Companion to Ethics*, ed. Singer, pp. 525–33.

Berger, Arthur Asa (ed.). *The Postmodern Presence: Readings on Postmodernism in American Culture and Society*. California: AltaMira Press, 1998.

Bhaba, Homi. *The Location of Culture*. London: Routledge, 1994.

Blackburn, Simon. *Dictionary of Philosophy*. Oxford: Oxford University Press, 1996.

Bloom, Harold. *The American Religion: The Emergence of the Post-Christian Nation*. New York: Simon and Schuster, 1992.

Bloustien, Gerry. "Fans with a Lot at Stake: Serious Play and Mimetic Excess in *Buffy the Vampire Slayer*." *European Journal of Cultural Studies* 5.4 (2002): 427–49.

Bogle, Donald. *Toms, Coons, Mulattos, Mammies and Bucks: An Interpretive History of Blacks in American Films*. 3rd edition. New York: Continuum, 1996.

Bordo, Susan. "Material Girl: The Effacements of Postmodern Culture." In *Literary Theory*, ed. Rivkin and Ryan, pp. 1099–115.

Bordwell, David, and Kristin Thompson. *Film Art: An Introduction*. 7th edition. New York: McGraw-Hill, 2004.

Bourdieu, Pierre. *Distinction*. Cambridge: Harvard University Press, 1984.

Boyette, Michelle. "The Comic Anti-Hero in *Buffy the Vampire Slayer*, or Silly Villain: Spike Is for Kicks." *Slayage: The Online International Journal of Buffy Studies,* number 4 (December 2001), http://www.slayage.tv/essays/slayage4/boyette.htm.

Bradney, Anthony. "I Made a Promise to a Lady: Law and Love in *BtVS*." *Slayage: The Online International Journal of Buffy Studies,* number 10 (November 2003), http://www.slayage.tv/essays/slayage10/bradney.htm.

Brantlinger, Patrick. "The Rule of Darkness." In *Literary Theory*, ed. Rivkin and Ryan, pp. 856–67.

Braun, Beth. "*The X-Files* and *Buffy the Vampire Slayer*: The Ambiguity of Evil in Supernatural Representations." *Journal of Popular Film and Television* 28.2 (2000): 88–94.

Breton, Rob, and Lindsay McMaster. "Dissing the Age of MOO: Initiatives, Alternatives and Rationality." *Slayage: The Online International Journal of Buffy Studies,* number 1 (January 2001), http://www.slayage.tv/essays/slayage1/bretonmcmaster.htm.

Briggs, Asa. "The English: How the Nation Sees Itself." In *Literature in the Modern World*, ed. Walder, pp. 189–95.

Bronfen, Elisabeth. *Over Her Dead Body: Death, Femininity and the Aesthetic.* Manchester: Manchester University Press, 1992.

Brooks, David. "Taste, Virtue and Class." In *Virtue and Taste: Essays on Politics, Ethics and Aesthetics*, ed. Dudley Knowles and John Skorupski (Oxford: Blackwell, 1993), pp. 65–82.

Brown, Curtis. "Art, Oppression, and the Autonomy of Aesthetics." In *Arguing about Art*, ed. Neill and Ridley, pp. 399–422.

Buffy the Vampire Slayer: The Script Book, Season One, Volume One. New York and London: Pocket Books, 2000.

Buinicki, Martin, and Anthony Enns. "Buffy the Vampire Disciplinarian: Institutional Excess and the New Economy of Power." *Slayage: The Online International Journal of Buffy Studies,* number 4 (December 2001), http://www.slayage.tv/essays/slayage4/buinickienns.htm.

Bunson, Matthew. *The Vampire Encyclopedia.* New York: Crown Books, 1993.

Bürger, Peter. "The Negation of the Autonomy of Art by the Avant-Garde." In *Postmodernism*, ed. Docherty, pp. 237–56.

Burr, Vivien. "*Buffy* vs. the BBC: Moral Questions and How to Avoid Them." *Slayage: The Online International Journal of Buffy Studies,* number 8 (March 2003), http://www.slayage.tv/essays/slayage8/burr.htm.

_____. "It All Seems So Real: Intertextuality in the Buffyverse." *Refractory: A Journal of Entertainment Media* 2 (2003), http://www.refractory.unimelb.edu.au/refractory/journalissues/index.htm.

Butler, Judith. *Bodies That Matter; On the Discursive Limits of "Sex."* London: Routledge, 1993.

_____. *Gender Trouble: Feminism and the Subversion of Identity.* London: Routledge, 1990.

Byers, Michele. "*Buffy the Vampire Slayer*: The Insurgence of Television as a Performance Text." Dissertation, University of Toronto, 2000.

Callander, Michelle. "Bram Stoker's *Buffy*: Traditional Gothic and Contemporary Culture." *Slayage: The Online International Journal of Buffy Studies,* number 3 (June 2001), http://www.slayage.tv/essays/slayage3/callander.htm.

Campbell, Richard, with Caitlin Campbell. "Demons, Aliens, Teens and Television." *Television Quarterly* 31.4 (2001): 56–64. Republished in *Slayage: The Online International Journal of Buffy Studies,* number 2 (March 2001), http://www.slayage.tv/essays/slayage2/campbell.htm.

Caputo, John D. "Mysticism and Transgression: Derrida and Meister Eckhart." In *Derrida and Deconstruction*, ed. Hugh J. Silverman (London: Routledge, 1989), pp. 24–39.

_____, and Michael Scanlon. *God, the Gift, and Postmodernism.* Bloomington: Indiana University Press, 1999.

Carlson, Marvin. *Performance: A Critical Introduction.* London: Routledge, 1996.

Carlson, Thomas A. "Consuming Desire's Deferral: A Theological Shadow in the Culture of Image." *Parallax* 10 (January–March 1999): 39–55.

Carroll, David. "Foreword: The Memory of Devastation and the Responsibilities of Thought: 'And let's not talk about that.'" In Jean-François Lyotard, *Heidegger and "the jews,"* trans. Andreas Michael and Mark S. Roberts (Minneapolis: University of Minnesota Press, 1990), pp. vii–xxix.

Carroll, Noël. "Art, Narrative and Moral Understanding." In *Aesthetics and Ethics*, ed. Levinson, pp. 126–60.

_____. "Why Horror?" In *Arguing about Art*, ed. Neill and Ridley, pp. 275–94.

Carter, Margaret L. "A World Without Shrimp." In *Seven Seasons of* Buffy, ed. Yeffeth, pp. 176–87.

Cartmell, Deborah, I. Q. Hunter, Heidi Kaye, and Imelda Whelehan (eds.). *Trash Aesthetics: Popular Culture and Its Audience*. London: Pluto Press, 1997.

Chandler, Holly. "Slaying the Patriarchy: Transfusions of the Vampire Metaphor in *Buffy the Vampire Slayer*." *Slayage: The Online International Journal of Buffy Studies*, number 9 (August 2003), http://www.slayage.tv/esays/slayage9/chandler.htm.

Chin, Vivian. "Buffy? She's Like Me, She's Not Like Me — She's Rad." In *Athena's Daughters: Television's New Women Warriors*, ed. Frances Early and Kathleen Kennedy (Syracuse: Syracuse University Press, 2003), pp. 92–102.

Churchill, Ward. "Literature as a Weapon in the Colonization of the American Indian." In *American Cultural Studies*, ed. Hartley and Pearson, pp. 179–85.

Clark, Daniel A., and Andrew P. Miller. "Buffy, the Scooby Gang and Monstrous Authority: BtVS and the Subversion of Authority." *Slayage: The Online International Journal of Buffy Studies*, number 3 (June 2001), http://www.slayage.tv/essays/slayage3/clarkmiller.htm.

Clark, Stephen R. L. "Enlarging the Community: Companion Animals." In *Introducing Applied Ethics*, ed. Almond, pp. 318–30.

Collins, Jim (ed.). *High Pop: Making Culture into Popular Entertainment*. Oxford: Blackwell, 2002.

Collins, Wilkie. *The Moonstone* (1868). Ware: Wordsworth Editions Ltd., 1993.

Connor, Steven. *Postmodernist Culture: An Introduction to Theories of the Contemporary*. Oxford: Blackwell, 1989.

_____. *Theory and Cultural Value*. Oxford: Blackwell, 1992.

Conrad, Joseph. *Heart of Darkness*. Ed. Robert Kimbrough. New York: W. W. Norton, 1988.

Crowther, Paul. "Postmodernism in the Visual Arts: A Question of Ends." In *Postmodernism*, ed. Docherty, pp. 180–93.

Culler, Jonathan. *Structuralist Poetics: Structuralism, Linguistics and the Study of Literature*. London: Routledge and Kegan Paul, 1975.

Dancy, Jonathan. "An Ethic of Prima Facie Duties." In *A Companion to Ethics*, ed. Singer, pp. 219–29.

da Ross, Giada. "When, Where and How Much is *Buffy* a Soap Opera?" *Slayage: The Online International Journal of Buffy Studies*, numbers 13 and 14 (October 2004), http://www.slayage.tv/essays/slayage13_14/Da_Ros.htm.

Daspit, Toby. "Buffy Goes to College, Adam Murders to Dissect: Education and Knowledge in Postmodernity." In Buffy the Vampire Slayer *and Philosophy*, ed. South, pp. 131–46.

Daugherty, Anne Millard. "Just a Girl: Buffy as Icon." In *Reading the Vampire Slayer*, ed. Kaveney, pp. 149–65.

Davies, Norman. *Europe: A History*. Oxford: Oxford University Press, 1996.

Davis, Glynn, and Kay Dickinson (eds.). *Teen TV: Genre, Consumption, Identity*. London: British Film Institute, 2004.

Davis, Robert A. "*Buffy the Vampire Slayer* and the Pedagogy of Fear." *Slayage: The Online International Journal of Buffy Studies*, number 3 (June 2001), http://www.slayage.tv/essays/slayage3/davis.htm.

DeCandido, GraceAnne A. "A Bibliographic Good vs. Evil in *Buffy the Vampire Slayer*." *American Libraries* 30.8 (September 1999): 44–47.

Dechert, S. Renee. "My Boyfriend's in a Band." In *Fighting the Forces*, ed. Wilcox and Lavery, pp. 218–26.

Deloria, Vine, Jr. "Indians Today, the Real and the Unreal." In *American Cultural Studies*, ed. Hartley and Pearson, pp. 44–52.

Dery, Mark. *The Pyrotechnic Insanitorium: American Culture on the Brink*. New York: Grove Press, 2000.

Devereux, Mary. "Oppressive Texts, Resisting Readers and the Gendered Space of the Spectator: The 'New' Aesthetics." In *Arguing about Art*, ed. Neill and Ridley, pp. 381–98.

Diehl, Laura. "Why Drusilla's More Interesting Than Buffy." *Slayage: The Online International Journal of Buffy Studies*, numbers 13 and 14 (October 2004), http://www.slayage.tv/essays/slayage13_14/diehl.htm.

Docherty, Thomas (ed.). *Postmodernism: A Reader*. Hertfordshire: Harvester Wheatsheaf, 1993.

Dowling, Jennifer. "We Are Not Demons: Homogenizing the Heroes in *Buffy the Vampire Slayer* and *Angel*." *Refractory: A Journal of Entertainment Media* 2 (2003), http://www.refractory.unimelb.edu.au/refractory/journalissues/index.htm.

Driver, Martha W., and Sid Ray (eds.). *The Medieval Hero on Screen: Representations from Beowulf to Buffy*. Jefferson, N.C: McFarland, 2004.

Dundes, Alan (ed.). *The Vampire: A Casebook*. Madison: University of Wisconsin Press, 1998.

During, Simon. "Postmodernism or Post-colonialism Today." In *Postmodernism*, ed. Docherty, pp. 448–62.

Eagleton, Terry. "Capitalism, Modernism, Postmodernism." In *Modern Criticism and Theory: A Reader*, ed. David Lodge (London: Longman, 1988), pp. 385–98.

_____. *The Ideology of the Aesthetic*. Oxford: Blackwell, 1990.

_____. "J. L. Austin and the Book of Jonah." In *The Postmodern Bible Reader*, ed. Jobling, Pippin and Schleifer, pp. 177–82.

Early, Frances. "Staking Her Claim: Buffy the Vampire Slayer as Transgressive Woman Warrior." *Slayage: The Online International Journal of Buffy Studies*, number 6 (September 2002) http://www.slayage.tv/essays/slayage6/early.htm. Previously published in *The Journal of Popular Culture*, vol. 35, no.3 (Winter 2001): 11–27.

Earnshaw, Steven (ed.). *Postmodern Surroundings*. Amsterdam: Rodopi, 1994.

_____. "Well and Truly Fact: Postmodernism in History." In *Postmodern Surroundings*, ed. Earnshaw, pp. 53–71.

Eaton, Marcia Muelder. "Aesthetics: The Mother of Ethics?" *The Journal of Aesthetics and Art Criticism* 55 (1997): 355–364.

Eco, Umberto. *The Limits of Interpretation*. Bloomington: Indiana University Press, 1990.

_____. *The Name of the Rose* (1980). Trans. William Weaver. London: Picador, 1984.

_____. "Reflections on *The Name of the Rose*." *Encounter* LXIV (April 1985): 7–19.

_____. *Six Walks in the Fictional Woods*. Cambridge: Harvard University Press, 1994.

Edwards, Lynne. "Slaying in Black and White: Kendra as Tragic Mulatta in *Buffy*." In *Fighting the Forces*, ed. Wilcox and Lavery, pp. 85–97.

Elam, Dianne. "Linguistic or Material Girl?" In *Feminism and Deconstruction: Ms. En Abyme* (London: Routledge, 1994), pp. 58–66.

Eliot, T. S. *Collected Poems 1909–1962*. London: Faber and Faber, 1985.

Erickson, Greg. "Religion Freaky, or 'A Bunch of Men Who Died?': The (A)Theology of *Buffy*." *Slayage: The Online International Journal of Buffy Studies*, numbers 13 and 14 (October 2004), http://www.slayage.tv/essays/slayage13_14/erickson.htm.

Falconer, Rachel. *Hell in Contemporary Literature: Western Descent Narratives Since 1945*. Edinburgh: Edinburgh University Press, 2004.

Fifarek, Aimee. "Mind and Heart with Spirit Joined: The Buffyverse as an Information System." *Slayage: The Online International Journal of Buffy Studies*, number 3 (June 2001), http://www.slayage.tv/essays/slayage3/afifarek.htm.

Fiske, John. *Television Culture*. London: Routledge, 1987.

_____, and John Hartely. *Reading Television*. London: Routledge, 2003.

Florescu, Radu R., and Raymond T. McNally. *Dracula: Prince of Many Faces. His Life and Times*. London: Little Brown, 1990.

_____. *In Search of Dracula: The History of Dracula and Vampires*. Boston: Houghton Mifflin, 1994.

Fossey, Claire. "Never Hurt the Feelings of a Brutal Killer: Spike and the Underground Man." *Slayage: The Online International Journal of Buffy Studies,* number 8 (March 2003), http://www.slayage.tv/essays/slayage8/fossey.htm.

Foster, Greg. "Faith and Plato: 'You're Nothing! Disgusting, Murderous Bitch.'" In Buffy the Vampire Slayer *and Philosophy*, ed. South, pp. 7–19.

Foucault, Michel. *Madness and Civilization*. Trans. Richard Howard. New York: Vintage Books, 1965.

Francis, Rob. "London Calling: *Buffy* from a British Perspective." In *The Watcher's Guide*, vol. 3, ed. Paul Ruditis (New York: Simon Spotlight, 2004), pp. 255–64.

Freud, Sigmund. "The Archaic Features and Infantilism of Dreams." In *Introductory Lectures on Psychoanalysis*, Penguin Freud Library, vol. 1, trans. J. Strachey, ed. J. Strachey and A. Richards (London: Penguin, 1991), pp. 234–57.

_____. *Moses and Monotheism*. Trans. Katharine Jones. New York: Vintage Books, 1939.

Frow, John. "Signature and Brand." In *High Pop*, ed. Collins, pp. 32–55.

Frye, Northrop. "The Bottomless Dream: Themes of Descent." In *The Secular Scripture: A Study of the Structure of Romance* (Cambridge: Harvard University Press, 1976), pp. 95–126.

Fukuyama, Francis. *The End of History and the Last Man*. Harmondsworth: Penguin, 1992.

Gaut, Berys. "The Paradox of Horror." In *Arguing about Art*, ed. Neill and Ridley, pp. 295–308.

Genette, Gérard. "Order in Narrative." In *Literature in the Modern World*, ed. Walder, pp. 142–50.

Gerbner, George. "Mass Media Discourses: Message System Analysis as a Component of Cultural Indicators." In *American Cultural Studies*, ed. Hartley and Pearson, pp. 141–51.

Gitlin, Todd. *Inside Prime Time*. Berkeley: University of California Press, 1999.

Goddard, Drew. "Foreword: Taste Our Steel." In *Seven Seasons of* Buffy, ed. Yeffeth, pp. xi–xii.

Golden, Christie. "Where's the Religion in Willow's Wicca?" In *Seven Seasons of* Buffy, ed. Yeffeth, pp. 159–66.

Golden, Christopher, and Nancy Holder. *Buffy the Vampire Slayer: The Watcher's Guide*, vol. 1. New York: Pocket, 1998.

Golden, Christopher, Stephen R. Bissette, and Thomas E. Sniegoski. *Buffy the Vampire Slayer: The Monster Book*. New York: Pocket, 2000.

Gordon, Joan, and Veronica Hollinger (eds.). *Blood Read: The Vampire as Metaphor in Contemporary Culture*. Philadelphia: University of Pennsylvania Press, 1997.

Gray, Herman. "African-American Political Desire and the Seductions of Contemporary Cultural Politics." In *American Cultural Studies*, ed. Hartley and Pearson, pp. 242–50.

Greene, Richard, and Wayne Yuen. "Why We Can't Spike Spike: Moral Themes in *Buffy the Vampire Slayer*." *Slayage: The Online International Journal of Buffy Studies,* number 2 (March 2001), http://www.slayage.tv/essays/slayage2/greeneandyuen.htm.

Grossberg, Lawrence. "Identity and Cultural Studies: Is That All There Is?" In *American Cultural Studies*, ed. Hartley and Pearson, pp. 114–24.

Habermas, Jürgen. "Modernity, an Incomplete Project." In *Postmodernism*, ed. Docherty, pp. 98–109.

Halberstam, Judith. *Skin Shows: Gothic Horror and the Technology of Monsters*. Durham, N.C.: Duke University Press, 1995.

Halfyard, Janet, K. "Love, Death, Curses and Reverses (in F Minor): Music, Gender and Identity in *Buffy the Vampire Slayer* and *Angel.*" *Slayage: The Online International Journal of Buffy Studies,* number 4 (December 2001), http://www.slayage.tv/essays/slayage4/halfyard.htm.

Hampson, Robert. "Conrad and the Idea of Empire." In *The Nineteenth Century Novel,* ed. Regan, pp. 498–507.

Hampton, Howard. "American Demons: *Buffy* Amok in D. H. Lawrence's World." *Village Voice Literary Supplement,* 20 May 2003.

Hannsberry, Karen Burroughs. *Femme Noir: Bad Girls on Film.* Jefferson, N.C: McFarland, 1998.

Haraway, Donna, J. "Ecce Homo, Ain't (Ar'n't) I a Woman, and Inappropriate/d Others: The Human in a Post-Humanist Landscape." In *The Postmodern Bible Reader,* ed. Jobling, Pippin and Schleifer, pp. 205–18.

Harris, Charlaine. "A Reflection on Ugliness." In *Seven Seasons of* Buffy, ed. Yeffeth, pp. 116–20.

Hartley, John, and Roberta E. Pearson (eds.). *American Cultural Studies: A Reader.* Oxford: Oxford University Press, 2000.

Harts, Kate. "Deconstructing Buffy: *Buffy the Vampire Slayer*'s Contribution to the Discourse on Gender Construction." *Popular Culture Review* 12:1 (2001): 79–98.

Haydock, Nikolas A. "Arthurian Melodrama, Chaucerian Spectacle, and the Waywardness of Cinematic Pastiche in *First Knight* and *A Knight's Tale.*" In *Studies in Medievalism,* volume XII, ed. Shippey and Arnold, pp. 5–38.

Heaney, Seamus. "Englands of the Mind." In *Literature in the Modern World,* ed. Walder, pp. 250–56.

Hegel, G. W. F. *Introductory Lectures on Aesthetics* (1886). Trans. Bernard Bosanquet. London: Penguin, 1993.

Held, Jacob M. "Justifying the Means: Punishment in the Buffyverse." In Buffy the Vampire Slayer *and Philosophy,* ed. South, pp. 227–38.

Helford, Elyce (ed.). *Fantasy Girls: Gender and the New Universe of Science Fiction and Fantasy Television.* Lanham, Md.: Rowman and Littlefield, 2000.

Hertsgaard, Mark. *The Eagle's Shadow: Why America Fascinates and Infuriates the World.* London: Bloomsbury, 2002.

Hibbs, Thomas. "*Buffy the Vampire Slayer* as Feminist *Noir.*" In Buffy the Vampire Slayer *and Philosophy,* ed. South, pp. 49–60.

Hill, Annette, and Ian Calcutt. "Vampire Hunters: The Scheduling and Reception of *Buffy the Vampire Slayer* and *Angel* in the UK." *Intensities: The Journal of Cult Media,* issue 1 (2001), www.cult-media.com/issue1/Ahillcalcutt.htm.

Hillis, Miller, J. "Introduction." In *Bleak House,* ed. Norman Page (Harmondsworth: Penguin, 1971), pp. 11–34.

_____. "Parable and Performative in the Gospels and in Modern Literature." In *The Postmodern Bible Reader,* ed. Jobling, Pippin and Schleifer, pp. 142–62.

Hills, Matt. *Fan Cultures.* London: Routledge, 2002.

Hogle, Jerrold, E. "Stoker's Counterfeit Gothic: *Dracula* and Theatricality at the Dawn of Simulation." In *Bram Stoker: History, Psychoanalysis and the Gothic,* ed. Hughes and Smith, pp. 205–24.

Holder, Nancy. *Buffy the Vampire Slayer: The Watcher's Guide.* Vol. 2. New York: Pocket, 2000.

_____. "Slayers of the Lost Arc." In *Seven Seasons of* Buffy, ed. Yeffeth, pp. 195–205.

_____, with Jeff Mariotte, and Maryelizabeth Hart. *Angel: The Case Files.* Vol. 1. New York: Pocket, 2002.

Holdsworth, Dick. "Ethical Decision-making in Science and Technology." In *Introducing Applied Ethics,* ed. Almond, pp. 130–47.

Homer. *The Odyssey.* Trans. Robert Fagles. Harmondsworth: Penguin, 1999.

Horkheimer, Max, and Theodor Adorno. *Dialectic of Enlightenment*. London: Verso, 1979.

Hughes, William, and Andrew Smith (eds.). *Bram Stoker: History, Psychoanalysis and the Gothic*. London: Macmillan, 1998.

Hutcheon, Linda. *The Politics of Postmodernism*. London: Routledge, 1989.

Ingram, Richard. "Democracy in the Era of Identity Politics: Lyotard on Postmodern Legitimation." In *The Political*, ed. David Ingham (Oxford: Blackwell, 2002), pp. 240–64.

Jackson, Helen Hunt. *A Century of Dishonor: A Sketch of the United States Government's Dealings with Some of the Indian Tribes* (1881). Norman: University of Oklahoma Press, 1995.

Jakobson, Roman. *On Language*. Ed. Linda Waugh and Monique Monville-Burston. Cambridge: Harvard University Press, 1995.

Jameson, Fredric. *Postmodernism, or The Cultural Logic of Late Capitalism*. Durham, N.C.: Duke University Press, 1991.

Janovich, Mark, and James Lyons (eds.). *Quality Popular Television: Cult TV, the Industry and Fans*. London: British Film Institute, 2003.

Jarvis, Christine. "School Is Hell: Gendered Fears in Teenage Horror." *Educational Studies* 27.3 (2001): 257–67.

Jarzombek, Mark. *The Psychologizing of Modernity: Art, Architecture, History*. Cambridge: Cambridge University Press, 1998.

Jay, Peter, and Caroline Lewis (eds.). *Sappho Through English Poetry*. London: Anvil Poetry Press, 1996.

Jenkins, Alice, and Susan Stuart. "Extending Your Mind: Non-Standard Perlocutionary Acts in 'Hush.'" *Slayage: The Online International Journal of Buffy Studies*, number 9 (August 2003), http://www.slayage.tv/essays/slayage9/jenkinsstuart.htm.

Jobling, David, Tina Pippin, and Ronald Schleifer (eds.). *The Postmodern Bible Reader*. Oxford: Blackwell, 2001.

Jowett, Lorna. "New Men: Playing the Sensitive Lad." *Slayage: The Online International Journal of Buffy Studies*, numbers 13 and 14 (October 2004), http://www.slayage.tv/essays/slayage13_14/jowett.htm.

Kaveney, Roz (ed.). *Reading the Vampire Slayer: An Unofficial Critical Companion to Buffy and Angel*. London and New York: Tauris Parke, 2003.

_____. "She Saved the World. A Lot. An Introduction to the Themes and Structures of *Buffy* and *Angel*." In *Reading the Vampire Slayer*, ed. Kaveney, pp. 1–36.

Keller, Donald. "Spirit Guides and Shadow Selves: From the Dream Life of Buffy (and Faith)." In *Fighting the Forces*, ed. Wilcox and Lavery, pp. 165–77.

Kenyon, Sherrilyn. "The Search for Spike's Balls." In *Seven Seasons of* Buffy, ed. Yeffeth, pp. 25–29.

Kershaw, Baz. "The Shadow of Oppression: Performance, the Panopticon and Ethics." In *The Radical in Performance: Between Brecht and Baudrillard* (London: Routledge, 1999), pp. 126–56.

Kilminster, Richard, and Ian Varcoe (eds.). *Culture, Modernity, and Revolution: Essays in Honour of Zygmunt Bauman*. London: Routledge, 1996.

Kilpatrick, Nancy. "Sex and the Single Slayer." In *Seven Seasons of* Buffy, ed. Yeffeth, pp. 19–24.

King, Neal. "Brownskirts: Fascism, Christianity, and the Eternal Demon." In Buffy the Vampire Slayer *and Philosophy*, ed. South, pp. 197–211.

Kristeva, Julia. "Romeo and Juliet: Love-Hatred in the Couple." In *Tales of Love*, trans. Leon S. Roudiez (New York: Columbia University Press, 1987), pp. 209–33.

Kryzwinska, Tanya. "Hubble-Bubble, Herbs and Grimoires: Magic, Manicheanism, and Witchcraft in *Buffy*." In *Fighting the Forces*, ed. Wilcox and Lavery, pp. 178–94.

Laclau, Ernesto. "Politics and the Limits of Modernity." In *Postmodernism*, ed. Docherty, pp. 329–43.

Lavery, David. "Afterword: The Genius of Joss Whedon." In *Fighting the Forces*, ed. Wilcox and Lavery, pp. 251–56.

_____. "Apocalyptic Apocalypses: Narrative Eschatology in *Buffy the Vampire Slayer*." *Slayage: The Online International Journal of Buffy Studies,* number 9 (August 2003), http://www.slayage.tv/essays/slayage9/lavery.htm.

_____. "*Buffy the Vampire Slayer*." In *50 Key Television Programmes*, ed. Glen Creeber (London: Arnold, 2004), pp. 31–35.

_____. "Emotional Resonance and Rocket Launchers: Joss Whedon's Commentaries on the *Buffy the Vampire Slayer* DVDs." *Slayage: The Online International Journal of Buffy Studies*, number 6 (September 2002), http://www.slayage.tv/essays/slayage6/lavery.htm.

_____. "Fatal Environment: *Buffy the Vampire Slayer* and American Culture." Unpublished conference paper, presented at *Staking a Claim: Exploring the Global Reach of Buffy*, Adelaide, Australia, July 2003.

_____. "I Wrote My Thesis on You!: *Buffy* Studies as an Academic Cult." *Slayage: The Online International Journal of Buffy Studies*, numbers 13 and 14 (October 2004), http://www.slayage.tv/essays/slayage13_14/lavery.htm.

_____. "A Religion in Narrative: Joss Whedon and Television Creativity." *Slayage: The Online International Journal of Buffy Studies*, number 7 (December 2002), http://www.slayage.tv/essays/slayage7/lavery.htm.

Lee, Alison. *Realism and Power: Postmodern British Fiction*. London: Routledge, 1990.

Leon, Hilary M. "Why We Love the Monsters: How Anita Blake Vampire Hunter, and Buffy the Vampire Slayer Wound up Dating the Enemy." *Slayage: The Online International Journal of Buffy Studies,* number 1 (January 2001), http://www.slayage.tv. essays.slayage11/leon.htm.

Levinas, Emmanuel. "On the Jewish Reading of the Scriptures." In *The Postmodern Bible Reader*, ed. Jobling, Pippin and Schleifer, pp. 319–33.

Levinson, Jerrold (ed.). *Aesthetics and Ethics: Essays at the Intersection*. Cambridge: Cambridge University Press, 1998.

_____. "Introduction: Aesthetics and ethics." In *Aesthetics and Ethics*, ed. Levinson, pp. 1–25.

Lichtenberg, Jacqueline. "Power of Becoming." In *Seven Seasons of* Buffy, ed. Yeffeth, pp. 121–36.

Little, Tracy. "High School Is Hell: Metaphor Made Literal in *Buffy the Vampire Slayer*." In Buffy the Vampire Slayer *and Philosophy*, ed. South, pp. 282–93.

Locklin, Reid B. "*Buffy the Vampire Slayer* and the Domestic Church: Revisioning the Family and the Common Good." *Slayage: The Online International Journal of Buffy Studies*, number 6 (November 2002), http://www.slayage.tv/essays/ slayage6/locklin.htm.

Lyotard, Jean-François. "Answer to the Question: What Is Postmodernism?" In *The Postmodern Explained to Children*, pp. 9–25.

_____. "Apostil on Narratives." In *The Postmodern Explained to Children*, pp. 17–22.

_____. "Brief Reflections of Popular Culture." In *Postmodernism*, ed. Appignanesi, pp. 181–82.

_____. "Heidegger and 'the jews.'" In *Political Writings*, trans. Bill Readings and Kevin Paul Geiman, ed. Bill Readings (Minneapolis: University of Minnesota Press, 1993), pp. 141–48.

_____. *Libidinal Economy*. Trans. Iain Hamilton Grant. Bloomington: Indiana University Press, 1993.

_____. *The Postmodern Condition: A Report on Knowledge* (1979). Trans. Geoff Bennington and Brian Massumi. Manchester: Manchester University Press, 1984.

_____. *The Postmodern Explained to Children: Correspondence 1982–1985* (1986). Trans. Julian Pefanis and Michael Thomas. Sydney: Power Publications, 1992.

_____. "A Postmodern Fable." In *Postmodern Fables*, pp. 83–102.

_____. *Postmodern Fables*. Trans. Georges van den Abbeele. Minneapolis: University of Minnesota Press, 1997.

_____. "Postscript to Terror and the Sublime." In *The Postmodern Explained to Children*, pp. 67–75.

Manns, James W. *Aesthetics*. Armonk, N.Y.: M. E. Sharpe, 1997.

Marinucci, Mimi. "Feminism and the Ethics of Violence: Why Buffy Kicks Ass." In *Buffy the Vampire Slayer and Philosophy*, ed. South, pp. 61–75.

Marshall, C. W. "Aeneas the Vampire Slayer: A Roman Model for Why Giles Kills Ben." *Slayage: The Online International Journal of Buffy Studies*, number 9 (August 2003), http://www.slayage.tv/essays/slayage9/marshall.htm.

McClelland, Bruce. "By Whose Authority? The Magical Tradition, Violence and the Legitimation of the Vampire Slayer." *Slayage: The Online International Journal of Buffy Studies*, number 1 (January 2001), http://www.slayage.tv/essays/ slayage1/ bmcclelland.htm.

McGinn, Colin. *Ethics, Evil, and Fiction*. Oxford: Clarendon Press, 1997.

McLeod, John. "Postmodernism and Postcolonialism." In *Postmodern Surroundings*, ed. Earnshaw, pp. 167–78.

McNally, Raymond T., and Radu R. Florescu. *In Search of Dracula: The History of Dracula and Vampires*. Boston: Houghton Mifflin, 1994.

McNeilly, Kevin, Christina Sylka, and Susan R. Fisher. "Kiss the Librarian, But Close the Hellmouth: It's Like a Whole Big Sucking Thing." *Slayage: The Online Journal of International Buffy Studies*, number 2 (March 2001), http://www.slayage.tv/essays/ slayage2/mcneilly.htm.

McQuillan, Martin. "A Glossary of Narrative Terms." In *The Narrative Reader*, ed. Martin McQuillan (London: Routledge, 2000), pp. 314–29.

McRobbie, Angela. "Postmodernism and Popular Culture." In *Postmodernism*, ed. Appignanesi, pp. 165–80.

Mendlesohn, Farah. "Surpassing the Love of Vampires; or, Why (and How) a Queer Reading of the Buffy/Willow Relationship Is Denied." In *Fighting the Forces*, ed. Wilcox and Lavery, pp. 45–60.

Merrick, Helen. "The Readers Feminism Doesn't See: Feminist Fans, Critics and Science Fiction." In *Trash Aesthetics*, eds. Cartmell et al., pp. 48–65.

Meyer, Kim Middleton. "Tan'talizing Others: Multicultural Anxiety and the New Orientalism." In *High Pop*, ed. Collins, pp. 90–113.

Mikosz, Philip, and Dana Och. "Previously on *Buffy the Vampire Slayer* ...." *Slayage: The Online International Journal of Buffy Studies*, number 5 (May 2002), http:// www.slayage.tv/essays/slayage5/mikosz%20and%20och.htm.

Milavec, Melissa M., and Sharon M. Kaye. "A Slayer's Solution to Aristotle's Love Paradox." In *Buffy the Vampire Slayer and Philosophy*, ed. South, pp. 173–84.

Miles, Lawrence, Lars Peterson, and Christa Dickson. *Dusted: The Unauthorized Guide to* Buffy the Vampire Slayer. New Orleans: Mad Norwegian Press, 2003.

Mitchell, A. J. *Visual Effects for Film and Television*. Oxford: Focal, 2004.

Money, Mary Alice. "The Undemonizing of Supporting Characters in *Buffy*." In *Fighting the Forces*, ed. Wilcox and Lavery, pp. 98–107.

Morreale, Joanne. "*Xena: Warrior Princess* as Feminist Camp." *Journal of Popular Culture* 32.2 (Fall 1998): 79–86.

Moss, Gabrielle. "From the Valley to the Hellmouth: Buffy's Transition from Film to Television." *Slayage: The Online International Journal of Buffy Studies*, number 2 (March 2001), http://www.slayage.tv/essays/slayage2/moss.htm.

Muntersbjorn, Madeleine M. "Pluralism, Pragmatism, and Pals: The Slayer Subverts the Science Wars." In *Buffy the Vampire Slayer and Philosophy*, ed. South, pp. 91–102.

Murphy, Kevin Andrew. "Unseen Horrors and Shadowy Manipulations." In *Seven Seasons of Buffy*, ed. Yeffeth, pp. 137–51.

Musgrove, Jan. *Make-up, Hair and Costume for Film and Television*. Oxford: Focal, 2003.

Nabokov, Vladimir. "On a Book Entitled *Lolita*." In his *The Annotated Lolita*, ed. Alfred Appel, Jr. Harmondsworth: Penguin, 1991, pp. 312–24.

Neill, Alex, and Aaron Ridley. *Arguing about Art: Contemporary Philosophical Debates*. 2nd edition. London: Routledge, 2002.

Newcomb, Horace, and Paul M. Hirsch, "Television as a Cultural Form." In *American Cultural Studies*, ed. Hartley and Pearson, pp. 162–75.

Nicholson, Heather Norris (ed.). *Screening Culture: Constructing Image and Identity*. Lanham: Lexington Books, 2003.

Nussbaum, Emily. "Must See Metaphysics." *New York Times*, 22 September 2002.

Olsen, Scott R. *Hollywood Planet: Global Media and the Competitive Advantage of Narrative Transparency*. Mahwah, N.J.: Lawrence Erlbaum, 1999.

Ono, Kent A. "To Be a Vampire in *Buffy the Vampire Slayer*: Race and (Other) Socially Marginalized Positions on Horror TV." In *Gender in the New Universe of Science Fiction and Fantasy Television*, ed. Helford, pp. 163–86.

Orr, John, and Olga Taxidou (eds.). *Post-war Cinema and Modernity: A Film Reader*. Edinburgh: Edinburgh University Press, 2000.

Orwell, George. *1984*. Harmondsworth: Penguin, 1984.

Overbey, Karen Eileen, and Lahney Preston-Matto. "Staking in Tongues: Speech Act as Weapon in *Buffy*." In *Fighting the Forces*, ed. Wilcox and Lavery, pp. 73–84.

Owen, Susan A. "Vampires, Postmodernity, and Postfeminism: *Buffy the Vampire Slayer*." *Journal of Popular Culture* 27.2 (Summer 1999): 24–31.

Pankrantz, Annette, and Michael Hensen. "Introduction: The Aesthetics and Pragmatics of Violence." In *The Aesthetics and Pragmatics of Violence*, ed. Michael Hensen and Annette Pankrantz (Passau: Verlag Karl Stutz, 2001), pp. 9–18.

Pasley, Jeffrey L. "Old Familiar Vampires: The Politics of the Buffyverse." In *Buffy the Vampire Slayer and Philosophy*, ed. South, pp. 254–68.

Pateman, Matthew. "Julian Barnes and the Popularity of Ethics." In *Postmodern Surroundings*, ed. Earnshaw, pp. 179–91.

_____. "Lyotard's Patient Pedagogy." *Parallax* 17 (October–December 2001): 49–57.

_____. "You Say Tomato: Englishness in *Buffy the Vampire Slayer*." *Cercles* 8 (2003): 103–13, www.cercles.com/n8/pateman.pdf.

Pathak, Zakia. "A Pedagogy for Postcolonial Feminists." In *The Postmodern Bible Reader*, ed. Jobling, Pippin and Schleifer, pp. 219–32.

Pearson, Matthew. "Vic Reeves and Postmodern Comedy." In *Postmodern Surroundings*, ed. Earnshaw, pp. 193–213.

Pefanis, Julian. "W(h)ither History." In *Heterology and the Postmodern: Bataille, Baudrillard, and Lyotard* (Durham, N.C.: Duke University Press, 1991), pp. 9–20.

Pender, Patricia. "I'm Buffy, and You're ... History: The Postmodern Politics of *Buffy*." In *Fighting the Forces*, ed. Wilcox and Lavery, pp. 35–44.

Playdon, Zoe-Jane. "The Outsiders' Society: Religious Imagery in *Buffy the Vampire Slayer*." *Slayage: The Online International Journal of Buffy Studies*, number 5 (May 2002), http://www.slayage.tv/essays/slayage5/playdon.htm.

Rainey, Lawrence. "The Cultural Economy of Modernism." In *The Cambridge Companion to Modernism*, ed. Michael Levenson (Cambridge: Cambridge University Press, 1999), pp. 33–69.

Rambo, Elizabeth. "Lessons for Season Seven of *Buffy the Vampire Slayer*." *Slayage: The*

Online International Journal of Buffy Studies, numbers 11 and 12 (April 2004), http://www.slayage.tv/essays/slayage11_12/rambo.htm.

Readings, Bill. "Pagans, Perverts or Primitives? Experimental Justice in the Empire of Capital." In *Judging Lyotard*, ed. Andrew Benjamin (London: Routledge, 1992), pp. 168–91.

Regan, Stephen. *The Nineteenth Century Novel: A Critical Reader*. London: Routledge, 2001.

Resnick, Laura. "The Good, the Bad, and the Ambivalent." In *Seven Seasons of* Buffy, ed. Yeffeth, pp. 54–64.

Ricoeur, Paul. *Time and Narrative*. Volume 2. Trans. Kathleen McLaughlin and David Pellauer. Chicago: University of Chicago Press, 1985.

Riess, Jana. *What Would Buffy Do? The Vampire Slayer as Spiritual Guide*. San Francisco: Jossey-Bass, 2004.

Riley-Smith, Jonathan. *The Oxford History of the Crusades*. Oxford: Oxford University Press, 1999.

Rivkin, Julie, and Michael Roberts (eds.). *Literary Theory: An Anthology*. Oxford: Blackwell, 1998.

_____. "English Without Shadows." In *Literary Theory*, ed. Rivkin and Ryan, pp. 851–55.

Rose, Anita. "Of Creatures and Creators: *Buffy* Does *Frankenstein*." In *Fighting the Forces*, ed. Wilcox and Lavery, pp. 133–42.

Roth, Phyllis A. "Suddenly Sexual Woman in Bram Stoker's *Dracula*." In *The Nineteenth Century Novel*, ed. Regan, pp. 465–74.

Said, Edward. *Orientalism*. New York: Pantheon Books, 1978.

_____. "Two Visions of *Heart of Darkness*." In *The Nineteenth Century Novel*, ed. Regan, pp. 508–17.

St. Cyril. *Catechetical Lectures. Patristic Fathers*, vol. 30, http://www.synaxis.org/ecf/volume30/ECF00001.htm.

Sakal, Gregory, J. "No Big Win: Themes of Sacrifice, Salvation and Redemption." In Buffy the Vampire Slayer *and Philosophy*, ed. South, pp. 239–53.

Sayer, Karen. "It Wasn't Our World Anymore — They Made It Theirs: Reading Space and Place." In *Reading the Vampire Slayer*, ed. Kaveney, pp. 98–119.

Schneider, Daniel E. *The Psychoanalyst and the Artist*. New York: Farrar, 1950.

Schudson, Michael. "The Politics of Narrative Form: The Emergence of News Conventions in Print and Television." In *American Cultural Studies*, ed. Hartley and Pearson, pp. 152–61.

Schudt, Karl. "Also Sprach Faith: The Problem of the Happy Rogue Vampire Slayer." In Buffy the Vampire Slayer *and Philosophy*, ed. South, pp. 20–34.

Sheehan, Paul. *Modernism, Narrative and Humanism*. Cambridge: Cambridge University Press, 2002.

Shelley, Mary. *Frankenstein, or The Modern Prometheus* (1818). Harmondsworth: Penguin, 1994.

Shippey, Tom. "Editorial Note." In *Studies in Medievalism*, volume XII, eds. Shippey and Arnold, pp. 1–4.

_____, and Martin Arnold (eds.). *Studies in Medievalism: Film and Fiction Reviewing the Middle Ages*, volume XII. Cambridge: D. S. Brewer, 2002.

Shustermann, Richard. *Surface and Depth: Dialectics of Criticism and Culture*. Ithaca: Cornell University Press, 2002.

Shuttleworth, Ian. "They Always Mistake Me for the Character I Play! Transformation, Identity and Role-playing in the Buffyverse." In *Reading the Vampire Slayer*, ed. Kaveney, pp. 211–36.

Siemann, Catherine. "Darkness Falls on the Endless Summer: Buffy as Gidget for the Fin de Siècle." In *Fighting the Forces*, ed. Wilcox and Lavery, pp. 120–32.

Simkin, Stevie. "Who Died and Made You John Wayne? Anxious Masculinity in *Buffy the Vampire Slayer.*" *Slayage: The Online International Journal of Buffy Studies,* numbers 11 and 12 (April 2004), http://www.slayage.tv/essays/slayage11_12/simkin_wayne.htm.

_____. "You Hold Your Gun Like a Sissy Girl: Firearms and Anxious Masculinity in *BtVS.*" *Slayage: The Online International Journal of Buffy Studies,* numbers 11 and 12 (April 2004), http://www.slayage.tv/essays/slayage11_12/simkin_gun.htm.

Singer, Peter. *A Companion to Ethics.* Oxford: Blackwell, 1994.

Skwire, Sarah E. "Whose Side Are You On, Anyway? Children, Adults and the Use of Fairy Tales in *Buffy.*" In *Fighting the Forces,* ed. Wilcox and Lavery, pp. 195–206.

Sokal, Alan, and Jean Bricmont. *Intellectual Impostures: Postmodern Philosophers' Abuse of Science.* London: Profile Books, 1998.

Sophocles. *Oedipus Tyrannus.* Trans. and Ed. Luci Berkowitz and Theodore F. Brunner. New York: W. W. Norton, 1966.

South, James B. (ed.). Buffy the Vampire Slayer *and Philosophy: Fear and Trembling in Sunnydale.* Chicago and La Salle: Open Court, 2003.

_____. "My God, It's Like a Greek Tragedy: Willow Rosenberg and Human Irrationality." In Buffy the Vampire Slayer *and Philosophy,* ed. South, pp. 131–46.

_____. "On the Philosophical Consistency of Season Seven: Or, 'It's Not About Right, Not About Wrong...'." *Slayage: The Online International Journal of Buffy Studies,* numbers 13 and 14 (October 2004), http://www.slayage.tv/essays/slayage13_14/south.htm.

Spah, Victoria. "Ain't Love Grand: Spike and Courtly Love." *Slayage: The Online International Journal of Buffy Studies,* number 5 (May 2002), http://www. slayage.tv/essays/slayage5/spah.htm.

Spigel, Lynn. "From Theatre to Space Ship: Metaphors of Suburban Domesticity in Postwar America." In *American Cultural Studies,* ed. Hartley and Pearson, pp. 363–72.

Stam, Robert. "Eurocentrism, Polycentrism, and Multicultural Pedagogy: Film and the Quincentennial." In *American Cultural Studies,* ed. Hartley and Pearson, pp. 373–82.

Stengel, Wendy A. F. G. "Synergy and Smut: The Brand in Official and Unofficial *Buffy the Vampire Slayer* Communities of Interest." *Slayage: The Online International Journal of Buffy Studies,* number 4 (December 2001), http://www.slayage.tv/essays/slayage4/stengel.htm.

Stoker, Bram. *Dracula* (1897). Oxford: Oxford University Press, 1998.

Stroud, Scott R. "A Kantian Analysis of Moral Judgment in *Buffy the Vampire Slayer.*" In Buffy the Vampire Slayer *and Philosophy,* ed. South, pp. 185–194.

Synnott, Anthony. *The Body Social: Symbolism, Self and Society.* London: Routledge, 1993.

Tabron, Judith L. "Girl on Girl Politics: Willow/Tara and New Approaches to Media Fandom." *Slayage: The Online International Journal of Buffy Studies,* numbers 13 and 14 (October 2004), http://www.slayage.tv/essays/slayage13_14/tabron.htm.

Tashiro, C. J. *Pretty Pictures: Production Design and the History of Film.* Austin: University of Texas Press, 1998.

Tertullian. *De praescriptione haereticorum.* Trans. T. Herbert Brindley. London and New York: S.P.C.K Publishers, 1914.

Todorov, Tzevtan. *Genres of Discourse.* Trans. Catherine Porter. Cambridge: Cambridge University Press, 2004.

_____. *The Poetics of Prose.* Trans. Richard Howard. Oxford: Blackwell, 1977.

Tonkin, Boyd. "Entropy as Demon: Buffy in Southern California." In *Reading the Vampire Slayer,* ed. Kaveney, pp. 37–52.

Topping, Keith. *Angel Hollywood Vampire: An Expanded and Updated Unauthorised and Unofficial Guide.* London: Virgin Books, 2004.

_____. "Changing Channels." In *Slayer: The Next Generation: An Unauthorized and Unofficial Guide to Season Six of* Buffy the Vampire Slayer (London: Virgin Books, 2003), pp. 22–26.

Tracy, Kathleen. *The Girl's Got Bite: The Unofficial Guide to Buffy's World.* Los Angeles: Renaissance, 1998.

Treptow, Kurt W. *Vlad III Dracula: The Life and Times of the Historical Dracula.* Portland, Oregon: Center of Romanian Studies, 2000.

Trow, M. J. *Vlad the Impaler: In Search of the Real Dracula.* Stroud: Sutton Publishing, 2003.

Turnbull, Sue. "Not Just Another *Buffy* paper: Towards an Aesthetics of Television." *Slayage: The Online International Journal of Buffy Studies,* numbers 13 and 14 (October 2004), http://www.slayage.tv/essays/slayage13_14/turnbull.htm.

_____, and Vyvyan Stranieri. *Bite Me Narrative Structures and* Buffy the Vampire Slayer. Melbourne: Australian Centre for the Moving Image, 2003.

Unwin, Stephen, with Carole Woddis. *A Pocket Guide to 20th Century Drama.* London: Faber and Faber, 2001.

Vasantkumar, N. J. C. "Postmodernism and Jokes." In *The Postmodern Presence,* ed. Berger, pp. 212–38.

Vattimo, Gianni. "The Structure of Artistic Revolutions." In *Postmodernism,* ed. Docherty, pp. 110–119.

Vidal, Gore. *Julian* London: Abacus Books, 1993.

Vint, Sherryl. "Killing Us Softly? A Feminist Search for the 'Real' Buffy." *Slayage: The Online International Journal of Buffy Studies,* number 5 (May 2002), http://www.slayage.tv/essays/slayage5/vint.htm.

Walder, Dennis (ed.). *Literature in the Modern World: Critical Essays and Documents.* Oxford: Oxford University Press, 1991.

Wall, Brian, and Michael Zryd. "Vampire Dialectics: Knowledge, Institutions and Labour." *Reading the Vampire Slayer,* ed. Kaveney, pp. 53–77.

Waller, Gregory. *American Horrors: Essays on the Modern American Horror Film.* Urbana: University of Illinois Press, 1987.

_____. *The Living and the Undead: From Stoker's* Dracula *to Romero's* Dawn of the Dead. Urbana: University of Illinois Press, 1986.

Warrior, Robert Allen. "Canaanites, Cowboys and Indians: Deliverance, Conquest, and Liberation Theology Today." In *The Postmodern Bible Reader,* ed. Jobling, Pippin and Schleifer, pp. 188–94.

Westerfeld, Scott. "A Slayer Comes to Town." In *Seven Seasons of* Buffy, ed. Yeffeth, pp. 30–40.

Whelehan, Imelda, and Esther Sonnet. "Regendered Reading: Tank Girl and Postmodernist Intertextuality." In *Trash Aesthetics,* ed. Cartmell et al., pp. 31–47.

White, Hayden. *Metahistory: The Historical Imagination in Nineteenth Century Europe.* Baltimore: The Johns Hopkins University Press, 1973.

Wicke, Peter. *Rock Music: Culture, Aesthetics and Sociology.* Trans. Rachel Fogg. Cambridge: Cambridge University Press, 1990.

Wilcox, Rhonda V. "Every Night I Save You: Buffy, Spike, Sex and Redemption." *Slayage: The Online International Journal of Buffy Studies,* number 5 (May 2002), http://www.slayage.tv/essays/slayage5/wilcox.htm.

_____. "There Will Never Be a Very Special *Buffy*: *Buffy* and the Monsters of Teen Life." *Slayage: The Online International Journal of Buffy Studies,* number 2 (March 2001), http://www.slayage.tv/essays/slayage2/wilcox.htm.

_____. "T.S. Eliot Comes to Television: *Buffy's* 'Restless.'" *Slayage: The Online Inter-*

national Journal of Buffy Studies, number 7 (December 2002), http://www.slayage.tv/essays/slayage7/wilcox.htm.

_____. "Who Died and Made Her the Boss?: Patterns of Mortality in *Buffy*." In *Fighting the Forces*, ed. Wilcox and Lavery, pp. 3–17.

_____, and David Lavery. *Fighting the Forces: What's at Stake in* Buffy the Vampire Slayer. Lanham, New York and Oxford: Rowman and Littlefield, 2002.

Williams, Raymond. *Keywords: A Vocabulary of Culture and Society.* London: Fontana, 1976.

Wilson, Steve. "Laugh, Spawn of Hell, Laugh." In *Reading the Vampire Slayer*, ed. Kaveney, pp. 78–97.

Winslade, J. Lawton. "Teen Witches, Wiccans, and 'Wanna-Blessed-Be's: Pop Culture Magic in *Buffy the Vampire Slayer*." *Slayage: The Online International Journal of Buffy Studies*, number 1 (January 2001), http://www.slayage.tv/essays/slayage1/winslade.htm.

Wisker, Gina. "Vampires and School Girls: High School High Jinks on the Hellmouth." *Slayage: The Online International Journal of Buffy Studies*, number 2 (March 2001), http://www.slayage.tv/essays/slayage2/wisker.htm.

Wyver, John. "Television and Postmodernism." In *Postmodernism*, ed. Appignanesi, pp. 155–64.

Yeffeth, Glenn (ed.). *Seven Seasons of* Buffy: *Science Fiction and Fantasy Writers Discuss Their Favorite Television Show.* Dallas: BenBella Books, 2003.

Zettel, Sarah. "When Did the Scoobies Become Insiders?" In *Seven Seasons of* Buffy, ed. Yeffeth, pp. 109–15.

Index

Abbott, Stacey 230 n.36, 233 n.33
Absolute good 45
Absolute knowledge 225 n.43
Academic scrutiny 110
Acathla 19, 198
Acting 100, 109; styles 24
"Action girl" stories 237 n.5
Actors' names 121
Adam 35–36, 94, 101, 113, 118, 120 123, 141, 187, 189, 204, 235 n.25, 236 n.4
Addiction to magic 96–97
Addison, John 130
Adoption 201
Advertisers 11; concerns 10
Advertising breaks 224 n.27
Aeneas 153
The Aeneid 153, 240 n.13, 241 n.15, 245 n.19
Aesthesis 21
Aesthetic(s) 1–3, 33, 34, 37, 45, 48, 51, 63, 86, 88, 164; analogue 201; attributes 101, 110; brilliance 188; of *Buffy* 89; choices 4, 96, 223 n.21; coincidence 97; of color 9; complexities 200; constructs 86; and culture 155; of culture 3, 7, 12, 44, 51, 57, 96, 163, 169, 182, 211; and cultural heterogeneity 183; "edges" 27; effect 25; of ethics 89; expression 182; games 88; of good 94; intensity 128; of involution 7, 110–11, 116, 170, 183; and knowledge 8, 16; obscurity 88; palette 90; of performance 11; possibility 208; practices 2, 92; premise 27; of representation 38; resolution 83; sign 92; sophistication 19; and television 8; tradition 93; unravelling 20; verisimilitude 28
Aesthetic-ethical dimension 9
Aestheticization of morality 94
Aestheticized television 203
African 61
Afro-Caribeanness 38

"After Life" 96
Ahistorical 9, 64
Alan Finch 102
Alcohol 186
Alderman, Naomi 48–50, 226 n.21
Alias 17
Alice's Adventures in Wonderland 120
All-American girl 187, 243 n.3
"All the Way" 150, 239 n.9
Allegorical recognition 25
Allusion 20, 121, 125, 147
Alternative credits 123
Alternative reality 27, 76, 97
"Amends" 149, 166, 171
America 45–46, 53, 56, 103; American culture 1, 4, 12, 104; American dream 135; Americanness 38, 50
Amy 78, 165
Analeptic 20
Anamnesis 50
Anarchism 18, 244 n.17
Andrew 28–29, 38, 44, 61, 95, 99, 117, 155, 171, 197, 211, 225 n.37
Angel 19, 36, 41, 44, 48, 55, 81, 87, 97, 117, 121, 124, 143, 152, 154, 162, 166, 178, 181, 190, 221 n.4
Angel 17–18, 21 33, 38, 44, 46–47, 49, 62, 66, 76, 82–83, 93–94, 97, 99, 104, 113, 113, 116–17, 123, 130, 142, 147, 149, 160, 166, 175, 184, 189, 190–91, 197–200, 224 n.10, 227 n.25, 239 n.5, 245 n.19
"Angel" 18, 19, 47
Angelus 19, 21, 41, 92, 94 105, 206, 237 n.7
Angle of vision 161
"Annabel Lee" 111
Anne 150
"Anne" 132, 142
Anti-hero 41, 241 n.12
Anti-humor 175

Anya 19, 20, 37, 46, 49, 58, 60, 62, 79–80, 87, 105, 114, 126, 131, 149, 162, 167–69, 175–76, 179, 181, 185–86, 191–92, 196, 198–99, 242 n.17; as Aud 175
"Anya" 185
Anyanka 76–77
Aphrodite 130–31
Apocalypse 18, 72, 75, 76, 84, 125, 139
Apocalypse Now 125, 146, 154, 161, 240 n.17
Appel, Alfred, Jr. 111
Arquette, Rosanna 119
Art 8, 155
Articulation of identities 7
Artistic diversity 183
Artistic productions 5
Atonement 93
Audience 3, 16, 19, 22, 25, 31, 38, 96, 112, 121, 124, 128, 139, 139, 162, 175–76, 180, 188, 190, 200–01
Augustine 42, 70
Auster, Paul 170, 241 n.10
Austin, J. 36
Auteurism 10
Authenticity 193

Backstory 102
Bacon-Smith, Camille 86
"Bad Girls" 55, 56, 102, 152
Bad Willow 76, 191
Baker, Jeri 104
Bakhtin, Mikhail 116
Balthazar 55–56
Bambi 168–69
"Band Candy" 134, 176–7, 179, 242 n.24
Banderas, Antonio 136
The Bandwagon 136
"Bargaining I" 130, 167, 169, 171, 179, 193, 243 n.4
"Bargaining I and II" 174, 205
Barker, Clive 104, 166
Barnard, Mary 129
Barnes, Julian 135, 170, 241 n.9
Baseball 63
Basement 147
Basquiat 178
Battis, Jes 139
BBC 59, 228 n.54, 230 n.30
The Beatles 242 n.23
Beck, Christophe 166, 181
Becoming/being 194
"Becoming II" 19, 82, 87, 113, 130, 166, 171, 198, 204, 206, 234 n.1
"Beer Bad" 73, 186, 210, 230 n.30
"Behind Blue Eyes" 179–80
Ben 44, 173–74, 240 n.13
"Beneath You" 172–3
Benson, Amber 10, 133–34
Bergstrom, Cynthia 92]
Beverly Hills 90210 88–89, 92
"Bewitched, Bothered and Bewildered" 165

Bhaba, Homi 223 n.16
Biblical 68
Big Bad 28, 29, 51, 55, 96, 134, 173, 240 n.13
Black and white 172–74
Black Death 53, 65
Black leather coat 97
Bleak House 141, 235 n.19
Blonde 89, 90, 92–94, 95, 97, 100
Blood 40
"Blood Money" 142
Blood of a Slayer 197
"Blood Ties" 130, 202, 232 n.19, 22
Bobby Ewing 200
"The Body" 114, 117, 136–37, 151, 166, 177, 202–03, 205–06, 210, 234 n.1
Body postures 100
Body switching 186
La Boheme 21, 177
Bowie, David 64, 177–78, 228 n.53, 242 n.23
Boyette, Michelle 241 n.12
Boys from the Blackstuff 209
Bradney, Anthony 18, 47, 224 n.9
Branding (of *Buffy*) 28
Brando, Marlon 155, 240 n.17
Brasseye 209
Brave New World 77
Breton, Rob 48, 225 n.41
Brideshead Revisited 54
British 38, 53, 54, 170
British Empire 83
The Bronze 17, 92, 117, 175–76
Brooks, Louise 132
Buchanan, Jack 136
Buffy 1–4, 6–8 10, 11, 15–16, 18, 20, 23, 25, 27, 29–30, 33–34, 36–37, 39–42, 44–45, 47–48, 50–52, 57, 59–63, 65–67, 71–75, 78, 83–90, 92, 100–01, 104–05, 109–12, 114–19, 121, 123–26, 130, 133–35, 139–40, 147, 152, 154–55, 157–58, 161–62, 165, 167–71, 174, 176, 178, 180–81, 183, 190–92, 197–200, 202, 208–11, 221 n.2 , 221 n.4, 221 n.7, 222 n.10
"Buffy" 134
Buffy and *Dracula* (links) 243 n.1
Buffy as Slayer 204
Buffy as vampire 187
Buffy film 3, 166, 231 n.10
Buffy nights 124
Buffy standard 11, 24
Buffy Summers 1, 3–5, 15–21, 28, 30–32, 35–36, 44–48, 52–56, 58, 60, 64, 67, 69, 72–77, 80–82, 84, 87, 90–97, 100–05, 112–13, 116–18, 120, 123–24, 127, 131–35, 137–38, 140–44, 146–48, 151, 159, 161, 164–68, 170–72, 174, 177–83, 185–90, 192–200, 202, 205–07, 223 n.3, 226 n.22, 235 n.25, 237 n.7; Buffy's dream 127, 133, 172, 236 n.5; Buffy's father 29; Buffy's house 114, 124; Buffy's mother 29

"Buffy the Bacchae Slayer" 239 n.5
Buffy the Vampire Slayer: The Monster Book 226 n.22
"Buffy versus Dracula" 102–03, 172, 188–89, 199
Buffybot 174, 188, 192–94
Buffyverse 17, 22, 27, 31, 37, 40, 48, 63–64, 71, 73, 97, 123, 155, 186, 194, 199–201, 205, 224 n.25, 224 n.26
Buinicki, Martin 225 n.33, 226 n.5
Bumpy 94
Bunny suit 162
Burton, Tim 167
Bye Bye Love 134

Caleb 66, 150
Callander, Michelle 33, 227 n.25, 243 n.1
Camera 53; angles 24; lens 24; work 128
Campbell, Caitlin 221 n.4
Campbell, Joseph 52
Campbell, Richard 221 n.4
The Canterbury Tales 235 n.19
Capitalism 169
Captain Sisko 154
Carroll, Lewis 120, 235 n.25
Carter, Margaret L. 27
Cartoons 63
Catatonic state 185
Catechumens 67–68
Catholic 65, 66, 67, 70, 74, 93
Catholic schoolgirl outfit 92
Cathy Come Home 209, 239 n.6
CD 4
Cecily 153, 162
Censorship 230 n.30
Chantarelle/lily 142
Chapman, Seymour 115
Character: analysis 136; characterization 20; development 18
"Checkpoint" 55
Cheeseman 135
China 62
Chips in the brain 105
"Chosen" 38, 97, 130, 144, 171–72, 207, 210
Christianity 43, 48–49, 62, 67–70, 74–75, 172–73, 229 n.1
Chronology 135
Chumash Tribe 42, 79–81, 210
Cinema 88; history 66; traditions 92
Circulation of signs 144
Citizen Kane 209
Class protector award 138, 184
Classical 11
Classical Greece 62
Classical narratology 110
Classical world 129
Classicism 126
Clem 46
Cleveland 186

Cliché 3, 122–23, 147
Closed knowledge 32
Close-up 127–28
Closing credits 224 n.27
Clothes 88–89, 91, 104
Coda 113
Coincidences 111
Collins, Wilkie 32
Collossians 69
Colonialism 41, 44, 67, 70, 82, 160
Color 91, 100, 105
Columbine shootings 232 n.18
Comedic: characters 232 n.25; effect 17, 165; value 167
Comedy 52–53, 60, 100
Comic genius 204
Comic hero 241 n.12
Coming-of-age tale 177
Commercial break 114, 121, 123–24
Commonality of Slayers 197
Communist 73
Company logo 124
Comparative media analysis 156
Computer 33, 35
Conflict of the Faculties 44
Connor 225 n.46
Conrad, Joseph 41, 67, 150, 153, 155–56, 159, 161
"Consequences" 20
Conservative 96
Consulting producer 120
Contemporary America 6, 9 62, 64–65
Contemporary culture 2, 88, 25 n.34
Contracts 10, 28, 121
"Conversations with Dead People" 102, 203, 234 n.1
Cop show 24
Coppola, Francis Ford 150, 154–55, 161
Copywright 124
Cordelia Chase 17, 26, 46, 53–54, 76, 91, 113, 117, 144, 162, 178, 186; Cordelia's visions 225 n.46
Corvinu, Matthias 65
Costume designer 92, 133
Costumes 24, 76, 105, 139
Count Orlok 104
Cratylus 141
Craven, Wes 92, 133
Cream 177
Credits 27, 114, 122
Creed, Linda 162
Critical vampirism 208
Critique 1
Crouse, Louise 133
The Crucible 78, 134
Crucifix 172–73, 241 n.13
Crusades 65, 74–75
"Crush" 85, 193
Cue 161
Culler, Jonathan 223 n.5

Cultural 1, 5–7, 37–38, 44, 208; aesthetic 46; analysis 7; assumptions 4; belonging 49; boundaries 7; capital 33; center 79; claims 2; context 64; criticism 208; difference 45; economy 160; expectations 49; extrapolations 168; forms 72, 111; heritage 103; history 62; hybrid 104; knowledge 155; memory 75; polyglot 12; practices 51, 182; processes 9; production 39; references 7; representation 23, 66; studies 208
"Culture" lobby 209
Curle, Richard 156
Cut 121; cutting technique 151
Cyclops 131

Dallas 200
Dan Vladislav 65
Danse Macabre 167
"The Dark Age" 166, 176
Dark hair 93, 99
Darla 41, 92–94, 96, 105, 228 n.54
Da Ross, Giada 221 n.6
Daspit, Toby 35
Davis, Robert A. 222 n.7, 224 n.30, 230 n.33, 235 n.21
Dawn Summers 29, 37, 39, 94, 114, 127, 148, 168, 174, 184–85, 191, 196, 199–204, 206, 232 n.19, 240 n.13
Dawson's Creek 92
"Dead Man's Party" 132, 150
"Dead Things" 18, 95, 132, 197
Dead time 136
Death of a Salesman 131–32, 134, 146, 149, 169, 181
De Burgh, Chris 149
Dechert, Renee S. 176
Deep Space Nine 154
Deer-stalker 169
Defamiliarization 28, 121, 123, 137; definition 235 n.19
Dehistoricization 3, 64–65, 75, 115, 222 n.8
Dehumanizing 77
Deictic 112
Demme, Jonathan 95
Demon 25, 47, 64, 68, 73–74, 75, 81, 90–91, 101, 104, 160 187, 196
Demon-human 189
De-mythologized 65
Deputy mayor 152, 197
Dery, Mark 71–72
Desert 206; desert-as-sandbox 206
Designs 105
Desperately Seeking Susan 119
D'Hoffryn 175
Dialogue 102, 128
Dickinson, Emily 133
Dickson, Christa 221 n.1, 224 n.10, 225 n.2
Diehl, Laura 228 n.52

Differentiation through language 228 n.51
Directors 10
"Dirty Girls" 99, 117, 150–52, 161, 167
Discourse 116
Discursive: nature 123; regime 9, 168, 177; space 95; structures 160
Disney 168
Dispatches 150
Dr. Jekyll and Mr Hyde 35, 122
Dominant culture 50
"Doomed" 9, 34
Doppelganger 134
"Doppelgangland" 97, 134, 168, 237 n.18, 238 n.29
"Doublemeat Palace" 10, 151
The Doublemeat Palace 169
Doubles 199, 238 n.29, 244 n.18
Doyle 117, 178; Doyle's visions 225 n.46
Dracula 66, 102, 104, 188–89; books 229 n.9; movies 233–35 n.35
Dracula (Stoker) 222 n.9
Dracula: Dead and Loving It 122
Dramatic irony 21
Dramatic lighting 24
Dream-Faith 171
Dreams 90, 103, 126, 185, 197; episodes 132; sequence 138
Dress and hairstyle (spike) 97
Dress symbolism 97
Drusilla 41, 51, 56, 76, 97, 99, 166, 204, 228 n.52
Duality 175
Dubbing 150–51
Duffy, Patrick 200
Dushku, Eliza 134
Dusted 221 n.1
Duval, Robert 154
DVD 4, 30, 114, 124, 127, 181, 242 n.28

Eagleton, Terry 8–9, 11, 223 n.17
Early, Frances 85
Early modern 3, 72
"Earshot" 27, 94–95, 138, 177
"Eastern question" 222 n.9
Easy Rider 239 n.6
Eclecticism 2
Eco, Umberto 2, 111, 114–15, 118, 123, 221 n.3, 225 n.34
Economic history 240 n.3
Editing 10; editing style 150
Edwards, Lynne 51–52
Eidolon 138, 144, 240 n.17; definition of 238 n.28
Elfman, Danny 166–67
Eliot, T. S. 156
Emotional intensities 113, 182
"Empty Places" 36, 198
"End of Days" 75, 127, 148
Engels, Friedrich 43, 75

England 58, 46, 49, 52, 54, 56–60 80, 169;
culture 83
Enlightenment 5–6, 41–42, 66–67, 70, 157;
Enlightenment Europe 104
Enns, Anthony 225 n.33, 226 n.5
"Entropy" 105
Epic poems 51
Episode's story 27; Episode's syntax 140
Episodic-syntactic 146
Erickson, Greg 224 n.18, 226 n.5, 229 n.1
Eschatology 19, 42–44, 62–63, 66–68, 70–
74, 75–77, 118, 159
Espenson, Jane 10, 79, 134, 176, 178–79
Espresso Pump 179
Ethan Rayne 134, 176
Ethical 44, 209; balance 99; choices 5, 7, 48,
155, 172, 183; complexity 30, 93; concerns
76; consequences 242 n.26; considerations
88, 192; corollary 97; decision 7, 197–98;
decision making 86; dilemma 101; dimen-
sion 232 n.18; diversity 45; doubt 87;
excellence 97; implications 103; obscurity
88; position and aesthetic appearance 94;
principles 22; questions 100; rules 102;
sign system 91; system 199
Ethnic: cleansing 227 n.26; construction 39;
difference 9, 39; differentiation 6; identity
39; purity 43
Ethnicity 5, 9, 38, 41, 45–50, 53, 59, 61, 83,
183, 102, 225 n.2, 226 n.21, 228 n.52
Ethnographic distinctions 7
Eudaemonism 87
Europe 6, 41, 43; Dark Age 62; history 67;
Medieval 62
Eurotrashed 103
The Evil Dead 239 n.5
Evil double 230 n.35
Evil vampire 172
Evil willow 97
Evil's being 105
Existential dilemma 196
Exogamous 119
Exposition character 176
Expressionist filmmaking 104
Extratextual 129, 169
Eye color 9
Eyes Wide Shut 161

Face 102; facial expression 128
Fairy tales 51
Faith 39, 55, 94, 99, 100, 102, 117, 134, 138,
148, 152, 162, 174, 185–86, 192, 196–99,
203, 244 n.19, 235 n.19; Faith-Buffy 233
n.27; Faith-in-Buffy 165
"Faith Hope and Trick" 32, 51
Faker 146
Falconer, Rachel 153
Fame Whore 122
Familial structure 114
"Family" 127, 201, 237 n.17

Family drama 58
Family ideal 245 n.20
Fan criticism 23
Fantastical 29
Fantasy 58
"Far Beyond the Stars" 154
Farce 53
Fashion 91, 99
The Fast Show 209
Fate 74, 243–44 n.8
FBI 26–27, 124
"Fear Itself" 144, 150, 162 181
Femininity 92
Feminist role model 231 n.12
Feminization 59
Fetishisistic 119, 193
Fictionality 27, 115
Fifarek, Aimee 235 n.24
Fight sequences 101; fight skills 101
Film 12, 91, 110, 125; studies 110; filmic her-
itage 103; filmic representation 172; filmic
tradition 122
Financial lives 169
Fincher, David 95
Finnigans Wake 22
Fire truck 233 n.29
Firefly 181
The First 148
"First date" 143
First Evil 97, 166, 171, 182, 191, 203, 239 n.5
First Slayer 64, 133, 135, 137, 171, 175, 182,
185–90, 196, 206, 244 n.9
Fish monsters 232 n.15
Five acts 27
Flashback 135
Flip chart 167
"Flooded" 205–06
Folk stories 51
Fonda, Peter 239 n.6
"Fool for Love" 51, 82–83, 143, 153, 162, 234
n.1
Foreknowledge 36
Foreshortening 24
"Forever" 177, 202
Formal: alienation 206; analysis 175; design
133; expectation 121; features 110; innova-
tion 128, 137; inventiveness 175; level 146;
qualities 112; shift 121; trick 165
Formalism 2, 210
Foster, Greg 87
Foucault, Michel 30, 225 n.32
Fourth wall 126
Frame 126, 187
Franchising 124
Francis, Rob 227 n.41
Frank N. Furter 179
Frankenstein 18, 113; Frankenstein's monster
94
Frankenstein (novel) 35, 119, 235 n.20
Frasier lens 137

Fred (Winifred Burkle) 153–54
"Fredless" 205
Free will 190, 243 n.8
"Freebird" 180, 182
French Revolution 43–44
"The Freshman" 138, 149, 166, 177, 204
Freud, Sigmund 50, 159
Friendship 237 n.8
Frost, Robert 138
Fury, David 10, 170

Gellar, Sarah Michelle 92, 133, 165, 193, 204,
    231 n.12, 239 n.5
Gem of Amara 143, 178
General culture 2
Generic 2–3, 53, 56; aspects 90; codes 52;
    disturbances 24; expectations 89;
    hybridization 103; television 147; tension
    52; variability 89; volatility 157
Genette, Gerard 116
Genre 36, 58, 94 117, 145, 221 n.7; busting 2,
    60, 92; fiction 157; and narratology 10;
    shifting 11; television 11, 221 n.6; warping
    17, 223 n.5
Genres in Discourse 139
The Gentlemen 133, 166–67
GEOS ratings 234 n.1
"Get It Done" 64, 182, 185, 189–91
Gidget 72, 243 n.3
"The Gift" 44, 99, 174, 196, 234 n.1
Giles, Rupert 11, 15–17, 21 26–27, 32–35, 38–
    40, 42, 44–46, 49, 52–54–58, 60–61, 64,
    73, 76, 79–80, 82–84, 91, 96, 113–15, 124,
    130, 133–34, 136–37, 142, 146, 150, 152,
    154, 159, 161–62, 165–70, 172, 174–81, 186,
    188, 190, 195, 199, 201, 205, 223 n.2, 227
    n.25, 228 n.45, 240 n.13, 241 n.3; Giles'
    dream 150, 164, 171, 173, 186, 189
"Gingerbread" 32, 78, 134, 165, 197, 225 n.41
Girl power 3–4
Glory 55, 95, 130, 173–74, 232 n.16, 232
    n.19, 240 n.13
"Go Fish" 232 n.15
Goddess 39, 144
Goddess Aphrodite 130
The Godfather 149, 155
Golden, Christopher, et al. 104, 226 n.22
Good and evil 86
"Goodbye Iowa" 35
Gordon, Howard 120
Gore, Tipper 78
Goth clothes 96
Gothic 28, 97, 119, 221 n.7, 222 n.9, 224
    n.30; Gothic horror 2–3, 30
Gourd 188
"Graduation Day I" 197
"Graduation Day II" 113, 132, 137–38, 148,
    171, 196
Grand narratives 42, 70
Grant, President Ulysses S. 83

"Grave" 162
"The Greatest Love of All" 162
Greco-Ibsen 135
Greek 69; comedies 129; literature 131;
    tragedy 126
Green, Seth 127
Green screen 151
The Green Wing 209
Greenaway, Peter 128, 236 n.6
Greene, Richard 231 n.6
Greenwalt, David 10, 104
Groundhog Day 169
"Grr arrgh" 124, 168, 170–71
The Grudge 239 n.5
Gunn, Charles 205, 226 n.21
Guns 18, 205–06
Gustafson, Gustav 204
Gutierrez, Diego 154, 161
Gwendolyn Post 38

Hair 88; hair color 9, 93
Halfrek 162
Halfyard, Janet K. 121–22
"Halloween" 96, 150, 176, 239 n.5
Hammer House of Horror 121–22
Hampton, Howard 170
Hanniganm, Alyson 127
Harmony 135–36, 183
Harris (surname) 46
Harris, Charlaine 38, 86, 94
"The Harsh Light of Day" 33, 136, 178, 232
    n.15
"The Harvest" 18, 26, 56, 75, 184, 187, 206
Head, Anthony Stewart 115, 167, 176, 179–
    80, 242 n.24
Heart of Darkness 4, 41, 125, 150, 153–57
Heavenly dimension 181
Heffner, Hugh 123
Hegel, G. W. F. 8, 43, 70, 223 n.18
Hell dimension 192
Hell in Contemporary Literature 153
Hellmouth 31–32, 91, 94, 103, 147, 186;
    Hellmouth-library 33
Hellraiser 104, 166
"Hell's Bells" 149, 151
"Helpless" 154
Henry IV 243 n.8
Hermeneutic 163
Hermetic 119
"Hero" 227 n.26
Herr, Michael 150
Hertzberg, George 119
Heterodox 32, 34
High art 7
High-brow 11
High cultural references 12
High School 64, 88, 99, 137, 200, 204; high
    school drama 2, 89, 100
Historical: attitude 66; concern 84; conse-
    quences 5; forgetfulness 77; frameworks

183; guilt 78; imagination 71; perspectives 65; present 79; representations 63; silence 83; site 63; sympathy 80; time 70–71
Historicity 3, 42, 63, 72, 160
Historiography 75
History 1–3, 9, 30, 41–42, 53, 62, 104, 118, 155, 209; as narrative 9, 63; of progress 64; of the world 190
A History of the World in 10½ Chapters 170
Hitler, Adolf 227 n.29
Hodges, Mike 176
Hoffman, Dustin 149
Hogle, Jerrold E. 222 n.7
Holden, Webster 102
"The Hollow Men" 156
Hollywood 74, 228 n.42
Holocaust 78
Homage 120
Home Improvements 119
Horror 3, 11, 25, 85, 88, 91, 94, 100, 105, 122, 192; horror genre 90; horror show 24; horror tradition 121
Houston, Whitney 162
Humanism 41
Humanity 6, 16, 41, 45–47, 53, 67, 103–04, 158–60, 161, 187, 189, 191–94, 202; humanity-as-becoming 199
Humor 17, 52, 127, 135, 222 n.8
Hunyadi, John 65
Hus 78–80
"Hush" 109, 132–34, 166–67, 234 n.1, 240 n.2, 245 n.21
Hutcheon, Linda 224 n.16, 224 n.17
Huxley, Aldous 77
Hybridized 145

"The I in Team" 206
"I Robot You Jane" 33, 192
"I Was Made to Love You" 95, 192, 202–03, 232 n.15
Iconoclastic 122
Iconographic: immediacy 88; simplification 172
Identity 16, 18, 39, 49, 123, 126, 151–42, 145, 155, 182–83, 192–94, 201, 226 n.22; identity and performance 138
Idol, Billy 97
Illyria 153
Image of Tara 188
Imagistic 129
Imperialist 73
In Memoriam 41
"In the Dark" 143, 178
Incest 119, 159
Index of fictionality 203
Indian 80–81, 83
"Indian" 230 n.38
The Inferno 242 n.15
The Initiative 34, 35, 48, 82, 99, 113, 124, 154, 204, 227 n.29

In-joke 179
"Innocence" 144, 232 n.15, 234 n.1
Insane asylum 195
"Inside Out" 243 n.8
Institute of Contemporary Art 210
Institutional: authority 32; knowledge 31; power 225 n.33
Interdimensional: chaos 185; portal 200
Interior 28
Internet 28, 200
Intertext 20, 105, 149; definition 234 n.7
Intertextual 89, 118–19, 128, 131; elements 111; link 120
"Intervention" 174, 188–89, 192
Interview with a Vampire 136
"Into Every Generation..." 232 n.15
"Into the Woods" 204–06, 237 n.17
Intradiegetic music 21, 117
Intratexts: definition 234 n.7; intratextual 119, 169; intratextual elements 111
Inventive aesthetics 209
Inverted double 175
Involuted games 125; involuted strategy 96
Involution 9, 20, 76, 88, 112, 114, 119, 121–22, 124, 126, 131–36, 140, 142, 145, 163, 174, 176, 186, 197, 226 n.7; aspect 185; chain 164; circulation 161; contacts 150, 189; contortion 120; drift 181; journey 165; link 92; possibility 128, 154; qualities 113; strategies 179; trajectories 166
Irishness 38
Ironic 122
Irrationality 34, 41
Islam 65–66
It's a Wonderful Life 76, 239 n.5

Jack Torrance 162
James Bond 57, 123, 205
Jameson, Fredric 222 n.8
Jarman, Derek 22
Jenkins, Alice 240 n.2
Jenny Calendar 21, 33, 35, 50, 166, 177, 189, 239 n.5
Jesse 184, 187
Jew 38, 42, 46, 48–50, 52, 54, 59, 61, 69, 81, 84, 236 n.1; Jews in Europe 81
Jimmy Olsen 239 n.4
John, Gospel of 63
Joke 175
Jonathan 27–29, 95, 122–23, 138, 161–62
Jonathan Creek 167
Jonathan Harker 222 n.9
Jordan, Michael 123
Jordan, Neil 136
Jove 131
Joyce, James 22
Joyce Summers 78, 94, 113–14, 124, 149–50, 166, 177–78, 201–04, 239 n.7
The Judge 45

Kant, Immanuel 44, 86
Katabatic 152–53, 173; katabatic journey 244 n.19
Katrina 197
Kaveney, Roz 63, 105, 235 n.29, 238 n.1, 238 n.29, 221 n.2, 230 n.35, 234 n.13
Kaye, Sharon M. 193
Kendra 38, 42, 51, 127, 186, 191, 205, 224 n.26
Kennedy 97, 191
The Key 200, 202
Kitchen appliances 205, 231 n.39
Knights of Byzantium 65, 228 n.47, 240 n.13
Knowledge 6, 7, 19, 30–34, 37, 50, 69, 183; categories of 18; forms of 87; gaining of 15; mode of 30; and morality 18; and narrative 15–16
Knox, Robert 41
Krzywinska, Tanya 73
Kubrick, Stanley 161–62
Kurtz 41, 153–55, 158–61; Kurtz-Snyder 162

Lack of speech 102
La Morte, Robia 33–34
Language in Buffy 241 n.5
Larry 150
Lavery, David 45, 63, 83, 119, 150, 208, 223 n.20, 241 n.11
Law 17
Law and Order 24
Leadman 204
Lee, Alison 22–21, 224 n.12–15
Legal declaration 124
Legal responsibility 121
Legends 51
Lennon, John 242 n.23
Lens 126, 161, 190
Leon, Hilary M. 227 n.25
Lesbianism 97, 128–29
"Lessons" 39, 169
Lestat 103, 233 n.34
Liberal agenda 79, 83
Liberalism 31, 72
Librarian 79
Library 32
Lie 19
"Lie to Me" 103, 142, 173, 181
"Lies My Parents Told Me" 173
Lieutenant Colonel Bill Kilgore 154
"Life Serial" 165, 168, 181, 241 n.4
Light 24, 53, 76, 91, 105 190, 206
Lighting 28, 104, 110
Lily 143
The Limey 150, 154
Linear 119
The Lion, the Witch and the Wardrobe 138, 144
Literalization of metaphor 151
Literary studies 110
Literature 12, 88

Little Britain 209
Little Ms. Muffet 138
"Living Conditions" 132
Loach, Ken 239 n.6
Loaded 178
Locklin, Reid B. 245 n.20
Logo 171
Lolita 54, 111
Long takes 136
Long walk 137
Longfellow, Henry Wadsworth 133
The Lord of the Rings trilogy 209
Lorne 117, 124, 162
Los Angeles 45
The Lost Boys 102
Love spell 165
Love story 58
Low-brow 11
Luke 75
Luke, Gospel of 68
Lynyrd Skynyrd 180, 182
The Lyon's Den 24, 209
Lyotard, Jean-Francois 2, 15, 36, 88, 41–42 44, 46, 49–50, 70, 78, 112, 157, 210, 221 n.5, 222 n.8, 223 n.1

MacDonald, Sharron 85–86
Madama Butterfly 131
Madonna 119
Mafia movie 56, 228 n.47
Maggie Walsh 34–36, 80, 133, 205
Magic 33. 57, 59, 64, 96–97, 123, 186, 223 n.3; magic spell 130
The Magic Box 58, 150, 167–68, 240 n.3
Magical ball of energy 200
Magical shift 28
Majority culture 50
Makeup 104–05, 138–39, 171
Male gaze 136
Male sexuality 93
Mall 63
Manicheansim 74
Map, Walter 65
Marcie Ross 25–27, 124, 150, 224 n.26
Mark, Gospel of 68
Marlow 41, 153–54, 157–60
Marshall, C. W. 240 n.13, 241 n.15
Marsters, James 59
Martial arts 101
Marxism 42, 70
Mary Poppins 50
Mary Poppins 59
Masculinity 88, 184, 228 n.46, 232 n.20
Masochistic 173
Masser, Micahel 162
The Master 53, 75–78, 91, 103–05, 113, 132, 147, 185
Masturbation 167
Material culture 8, 9, 10
Materially present aesthetic 8

The Matrix 28, 74, 101, 120, 149, 233 n.29
Matthew, Gospel of 68
Mayor Wilkins III 94, 100, 113
McCarthyism 78
McClellan, Bruce 229 n.7, 233 n.32
McIntosh, Todd 104
McMaster, Lindsay 48, 225 n.41
McNeilley, et al. 24, 32, 123, 147, 223 n.3, 224 n.22
McQuillan, Martin 116
Mechanics of slaying 193
Medieval Europe 104
"Memory of a Free Festival" 177
Metafiction 22–23, 29, 124
Metanarrative 42
Metaphor 25, 175
Metatextual 159, 203
Metcalf, Mark 76, 104
Middle-brow 11
Mikosz, Philip 110, 115, 122
Milavec, Melissa M. 193
Miles, Lawrence 221 n.1, 224, n.10, 225 n.2
Miller, Arthur 78, 132, 134–35, 137, 169
Miller, Hillis J. 141
Mime 167
Mina 185
Misdubbing 171
Mise en abyme 124
Mise-en-scène 155
Miss Kitty Fantastico 126–28, 131, 141
Mr. Trick 51
The Modern 50
Modernist 156; epistemology 35; poetic practice 129; tradition 104
Modernity 1, 3, 6, 34–35, 41–43, 51, 52, 59, 61, 70–71, 73, 75–78, 84, 87, 105, 135, 155–61, 163; 221 n.2, 222 n.9
Modes of discourse 157
Modes of production 208
Moloch 192
Money, Mary Alice 227 n.27, 227 n.33
Monologue 137
Monsters (ugly) 94
Montage 28, 114–15, 117–22, 155, 182, 231 n.10
The Moonstone 32, 225 n.35
Moral: absolutes 20; ambiguity 173; ambivalence 175; category 47; choice 85; degeneracy 85; dilemma 20; eclecticism 87; law 18–19, 87; legitimacy 44; makeover 100; order 198; philosophy 87; principles 22, 231 n.6; rehabilitation 244 n.19; relativity 20; simplicity 19; structures 174; system 7; universe 172; values 5
Moritsugu, Jon 122
Moss, Gabrielle 222 n.11, 222 n.12, 223 n.13
Mothers Opposed to the Occult 78, 225 n.41
Mrs. Dalloway 156
Multicultural 48
Murnau, Fredrich Wilhelm 104

Murphy, Kevin Andrew 230 n.30
Music 53, 85, 176, 178–79; musical 63, 11, 181, 190
Music for Elevators 179
Mutant Enemy 170
My So-Called Life 4
Mysticism 33–34, 144
Mythic 104, 115, 118; history 64; mythically ordained 64; past 84; state 26; time 64, 75; values 5
Mythological coherence 244 n.13
Mythology 29, 41, 43, 53, 192
Mythology of the Slayer 189

Nabokov, Vladimir 111, 228 n.43
The Name of the Rose 2, 225 n.34
Naming 141
Nancy-boy 143
Narrative 8–9, 15, 16, 19, 33, 43, 63, 75–76, 101, 110, 113–15, 116–18, 137, 155, 160, 163; completion 81; complexity 19; concerns 111; eschatology 83; expectation 26; of modernity 44, 157; narrator 158; organization 16; patterns 114; play 76; power 118; prompt 198; reminder 204; requirements 168; scheme 114; space 123; structure 17, 173; trajectories 16, 84; universe 87
Native Americans 78
Naturalism 157
Nazi 227 n.29
Nerf Herder 132
Nest, Heinrich Joseph 104
Networks 11, 181; network constraints 10
"Never Kill a Boy on the First date" 15, 71, 133, 188, 205
"A New Man" 34, 80, 176
"New Moon Rising" 126, 140, 236 n.3, 244 n.17
New World 56
"A New World" 242 n.15
New York 45
New York Trilogy 170
Nichols, Mike 149
Nielson ratings 223 n.21
"Nightmares" 131–32, 134, 149, 161, 181, 187, 194, 231 n.10, 243 n.4
Nihilism 5, 191, 194–95, 224 n.11; nihilistic hybrid 186
Noir hero 18
Noir shadows 24
Non-narrative 142
Non-normative sexuality 205
"Normal Again" 17, 23, 28–30, 109, 117, 154, 161, 199, 224 n.25
Normative masculinity 95
Normative teen culture 230 n.33
Nosferatu 104, 121, 166
Nostalgia 64, 66, 73
Not-Adam 187, 204
"Not Fade Away" 153, 162, 232 n.14

Index

Noxon, Marti 10, 103, 170, 244 n.9
Numerology 197
Nursery rhyme 133, 237 n.17

O'Brien, Richard 179
Occult knowledge 35–36
Och, Dana 110, 115, 122
Odyessus 17, 131, 153, 177; and the Cyclops 237 n.13
The Odyssey 131, 153, 245 n.19; and Oedipus 237 n.14
Oedipus 131
Oedipus Tyrannus 131–32, 159
Off-center framing 150
The Office 209
Olaf 94, 175, 232 n.16
Olivia 133, 166–67, 172, 178
Olsen, Scott R. 223 n.14
"Once More with Feeling" 4, 109, 132, 162, 171, 176, 180–81, 191, 194, 196, 203, 233 n.29, 234 n.1, 245 n.21
One-off television shows 11
One-shot 137
Ono, Kent A. 46, 225 n.3
Ono, Yoko 242 n.23
Open knowledge 32
Opening credits 10, 27–28 120, 239 n.6
Opening fade 164
Operatic atmosphere 21
Oracular 185
Organ 121–22
Orientalism 236 n.6
Orthodox knowledge 32
Osiris 130
"Out of Mind, Out of Sight" 25–26, 124, 150, 170
Overexposed 24, 206
Overextended shadows 28
Ovid 129
Owen 133, 187–88, 243 n.5
Oz 33, 46, 113, 127, 130, 138, 149, 178, 191, 200, 205, 242 n.24

"The Pack" 18, 144, 182
Pagan 67
Pale skinned 102
Palimpsest 155
"Pangs" 11, 65, 76, 80, 82–84, 133, 137, 210
Panning shot 91
Paratext 28, 124, 170–71; definition of 234 n.7; paratextual 111, 119, 203
Parenthood 223 n.20
Parodic relationship 135
Parody 3–4, 17, 24, 52, 53, 103, 143, 230 n.30
Parousia 70
"Passion" 21, 23, 109, 239 n.5
Pastiche 24, 52, 123, 222 n.8, 222 n.10; pastiche of realism 111
Pastoralism 135
Pathos 19, 188, 191

Paul of Tarsis 42, 68–70
Pax Brittanica 67
Penelope 131
Performance 126; and ethnicity 236 n.1
Performativity 39, 48–49, 51–52, 61, 139, 192, 228 n.52
Peroxide hair 97
Peterson, Lars 221 n.1, 224 n.10, 225 n.2
The Phantom of the Opera 122
Phaon 129
Phillips, Ambrose 130
Physiognomic change 94
Picard, Jean-Luc 56
Picasso 22
Pigtails 166
Pike, Luke Owen 40, 43
The Pillow Book 128
Pinhead 104
Pirandello, Luigi 243 n.8
Plato 87, 141
"The Play's the Thing" 239 n.5
Pleasantville 92
Plot 116; complexities 200; development 127; features 181; mechanism 56
Poe, Edgar Allan 111
Pogo (postmodern gothic) 167
Political 44; correctness 56; history 62
Poor Cow 239 n.6
Pop culture 2, 6, 11, 12, 58, 74, 210, 225 n.37, 230 n.35; lecturer 35
Popular production 7
Pornographic fantasy 152
Post-Enlightenment 6, 75, 155
Postmodern 1, 3, 6, 23, 50, 64, 66, 72, 73, 74–75, 78, 87–88, 103–04, 157, 224 n.30, 229 n.7; America 6; atheology 229 n.1; cultural turn 11; gothic 222 n.7; humor 242 n.17; present 84; theory 22
The Postmodern Condition 15, 70, 221 n.5, 223 n.1
Postmodernism, or The Cultural logic of Late Capitalism 222 n.8
"Potential" 148, 203
Potential slayer 148, 151
Pound, Ezra 129
"Power Play" 232 n.14
Powers That Be 74, 190
Pragmatism 235 n.29
A Prayer for the Dying 176
Praying mantis woman 94
Preachers 63
Prehistory 18, 64
The Prelude 41
Premodern 1, 5, 41, 51, 74
Pre-Raphaelite 97
"Previously on..." 27, 114–15, 117–21, 123–24, 191
Primals 182
"Primeval" 35, 73, 101, 113, 120, 148, 169, 185, 187, 233 n.29

Principal Flutie 18, 159
Principal Snyder 34, 94, 154–55, 158, 160, 199, 240 n.17; Snyder-as-Kurtz 159
Principal Wood 143, 173, 189–90
Producers 10
Production 101, 109; requirements 53, 133; team 11, 94; techniques 111; value 4, 7
Production-heavy genre 181
Program writers 200
"The Prom" 138
Prophecies 36, 162, 190–91, 205
"Prophecy Girl" 113, 147, 190
Prophetic dreams 117
Propp, Vladimir 116
Proscenium arch 126
Protestantism 66
Pruitt, Jeff 101
Pseudo-parodic 152
Public space 180
Puccini 132
Punk aesthetic 97
Puns 111
Puppet show 190
"The Puppet Show" 132, 149, 159, 162
Puppet vampire 171

Quark 154
Quasimodo 85

Rabbits 150
Race 227 n.27
The Races of Men 41
Raimi, Sam 239 n.5
Rational ideals 32
Rational knowledge 34
Rationalism 31
Reading the Vamire Slayer 221 n.2, 222 n.7, 224 n.11
Readings, Bill 47
The Real 136
Real-seeming 23–24
Real time 137
Realism 22–23, 25, 45, 48, 64, 91, 111, 137, 203; as technique 11, 23–24, 28
Realist 156; codes 23; fiction 24; genre 24; production 25
Reality effect 123
Record collection 178–79
Redemption 152
Reed, Lou 178
Reformation 70
Religious principle 87
Renaissance 129
"The Replacement" 193, 230 n.35, 238 n.29
Representation 139
Representational: critique 83; economy 28; heterogeneity 47–48; history 92; realism 24; strategies of evil 96; traditions 88
"Reptile Boy" 232 n.15
"Restless" 7, 57–58, 94, 103, 109, 110, 113–14, 117–18, 120–21 124, 127–28, 132–33, 136, 138, 142, 149, 151–52, 154, 156, 162, 167, 169, 173, 179, 180–82, 184, 188–90, 196, 199, 204–06, 210, 235 n.25, 238 n.1, 239 n.6, 238 n.27
Resurrection spell 192
Rice, Anne 136, 233 n.34
Riess, Jana 237 n.7
Riley, Finn 34–35, 99, 113, 135–36, 141, 143, 146, 166 179, 187, 204–05, 239 n.9, 244 n.17
Ripper 166, 177, 223 n.3, 242 n.24
Ritual 130
Rivkin, Julie 39
The Rocky Horror Picture Show 179
Romanticism 41, 119, 156; romantic gothic 167
Roseanne 223 n.20
Rosencrantz and Guildenstern Are Dead 147
Ross, Gary 92
Roswell 221 n.4
Rothko 22
Rousseau, Jean-Jacques 43, 70, 75, 160
Ruskin 22
Ryan, Michael 39

Sadomasochistic 76, 179
Said, Edward 236 n.6
St. Cyril 67
St. John Thania 134
St. Peter 69
Saint-Saens 167
Sandbox 150–51
Sandy 237 n.17
Sapphic ode 129
Sappho 129–31
Sarah, George 179
Saviour 173
Sayer, Karen 120
Scar 184–85
Schnabel, Julian 178
Schneider, Daniel E. 134
"School Hard" 204, 230 n.36
Schrek, Max 104
Science 118
Science fiction 4, 76
Scientific rationalism 30–31, 34–36
Scoobies 18, 23, 25–26, 28, 32, 35, 45, 78, 100, 113, 147–48, 152, 167, 178, 185
Scooby Doo 25
Scooby family 127
Scooby Gang 18, 47–48, 91, 94, 97, 127, 163, 178, 193, 201
Score 167
Scream 3, 71, 92
Scream 2 92, 133
Script book 4, 181
Seasonal narrative 128; seasonal structure 84, 210
Secret 224 n.7; of Buffy's role 26; identity 17; knowledge 17

"Seeing Red" 96, 162, 206
Seidel-Arpaci, Annette 48–50, 226 n.21
Seidelman, Susan 119
Seinfeld 209
Self 201
Self-ironic writing 176
"Selfless" 19–20, 87, 149, 151, 162, 175–76,
    234 n.1
Self-referential 23, 55, 103, 105, 125
Self-sacrificing 184
Semi-parodic 89
Sergeant Cuff 225 n.35
Seriality 110, 133–15
Sesame Street 103
Sets 24; construction 204; dressing 204
Seven 95
Sex Pistols 56, 59, 168
Sexual fantasies 151, 163, 166
Sexuality 5, 193, 228 n.52
Sexualization 231 n.12
Sexually disturbed 96
"Shadow" 193, 239 n.9
Shadow Men 64, 190, 196, 199, 244 n.9
Sheen, Martin 150, 154–55
Shelley, Mary 118–19, 235 n.20
Sheridan, Philip 83
The Shield 209
Shimmerman, Armin 154
The Shining 161
Shuttleworth, Ian 233 n.277
Sid Vicious 56, 242 n.24
Siemann, Catherine 72, 243 n.3
Signification 92; of goodness 95; signifying
    practices 90, 168
Silence 136
Silent movie 11, 172, 190
The Silence of the Lambs 95
The Simpsons 166
Sinatra, Frank 123
The Singing Detective 209
Sitcom 11, 60
Six Characetrs in Search of an Author 243 n.8
Skimpy outfit 97
Skin color 9
Skip 243 n.8
Slapped girl 170
Slayage 10, 221 n.4, 221 n.6, 222 n.11, 222
    n.7 223 n.19, 223 n.14, 223 n.20, 223 n.21,
    223 n.3, 224 n.21, 224 n.22, 224 n.23, 224
    n.30, 224 n.9, 225 n.33, 225 n.41, 227
    n.25, 228 n.52, 233 n.32, 33, 235 n.21, 24,
    237 n.15, 240 n.13 , 242 n.16
Slayer 1, 3–5 16–17, 20, 25, 29–31, 34, 36 51,
    53–55, 71, 74–75, 79–81, 90, 99, 143, 169,
    172, 183, 186–87, 191, 196, 198, 199, 202,
    205–06, 224 n.26; Slayers 73, 184, 207;
    Slayer's handbook 205; Slayers in training
    37, 100
"Slouching toward Bethlehem" 162
Slow motion 24, 150, 152, 182

"Smashed" 134, 165
"Smile Time" 190
Snobbery 110
Soap opera 11
SoCal 45–46, 91
Social semiotics 92
Socialist 73
Sociological analysis 226 n.17
Soderbergh, Steven 150–51, 239 n.6
Sokal, Alan 112
"Some Assembly Required" 119–120
"Something Blue" 130, 165, 205
Sonata form 113, 234 n.13
Soul 19, 40, 69, 99, 173, 226 n.5, 241 n.14
Sound effects 24, 85
Soundtrack 167
South, James B. 96, 231 n.43
Southern California 24, 45, 63, 89, 91
Speech patterns 89, 100
Spell 58, 95–96, 105, 120, 144, 150, 167–68,
    181, 194, 203
Spike 38, 41, 49, 51–52, 54, 56–60, 62, 66–
    67, 76, 79, 82, 84, 94, 97–99, 105, 120, 136,
    142–43, 150m 153, 162, 165–66, 168–69,
    172–76, 179–81, 189, 191, 193–96, 198, 201–
    02, 206, 227 n.29, 230 n.36, 232 n.25, 235
    n.25, 241 n.12
"Spin the Bottle" 55, 117, 124
"Spiral" 168, 228 n.47
Spirit guide 188
Spliced 118
Spungeon, Nancy 56
Stam, Robert 119
Stamp, Terrence 239 n.6
"Standing in Your Way" 182
Star Trek 155, 209, 230 n.35
Star Trek: The Next Generation 56
Starlike quality 28
Steadicam 161
Stendhal 157
Stengel, Wendy A. F. G. 223 n.14
Stoker, Bram 66, 102, 185, 222 n.9
Stoppard, Tom 147
Story 116; and plot 118; story arcs 20
"Storyteller" 23, 44, 109, 117, 150, 152, 167,
    170–71, 176, 211, 229 n.6, 242 n.18
Street fighting 101
Strong, Danny 28
Stroud, Scott R. 86
Structural feature 90, 120
Structuralist theory 115
Stuart, Susan 240 n.2
Studio 238 n.27
Stunt coordinator 101
Stunt doubles 101
Stylistic choices 174
Stylistic differentiation 164
Stylized shot 126
Subhuman 199
Suicide 184

Sumptuous colors 128
Sunnydale 17, 24–29, 31, 39, 45, 48, 51, 55,
   58, 71, 76–77, 86, 90, 97, 104, 113, 117, 168,
   171, 176, 186, 207, 237 n.7; Sunnydale
   High 25, 53
Superhuman 192, 198
Superman 239 n.4
Superscripting 203
"Superstar" 27–28, 95, 109, 122–23, 138, 224
   n.25
"Surprise" 45, 127
Sutherland, Kristine 239 n.7
Sweet 194, 242 n.26
Symbology 98; of good and evil 9
Symonds, Adington John 131
Syndication 124

Tabron, Judith L. 223 n.21
"Tabula Rasa" 23, 57–58, 97, 150–51, 162,
   169, 180, 228 n.47
"Tales of Brave Ulysses" 177
Tara 18, 55, 57, 60, 85, 96–97, 103, 113–14,
   126–30, 132, 134, 136–38, 144, 151, 167,
   169–71, 179, 182, 192, 197, 199, 206, 221
   n.21, 230 n.30
"Tara" 127, 236 n.5
Taxonomic 34
"Teacher's Pet" 31, 232 n.17, 239 n.11
Teaser 27, 114, 120–21, 124
Techno-pagan 33, 35
Techno-scientific 77
"Ted" 102, 192, 197
Teen drama 4, 100
Teen romance 58
Telemachus 177
Teleology 63, 75, 84, 231 n.43
Television 3, 4, 10, 32–33, 63, 84, 88, 91,
   145; aesthetic 9, 11–12; as anti-aesthetic 9;
   as art 12; contemporary U.S. 103; criticism
   110; drama 31, 109; formal limits of 24;
   history 11; iconography 93; production 10;
   serial 10, 114; shows 51; realism 89; serial
   drama 111; space 126
Televisual spectacle 101
Televisual traditions 92
Telos 42, 44
Tennyson, Alfred Lord 41
Tensor sign 112
Tepes, Vlad 65
The Terror 43–44
Tertullian 67
Thanksgiving 63, 78–79, 81, 83
Theatre 126
Theme and style 183
Theory of Literature 115
3rd Rock from the sun 119
"This Year's Girl" 100, 132, 196, 205
Thriller 17, 24, 32
Time 181
Time Warp 179

Todorov, Tzvetan 139–40, 224 n.8
Tomashevsky 116
Tonkin, Boyd 45, 222 n.7, 226 n.17
Torrance High School 231 n.9
Total knowledge 36
"Tough Love" 169
Trachtenberg, Michelle 202
Trademark 170; logo 224 n.27
Transformer 178
Trespass story 25–26
"Triangle" 232 n.16
Turnball, Sue 10, 24, 224 n.21, 225 n.37, 229
   n.6
TV 73, 210
'20s movies 173
24 209
Twin Peaks 137, 209
Twinkie bars 63
"Two to Go" 195, 198
Typology of television criticism 10

Ubervamps 167
Uber-witch 96
Ulysses 22
Uncle Rory 151
Unheimlich 27
U.S. political concerns 66
Universal humanity 39
UPN 10, 191, 205
utilitarian 174

Vamp Willow 76, 97, 168, 237 n.17, 238 n.29
Vampire Slayer 64, 89, 101, 115
Vampire with a soul 23
Vampires 1, 4–5 16–17, 27, 47, 51–53, 74, 76–
   77, 82, 92, 94, 97, 101–02, 104, 117, 132,
   160, 173. 227 n.25, 230 n.36; bats 170;
   brothel 205; vampireness 38; vampire-
   paramour 142
Van Dyke, Dick 59
Van Helsing 185
The Velvet Underground 178
Vengeance demon 162
VHS 4, 124
Victorian 41, 54, 56–57
Video 113, 124, 149, 154, 164
Vietnam 149
Viewer 2, 11, 20, 114, 118, 120, 126, 147
"Villains" 18, 97, 169
Violence 17, 101, 195
Visual irony 172
Visual pun 164
Visual representation 96
Visual signs 85
Voice-over 143, 162

Wachowski brothers 1120
Wall, Brian 87, 136–37, 221 n.2, 224 n.11,
   225 n.43, 240 n.3, 244 n.13
Waller, Gregory 223 n.6

Wardrobe 99
Warhol, Andy 178
Warren Meers 18, 28–29, 39, 95–97 192–93, 197, 206
The Waste Land 156
Watcher 17, 53–55, 57, 79–80, 91, 162, 164–65, 173, 176; Watcher-librarian-mentor-guide 179; Watchers' Council 18, 32, 38–39, 47, 54–55, 58–59, 65–66, 74, 161, 167, 197–98
The Watcher's Guide Volume 3 228 n.41
The Watchtower 92
WB 10, 170, 221 n.4, 221 n.1 232 n.18
"We" 159–60
"The Weight of the World" 185
"Welcome to the Hellmouth" 1, 17, 52–54, 81, 88, 91–92, 96, 138, 168, 175–76, 185, 210, 224 n.10
Wesley Wyndham Price 38, 52, 54–55, 60, 94, 113, 152–53, 240 n.13, 242 n.15
The West Wing 155, 209
Westerfeld, Scott 25, 27
Western 2, 56, 228 n.47
"What's My Line I" 125
"What's My Line II" 57, 127, 205
Whedon, Joss 3–4, 10, 34 52, 60, 92, 101, 104, 120, 128, 135, 149–50, 154, 156–57, 164, 170, 177, 181, 191, 221 n.1, 222 n.11, 223 n.20, 227 n.25, 233 n.29, 233 n.33, 236 n.4, 238 n.27, 239 n.4, 239 n.6
"When She Was Bad" 46, 132–33
"Where the Wild Things Are" 151, 179, 186
The Who 179
"Who Are You?" 100, 134, 165, 186
"Who Killed Bambi?" 168
Whodunit 17, 32
Wiccan 35, 138
Wilcox, Rhonda V. 119, 156, 228 n.51, 244 n.19, 224 n.23, 235 n.22
Willard 155
William the Bloody Awful 57–58, 82, 162
Williams, Raymond 5, 223 n.15
Willow Rosenberg 11, 15, 17–19, 28, 35, 38–39, 42, 46, 48–50, 53–54, 57–60, 73, 76, 78–81, 84–85, 91, 94, 96–97, 99, 113, 119, 124–27, 129–32, 134, 136, 139–42, 144, 146, 149–51, 159, 162, 167–68, 175–76, 179, 181–82, 191–92, 195, 197, 199, 205–06, 209, 223 n.21, 236 n.1, 237 n.8, 238 n.27; Willow's dream 128, 134, 137–38, 143, 145, 151, 164, 169, 181, 184, 188
Willy Loman 134
Wilson, Steve 147, 227 n.40
Winslade, J. Lawton 237 n.9
"The Wish" 76–77, 97, 104–05, 109, 134, 168, 186–87, 238 n.29, 245 n.21
Wisker, Gina 237 n.15
Witch 81, 84, 139, 237 n.9
"The Witch" 165, 186
Without dialogue 133
Wolfram and Heart 44
Wolf's Howl 121
Wordsworth, William 41
Writers 10, 21, 109, Writing staff 11
Writer's response 23
Wuthering Heights 235 n.19

Xander (Alexander Harris) 15–17, 19, 21, 23, 31, 33, 36, 41, 57, 58, 67, 73, 76, 78–79, 87, 91, 94, 96, 99, 103, 105, 113, 122, 124, 130, 132, 138, 144, 148, 150–52, 154–55, 158–59, 161–65, 167, 170–71, 175, 179, 187, 189, 191–92, 199, 210, 203–5, 237 n.7, 238 n.29, 239 n.4, 240 n.17; Xander's dream 145–46, 149, 155, 162, 184, 188, 206
Xena Warrior Princess 239 n.5
The X-Files 4, 26, 86, 120, 209, 221 n.4
X-Men 74

Yeffeth, Glen 224 n.25
"The Yoko Factor" 127, 133, 143, 172, 180, 184
Young Americans 64
Young Buffy 185
Youth culture 57, 122
Yueh, Wayne 231 n.6

Z-Cars 209, 239 n.6
"The Zeppo" 147–49, 151, 161, 239 n.4
Zryd, Michael 87, 136–37, 221 n.2, 224 n.11, 225 n.43, 240 n.3, 244 n.13